BACK TO THE DRAWING BOARD

BACK TO THE DRAWING BOARD

Don Ainley

Book Guild Publishing
Sussex, England

First published in Great Britain in 2008 by
The Book Guild Ltd
Pavilion View
19 New Road
Brighton, BN1 1UF

Typeset in Times by
Ellipsis Books Ltd, Glasgow

Printed in Great Britain by
CPI Antony Rowe

A catalogue record for this book is available from
The British Library.

ISBN 978 1 84624 239 7

Nurse Clara Tattersall 1891–1968
The gentle, patient lady responsible for this book

Contents

Foreword

I once sat down to see just what I could do with the versatile English language, having been inspired over many years by the imaginative stories of Ed McBain, O. Henry, Bill Bryson, Nevil Shute, John Steinbeck, Charles Dickens, Leslie Thomas and Michael Crichton, masterly word-smiths all.

Being less imaginative and much less creative, I chose the easier route via autobiography.

Time distorts memory all too easily as life becomes but a sequence of incidents, some coincidental, accidental, others intentional. We blunder through them en route to somewhere unknown, loading the memory banks. Someone once aptly wrote, 'Don't live life by each breath you take, but by what takes your breath away.'

I did the blundering, the reader may enjoy the memories.

St Annes-on-Sea
England 2007

1

One Solitary Bang 1940,
Somewhere in England

The sudden, sharp crack of a rifle shot pierced the still air, bouncing over the village roofs to echo from the steep hillside opposite. With harsh curses four startled rooks rose rapidly to gain the safety of height, then continued to squawk their annoyance as they began to circle lazily in the rising thermals. The village was unknown as place names had been deliberately removed, even the mileage indicators to distant coastal cities had been chipped away, along with both place names on the stone post at the roadside, leaving just two useless arrows.

Shortly before the bang three lads, with a younger one, had been standing in the stone-cobbled lane (the stones known locally as 'sets', probably because they were set into position with hot tar) where the noise occurred. The nine-year-old Donald had carefully positioned a live .303 bullet in a nick in a high dry-stone wall. This stretch of wall would have been built with an extra wide base as it retained a steep field – beyond that further but less steep fields marched up the hillside, to finish where the heather moors began. On most public highways these tapered walls were surmounted by semi-circular top stones, cemented in place. The walls dividing farm fields relied on gravity alone.

Each of the three older lads carried a 'spike' stuck through a loop in their braces. They were simply recycled steel spindles from spinning

1

frames and always readily available from the scrap pile in the cotton mill yard, but they were never allowed to be taken to the infants school. Both ends being pointed made them infinitely useful. The lads had practised drawing these spikes much as a film cowboy draws his gun, and knew they could draw and throw long before any German parachutist could retrieve his bayonet and fit it to his rifle. They were ready for anything from live Germans to live rats on the canal bank.

The older Donald now carefully held his spike to the exposed end of the round to act as a firing pin. The younger Donald, eight years old, was now about two feet away from the bullet, standing with fingers in his ears and eyes closed. The other eight-year-old, John, just as close, now shouted to his young brother, 'Gerrout the way or you might get killed dead.' The young Keith, known as Tod, short for toddler, hands in pockets, walked backwards to a point in the middle of the lane, but slightly offset from the action. He sulkily shouted, 'You're always rotten to me.' He then spotted a bubble which had formed in the tar between the 'sets' from the previous day's sun and became intent on kicking it with his tiny clog.

The elder Donald shouted 'ready' and crashed a rock larger than his own fist into the other end of the spike. The recoil pushed him onto his back in the road so that the flying sharp chips of stone missed him. Lethal spike clanged on the sets and rolled to the opposite wall. The net result was one loud bang across the village, one bullet simply disappeared deeper into the wall as dust shot out of nearby nicks between the stones, one grazed elbow and frayed jacket arm. John complained, 'I thought the wall woulda come down' as he moved into the stench of cordite to retrieve the spent case to add to their stock of items to swap in the school yard. He prised it out of the wall with his spike, picking it up from the cobbles and shrieking 'Ouch!' as the still hot metal burnt his fingers. An old woman, labouring up the hill with her meagre groceries in a carpet bag, reached them and said, 'Yer'll kill yersens messing about with fireworks like that. I'll tell yer mother when I gerrup there.' The younger Donald felt cheated, he expected at least a few large stones to fall out. All three knew of a certain stone wall which fell into this lad's kitchen without any explosion. Tod said, 'I want to wee and I'm 'ungry. I missed it, yer oughter bang another.'

At the end of the long summer holiday, the three older lads would return to school to be issued with gas masks. Tod was given a small Mickey Mouse version. He grew to love this, it became his 'bestest toy'. Bored at home all day, he frequently wore it. At that time his second 'bestest' toy was a battered tin car without tyres. He kept this in an old biscuit tin with a dead bird and dead mouse. He loved to stick a pin in the maggots. One morning John left the lid off by mistake, and their mother, guided by the weird smell, found it under their bunk bed. With a panicky scream she shot downstairs and dumped box and contents into the dustbin, never noticing the tin car which, during her flight, had slid under the bird's wing. Tod never complained but begged John to kill him a rat on the canal bank and to 'Gerra bigger tin'.

The three older lads would probably have swapped their gas masks for something more exotic had it not been for the headmaster's stern warning about poison gas, mustard gas and laughing gas which the wicked Germans had used during the 1914–18 war. The terms 'mustard' and 'laughing' puzzled the three pals and the rest of the school. The head stressed that the Huns would do it again. The word 'Huns' also left the whole school puzzled, until one girl said her granddad told her that Huns were Germans in disguise. The adults in the village would have perhaps slept easier in their blacked-out bedrooms had they known of the junior Home Guard living amongst them. Lads of varying age held a mixed armoury of pre-war air pistols and air rifles (although pellets for these were to become ever more difficult to obtain), pre-war shop-bought powerful aluminium catapults, less powerful ones made from the Y-branch of a tree and some old inner tubing, bows and arrows in profusion, and perhaps forty lads had the trusty oft-sharpened 'spikes'. Even the youngest all had pea-shooters, which could fire a poisoned dart! One enterprising lad had tried to convert a normal bow into a cross-bow using an old pair of his father's braces. At the first test firing, at a target rat on the canal bank, the braces lashed his face as they tangled round his neck, his finger stung like mad as the bow shot from his hand and flew into the canal. He only found the arrow as he stepped forward and promptly trod on it.

However, the adults were well aware they had a lamp lighter who, at dusk in winter, would reconnoitre the surrounding lanes armed with a

3

long pole to turn up the gas lamps, creating little light as the lamp panes were painted blue to match the bus windows. He then went home for his tea, changed into his air raid warden uniform consisting of tin hat, whistle, arm band and canvas satchel containing a flask of tea and sandwiches. His stentorian shout 'Put that light out' was heard throughout each evening. After a few months he began to imagine slits of light between badly drawn curtains. The village was also guarded by one police constable with whistle and truncheon, plus the vital telephone. He used this to warn the night watchman in one local mill, whose duty was to climb the endless fire escape stairs to the roof, as he went to hand crank the air raid siren. Partly deaf, he would go back down to await the second message relayed from the constable. He then had to climb back up to crank the continuous 'all clear' signal, then to suffer a second dose of temporary deafness.

The villagers were even more reassured by their one and only Home Guardsman. He was known to have a real rifle, an unknown amount of live ammo, full khaki uniform, the lot. This gear he took to work every day as a bank clerk, the uniform carried in a suitcase. He even had to repeat this when attending chapel each Sunday, the whole lot parked in the pew beside him. This stalwart had a club foot.

The council caretaker, who possessed a shotgun, once a month had to pin a target on the green door where the council grass mower was now locked away 'for the duration' due to the shortage of petrol. Surveying the Home Guard's efforts his head shaking increased as month by month he removed the unmarked target and surveyed the increasingly splintered door. With a pencil he would punch a random three holes in the target and hand it to the council clerk to post off to some distant army command. Only the clerk knew the address and had had to sign the Official Secrets Act to get it. At least the caretaker knew the rifle would fire and he could grab it in the event of hostilities, although dashing the quarter mile to defend the gas works would be thwarted by leg shrapnel collected in the last war. Each month he witnessed the marksman's efforts and duly repeated this to laughs all round the British Legion clubhouse. In their wooden shed the committee, on his advice, had bought their very first fire extinguisher.

Our three young heroes, Donald, Donald, and John, were never bored:

4

they needed no soppy youth clubs or organised after-school activities: later in the war they even flew their own Flying Fortress, cunningly disguised as a sycamore tree. It was perfectly natural to them as they knew many Fortresses limped back to Lincolnshire with but three crew alive, the rest hanging dead in harness or even blown right out of the aircraft. On this summer morning, during the 'phoney' war period of 1940, they were simply adapting to war-time England, running their own exercises. In contrast Tod was bored every ten minutes.

The three youngest had been born in this very lane, in the huddle of poor cottages dug into the hillside. Not so the elder Donald – it hadn't always been like this for him, born two counties away to a quiet respectable couple, if living in a detached bungalow in its own grounds, a free perk with his father's job, can be classed as respectable. Nor had he been evacuated to this narrow valley to avoid the expected bombing of Manchester. Instead, when four years old, something happened to plummet him and his mother into total poverty lasting for years. Had he been born a year earlier he could have been living in a luxurious town house and also a country house with a family of millionaires, safe in eastern Canada. He never mentioned this as he knew no-one would believe him. On his first day at this village infants school, his fourth such school to date, the kids hadn't believed it when he said he'd previously lived at Hoyland, a village near Barnsley. They thought he was Irish. By age twenty-one he was known to colleagues as a 'lying sod', by twenty-eight, this role was firmly established.

It could be interesting to explore this one lad as he survived into adulthood, moulded by poverty and later by shrewd and talented employers to become a complicated character, able and willing to take calculated risks and react rapidly. He could tell the story himself, but it is 1940, he is only nine and much too busy. He still has three more live rounds and knows of a local handicapped man with exactly the weapon to fire these.

2

The Lad's Tale

Long, long ago on the 3rd June 1931 I was born in Altrincham General Hospital when my parents lived at 26 Ashley Road, Altrincham, Cheshire, England. I was christened Donald (my mother was half Scottish) and William (after my father). Number 26 was a detached bungalow that went with my father's job as Head Gardener at what was then the Bowdon Hydro Hotel across the road, now a 'Quality Hotel'. Vague memories include our black cat which spent a lot of time on the bungalow roof, deer grazing in Dunham Massey Park, a dog and children swimming in a smooth stretch of water above a weir on the River Bollin. Nearby was a wooden footbridge and white-painted wooden mill with a waterwheel. I remember my father one day telling me to go into our garden to get some lettuce for tea. I picked the whole row. I was then perhaps three years old.

My mother was born in Midgley, a village near Halifax, West Yorkshire, trained as a nurse at a children's hospital in Rochdale and emigrated to Canada, where she first got a job living in a private home nursing an incurable. The second job was with a family called Doughty; when the mother had produced her twentieth child – a doughty woman indeed – the grateful Canadian government gave the family a scroll and CAN$5000. An ancient sepia photograph shows two of the younger children cleaning the whole family's shoes on the veranda steps.

Another such job for my mother was with a very rich family in St. John, New Brunswick. Their name was Bullock, the father and both sons all millionaires in timber and oil. The father had been Mayor of St. Johns on three occasions. One old newspaper cutting shows one of their huge log rafts being pushed down-river. The sons were both married, yet the whole family lived together in a huge town house with servants and five cars. In summer the whole ménage moved en masse to their country mansion, with ice delivered weekly to their stone ice storage house buried in the garden. The lady of the house had some form of slow cancer. My mother nursed her for four years, and was treated as one of the family. When she met and married my father he was simply absorbed into this family as a chauffeur. Each year my mother accompanied the lady on her visit to some clinic for a week's treatment, involving a long rail journey through 200 miles of nothing but forest – some of it was theirs, the single track railway forming a fire-break through the timber.

After Mrs Bullock finally died my parents came back to England. The Bullock family must have been very grateful to my mother, for each Christmas she received a card signed by all the family with a money order for CAN$100. In 1935 she must have included a letter with her Christmas card to let them know that my father had left home for good. I was four years old when he left to seek work back in Canada, never to be seen or heard from again. In 1938 Mr Bullock Snr included an invitation to her to go back to Canada with me, to live with the family and act as a paid nanny to the grandchildren, as he felt war was imminent in Europe. She would not go, why I don't know, she had a brother and three nephews in New Brunswick. How different my future might have been had she returned.

My father was born in Elland, near Halifax in West Yorkshire, but first met my mother in Canada. The name Ainley, spelt thus, is peculiar to Elland and Huddersfield about 7 miles away. In the thirteenth century one Sir Richard Aneley went to the Middle East as a crusader to force Christianity on the heathens in those parts. He lived at Elland Hall which centuries later became the head office of Nu-Swift Fire Extinguishers Ltd. On his return he found that some nearby squire had lock-picked Lady Aneley's chastity belt, so killed him with his trusty sword on the

8

river bank near the Hall. For this he was hanged at York. (I remember in 1980 looking in the New York phone book – just one Ainley, the rest were all Aneley, Ayneley, Aynesley or the Scottish spelling Ainslie.)

To this day the hill which climbs from Elland in the Huddersfield direction is called 'The Ainleys', half way up is the 'Ainleys Industrial Estate', the top of the hill is called surprisingly 'Ainley Top', now the site of a hotel near the M62 motorway, and the hotel includes the 'Ainley Suite' and the 'Ainley Conference Centre'. Despite this when my son and I separately rang to reserve rooms when attending my niece's wedding, we were both asked to spell our name! When we arrived to register, the young receptionist must have thought we owned the place!

3

The Lad's Relatives

My mother's father was born in a tiny hilltop village in the Pennine countryside. He never learned to read or write – on my mother's birth certificate the then registrar has printed 'X – the mark of John Tattersall' in neat copperplate writing – yet when adult he simultaneously owned two farms and two quarries. In his spare time he raised two sons and three daughters. He sometimes moved hewn stone over a mile down the steep cobbled hill to the station in the main valley for onward transit by rail. At that time Bramwell Bronte was the railway goods clerk. On one occasion the horse-drawn cart of heavy stone ran away down hill and the carter was crushed to death under his own cart wheel.

My grandfather was once a witness in a court dispute over the closure of a rough cart track on the edge of the moor above the farm. This track had saved the locals a two-mile trek since times immemorial, but one George Bedford Whittaker, of Whittaker's Brewery in Halifax, rented the shooting rights on this moor and decided to close the track at both ends. Another witness, known only as 'Samson', and also unable to read or write, lived in a square, windowless, stone shed roofed with grass sods. Built in the corner of a field it was originally intended for animals. He did odd jobs for all the local community, was famous for his grouse stew, rabbit stew, and dandelion soup, and had no idea what date he was born. To reach the court at Wakefield in those days required a full day's journey, and the two biased witnesses no doubt stressed the community benefits of the track remaining open for all time. The judge agreed and Whittaker was faced with a huge bill for costs.

By a strange coincidence my wife's grandfather owned a large quarry outside Huddersfield, which later supplied the exact matching stone required to repair Buckingham Palace after wartime bomb damage. In those days anyone with land who wanted to build anything simply dug a hole in the hillside to get at the stone. Sometimes it was easier to hack away at a few small quarries rather than continue with one ever-increasing hole: serrated hilltops bear witness to this activity to this day on many Pennine skylines. As a lad in wartime, I too had an interest in quarries, not pecuniary but involving the endless search for spent or unused ammunition discarded by the Home Guard.

John Tattersall's eldest son was my Uncle Harry, who gave a wrong age when recklessly volunteering for the army. He went into the 1914–18 war, somehow survived to be gassed and was invalided out as a company sergeant major. After convalescence in an army hospital somewhere in the south of England he was advised to live in a dryer climate than West Yorkshire due to lung damage. He emigrated to New Brunswick, Canada and was eventually awarded a disability pension of 1shilling and 6 pence per week, in today's money exactly seven and a half pence! On receipt he swore he would never set foot in England again and never did. He worked until retirement as a plate layer, i.e. track maintenance on the Canadian National Railway, with a break during the war when the Canadian Army asked him to wear a company sergeant major's uniform to train their troops on home soil. Just like the Amish sect in America, he and his workmates together built a house for each of them from logs which years later they covered in clapboard and painted white. Harry married and raised three sons, Gerald, Douglas and Cyril. On retirement from the railway he got a job as an armed bank guard so that when he finally stopped work he was already getting a Canadian state pension, plus another from the railway, a small one from the Canadian Army, another small one from the bank, and 7½ pence per week from Britain, so was able to continue running his huge American car!

Harry's son Cyril always preferred America and worked just over the border in Maine. He went into the US Army in 1941 and survived the Normandy landings right through to Berlin. Whilst there awaiting demobilisation he was accidentally run over by a US Army six-wheeler truck which left him with one leg an inch shorter than the other and delayed his exit from the army by many months. War can cause such strange flukes, as when my wife's Uncle Noel, having joined the British Army straight from college, went through the Anzio beachhead landings in Italy winning a Military Cross, further north in Italy won a bar to the cross, by then an acting major, all without a scratch, but tore his eyelid when drunkenly falling out of a jeep, appropriated for an illicit night out with his pals. A horrible fluke also happened to his older brother, my wife's Uncle Geoffrey, who had just gained a degree in Civil Engineering in 1940, was then called up into the RAF and was set to work building airfields throughout Britain. Never having suffered a scratch, he too was awaiting demobilisation when an RAF plane crashed into a hangar and killed him in the last week of the war.

The only one of my Uncle Harry's family I ever met was Douglas, who years later stayed with us for a few days en route to Suffolk to discover some relatives of his now dead mother. His American-born wife Ella was very attractive and seemed to live on about 20 different pills a day, had a weird diet and was desperate to preserve her looks and body to keep everything presentable for the embalmer. She filled the bathroom windowsill and also her dressing table with jars, bottles, sprays, vitamins etc., all of which she had hauled across the Atlantic. Doug, on leaving school, learnt to be a motor mechanic, later specialising in bodywork repairs, working his way up to become a foreman in a General Motors main dealer in Sudbury, Ontario. Around age 50 he developed a serious stomach ulcer which his doctor insisted would mean major surgery with only a 50/50 chance of success.

Doug had a friend who saved his annual holidays and over Christmas went north shooting bear or elk. He told Doug of the ancient Indian cure for stomach problems. It seems that in all the remote frozen settlements up north the general store would always have a basket on the counter containing dried beaver droppings, to be taken in a glass topped up with gin to mask the vile taste. The friend wrote to one such store run by a friend and got some posted back. Doug's ulcer receded; provided he ate the minimum fat he had no further pain. Doug duly reported the progress to his doctor who promptly condemned the tale as just more Indian folk-lore. I remember suggesting to Doug that the doctor and all his colleagues should have been pressing Canadian medical authorities to research the chemical contents of the particular bark eaten by the beaver, the exact tree, local soil and the beaver's full digestive tract to find the chemical process that could perhaps help prevent ulcers. Doug had at least avoided the risky operation. He never went back to the G.M. dealers – instead he got a new job as a crash claims investigator with a large insurance company. He had higher pay and a company car as a result of eating beaver droppings.

Harry's sister, my Aunt Laura, married Fred Spencer who after the 1914–18 war returned to take over his father's farm, on a hilltop above Halifax. They had seven children although the last one, Charlie, died very young. Sadly, Fred also died, long before I was born, leaving Laura to run the farm helped by her growing family. She was plump, placid, rosy cheeked and always friendly, wore clogs in the farmyard, slippers indoors. Her busy life was an endless round of washing, ironing, cooking, milking, mucking out. More of this wonderful, caring woman later. Fred had been in eastern Mesopotamia (now Iraq) during the 1914 war. Strange that he was stationed not far from Habbaniya, as many years later I flew freight there, into the then RAF camp.

Harry's brother, my Uncle Arnold, just disappeared during the London bombing. All I ever learned from my mother was that he had become 'something high up on the railway' and as far as was known had never married or kept in touch at all. He was assumed to have been killed during the bombing but how or when none of the family knew.

Another of Harry's sisters, my Aunt Beatrice, who again I never met, was somewhat peculiar. Her husband had once been station master at Brighouse in West Yorkshire, moved to be station master at Harrow on the Hill, Middlesex, then retired. In those days Christmas cards were always made from an outer card with an inner folded paper carrying the greeting and signature under the message of good tidings. The two folded pieces were held together with a ribbon passed through holes in both, or a coloured string round the double folds. For years Beatrice sent the second-hand outer bit only, duly signed with centre fold removed as a Christmas card to my mother. By the time I was a teenager I told my mother to cross out the signature, sign it herself and return it without a stamp, just after Christmas of course. But my mother was far too gentle and never did. This distant aunt must have known of my mother's struggle, yet throughout my childhood never once sent me a birthday or Christmas present.

She too had one son, also called Donald. I never saw him either. He became vicar of Chelsea, Dean of a Theological College in Edinburgh or Aberdeen and finally ran a retreat for clergy in York. On one occasion he somehow traced my address and wrote to inform me that his wonderful mother had passed on, no flowers please but donations could be sent to some charity or other. Fat chance, I never even replied. I later saw his own half-page in-depth obituary in the *Daily Telegraph*, which generated glowing responses praising this wonderful man in subsequent letters to the editor. I too could have written outlining the strangeness of his wonderful mother, I just didn't bother.

4

Gypsy Lifestyle

We were living in furnished rented accommodation in Altrincham when my father left us, intent on seeking work back in Canada. It was 1936 and we never saw or heard from him again. My mother was left with two suitcases, very little cash and a five-year-old boy, no home, furniture or job and no social services then available to turn to for help. A return to hospital nursing was out of the question so she promptly got a job as housekeeper to a recently divorced senior clerk in a bank. He had just bought a house in Gatley, near Altrincham, but she could not move in until some alterations and decorating had been completed.

With two weeks to wait she decided to visit an older nursing colleague from Rochdale, a spinster now living in Paisley, Scotland. This was how I came to see across the River Clyde the huge *Queen Mary* being fitted out in John Brown's shipyard, and the large neon sign showing the outline of a sewing machine, the needle appearing to rise and fall, mounted on the roof of the Singer factory at Clydebank. An ancient photograph shows me as a babe-in-arms, my mother and father with this old friend in the garden at Bowdon, so she must have visited us just after I was born. In Paisley I was told to call her 'Granny' Cordner.

We returned to live in Gatley, where I went to my first infants school – Gatley Primary, it was straight across the road from our house. I have no memory of teachers, children or inside that school but the single report states that I was seven years old and had attained 10/10 in 'memory work' and 8/10 in composition. I do remember helping, or more likely hindering, Edward Price, my mother's employer, to lay a coloured concrete garden path in a crazy paving pattern. Eventually he decided to get married and we were on the move again.

My wonderful, caring Aunt Laura wrote to my mother: 'Stop with us over here as long as you want, I could do with some help, he's never seen his cousins.' To me the farm was wonderful, all sorts of smells and activities. One job I had was to wind a butter churn endlessly, using cream skimmed from huge bowls of milk. The square jar was glass with a wooden paddle inside. The liquid very suddenly solidified into butter, so dense I could hardly turn the paddle. Another job was to crush with a mallet the huge blocks of salt used to rub into the divided pig hung in the dairy to cure.

One day a wooden threshing machine arrived, pulled by a steam traction engine. Parked in the farmyard the engine was positioned to drive the thresher with a wide leather belt from the flywheel. Soon after starting the belt flew off and caught the labourer straight in his stomach. I saw him double up entangled in the belt, but at that point my aunt shoved me back into the farmhouse. In the evening I learnt that he had been killed.

I also remember pushing a sack cart with a cardboard box on it along the dirt road to the pub to collect beer bottles and Woodbine cigarettes in an open-ended paper packet for my cousins working in the fields, I got a bottle of pop for doing this. The landlord seemed very secretive about selling to me, it all occurred in the back yard of the pub with the big gates closed.

Aunt Laura's eldest daughter, Audrey, was married to a foreman in the huge local quarry and lived nearby, while her brothers and sisters lived on the farm, the youngest, Edith, being a teenager about to leave school. We kept in touch for years as first John was called up into the army, then Robert into the air force where he remained for the full 22 years, Alec into the navy, then Annie joined the Land Army and was sent to a farm in Kent. She eventually married a greengrocer in Hythe but never returned to live in Yorkshire. After the war John returned and

worked in the same quarry as his brother-in-law. Alec returned and started
long distance truck driving. Edith began work in Marks & Spencer and
later married a Bradford monumental mason. In the end my aunt had to
give up the farm as she and Edith could not run it on their own, so they
moved into a terraced house in the village.

We must have only stayed on the farm for a few weeks and I never
went to the village school with Edith. My mother got a job housekeeping
for a single farmer in another village about 10 miles away. Here I did
go to the village school, I got a lift there every morning with the father
of a local pal and after school caught the single-decker bus back home.
This bus had to fight the moorland route to Rochdale in winter and
carried four shovels – when the bus got stuck in snow the passengers
alighted and started digging. For this help the driver always stopped by
each scattered home, ignoring the bus stops. In the early years of the
war a dummy runway was created on the moor using two long rows of
oil drums filled with oily rags. Despite the blacked-out valleys each
evening the local water-board man, who looked after valves etc. on the
two reservoirs, lit these drums as a decoy for German bombers en route
to Manchester.

On Saturday mornings I helped the farmer to deliver milk carried in
huge churns in his horse and cart. People just left a jug out on their
doorstep with a saucer on top to prevent birds pecking at the cream.
Sometimes they left a note in the jug ordering fresh eggs with or without
hen muck and the odd feather. Later came glass milk bottles with a cardboard disk inserted into the bottle neck. In the centre of the disk was a
partly-punched smaller disk, this was pressed open to pour the milk.
Birds soon learned to do this to get at the cream.

The farmer married so we moved on once again, this time to live-in
with an elderly lady who was convalescing from some illness. This was
in an end-of-terrace town house at Park Square, central Leeds. Today all
the houses are used as offices by doctors, dentists, solicitors and accountants – pre-war each house would be occupied by rich merchants with
servants. The three weeks we stayed there was my first introduction to
the nightly sound of sirens, anti-aircraft guns and bombs, for on the east
side of Leeds was a Royal Ordnance factory making tanks. To the south

east a ring of anti-aircraft batteries tried to get the bombers before they reached the factory.

One night the sirens sounded as usual and I was bundled, and told to stay, under a stout kitchen table in the cellar with the family Alsatian, my mother upstairs in the lady's bedroom. I was far more scared of the huge dog than the bombs, it just whined all the time and jumped every time the guns fired. I heard the loud growl of an aircraft directly over-head, then a muffled crump, followed by further bumps that seemed much nearer, and the aircraft noise diminished. Much later the all-clear siren sounded. Next morning on going outside I found the street at the end was cordoned off, with a constable and air raid warden on guard. Piled against the wall and over the footpath was a huge pile of sooty bricks, poking from the top of this pile the four (one bent) fins of a sizable bomb. Looking up, I saw that nothing remained of the chimney. The constable said they were awaiting the army bomb disposal squad. We were lucky.

I also remember watching an American army jeep being driven up and down the very wide stone steps leading up to Leeds Town Hall, two stone lions guarding the steps, with a bored officer standing around in a white rubber raincoat.

Soon the lady recovered her health. In this short time I had recorded three firsts – a live German bomb, a real jeep decked out in white-walled tyres and a raincoat made of rubber.

We were as ever welcome back at the farm. It was nice to see this natural smelly world again rather than the city under siege, but the stay was brief as my mother then got a job nursing an elderly bed-ridden miner in an advanced state of silicosis. I saw him for perhaps five minutes when we first arrived, when his daughter took us upstairs. I thought he must be dead, I had never before seen a grey-faced man with dark pouches under both eyes.

The house was in a long brick terrace in a mining village called Hoyland Common, outside Barnsley, South Yorkshire. I never went to any school here so the miner must have died very soon. When he did his daughter claimed the house and paid my mother. Both suitcases packed, we got a bus into Barnsley centre where a helpful inspector worked out that it would be impossible to reach Halifax in time to get the last bus to the farm. A hotel being out of the question he suggested 'Try the police station.' We found this, the story was duly told, and the sergeant replied, 'You can't walk the streets all night with a little lad, all we can offer you is a cell and it's a bit rough.' A constable was promptly sent to the sergeant's home for sheets, blankets and pillows. He showed us the toilet and we were duly installed in adjacent cells but separated by iron bars. 'I'll get you a good breakfast but you will have to be out of here early before t'Inspector clocks on. Goodnight Missis, goodnight lad, don't worry.' We ate the breakfast, my mother thanked him and we went back to the bus station, her greatest crisis to date solved by a beefy, blunt, practical Yorkshireman in double quick time. We were back on the farm by early afternoon, Aunt Laura laughing at the police station drama: 'Could have been worse, I'll get t'kettle on.'

Through the *Yorkshire Post* my mother quickly found another job in the picturesque village of Clapham, near Settle in North Yorkshire, although the postal address at that time was Clapham, via Lancaster in Lancashire. Here we settled down to an amazing eight months' stay whilst she nursed a terminally ill man. To get to school I simply crossed the road, climbed over the wall and down the bank, crossed the stream on stepping-stones, climbed up the other bank, clinging to tree roots, and went straight into the school yard. Just like Gatley, no excuse for ever being late. I was one of only ten pupils in the whole village school. One elderly school-ma'am taught everything in one classroom, every Friday she brought us treacle toffee and each kid in turn broke it up with a tiny hammer. Perhaps a mile from the village was the tiny station on the Settle/Carlisle line, and on Saturdays I went there with sandwiches to watch the long double-headed freight trains, the guard in his van always waved.

My jobs at home were to chop wood and saw and split the logs stored in the dry garden shed, to pick vegetables as required and to very care-fully clean the glasses of the oil lamps around the house. I never saw any kids after school, as some probably lived on remote farms. From leaving Altrincham I never seemed to have toys, toy cupboards, garden swings etc., but I must have had at least a tennis ball and always a penknife. Birthday presents would be one orange and a bar of chocolate,

Christmas would be an orange, an apple, chocolate and some liquorice allsorts, I once even got a Dinky toy. I seemed to exist in a world of dying adults and precious little else, although I doubt it would bother me at the time as there was always a cat to stroke, birds to watch and some puddle or stream to skim stones across.

The village had a real Squire complete with old Rolls Royce, manor house, and servants. He owned the whole village and surrounding farms, small lake and huge waterfall pouring from Ingleborough mountain and his own little forest with a saw mill. I remember the huge saw let into the floor of a shed, the fierce whine as it sliced logs into lumber increased as it completed the cut and could be heard around the whole village. I remember the smell of released sap and resin as the flat leather driving belt came and went through two slots in the wall, beyond which was a lean-to windowless stone shed housing the engine, but I never knew what type of engine. I was never allowed to even stand by the open door in case flying sawdust went into my eyes, instead I had to peer between cobwebs through the dusty window. I suppose I was always happy if I could watch any kind of machinery. My mother was equally happy every night when she knelt and prayed to her God.

It was 1995 when I next returned to Clapham. The village was very quiet in mid week, just the distant hum of traffic on the by-pass to Settle and the sharp squawk of a few crows. One sell-everything-post-office-plus-sandwiches remained and a women's hairdresser, with one private house offering milk, cream, fresh farm eggs and camping gas cylinders. The Squire was long dead, his home now a residential education centre for adult special study courses run by the County Council. I found the house where I lived and the stepping-stones, but went the long way round to the school. To my surprise it was still open. I went in and spoke to the headmaster. He now had one full time and one part time teacher and there were now forty pupils. He had record books from the day the school was built, in one there was my name and the dates showed that I had attended for eight months, all recorded in beautiful but faded copper-plate writing. I mentioned a photograph I had at home of us ten children and promised to post it to him for the school scrapbook. Before my wife and I drove away we sat on the village seat listening to the tinkling, clear stream, having already found the old saw mill, still active judging by the strong smell of resin, the blacksmith's shed, now a base for a mountain rescue team, and the closed station, now a private house and on sale. Just then a freight train of empty hopper trucks rumbled up the line, no doubt bound for the siding at some distant lime stone quarry, powerful diesel pulling but no guard's van at the end, just a dim red lamp on the last truck.

Back in the car we finally left in the Settle direction. I noticed that opposite the New Inn the old barn had had its huge doorway glassed in to form a shop selling sheepskins, candles and the usual tourist ware with cream teas available but only open weekends. Further on a huge glass Mercedes showroom, directly opposite a similar one for Audi cars, both new and in fields at the extreme edge of the village. Long shadows formed and re-formed on these buildings as a cloud moved to allow the sun to give a last lick of gold paint to the rural scene.

A nostalgic day for me – changes everywhere but nothing really changes.

5

Topography

Viewers of the BBC TV series 'The Last of the Summer Wine' may get the impression that summer wine country is centred on a few villages surrounding Huddersfield, West Yorkshire. However, in reality summer wine country covers at least seven hundred square miles of similar villages in Pennine hills drained by streams joining rivers running into the North Sea on the east side, and similar streams draining into Morecambe Bay and the Irish Sea in the west.

In the sixteenth century the valley would have been completely wooded, fast streams in each branch valley draining the heather moors above the tree line, the heather growing on sometimes a very deep layer of peat, beneath that the millstone-grit rock or limestone. Today you can clearly see some of this barren moonscape when descending into Manchester airport. The Romans first built the few roads over these moors, much later packhorse routes were established over the hilltops, avoiding the valleys where thieves lay in wait to steal their cargo.

Some years before the M62 linked Liverpool with Hull, a test section of motorway was built at the highest Pennine crossing point. Two problems developed: first test boring showed nearly 100 feet of peat, and second, recorded winter wind speeds proved that drifting snow would block the route. To counter this it was thought that huge slanting wooden roof covers would have to be built, as on some Alpine routes. Low cloud could also cover these hills. The route was therefore changed by making a huge cutting through a hillside, the bedrock of which was then hauled to form the embankment for a new reservoir nearby which also kept the motorway reasonably level. A cunning but expensive solution, yet the route is still sometimes closed briefly due to sudden drifting snow and is now fully lit to counter the low cloud. A red-lit sign in Oldham warns of weather conditions up on the tops.

One Pennine valley, and one sprawling village in that valley where I spent my most formative years, have left the strongest memories of the area and the locals. Water power and the extending industrial revolution added road, canal and railway to the existing river in the main valley, leaving little space for houses, mills, shops, schools, and churches. Steam power meant even larger mills cluttered the valley, sometimes the whole length of a four-storey mill would be lapped by canal or river. Some mills had an external hoist to unload cargo from barges. The railway occasionally had to run on a viaduct and through a short tunnel. Somehow in our village they had managed to include a tip, small gasholder, council offices, recreation ground, rail sidings and bowling green.

Some churches were built two storeys at one side, four at the other, providing a Sunday School underneath. In one small town, to get sufficient draft for the boiler fire, one mill level with the canal had an eight foot square tunnel from the boiler house built on and up the sloping surface of the hill, which then changed to a normal tall chimney. The base of the chimney was far higher than the mill roof. Some corners of this town never see the sun all the year round. There is one street which climbs the hill at a compound angle such that if parking a car the passenger door would jam the footpath and exiting the driver's side means you fall out rather than step out.

In contrast to this clutter, one steeply wooded branch valley, with rippling stream, is to this day a hidden oasis of such natural beauty that each year Swiss people meet there to admire the bluebell carpet, the one place in England which most reminds them of home. Swiss visitors never saw the stream running multi-coloured when the local textile dye-house dumped their effluent.

Many years later, deep in these woods a boy scout troop had an old hut used as a base for hiking on summer weekends. Someone gave them an old but still vivid orange truck tarpaulin with which they mended the leaking roof. Someone else reported this to a distant town planning official who ruled that the orange colour was quite out of keeping with the surroundings despite the vivid orange sunsets above the hut. It must be green or nothing, so the scouts promptly painted the tarpaulin, knowing that the green paint would peel off after only one winter. The official, smugly satisfied, waited for his OBE in the six million pound extension behind the town hall, thinking this a very satisfactory outcome really – only two site visits, three planning committee presentations, a discussion at a full council meeting and the establishment, at his suggestion, of a permanent sub-committee to vet similar violations with of course a permanent full time secretary (also at his suggestion). Another job well done. He never saw the multi-coloured effluent either, and the offending orange tarp had only been visible from an aircraft.

6

Sounds of the Village

To preserve the location of one vital foundry and machine shop, the Pennine village where I lived for most of the war shall remain nameless. This exact spot was a target pin-pointed on maps held by the Luftwaffe throughout the war, very likely stolen by the Soviet air force and held for fifty years of subsequent cold war. Although as a child I would never notice it, the hive of activity in this valley must have generated endless noise, both night and day.

In daytime, downtown there was one ancient business, where two elderly brothers made clogs in two styles. The low ones were like shoes but fastened with a metal clasp, generally worn by women and children, the high ones were built like a boot but even the laces were narrow strips of thin leather, these worn by men. In both, stockinged feet stood direct on bare wood three quarters of an inch thick. Narrow grooved 'irons' shaped to match the outer edge of sole and heel were nailed to the wood, the nail heads flush in the grooves. The shaped leather uppers were also nailed to fit a rebate cut in the edge of the wood. For quietness and to give better grip old cycle tyres were cut down and used as an alternative to irons. Kids loved to skid their feet on the cobbles to make sparks from the irons. When irons or rubber wore down you went to the cloggers to get re-shod like a horse, this was a while-you-wait service. If you ordered a new pair from the combined talent of these two brothers, they would first measure both feet. In two hours the clogs would be ready, smelling of the dubbin rubbed into the leather. They were extremely warm, dry and ideal for snowy weather. Kids loved to skate on ice and walking with irons on soft snow caused a hard compressed lump of snow to build up between the irons. A swift kick loosed this projectile at the nearest kid, a change from throwing snowballs. One day I jumped off a wall, landing flat on my feet. Both clog soles split straight down the centre. I walked home in socks to put on my only pair of boots. Next day at lunchtime I ran down to order a new pair of clogs, and after finishing the paper round I collected them at teatime. Fortunately my mother had just received her annual grant of £15 from the 'Sam Dugdale Trust Fund', a local charity set up by a long-dead mill owner to aid needy village children. On the way home I scrounged from the Co-op some brown paper to stuff inside the clogs, as the cloggers always made children's sizes deliberately over large to fit growing feet for as long as possible.

My mother cleaned house for a woman who had told her to apply for this grant, her husband being one of the trustees. With his father and brother he ran a four-storey mill which was the quietest enterprise in the village. They took in scrap rags and sorted them into wool, cotton, or worsted, then baled each separate material and sold them on.

As late as the 1960s postmen in a nearby town wore clogs, and to this day my wife's cousin still makes clogs, boots and riding boots in Newton Stewart, Dumfriesshire. Our clogger's shop was heated by an old iron stove, and in one corner there was always a bale of straw used for making or repairing horse collars, leather galore was scattered at random all over the shop with large sheets stored on a rack to breathe. They also made full tack for horses and the polished saddles gleamed. In contrast the shop was swept out yearly and the outside had last been painted in the previous century. It looked like something from a wild west film but we kids would always call in passing, just to watch the action. The two brothers' constant hammering contributed their steady share of local noise.

Round the corner many more decibels were generated by the village blacksmith, who heated and hammered endless bits of metal all day long, the sound amplified by the open-ended corrugated iron shed where he worked. This was another favourite port of call, we could never understand why the horse didn't flinch when hot iron was nailed onto its hooves. The blacksmith wore a long leather apron, probably made to measure by the cloggers. Sometimes we would see him heat to red the new steel rim for an old wooden cart wheel, then drop it in place when the wood burnt, giving off acrid pungent fumes which made our eyes water. In his rare quiet moments he would shave new spokes for a damaged wooden cart wheel.

At some time long ago, he or his father (retired but occasionally seen out in a wheelchair pulled by a huge Alsatian) had rigged up a fan to the forge. This was an old weather vane on a steel bar which protruded up through the corrugated iron roof, driving a fan at the bottom which, as long as there was any breeze, would cause the glowing coke in the forge to burn white-hot. This allowed more time for hammering without having to constantly pump the leather bellows. No doubt any rash thief intent on stealing steel bars by night would also receive a good hammering before being savaged by the huge Alsatian.

Across the main road, in a ramshackle jumble of lean-to shacks, a battered sign board proclaimed this to be the headquarters of 'Rigour and Mortice Ltd Joiners and Funeral Directors'. (The name, fictitious of course, reminds me of a present-day firm of genuine funeral directors in Blackpool called Box Brothers). Sawn lumber, split logs with bark still on the edges and odd stacked ladders poked out in all directions. Their contribution to the valley symphony was the sudden penetrating whine of a circular saw slicing wood, rising to a scream as the blade completed the cut. Their saw was driven by an ancient single cylinder gas engine which ran all day and added its own bass exhaust notes. Five minutes' daily oiling ensured this would run for another fifty years. The brass nameplate on the engine, polished weekly by the apprentice, showed it was built in 1894 – the crankshaft had revolved millions of times but it had only travelled three miles from where it was made. This firm supplied the blank spokes to the blacksmith.

A powerful percussion plus trombone element was added to the din by the distant whistle of a long freight train climbing up the valley, repeated much louder as it approached our station with the protesting staccato bark of the hard-thrashed engine exhaust drowning the rattle and bump of shunting in our local goods siding. Shortly after, the long warning whistle would repeat as the train approached the next station up the valley. The driver 'had the road' through to Liverpool docks, signals green, points set specially for him, and he let you know about it. These war cargo trains were much longer than the pre-war mixed freights which rattled through the valley stopping at every station. A variation in the percussion was included with the regular bang of wheels hitting rail joint gaps, rising in a crescendo and then diminishing. These heavy 0–8–0 steam locos, shiny black when they left the builders in 1919, had never been cleaned since 1939.

Occasionally on still summer evenings the other sounds would be augmented by mortar fire suggesting the Germans had arrived. However they were merely fog signals stolen from the plate-layer's hut and placed on the railway line by the Blacko Gang in case anyone in the village had nodded off. Sometimes soloists would play their minor parts – the shout of the local constable chasing kids, the bawled evening shout 'put that light out' from the air raid warden, the panic soprano of a calf stuck in a swampy field promptly answered by the hoarse bellow of a cow complaining about all the noise, even the high drone of a loan aircraft trying to find Yeadon, near Leeds. One day I was startled by the sudden undulating roar of a Merlin engine, as a Spitfire shot past. Standing outside my front door, I could see the RAF roundel painted on the top of the starboard wing. I was actually above this aircraft – at this dangerous low level he was a split second away from four mill chimneys, seconds later he would reach five more and so on up the valley. He must have had a death wish but he could have stopped production at any one of the mills. From where I stood I could look down on the tower of the Congregational Church yet our house was but a little way up the hillside. The Spitfire growl receded without any subsequent bang so he must have weaved or climbed out of the valley.

Winter would add repeated bangs to the melody, from legitimate railway fog signals on murky days and nights. Night time would bring first the wailing rise and fall of the air raid warning siren, followed by the steady growl of German engines seeking the one vital foundry. They never dropped bombs but in the fields nearby we would find the remains of burnt-out flares, each a perforated distorted metal stick stuck in the grass in a pile of grey magnesium ash. Huddled in the air raid shelter we never saw the brightly lit valley. Foiled once again the growl would diminish as the Luftwaffe headed for Liverpool, Manchester or Sheffield. Then the long continuous single note of the 'all clear' siren would complete the slow movement of this concerto.

One last desperate attempt to take out the foundry provided the valley with the greatest single blast of concentrated explosive sound ever experienced by local residents. On the night of 23rd December 1944, with no prior warning siren, a V1 flying bomb landed in a field around a quarter of a mile from the target. Strange how this exact spot was close to where centuries before Oliver Cromwell had hurled cannon balls from a higher vantage point when trying to destroy a church. The blast lifted the roof cleanly off a small detached bungalow nearby and deposited it in the field – the elderly occupants suffered not a scratch but would no doubt be puzzled to see stars above their bed, perhaps thinking thieves had taken the whole roof in a determined effort to steal the lead flashing. I now know from research that a few V1 weapons reached Birmingham and Manchester, previously I had always thought that their rocket fuel was only sufficient to reach north London. Based on this false premise I wrongly assumed that it must have been an experimental weapon either ship-launched from the North Sea or even air-launched from a lone bomber. I was wrong on every point, proving that one should never assume anything, particularly concerning German engineering. It was most likely launched from the North Sea German coast around Wilhelmshaven. I missed this big bang as I had moved away by then but my old pals John and Keith were woken by it.

Sixty years later I have a large photo of the central and east Pennines, taken from a satellite 11,028 miles above the earth. Even with a good magnifying glass you can barely distinguish hills from valleys. I also have photographs of the whole 700 square miles taken from an aircraft at 5500 feet, on these any woodland obscures buildings etc. in the valleys. It is not at all surprising that, try as they might and even using flares, they could never locate that foundry, yet many individual German planes must have flown directly over it. The foundry made aluminium bronze selector forks for truck and tank gearboxes, probably the only source in the country. A big hole in that foundry would have caused a much more serious hole in the British war effort.

In similar Pennine countryside, Rolls Royce had taken over an empty cotton mill to avoid disrupting aircraft engine production, as their Derby and Coventry factories were frequently bombed. Years later a section leader in their design office told me that in the designation RB-254 (a huge fan bypass engine for modern jet airliners) the R stood for Rolls and the B for Barnoldswick, in Lancashire, where this successful engine was partly developed.

During the war all manner of sounds flooded this Pennine valley. Today there is just the hum of traffic on the only road to stay open twixt Yorkshire and Lancashire in snowy winters, the occasional rattle of a two-coach diesel train and shouts from footballers at weekends on the long filled-in tip. The cows have nothing left to complain about, that is if there are any cows now left in the valley. The dense yellow fogs we used to experience are no longer seen. I remember the occasion when as a lad I once travelled back on the bus from the nearby town; the conductor walked all the way in front of the bus shining a torch on the kerb and shouting instructions through the driver's open sliding window. When I got off he had already walked four miles and he had a further four miles to the final destination, and then they had to get back. With no smoking chimneys nowadays, the early morning mist soon lifts from the valley and the air is clear and clean. The station is long closed, many houses demolished – the massed sounds never to be heard again.

7

The Grenshaw Family

Looking back I think my mother used the *Yorkshire Post* to search for jobs, for we very quickly moved to a valley village about nine miles from the farm, where she was to act as live-in housekeeper and general dogsbody in a rather strange establishment. The Victorian detached house was the largest house in the village and set in its own belt of woodland, carpeted in May with bluebells. A long winding drive led to the house and part way along it was a separate garage. Below the woods a large stream was fed by a much smaller stream running down through the wood, all perfectly natural, unlike the household we joined.

Cecil Grenshaw was Australian. Orphaned when fourteen he had been placed to live with and work for a farmer who on one occasion, thinking the boy to be idle, tied him to a fence and birched him, whether by one stroke of a leather cat-o-nine-tails or a branch from a tree is not clear, but the marks on his back would remain for the rest of his life and were very clear indeed. They still looked like long burn scars twenty-seven years later; I first saw this grim sight when he took his son and me to the local public swimming pool. We went on a Saturday lunchtime when everyone was at home eating, only the male attendant present to issue tickets at the entrance turnstile, so no one would see these scars. He was a salesman for a local paint manufacturer and used a pre-war black Austin 10 car for his job.

His wife was very peculiar – she thought she had lived in a previous life as a Victorian, and always wore crinoline-type dresses with a cape and bonnet when outdoors. She fully expected to have yet a third life after this current one, planning to return as a butterfly. In summer she caught butterflies with a net on a pole, examined them through a magnifying glass, muttered and released them. She had tried various odd-ball religions and was by then a Christadelphian. Her husband, being Australian, probably believed in beer and sunshine but would get little of either in wartime Britain.

They had one son, Christopher, a year older than I, quiet, normal and generous, who was probably more than glad I had gone to live there. Each morning his father took him to a small expensive boys' school in the nearby town wearing a full uniform in green and gold, dropping me off at the local junior school en route. The locals branded this family as weird, posh and rich – initially at school I was just branded posh as I came to school in a car. Chris had some amazing toys, one such being a complex clockwork tin-plate travelling dockside crane. From one single lever on the cab the hook raised or lowered, the jib too, the cab swivelled in either direction and the whole crane travelled either way on its miniature rail track. It was about three feet long and two feet high. He also had a clockwork open car with steerable wheels and three working gears, operated by a lever positioned as in a real car. With wheels set fully left in the lowest gear it would run round in a small circle. Change to second and it made a larger circle and in top gear it made an even larger circle. At my age then I could never figure out why. On both toys everything was enclosed so you could not see any gears. They were made pre-war by a German firm called Schuco. I could play with these toys whenever I liked. Chris also had a huge Canadian sledge made of bent cane and with a wickerwork double seat high off the ground. Together on this we shot down the steepest fields because the more weight, the faster it went.

A retired long-term paying guest in this ménage had been a music master in some boys' school. His own baby grand piano was in the lounge and he played it frequently. Another lodger was a German Jewish refugee who ran his own small factory in a disused mill in a nearby town. He made bitter plain chocolate bars which were included in survival packs in RAF rubber dinghies etc., and every week he brought us home one bar each but never ate any himself. He also bought his own black bread from somewhere or other and every night tuned his radio to German news programmes. Also staying long term were two 'government' engineering inspectors seconded to a local machine shop – the Luftwaffe target.

My mother and I slept in a single-storey extension at the back of the house, requiring buckets when the glass roof leaked in two places. I could not get to sleep for the sound of rain dripping into the buckets, the German news next door and the distant piano. It was my introduction to some of the sounds of this valley.

Cats were banned from the grounds and must be chased away if seen as the lady of the house thought they were children of the devil spying on humans. Coal was not delivered in sacks, instead one ton was delivered by horse and tipping cart, dumped into the side yard and covered with a tarpaulin held down by stones. My only job was to bucket this and deliver one bucket to the hearth in each downstairs room. The only heating upstairs was by hot water bottles, our shed at the back had no heating at all.

In my whole life my only experience of foretelling the future occurred whilst living in this house. Across the valley was a single farm with fields stretching up to the next hamlet. One night I dreamed that there was a small town on this hillside – when I woke in the morning the dream was quite vivid but outside I saw farm and fields were still there, no sign of any town. This exact dream repeated some nights later and for yet a third time. The small town with shops was always the same. This would be around late 1940 or early 1941.

In the 1960s the whole farm was compulsorily purchased by the local council and houses, flats, shops and a working man's club were duly built with the bus route diverted to serve them. Perhaps I had come under some spell from this weird woman, or even the cats. Very strange, it could have been a useful asset if I'd wanted to buy land, or back horses!

8

Laneside

At some point my mother must have decided she would prefer to have her own home. It would be the very first since Altrincham, so she rented a one-up/one-down cottage for one shilling per week with a huge stone coal shed built on to it. There were six steps up to the only door, three sash windows, a balcony with railings round (this was the coal shed roof) and a long-distance view across and up the valley. It was at the other end of the village to our previous 'home'. The whole rear of the ground floor was dug into the hillside. It was number two in a cluster of eighteen homes with the simple postal address 'Laneside'.

Inside there was a single gas light with asbestos mantle, and a large cast iron range with an oven on one side and water boiler with tap on the opposite side. At the back was a crane to hang the kettle on, which in use swung out over the fire. The chimney drew very well for a coal fire. Beside the oven, in a floor to ceiling cupboard, was a glazed earthenware sink with one cold tap. Under the stairs was a reinforced air raid shelter.

The cottage was much nearer the school and my mother easily got work, cleaning, dusting and polishing for a few local mill owners' wives and the wife of a bank manager. It brought in enough money and she was often given vegetables etc. with her wages. She never did return to any form of nursing – after all the turmoil perhaps she needed a quiet, organised life, locals and employers left to assume she was a widow.

Aunt Laura, Audrey and Edith visited us to see the cottage one weekend. Laura arranged for a spare bed to be brought from her farm in her local butcher's van. At a sale room my mother bought a table, chairs and other essentials, neighbours gave her spare curtains and bed linen, one even gave her a Singer sewing machine. The coal man called and added one free bag to the bag she bought – every person helped her who could, it was typical of village folk in those days. The local mill manager whose house she cleaned even called one evening to offer her a job in the weaving shed, but she declined.

I very soon knew the kids in this group of small cottages – it was the first time I had ever put down roots and developed a close knit circle of pals. In this cluster of homes clinging to the hillside were one family of five daughters, their father boiler-man at the local mill. Perhaps mill boiler-men were exempt from conscription as no boiler, no production – I'm not certain of this but it could well have been a reserved occupation, and due to the continuous shovelling of vast quantities of coal would not be a job where women would replace men. Next door lived an evacuated London woman with her young son and daughter. They were permanently forbidden to play with us northern roughnecks and they always walked well behind us to and from school. At first we imitated their London accent but soon left them alone, where and what their father was we never knew. Across the lane lived one small boy called Stuart, he too forbidden to play with us. He had a permanently hoarse voice and had not yet started school. His father worked nights in the machine shop sought by the Germans. To get to his house you had to go through a high door in the wall and along a balcony supported by another high wall topped with railings. One day during the holidays we knocked on the door of the sleeping man and ran away along the balcony into the lane. Parked by the door was the coal man's cart – the coal man emerged wearing a very wide leather belt and his protective leather back cloth, no doubt both tailormade for him by the village cloggers. With a sack of coal on his back he was about to go through the gate when Stuart's father in pyjamas and slippers threw a bucket of water over him. We hurtled gleefully down the lane to avoid the joint wrath of these two who just stared at each other in speechless amazement. At a safe distance we could see white lines left as rivulets of coal dust ran down the coal man's face.

In one house lived a little old spinster called Elizabeth who gave my mother an enormous carved sideboard. This same coal man having completed his deliveries much further up the hill, returned and moved it from Elizabeth's down the lane to our cottage on his now empty flat cart. It was wartime and the villagers helped each other where possible, the only reward a cup of tea. Old Elizabeth was always first to rush out with bucket and shovel to collect the horse droppings for her rose trees. The huge sideboard was too long to place against the only available wall, as it would block off the door to the understairs air raid shelter, so it remained about a foot from the wall for ever, the central dip in the ornately carved back just cleared the single gas lamp.

The two cottages immediately next to ours each had a third storey forming a separate bungalow above, access was by the stone flagged path which ran round the back of the whole block. A retired joiner lived in one, the other was occupied by an Irish couple. The woman always wore bulky long dresses with a long apron, smoked a long white clay pipe and had no teeth. There would be gas available but we thought that she used paraffin for heating and cooking and had an oil lamp, the coal man never delivered and she would not buy firewood. If she spoke as we passed it was impossible to understand her. We never once saw the husband so he may have been bed-ridden, but we had heard her muttering to someone indoors.

An old widow lived with her spinster daughter in the cottage below. She supplemented her pension by re-selling loaves of bread delivered each week by van from the nearest town. Everyone in our cluster of houses bought from her as it left more room in shopping bags when visiting the Co-op.

Double decker buses were fitted with a huge rubber bag extending the length of the roof and the bus towed a trailer fitted with stove and coal bunker. A large pipe fed warm coal gas up into the bag, another pipe in the front fed it down into the engine compartment. The whole device was intended to save petrol. The conductor's second job was to rake out and top up this stove as necessary at certain bus stops, but never at the town centre terminus. There was then no bus station in the town, each bus route started from a different street. The street where our route started and finished was paved with parquet style wooden blocks, hence no hot ashes were allowed.

In front of our end terrace house the ground was supported by a retaining wall which, although the top was flat and level, increased in height as the lane sloped down. At one point the wall changed direction and then lost height as it carried on at an angle into the steep field. There it became the boundary of a vegetable garden, now abandoned but with strawberry plants spreading everywhere, bonanza time for us in summer. It had been tended by a retired postman but he never bothered with it any more. The lane had no footpaths and across from our house was a wall about four feet high, beside the wall a mature sycamore tree. We found that if our vital rope was tied to a branch and the other end passed across the road, by gripping this end a lad could run along the flat stone wall to get enough momentum to swing right over the lane and land in the tree, caught and held by another lad already up the tree. We had repeatedly practised this, sometimes falling in the road, sometimes going over the wall and missing the tree to fall in the undergrowth of brambles. We had eventually all mastered it and knew the exact distance to run to start the swing.

At dusk one winter evening, an old woman who lived much higher up the lane was climbing the hill carrying two large shopping bags. Just then a body flew straight across in front of her at shoulder height and disappeared. She cried out, dropped the bags and sat down in the lane. Up the tree we all kept silent. Eventually she recovered enough to knock on the nearest door, blurting out, 'There's Germans landing on parachutes . . . tell t'police!'

'Oh, no, it will be just them damned kids.'

She sat on the low wall for a little while, then even more slowly set off up the hill. When she was well away we got down from the tree. It was fully dark by then and John tripped on a bottle of lemonade she had left in the road.

Under the junior school, what had once been a covered playground was converted into a woodwork room by filling in the supporting arches with glazed windows, the room fitted with joiner's benches, each with two vices. The peripatetic woodwork master always began the lesson by getting some lads to saw up small boards, then to split these with chisels into narrow sticks which, at the end of the lesson, he loaded into the wicker basket on his bike. This was his firewood for the week! If any lad misbehaved he hit him with any handy piece of wood, or threw it at culprits further away. One lad who came weekly for that one lesson at our school, with a few mates from another junior school up in the next village, was hit by accident instead of the real culprit. Wearing clogs, the aggrieved lad just walked straight to the teacher, kicked him savagely on the shin and continued out of the room without a word, never to return. Another time the teacher missed his target and the wood went through the window. Some while later all these windows were fitted with wire mesh screens on the outside, the headmaster announcing that this was 'to stop balls from the playground and in case of air raids'.

There can't have been many schools where uncle and nephew attended as pupils at the same time, yet they did at this school. Both lived at the somewhat grandly named General Rawden Hotel, one of the three pubs in the village, each owned by the three breweries in the nearby town. Roy Sharratt's father was the licensee, Roy's much older sister lived and worked at the pub, her husband away in the army. Her only son, Bobby Storah, was Roy's nephew.

Old Elizabeth taught my mother to make a 'bitted' or 'rag' rug, all poor local people made these. First, for one penny, you bought an old hessian sack from the Co-op. Cut down both long edges and opened out flat this became the standard size rug, then any scrap bits of woven cloth, anything of any colour or pattern were cut into pieces 1 inch by 2 inches, these being inserted through the sack leaving a loop at the rear. A long length of twine knotted into the corner of the sack was then progressively fed through each loop to retain each 'bit'. The nearer you placed the 'bits' together, the denser the finished rug. The insertion tool was a wooden spike with a spring loaded hollow prong at the end, which gripped the 'bit' as it went through the sack, as you pulled it out the grip released itself. Elizabeth loaned hers to my mother. Together we eventually finished the rug and it was duly laid in front of the hearth, very soft to walk on but if you dropped anything tiny on it you had to find it by shaking the rug carefully.

Early in September we started to collect wood for the November bonfire. As the pile grew on the narrow strip of spare land opposite the cottages we could see a much larger pile being accumulated down across the main road on the edge of some allotments. Some older kids lived down there in three rows of terrace houses, one house in the terrace beside the main road being the home of the local policeman, but without a 'Police' sign, just a large Constabulary badge fastened above the door. We heard at school that some of these kids had fireworks, which of course we could not afford. We offered them a deal, in return for some treacle toffee made by our mothers we would like to come to their 'plot'. This was agreed, and they mentioned the constable's ruling that 'the fire must be out by 7 o'clock sharp, spray it with the hosepipe from the allotments so that the German bombers don't see it.'

We were left with a large varied pile of scrap wood, but the teacher's firewood had given me an idea. If we could get hold of a saw and use John's father's axe we could start to sell bundled firewood. We went to the retired joiner at the back, and proposed our second deal of that day. If he initially loaned us a saw, we could start paying for it as and when we sold firewood.

'You can 'ave it, I can't use it with me rheumy 'ands,' he said. Beside our cottage and at bedroom level was a disused one room dwelling which John's father had rented for 6 pence a week, where he kept the canaries which he had bred and sold, the empty cages still left on a long bench. John's mother still paid the rent and the third deal was that once selling we would refund her the rent. In less than two hours we moved all the bonfire wood into this one dry room and we were in business. John's mother insisted 'Keith must never touch that axe, or the saw, so see to it'. Keith's job, therefore, was to load the sticks into an old paint tin half filled with sand. With the dangerous scissors, which his mother knew nothing about, he then had to cut set lengths of twine, bought from the Co-op, for us to tie the bundle of sticks as he couldn't make knots. Keith frequently dropped the ball of twine, which promptly rolled away, unwinding itself as it went. We took turns, one held the wood while the other one sawed, the third one chopped. Lifting the now tied bundle out of the tin was the last job on our assembly line and we soon had a good stock of bundles.

We found a broken radio chassis on the tip, noticed two fine copper wires leading from the largest component which at the time we didn't know to be a transformer. Back home we soon taught Keith to bind the wire round the bundles, twist and cut both ends with the scissors. 'Why didn't you fetch this before, it's better than messing about with string.' He once begged to have a go with the axe; we found one block of wood free from knots, propped it up so that he could wield the axe with both hands and he made a mighty stroke – both pieces shot away across the room. 'Don't ever tell anyone, now get winding some bundles.' We never found another scrap radio but it was months before we had to buy any more garden twine.

In a distant field the local farmer, who delivered our milk and eggs when not re-building his walls, had a part-collapsed disused lone hen-hut. He agreed we could have it for the 'plot' if we shifted it. More wood for the business, this time designer firewood with one side of each stick whitewashed – it would burn more slowly to give a greater chance for the coal to ignite, or so we could tell the customers.

Years afterwards, when chatting to a retired farmer in a pub, I learned of one war-time rule concerning food rationing. A few locals kept pigs but there were no large-scale breeders in the area. A farmer would kill a large pig and sell the cuts to his close pals. He then rang the constable and the Ministry of Agriculture area inspector, who by law had to witness the slaughter of his pig (this being a second, smaller animal of course). The inspector then signed a certificate that went with the carcass to the curer. When the inspector had departed the local constable was then rewarded for his ham acting with a large piece of gammon reserved from the first animal.

Around that time one lad at school announced that he was leaving the village, his mother moving to the next town to live with her sister while both their husbands were away in the army. I went to the papershop with him after school and took over both his morning and evening rounds. This entrepreneurship produced (a) spending money, (b) cash to purchase a new second axe, (c) our very first firewood customer – the papershop. Each Friday afternoon my route to the papershop was via the tip to check what wood had been dumped. Saturday morning John and I pulled both bogies loaded with firewood and we started to deliver both papers and firewood, as the previous Saturday when I called to collect the newspaper money I had mentioned that firewood bundles would be available. On the way back we trawled the tip for wood, hauled it round to the Co-op, John guarded both bogies whilst I went in and got the groceries which both our mothers had listed and we hauled everything home.

As with the shanty town dwellers on the outskirts of Mexico City, the tip had become a vital part of our economy. One Sunday we were busy sawing and chopping when the retired joiner called round. He returned home to get a file and oilstone to sharpen both axes and went to great lengths to show us how to sharpen the saw by filing a new cutting edge to each tooth, but at a slight angle. He called it 'touching up'.

In the space of two weeks we had established an ample renewable stock of free raw material and an existing stock of finished products. We were fully tooled up with our own transport, we had an expanding cash-only customer base, weekly repeat demand for a fully consumable product, a young, alert and money-driven staff, no bad debts, no long-term debts and we were not committed to any long-term leases. We had no auditors' fees to pay as we kept no books, We had no local competition and were paid to deliver by the mighty newspaper industry!

I once found a bike frame on the tip, short of saddle, mudguards and rear wheel. The local cycle shop found me an old wheel to fit it and an old saddle stem and I bought a new saddle. The cycle shop man promptly became one more firewood customer. I was now mobile and used the bike to and from the papershop on weekdays, it was fine on the main road or canal bank, other routes were much too steep. Having no electricity meant that our radios ran on wet accumulators, rented for one penny a week, kept on a slow charge at the cycle shop and exchanged every fortnight.

Once a month lads from the school were asked to pull a plumber's handcart round the village collecting waste paper and cardboard to be recycled – we took this to an empty house for temporary storage. I went on this expedition just once, more time was spent chasing paper which blew off the cart into the middle of the main road, it was easier to stay in school. On one Friday detour to the tip I found a huge pile of what looked like old roof timbers, it looked as if a tipping lorry had dropped a full load. The plumber's cart was normally left in a disused, corrugated iron garage behind the Catholic church, so on the Saturday our gang borrowed it to shift this wood, much of which was too long for the cart and overhung it, but we tied it on with an old clothes line. As we struggled up the steep lane Norman's father, on his way home from work, caught up with us and gave us a helping push. One month's firewood in just one trip!

The managing director of the local cotton mill sometimes drove past our house to work in his immaculate pre-war black Riley, petrol supply permitting, otherwise he marched there with his two terriers running loose ahead of him, sniffing at everything, particularly the telegraph poles. We found a dead cat one day and presenting it to him with a 'please sir, your dogs have killed our cat' were rewarded with 'so sorry lads' and one shilling! We were tempted to keep the cat and try this again but saw maggots on it so slung it in a field.

Once, on the tip we found a long thick rope. We tied some evenly spaced knots in it and used it to climb the lone sycamore which we then adopted as our personal Flying Fortress. Keith was allowed to proudly carry this rope wound across his chest like a bandolier, compensation as he was too small to climb the tree.

9

Pals

Pals I had during the junior school years were John and his younger brother Keith, Norman, Granville and another Donald. We all walked up and down the same lane to school, sometimes taking a short cut across a field if there was no bull in it that day. We all had homemade sledges and homemade 'bogies', the latter being two old floorboards battened together with one old pram axle pivoted at the front and a second fixed axle at the rear, steered or pulled by a rope attached to the front axle. Norman used his to hurtle down the steep lane from his home, leaving it in our coal shed, then collecting it and pulling it back home up the hill after school. He never came back to play with us in the evenings because he lived perhaps a mile further up the lane, in a cottage attached to a farmhouse. They had no piped water, instead used the farm well which had never been known to run dry, and collected rainwater from the roof for the garden. They had no electricity or gas, his mother cooked on the old iron range and a paraffin cooking stove. Lighting was by three beautiful old brass oil lamps with double wicks giving a steady golden glow, the lamp glasses always spotless. This continued until the 1950s when rural electrification was extended to include their hamlet. There was a small Baptist chapel nearby which my mother used to attend, the inside whitewashed every year and heated by a pot-bellied iron stove burning coke. This was mounted on a stone plinth near the centre of the building, a stove pipe angled from it up to the wall giving off additional heat Canadian style.

Within a five-minute walk lived a third Donald, eldest of three brothers. Their surname nearly rhymed with maggot so naturally they were known to all the school kids as 'the Maggots'. Near the school was a large shed, the garage for the large truck run by a one-man transport firm. Jim Meadowcroft hauled textile goods around the mills in the valley. Outside this shed he always left a pile of large empty wicker skips used for carrying full yarn bobbins. One day coming from school we grabbed Stuart, the youngest 'Maggot', stuck him in a skip and sat on the lid for fun. His brothers were walking in front and never saw this. His mother appeared twice at the end of their terrace to shout for him to come home so we finally let him out. He must have told her about the kidnap, for the next time we passed their house she shouted from a bedroom window, 'You scruffs keep away from here, or else.' The window banged shut. We learned later from Donald that they were banned from playing with us. Pity really, we needed more crew for the Flying Fortress.

When Norman and I passed the County Minor Scholarship to go to the senior school he got a bike and in summer we cycled all the way. At the point of the main road where we had to turn right by the fish shop dual tramlines remained in the middle of the road, although in other portions of the road they had been lifted for scrap steel for the war effort. To date, due to my gypsy lifestyle, I had already attended four infant/junior schools; on the very first day at my fifth school we both got our front wheels caught in the rail groove and fell off in a heap, arriving grazed and bruised. Perhaps an omen for I got many more bruises at this school over the next five years.

Normally we would have had to attend in full school uniform: cap, blazer, grey flannels, black shoes, school tie, white shirt and school pullover. Because wartime had brought clothes rationing the rules were relaxed, only cap and tie were compulsory. My mother sometimes sold our clothing coupons to the mill manager's wife.

Being the same age Norman and I both completed apprenticeships and were conscripted into the RAF going together to RAF Padgate, near Warrington, for eight weeks initial training. He then had a fortnight's embarkation leave during which he married a local infants school teacher and they honeymooned at Blackpool. He then went to the Far East for the remainder of his two years. Whilst he was away she died in her sleep, only then did her parents find out she was diabetic. I had been posted to RAF Dishforth in North Yorkshire near Ripon. I got home most week-ends and reading of Norman's wife's death in the local paper went to see his parents, his mother was distraught. The RAF did not allow him home for the funeral and this really sickened her.

I did an extra year in the RAF and on return from the Middle East found that Norman had emigrated to Australia. I never saw him again. There he remarried and had twin sons but like my Uncle Harry in Canada he too experienced British government at its caring best and distanced himself as far as possible from it.

My pal Granville was tall for his age, lanky and clumsy. Apart from walking to and from school we saw little of him, he always wore high laced-up clogs and worked on his father's farm before and after school. He had around four miles per day to walk and no bus available. We only played together in the school holidays. His father's farm had no gas, electricity or piped water.

The other Donald lived in the next terrace to John and Keith. This block was built at an angle to the lane on a steep slope, his house being partially dug into the hillside, such that half their kitchen window in the end of the terrace was below the field level. The recessed window was protected by a dry stone wall built to stop cows falling into the recess.

Once after school we were playing cowboys in this field. I shot John who, clutching his chest, fell backwards against this little wall, then pitched forward onto the grass. In slow motion, most of the wall tumbled with a deep rumbling sound down into the kitchen, taking most of the window with it. Directly behind the window the kitchen sink was shattered by huge half-round top stones and water spurted upwards from a drunken pipe, the tap had disappeared under the stones. We all shot away up the field as Donald's old grandmother ran from the house repeatedly screeching out 'There's a bomb dropped, there's a bomb dropped.' Rattling down the lane in clogs and shawl, she sped to find her daughter and son-in-law in the mill. Crossing the main road, at the bus stop, she repeated this to the conductor who was somewhat puzzled as he had heard nothing in the way of sirens or aircraft. Donald's father ran all the way back from the mill, entered the still wide open house door and found all the debris, then promptly turned off the water. The kitchen floor being bare stone flags had a small grate at one corner so the water had really done the least damage, simply running away down the grate.

We just ran and ran, eventually ending up three fields distant where, panting, we held a council of war. Leaning against the wall (kids never learn) hands in pockets as usual we debated what best to do in the worst crisis of our war to date. The eventual consensus was that (a) a badly built stone wall had simply collapsed due to vibration from the constant drone of German bombers, (b) this had nothing to do with us as we had been away playing in the woods, (c) we knew, saw and heard nothing, (d) we would go right round and approach quite openly up the lane, Donald would go inside and rush out again to invite us to look at the disaster, when we would all feign amazement.

It all worked exactly as planned. When we went in Donald's father and the farmer who had been summoned from milking were shifting rocks back out into the field and we were roped in to help. Keith shot into his own house for a treacle sandwich and stayed there. We had actually got away with it, amazing! The next day we saw the plumber's van in the lane and the farmer in the field re-building the wall. All would soon be well again but Donald's grandmother would never forget it, nor the ride back home in the mill owner's car.

John was a year younger than I, although a quiet lad he took full part in all our exploits. He left the local school to become an apprentice with the local painter and decorator, but badly affected by the smell of paint and turpentine he soon left to start work in a carpet factory. He stayed in carpet manufacturing right up to retirement, by which time he was chief inspector in a large group. I was best man at his wedding, he was best man at mine. John's wedding some 45 years ago was the only time I got drunk through mixing drinks. I had a blinding hangover through that Sunday and swore I would never do it again – I never have and stick to beer. When called up into the army (conscription continued in Britain long after the 1939–45 war had ended) he was first posted to

Elgin in Scotland, then the Middle East, but returned unscathed and continued in carpets.

George, John's father, was in the army, posted to the Azores just before we moved to the village, no one saw him for four years. He had previously worked at the railway goods yard. He was in the Royal Engineers where for the remainder of the war he maintained air conditioning and refrigeration plant for military units stationed there. He returned safely and from there on became a communist, although he took no part in politics. John's mother remained a staunch practising Catholic until she died in her early nineties. George had a deep fear of debt, so would never take on a mortgage. Instead when the eighteen cottages were demolished as being unfit, the family rented a roomy council house with all mod cons such as electric lights, back door, bathroom and separate toilet. For some reason the kitchen, bathroom and toilet had unplastered walls, they were simply painted light green.

I well remember John and Sheila becoming engaged, Sheila being a Sunday school teacher at the Methodist chapel. One Friday evening I was at their house when the local Catholic priest visited to warn John that he would be excommunicated if he went ahead with the marriage. John's mother, knowing her priest was coming, had retired upstairs not wishing to see him humiliated. Faced with one irate communist and John who had never been inside a church since he stopped attending Sunday school at around ten years old, also Keith who had been completely indifferent to any kind of religion, and me ready to burst out laughing, the priest muttered something (probably a curse) and promptly left. George shouted 'Don't threaten my son with your black-magic and don't ever set foot in this house again.'

Keith was five years younger than John, just a toddler at that time and we were always having to wait for him to catch up. He loved being in our gang and desperately clung onto us as we hurtled down steep lanes or fields on our bogies. He then very importantly pulled the pile of bogies back up the hill. Today he is a proud grandfather with golf as his hobby, having years ago given in and allowed Sylvia to marry him after courting for seven years. Their wedding was a very lively occasion.

Maureen, their sister, was then just a babe in arms. When air raid sirens sounded John, Keith and mother with babe in arms ran down the lane to our house, Maureen mummified in a blanket, the others wearing top coats over night attire. Our house had old railway sleepers fitted vertically under the staircase to strengthen it to use as an air raid shelter. The six of us squeezed in together to keep warm. The smell of old creosote on the sleepers and paraffin from the hurricane lamp was trapped in that cramped triangle. When the all clear siren sounded we all un-squeezed, they went back home to bed and my mother said a prayer.

Next to John's cottage was a triangular stone-flagged yard which narrowed to become the path that in turn led round to the back of the block. To one side of this yard was a cluster of stone-built cubicles each the width of a door, with a gap at both top and bottom of these doors. A series of single overlapping stone slabs formed the roof. The interior, whitewashed once a year, had a lift-off seat with large hole in the middle, the bare boards scrubbed weekly. On a nail inside the door hung torn squares of the local newspaper. These cubicles were tub toilets, one per house, emptied weekly by the council truck. The whole cluster was commonly known as 'the bogs'. Just as John's family came down the lane to our air raid shelter, so we and all the other residents went outside and up the lane to the toilets, not a place to linger on a cold winter night.

In a complicated exchange I once acquired from some lad at school the mould for making one lead soldier. This was in two halves, you first held the inside of each over a candle to put a sooty deposit on the surfaces to aid release. The two halves, made from some kind of ceramic, when secured together with an elastic band left a small vent at one end, with a larger pouring hole at the other. I melted some scrap lead from the tip in a soup ladle on the fire and poured it into the mould. When cool there emerged the detailed figure of a Scottish soldier in a kilt, although the rifle was a bit short. Once cleaned of black soot, it was painted with some olive drab from a model aircraft kit, kilt and bare knees all in olive drab. I soon tired of this labour intensive effort and swapped the mould for something else. I learnt two things, however: never to allow even the smallest drop of water to hit the surface of molten lead as this causes the whole ladleful to fly out into the fire, and second that toothpaste tubes in those days were possibly made of lead. A rolled up empty tube when put in the fire would suddenly unroll itself with a bang and then melt.

Just once we walked the three miles to a run-down cinema on the fringe of the town. This showed old black and white cowboy and gangster films and after each Saturday matinee a man with a tank strapped on his back walked the aisles spraying scented disinfectant. It was known as the 'flea pit', real name Palladium, the matinee known as the 'three penny rush'. Here we joined a long queue on the pavement to enter and be frisked by the male usher who threw confiscated catapults, pea shooters and other weaponry onto an increasing pile in the foyer. He was helped by an usherette who did more wrestling than frisking. However they did not take the bags of cream buns which were later thrown at the screen. The national anthem completely ignored, there was a mad rush to get out to select a better weapon. As we were not 'carrying' we just ambled out to find all that remained of the pile was a pair of toy handcuffs. The gangster film was good and the Pathe Newsreel showed bombers over Germany at night, but we never went again as it was too far to walk and we could not afford both bus fare and entrance charge.

One lad at school called Ken lived at the far end of the village. He, along with his mother, older brother and sister, had been evacuated from the Liverpool bombing to our relative safety. After the war he returned to Liverpool to work as a steward on the transatlantic liners as had his father before the war. Years later he left the sea to scttle in Bermuda helping to run a restaurant, his hobbies then scuba-diving and under water photography. He became so competent that *National Geographic* magazine published lots of his pictures of multi-coloured rare fish. His brother and sister both married locals and remained in the village, his brother becoming a tool-maker in the machine shop sought by the German bombers. On first hearing the sirens in our village his mother must have wondered why ever they had been moved to live here.

On the grapevine Ken had heard that three miles up the hill on the highest fringe of the nearby town was an abandoned quarry where the local Home Guard practised. He thought it might be worth exploring in the holidays. There might be an old hut with dynamite left in it as in cowboy films, and the Home Guard might also have left something of interest. We set off and found it on the edge of moorland but could not understand why the flat quarry floor was covered with a deep layer of black sand. There was no hut, no dynamite but lots of spent cases from .303 rifle rounds and some wooden targets fastened to the rock walls. Collecting every single case (excellent barter for swaps) we also found a few live rounds, bonanza! Poking in the sand with his spindle Ken found a black Colt .45 revolver stamped with the arrow-head indicating War Department issue. Alas all six cylinders were empty but in swap value this was priceless. We agreed to return to the quarry the next day but found only still more spent cases, despite kneeling and prodding as if we were searching for landmines.

Years later I found out that this curious black sand was moulding sand dumped by a foundry. It can be re-used a few times in moulds but the repeated heating ruins the chemical binder coating each grain and it is then useless.

Walking back home it was exciting to handle live rounds and spent cases, imagination running wild, we in the Fortress crew thinking of a whole burst of them stitching their way along the cockpit of a German fighter, although we knew the Fortress gunners used the heavier .500 calibre rounds. Had we jammed it in a normal wall dividing two fields the round might have gone straight through the wall and wounded or even killed a cow. We were lucky the constable was nowhere in sight. Oh! What tales to tell at school after the holidays!

One day in the village two lads were brawling on the pavement, our gang and other lads clustered around watching. Approaching in the distance the village policeman broke into a run shouting 'pack it up and go home', waving his cape in one hand. Some of us had ruefully experienced his use of this cape, the brass hanging chain at the collar really hurt when he lashed out with the cape. He wasn't a man to bother with juvenile courts, probation officers etc., just an efficient copper who dispensed his own brand of rapid justice followed by a visit to the boys' parents to describe the degree of wickedness, never a mention of the punishment already inflicted. The two lads had got up and we were just beginning to move away when Ken pulled out the gun, pointing it straight at the policeman. The policeman stared at it, thinking it to be a toy gun, and just turned to walk away. Ken was instantly famous throughout the school as the only lad to have pulled a gun on a cop in true gangster fashion. All the lads were familiar with this gun, as for one half-penny they were allowed to hold it in the toilets at break time but the young fingers could not pull the stiff trigger. Much later Ken swapped it with one of the Blacko Gang for an old bike!

Occasionally we would tangle with this Blacko Gang, their leader one Ted Black, whose father was manager of the local Co-op. His gang of five or sometimes more would trawl the tip as we did. Whoever got there first would start a pitched battle across the tip prising up anything to throw at the opposition, our objective to force them back down the steep slope into the river, theirs to force us in the other direction into the canal. Sometimes battle would cease at the shout of the recreation ground care-taker, rapidly approaching waving a walking stick. We ran one way on the canal tow path, they the other way along the river bank. Even at that early age we already, albeit unwittingly, knew and used the divide and conquer technique, although in our case it was more accurately divide and survive.

The Co-op emporium was massive for the size of the village. It was run by Ted Black's father with the help of Ted's older brother Edgar, both attired in fawn warehouse coats. The son had started at 14 straight from the village school, to learn the crafty art of retailing, along with his other varied duties such as unloading trucks, polishing apples, serving as barman at wedding receptions or funeral teas, taking orders for coal, fitting shoes, sweeping the bare wooden floor weekly (merely a system of rearranging layers of dust). His final job of the day was to drop the orders for coal into the Co-op coal office on the railway sidings on his way home. Next to this office were stables housing the black horse kept for funerals and the brown horse for coal deliveries. In a lean-to shed against the stables were kept the coal cart and the horse drawn hearse painted black with side windows and black curtains. A carved wooden rack for flowers was mounted on the roof. I remember once seeing this rig in action, someone had cut down a whole rhododendron bush in full flower and tied it on this rack with black ribbon. On hooks in the stable wall hung varied bits of horse tack, a separate hook holding the black frock coat and top hat for the hearse driver, Mr Black himself.

The Co-op building was two storeys high on the road side, four on the canal side. From a separate entrance at street level one staircase led down to what was known as 'The Co-op Hall', a second staircase led to a storage area below. A disused hoist overhung the canal which would originally have been used for unloading deliveries direct from canal barges. The Co-op Hall was used for lectures with slides, wedding receptions, funeral teas, meetings of any local organisations, whist drives, dances with a pianist and for the annual general meeting of the Co-op itself, when the manager presented audited accounts to the committee and any members who may have attended to query why the cash-back dividend was again so low. This cash was paid out at the AGM or for just one week after it in the shop – if you did not claim it you waited until the next AGM.

Inside the shop the main grocery counter was well organised and run by the two women assistants. The rest of the whole place was a shambles run by father and son, with beds, furniture, fork handles, Wellington boots, rolls of wire netting, bundles of thick-stick firewood at four pence (ours was three pence), wash tubs, galvanised buckets, coal scuttles, tools, sacks of potatoes, even toilet rolls kept in a sack.

Whatever you wanted they had it, if only it could be found, which might entail a long wait. The son had been taught window dressing by his father, his best creation two huge piles of cornflake packets with a roll of linoleum balanced artistically across them. He cleaned the huge shop windows twice a year on the outside, alternate years he cleaned the inside. Above the windows outside were two white globe lamps held on cast iron wall brackets, never lit even on the dullest foggy days. The whole place looked like the general store in River Bend, South Dakota circa 1890. Long after the main building had been built a small single storey brick shed had been added. This was the butchery department with one elderly butcher selling the meagre ration but with rabbits and tripe always available.

We realised from a map that the river in our valley eventually ran into the North Sea so, foregoing the penny had we returned it to the Co-op,

58

we put a fake coded message in a pop bottle. Purporting to come from a German spy it read 'send more currency and earmuffs'. We knew it would float right across the North Sea to Wilhelmshaven where it would be picked up by the Gestapo. We carefully launched the bottle into the river, it probably went down river but one hundred yards and may to this day be still bobbing about between stones and dead undergrowth.

Around this time I entered a competition to design a 'Wings for Victory' poster. I won it with a pencil sketch of a foggy day at sea, the stern of a merchantman just visible through the fog, a Spitfire flying overhead just above the belt of fog. I very proudly collected the six shillings postal order at the British Legion hut and shook hands with the Council Chairman. I was so rich I could have bought 36 vanilla slices at the Co-op. I didn't, but added some more savings to buy a second axe for the firewood business, this also from the Co-op.

Midway through the village was one three storey terrace, with the usual bungalows on the top deck, these accessed by very long steep stone steps at each end of the block. Dustbin men had to carry full metal bins down these in icy winter weather. Part way along this block was Corletts wholesale sweet warehouse. The owner always stood guard at the large loading bay door every afternoon until all the school kids had passed down the road, just in case some kid nipped inside to steal a full jar of boiled sweets. Fastened to his outside wall was a machine which dispensed bubble gum, every fifth halfpenny inserted produced two gums. We older ones used to politely let the younger kids feed in four consecutive coins and then quickly push them aside so we could insert the vital fifth coin, our early version of 'you lot buy four, we get one free'.

It was some time during this period that my mother realised she could earn money more easily on clean war work in a factory in the nearby town, instead of going out every day in all weathers to clean people's homes. She got a sitting down job assembling detonators for use by the army, these were the diameter of a pencil but just over an inch long enclosed in a brass case and had to be spaced evenly along a fine insulated cable. For a powerful landmine to work effectively the track of a tank needed to pass directly over it. This rarely occurred, so a string of these detonators would be buried in shallow soil or hidden in the grass around the mine. When a tank track compressed any detonator it set off the whole string which provided enough vibration to trigger the mine. Mother once accidentally brought one home in her shopping bag. When she emptied debris from the bag into the fire at home it blew hot coal out and charred the bitted rug. Afterwards I found a distorted brass casing – from then on she emptied her shopping bag into the scrap bin at work.

To avoid the daily bus journeys she later found a house to rent only five minutes walk from the works. We moved into the town and my days in the village ended. John and Donald got my share in the firewood business and some other kid took over the paper rounds. In some ways I was glad to be rid of all the manual work as the homework from the senior school was by then increasing, but I missed the close pals and knew no one in the town.

Before I left, one frightening accident occurred at the junior school. The lower tarmac playground sloped down to a high retaining wall above the footpath on the main road. On this wall was mounted close-spaced metal railings, each upright topped with a decorative cast iron spike, not at all sharp, in fact the end was rounded off and would be covered with many layers of black paint applied over the years. Matching railings, but in this case mounted on a low wall, divided the playground into boys' and girls' areas. One young girl, perhaps seven, in her lunch break was climbing this railing when she slipped somehow and impaled herself on one of the spikes. Where it actually entered her we knew not, but she started to scream. Blood trickled down the railings, the pitch of the constant scream increased and blood flowed down the wall and down the tarmac. The headmaster rushed out of school with both women teachers, one woman went either side of the railings and tried to support the girl's weight. The whole playground was silent, every child just remained motionless, a dropped lone tennis ball rolled ignored down the tarmac. The girl suddenly stopped screaming as the headmaster dashed back into the school to phone for an ambulance, on return he ordered us to get our coats and go straight home and return in the morning. I did not know the girl's name, but of course we all knew her by sight. The head then went across the main road to the constable's house, he was out somewhere, but his wife came over. I remember the sun glinting on the dark pool formed against the wall.

The next day there was no trace of blood anywhere. We never knew what happened later, whether she lived or died, but she never returned. For some days everyone was very subdued with many curious glances at those railings, one girl was sick in the playground that day. It was a truly shattering experience for a whole school of young children, three teachers, one constable's wife and the ambulance men. Some days later the dividing railings were removed as scrap metal for the war effort.

Years later I became a manager at this school. I was the only one in this group to have actually attended the school as a child, but at the meetings I never mentioned the tragedy. After the war the railings had never been replaced and even the low dividing wall had at some time been removed.

10

One Memorable Day

One night each week I cleaned my boots to attend an organisation at the Methodist Chapel Sunday School. The 'uniform' was a shiny black leather belt carrying a pouch, a white belt draped at an angle over one shoulder topped off with a round pill-box hat with chin strap, round this hat the words 'Life Boys'. This was the junior section of the 'Boys Brigade'. This uniform was worn over varied trousers, patterned pullovers, all manner of jackets and scarves. Standing on parade we must have looked like a rehearsal for some comic opera, the costumes not yet delivered.

Once a year I polished the boots even more thoroughly for the Armistice Day Sunday parade. This assembled at the top of the village, marching through to turn left onto Station Road and then to the war memorial on the recreation ground. An adult Boys Brigade officer led the parade, ten paces behind him two others carried a banner aloft. Then followed the Boys Brigade band, big drum banging, brisk tapping of side drums and bugles blasting, then came the Girl Guides (we had no scout troop in this village), the St. John Ambulance Brigade contingent, followed by decked out girls from three sunday schools also carrying huge banners.

Behind these came one part time fireman in uniform, one limping character in Home Guard uniform carrying a rifle, the air raid warden in tin hat and armband, a stirrup pump in a sling on his back. Three paces further back came the village policeman shouting 'left, right' but sometimes hesitating, trying to match his shouts to the foot-fall. Bringing up the rear we Life Boys had to hop, skip, jump and run to keep up with this proud throng, and behind us and sometimes amongst us ran two barking dogs. This entire spectacle was watched by villagers lining the pavement, prams, babes in arms and one old woman knitting gloves for the troops.

A sudden prolonged train whistle drowned out the whole band, and my eyes swung to the railway, less than a hundred yards away across the river. I saw a long string of low trucks carrying tanks trundling through the valley – never having seen a real tank before I stopped to watch. The lads following bumped into me, a dog's paw was trodden on, snarling, the dog promptly bit one lad and we finished up in a tangle on the road. A message was relayed along the pavement and a St. John Ambulance lad ran back to help. We sorted ourselves out and had to run like mad to catch up, leaving the injured lad and his attendant in the road.

The vicar, Catholic priest, Methodist minister and limping British Legion veterans with their Hon. President, a lieutenant colonel in full army uniform with revolver had all made their individual way to the cenotaph. The lieutenant colonel was also a local mill owner who employed many of the adults present. We duly joined them and arranged ourselves in a semi-circle.

For the twenty sixth time one medal-bedecked veteran, further burdened with his Chairman of the Urban District Council chain of office, started the solemn ceremony by accompanying the singing of a hymn on his mouth organ, perhaps a cherished gift from a dying comrade in a distant muddy trench. The vicar then read a prayer and ended with a blessing, his high outstretched arms enfolding all God's creatures including two puzzled rabbits watching from the river bank and one equally puzzled but cautious rat on the canal bank. Being November, at this stage the Blacko Gang at the far end of the tip started to let off fireworks, not exactly part of the ceremony yet no doubt a little nostalgic for the veterans. Blacko was the leader of our sworn enemies, being one Ted Black whose father was manager of the Co-op.

Just then came an almighty blast from a shot-gun. The caretaker of the library, council offices, recreation ground and the slipper baths also fancied himself as Principal Rodent Control Officer Grade I, as we might call him nowadays. He decided that this sacrosanct occasion should not be viewed by vermin, God's creatures or not. He let fly at the rabbits, missed and the rabbits promptly disappeared underground. He turned the second barrel on the rat, again missing but his pellets rattled on an empty oil drum floating on the canal. The rat, thinking this was machine gun fire, promptly dived under water with a plop. Blacko's gang ran off before he could reload. Slipper baths were simply a public bath house where for six pence in old English money you got a towel (better to take your own), a minute piece of carbolic soap and a hot bath in your own private cubicle, frequented weekly by half the adult villagers, who didn't have a bathroom at home.

It was only to be expected of a diligent caretaker, particularly as both the council chairman and past chairman were present, and clearly indicated that he was ready for German parachutists who were expected any moment, the recreation ground and bowling green being the only flat drop zones in the village.

The age old ceremony ended with a lone bugler playing the 'Last Post' a little off key while banners were dipped towards the cenotaph column, one clumsy lad dropping his onto the vicar's shoulder. The band quietly marched away to the beat of a single side drum, other people drifted homeward, veterans and colonel went into the nearest pub, the colonel was buying. The old woman, still knitting, trudged home, but for us lads the best was yet to come.

Every rat in the village risked air rifles and pistols, arrows, catapults and thrown steel spikes, also a chance encounter with one old chap who for his Sunday morning walk patrolled the canal bank carrying an axe, ever mindful of possible parachutists. I remember as a lad watching a rat cross the main road to the bus stop, the few women there lifted their skirts and screamed, one brave man stamped on it in the gutter. The rat shook itself and limped back across the main road, then down Mill Lane back to the canal.

Knitting for the troops was a wartime practice when worn knitted items would be unravelled and re-knitted into balaclavas, gloves and scarves and clever women who could turn a heel produced socks. Known as 'comforts' they were duly given to the troops. Interesting to imagine a private huddled in an army greatcoat, thick as a carpet, with mauve and yellow gloves where some woman used up her old yellow jumper before finishing the gloves. Perhaps the army insisted on brown or green or permitted a mixture for camouflage.

Two hours later on that cold frosty day, clear sky promising an even colder night, the hazy watery sun not even creating shadows, we three lads leaned, backs against a wall, hands in pockets. We often stood thus whilst planning our next move. The toddler Keith was kicking at a frozen cowpat to reveal the worms and centipedes keeping warm underneath. To the west we detected the faint but increasing drone of high flying aircraft, but at first we couldn't see any. We knew they couldn't be German as they never came from the west and they never came in daylight. Soon tiny silver specks appeared, they grew closer and multiplied to cover the entire span of sky limited by the surrounding steep hills. It continued, the leaders now overhead in a neverending polka dot pattern. Not squadrons, nor even wings, instead a total aluminium armada, they were either unpainted Flying Fortresses or Liberators bound for RAF bases in Lincolnshire and elsewhere.

They were our buddies up there, numbers, height, speed and call signs unknown and radio silence maintained. They would soon know full well the long run through flack and fighters to bomb the ball bearing factories at Sweinfurt, the harder and colder slog back through more flack and fresh fighters. We bombed Sweinfurt and many other swine every week but we always returned, our leaky airframe cunningly camouflaged as a tree. We too braved the cannon fire, mostly stones thrown up at us by young Tod, too small to climb the tree and be a gunner. Soon bored he would switch his aim to the nearest cow, he rarely hit one but when he did the cow's bellow would be echoed by his gleeful shout. When the cow moved out of range he just sat on the wall shouting 'when-you-gonna-land-it-I'm-'ungry'. He was already a past master at the all-in-one-word language. As though his stomach mattered when we were struggling with a bouncing aircraft over Essen. From newspapers, war films, newsreels and radio we already knew the map of Germany better than our native land. At that time my idea of even Scotland was limited to an outline shape on a tartan biscuit tin in the Co-op and I knew that somewhere on that outline was one big ship and a sewing machine on a roof.

The sun gone, the last specks were now black against the spreading dusk to the south east. Soon the parallel white lines also merged into darkening misty blue but the faint drone seemed to last for ages. Young Tod's whine 'I'm-'ungry-'n-cold-'n-let's-ger-'ome-it's gerring dark-we-might-get-losted' turned off this magic lantern.

It hadn't been a mirage, nor had we fallen asleep because the following summer we experienced two repeats, both longer-lasting, against a vivid blue sky watched lying on our backs on warm grass.

As the winter developed our aircraft was grounded due to bad weather, the main problem being hoar frost on slippery branches and all our camouflage had been blown off. It would be late spring before we next climbed to seek the wide blue yonder over that eastern skyline, camouflage freshly restored perhaps for a straight line run to Berlin, secondary target Wolfsburg, weather man decides and is always wrong. If we hadn't needed all available timber for the firewood business we could have built a tree house in the shape of a cockpit. Our buddies up there climbed through a hatch to board their aircraft, we climbed up a knotted rope and when we landed had to take it away with us in case some other kids stole it. Our rear gunner sitting five feet below us at the end of a sagging branch must have confused the Luftwaffe fighter pilots. Had the Blacko Gang known of our aircraft they would have raided and cut off all the branches.

In one single day we experienced a marching band, live firing, medals, tanks and the greatest free air show on earth. All this in one small spot on the map, later famous as the only village in West Yorkshire to receive a flying bomb, the birthplace of he who invented logarithms to the base E, where multi-tasking for caretakers originated and once Bramwell Bronte was station master and goods clerk. I'll remember that day for ever.

Within twelve years I was to see an even deeper blue sky, gradually obscured with flying objects spaced so close together that the powerful sun was slowly blotted out completely. This show lasted all day. Taking off from Aden for the 2600 mile one-way trip, they all crashed on an airport. None was armed, none was aluminium.

11

Senior School

My five years in the senior school are best remembered by linking each teacher with the subject they taught, starting with the very top man.

To first formers the Head was some sort of powerful god. He taught us History of Britain in Roman Times – for me drawing Hadrian's Wall and decorated columns of Roman baths came easily. In year two or three he spread word of one Palmerston and his Foreign Policy. To me this was totally boring as were the Napoleonic Wars because no aircraft were involved. No mention of slavery, window taxes, tea in Boston, press gangs, suffragettes, Indian mutiny, corn laws, slaughter on the Somme, despotic kings, ten-year-old boys and twelve-year-old girls working down mines, young princes slaughtered in a tower or other delightful festering parts of our great and glorious heritage.

From day one he got instant attention, we dare hardly move, he had ultimate power but was quietly spoken, tall, polite and scholarly. As well as at lessons we saw him briefly each morning at assembly. It was here that in later years we began to sense the full power of this man. The large mid-corridor school hall doubled as a gym, one end wall covered with climbing bars, the other end a stage with piano, the collapsible vaulting horses stored under this stage. Wooden beams lowered from the ceiling, climbing ropes hung down and when not in use were retained with braided tie-backs to the outer wall.

School theoretically commenced at 9.00 am but you had to be in the hall, in your row in your exact form by exactly 9.10 am or you received 1 hour's detention doled out by the teachers stationed at each end of the hall. Precisely on time the staff mounted the stage followed by the two guards, followed by the prim senior girl who played the piano. The teachers sat down, Headmistress always central. The Head walked to the lectern. Around 540 of us all stood, propped up by each other. The first form nearest the stage, prefects at the back, in line with the entrance gap ready for their privileged orderly exit.

The mini-revival meeting started by all the staff rising, the Headmistress stepped forward a pace and muttered a brief prayer, one verse of a hymn was then sung by all the throng, only five hymns, a separate one for each weekday repeated every week, a cunning ploy to ensure that by the end of one term you knew all words and music perfectly. The Head gave out his routine announcements etc., marched off the stage followed by the staff and pianist, her one perk to avoid the melée, the staff and prefects making their common exit. Then and only then we sardines tumbled out, trodden on or crushed, sometimes both en route to various lessons. The exact format was repeated every day.

One morning in my second or third year the Head was missing. The Headmistress announced 'the Headmaster will be a little late this morning, you may talk but I want instant quiet on his arrival'. Puzzled we muttered and waited. At 9.20 he strode straight to the lectern amid dead silence. 'Good morning school, I apologise for keeping you waiting. I have today expelled W (girl) and XYZ (three boys) for utterly disgraceful behaviour in the physics lab last night resulting in damage to the classroom door.' He marched straight out ignoring the hubbub, revival meeting abandoned, staff and pianist departed. We as usual tried to depart in one piece. As the four he mentioned were all in the fourth form we did not know them but we could visualise the very well-developed girl playing hockey. Not only the hockey stick bounced up and down; she had quite a fan club.

It was perhaps a fortnight before the whole story filtered down to form 2a and spread from some prefects beating it out of the fifth former whose brother was one of those expelled. Seems that the four accused, knowing somehow that the physics lab would not be occupied for the final period of the previous day, rushed to it after their last class, and once inside managed to jam the door. Obviously all pre-planned.

In the much-loved TV series 'Rising Damp' the late Leonard Rossiter played the part of the shifty, leering 'Rigsby' running a seedy doss-house, greasing round the female tenants and castigating the males. Wearing a blue smock he would have been perfectly cast as the caretaker in our school. That particular day he had expected to start work early in what he thought to be an empty room but found he could not open the door. He shouted out and getting no answer, promptly went to the Headmaster. The Head with all his executive power told him to break it down and capture those responsible (or irresponsible), after all he was the Head and with an MA, his lackey a mere caretaker with a BO. The latter, well versed in the powers of Headmasters and knowing that mending the door would fall to him, decided that he'd best first reconnoitre the whole situation. Hurtling downstairs, kids flying in all directions, from one of his many cubbyholes he grabbed his longest extending ladder, once outside he propped it against the wall, shot up it and peered into one of the lab windows. Lads homeward bound stopped to watch, some just puzzled, others hoping the place was on fire and they might (a) see the caretaker burn with it, (b) sell the story to a newspaper, (c) be interviewed on the radio.

The four defendants meanwhile had eagerly commenced a most commendable, dedicated self-study session in advanced physiology, biology and the natural world. What the caretaker saw would have packed all those tiered benches in the physics lab five times over with queues to the Scottish border. This was far better than, when some years ago, he had barged into the library at five o'clock to find a female teacher sitting on a prefect's lap with her blouse undone. They had been kissing. He had told no one about this, but whenever he passed this teacher he always winked as she turned away.

On four blazers, one skirt and a cardigan spread for comfort on the long demonstration bench the girl lay on her back, still wearing some of her clothes, shoes, socks, watch and shiny decorative hairclips. One lad was kissing her lips, the second appeared to be counting her ribs, the third exploring below her waist. They looked like surgeons engrossed over an operating table. Being a caretaker he must have seen most tricks but this topped the bill. Desperate to join this study group he shot back down the ladder, jumping the last three rungs to land straight on to the foot of one lad who had been watching this curious performance. This lad's parents next day were informed by the X-ray department of the local hospital that two bones were broken and he should not play football or do PT for three months and yes, it will itch when the plaster is on. Ignoring the screaming lad and bouncing others aside, he hurtled inside, grabbed a bucket and shot up the stairs where at the second turn he sent the English Literature teacher flying and the homework books and briefcase flying further. His legs were in perpetual motion from leaving the top of the ladder to this abrupt halt, pursued by a horde of Pied Piper kids. Recovering he held the bucket with the open end against his chest, dashed up the last few stairs and leapt across the corridor. Reconnoitring completed, he was now on a priority mission, his orders direct from the top man himself. He hurled himself bucket first at the door, the wood frame splintered and he shot inside. The noise and flying bucket brought the self-study to an abrupt halt with angry screams from the caretaker who had left his fingers between bucket and door, from the lad on top who had been clonked on the head by the bucket handle, from the kissing lad who had been hit by the bucket rim and from the girl who was just annoyed at the interruption and had also lost two hairclips in this rapid action.

Sucking his crushed fingers he ordered the two main participants to get dressed, staying very, very close indeed to the girl in case she escaped, perhaps difficult as lads six abreast were still trying to get through the door. Mission accomplished, he marched the study group to the Headmaster. Rumour mill wheels already turning, one lad stuck in the doorway afterwards swore on the caretaker's grave he had seen the caretaker tearing the girl's clothes off, and sucking his fingers where the angry girl had bitten him.

Once inside his study the Head, calm and polite as ever, intoned: 'Shut the door, now then caretaker, what is this all about?' Smirking the man gave it to him, naturally omitting any mention of injured kids or flying homework. The Head sternly addressed the girl.

'What have you to say for yourself? Do you dispute any of this?'

'Nothing sir, no sir, it will not happen again sir, can I go back to find my hairclips, my boyfriend gave them to me sir.'

'What boyfriend?' shouted her most intimate accomplice.

'Quiet you'

The same two questions repeated three times produced the same answers, the last boy's 'it won't happen again sir' countered by the Head's 'I'm sure it won't, for any of you, collect your hairclips and all report to me at 9 am tomorrow. Now go.'

Crafty and true to his craft of taking care of himself, his smirk changing to a 'see what a good caretaker am I' smile, the caretaker thought it the best time to suggest that the much more competent woodwork teacher would be better qualified than he to mend the door. 'I think not, he is far too valuable to be doing odd jobs, he suffers from arthritis so the stairs are out of the question. See to it as soon as possible, close the door.' Under his breath the caretaker cursed the Headmaster, arthritis, oversexed kids, all other kids, shattered door frames and idle pampered cabinetmakers as he dashed off to find his cleaning women. He gave them the full story in which his cold nerveless dedication and strong moral sense made him the hero of the whole episode. Four female voices frequently interjecting 'ooh', 'ah', 'by gum', 'whodathoughtit', more 'oohs' and one 'ee by gum' topped off with 'wait while our Meg hears this'.

The now purpling fingers evoked sympathetic female advice such as 'bathe them in cold water', 'no, hot water is best at night', 'no, warm vinegar will help'. He rather thought he would try the fourth woman's recipe of warm vinegar with mustard. He also suggested that they take on some share of his night's grafting in view of the state of his poor fingers. They grudgingly consented – but for one night only.

Later, in the working men's club, swollen fingers stinking of vinegar and mustard, he hinted to his cronies of dark deeds at school that day. For the price of one pint the cronies got the full tale, including the heroism but no mention of morals. One fell out of the chair laughing. Wilf, who cut the grass in the school playing fields, lurched across thinking someone was telling jokes 'I heard one today. Police and a bomb disposal crew were called to investigate a suspicious object in a car in Liverpool. On arrival they found it was a tax disc.' Then the caretaker remembered one, 'A woman knocked on the door of a hostel in London. The lady who ran it opened the door and gasped, "Oh! you poor thing, your ankle is in plaster, your arm in a sling and your head bandaged, whatever happened to you?" "My husband hits me with a brick." "Come in, we must ring the police, the man is a fiend." "No don't ring them, they have charged him already." "Charged him with what?" "Stealing a brick."'

The steward's shouted words 'It's after time, hop it' ended this amazing day.

The caretaker never realised that if one hundred boys had asked him, he, the only one able to tell them precisely what had happened, could have remained silent and extracted revenge for years of his own fruitless enquiries. For four kids this would never, ever happen again.

In our modern world, the caretaker would have been sacked by the education authority for damaging the fabric of the school and fined by the Health and Safety Executive for leaving a ladder against a school wall overnight. The union representative for the Head would have stressed that the Head only vaguely remembered asking the caretaker if he could do something about a sticking door somewhere. Parents of one injured boy would have issued a writ against the Head, the caretaker, the Education Authority and any one else their lawyers could think of.

Ever more embellished versions of this story were still a hot topic round the town six months later. A local soldier returning from leave to his anti-aircraft battery in south Leeds relayed it to his mates who didn't believe a word of it. The Ministry of Information could have used it to boost morale countrywide or as a useful alternative to 'only two of our three hundred and seventeen bombers failed to return'. They didn't however as big brother and the bishops would not want the rapid spread of such a practice to become embedded in the standard school curriculum.

Nearly 600 in the school now have a problem, they will never know just what happened when the four returned home to report the drastic termination of the happiest days of their lives. Not so the reader, we can pause just for fun to play 'fly on the wall'.

One of the three disconsolate lads arrives at his Yorkshire stone terrace home, the time 10.45 am.

'Eh, wot you doing back 'ere?'

'Er, well . . . I got expelled'

His mother, hand to throat, sits down abruptly, a half-crushed cat leaps snarling to the floor.

'Oh my god, wha . . . whatever for?'

'Playing with a girl'.

'What's wrong with playing with a girl, what were you playing at, what happened?' Rising panic and fear in her voice.

He provides a brief muttered outline of events, playing it down.

'What were yer cousin John doing?'

'Kissing her.'

'What did t'other lad do?'

'Had her blouse undone, he kept gerring in my way.'

'Oh God, [sob] Oh my God!' this in a loud anguished shout, trembling now.

'What did you do?'

'Nowt much, just . . .'

'Oh no! You never learnt this at Sunday School, it's that damn school.'

'It was 'er idea, she showed me.'

'Oh my God, we're ruined, what will your father do, what will the neighbours say?'

No answer, he just stares at the cat, reliving every moment with a slight smile.

'It's nowt to laugh at.' Smile disappears.

She slumped lower in the chair, one shoe falls off unnoticed. The cautious cat moves further away.

She thought of the birth pains, then fourteen years of washing, cooking, ironing, even stoning the doorstep so that he would always return to a neat home, how could her God allow this to happen.

Neighbours and friends might never again sit with her at Beetle Drives or whist at the club, they might even have to move – Higgins Street perhaps, near the tip and her hypochondriac mother.

She remembered the couple at number 17, the husband's incident with that Salvation Army girl, their son now in jail for refusing call up to the army and he wouldn't take the option of working down the pit either. Nobody sat with them anywhere at all, and their gas was turned off although this was an accident and quickly restored.

With some guilt she thought of the shifty Herbert Briggs, long-time member of Hilltop Primitive Baptist Chapel, excluded after a female in the congregation anonymously complained to the minister that he was too primitive and had very cold hands. He did not move across town, he just hanged himself. Took her months to get over it, she being the complainant.

'You stupid great lump, we send you to a posh school and this is what you do to us.' She is rapidly developing a death wish. The lad grins, facing the fireplace she could not see his face, the grin fades at the thought of his father's belt.

Promptly at half past two the door sneck rattles, enter the father, tired from his 6 am start at the dark and satanic Jerusalem Mill. Sobbing, she tells him the desperate story. To her amazement he takes it in his stride, doesn't even touch the stout leather belt at his waist.

'Na'then, I'll get him on at't'mill int' morning, we're working seven days a week ont' khaki stuff and they're seeking 'ands. Ee won't 'ave any time for wenching. Ee's better back in clogs, to 'ell with these fancy grammar schools, they learn 'em nowt but evil. Any road, another wage'll be 'andy.' At this, much relieved, the lad laughs and, hand on his mother's shoulder said, 'Don't worry, we'll be all right.' She could not speak, not one single word.

This father is after all just a hard-working northern bloke dreading call-up to the forces. When asked to pay for anything his expression would change from shock to amazement to absolute agony to stuttering the two most commonly used words in Yorkshire, simply '**HOW** much?' snarled on a rising note.

The fly takes off low, as it buzzes past, the cat swipes with one paw but misses.

Let us pause yet again to experience the next boy's home coming and sympathise with the fly on this boy's wall.

Peter Raymond Alec Bridgecombe does not go home, instead he catches a bus to his father's surgery. Once there the receptionist naturally thinks he is ill. 'What's wrong with you Peter?'

'I need to see my dad'

'What shall I tell him?'

'Nothing, I just need to see him.'

She pops her head round the doctor's door and tells him. 'Right, just give me five minutes, then send him in. Wonder why?'

'He won't say doctor.'

The boy recounts the whole story. 'Whatever were you thinking of?' He repeats this, he would have to do something about this very rapidly.

'Sorry Dad, didn't mean to.'

The doctor shouts, 'Miss Clements, no more patients for the next hour please.'

The boy glumly stares at the skeleton while the doctor gets directory enquiries for the number of an old public school in the Yorkshire Dales, where a pal from his university days is teaching geography and geology. The school secretary answers. 'Are you a parent?'

'No, not yet, will you please ask David Hamlin to ring me urgently, it is very urgent and personal.' He gives her his surgery and home numbers.

The receptionist brings the boy an apple and a bottle of orange juice when she returns from her lunch on the high street. The father says gravely, 'This is serious, very serious, your mother just won't believe it'

'I know, I am very sorry.'

The doctor is wondering how he would manage to pay the fees, dreading the cost.

Eventually the receptionist connects David Hamlin BA, after the 'long time no see' preamble the doctor gives him the woeful details.

'Oh dear, I see now why it was urgent, I'm sure we can fit him in with the fourth form lot. Don't worry, could happen to any lad, boys will be boys. I'll talk to the Head at lunch and get straight back to you, be glad to help and I will keep my eye on him. There will be no more girls, he will be too exhausted from cross country running, the cadet force and open air PT in the rain. He'll soon settle here.' He fails to mention the incident some months earlier when the assistant matron was found in a dormitory after lights out.

He rings again as promised. 'The fees are £1,300 per year payable per term in advance with some optional extras but ignore them for the moment. The Head suggests you pack his clothes and bring him over as soon as possible so as not to interrupt his education. We'll sort out the uniform later.'

Doctor and son return home, Mrs Bridgecombe also now back from her quarterly lunch meeting of the War Bonds committee. Given the news she clutches her husband, totally speechless, then begins to sob. She doesn't think about neighbours, she doesn't think about anything, her mind just switches off with shock. She pulls the boy to them, the only sound the boy's stifled 'Sorry Mum'.

Both parents so wanted him to become a doctor, the boy's secret ambition is to fly fighters in the RAF but he has never mentioned it. They spend a very miserable evening and the radio news does nothing to relieve this. Next morning the doctor rushes round to his bank manager. Adroitly hiding the true situation he explains the suddenly available place at this well-known public school in Yorkshire, adding how lucky as there is normally a two-year waiting list. Doctor and bank manager had together attended the same school the son has just left. Half an hour later, their account credited with £2,000, he rings his wife. She furiously starts ironing and packing. On the Friday a local army doctor home on leave holds the morning surgery, glad to help out in civvies of course, while the parents deliver the boy to his new school. One elderly patient was somewhat surprised to be told, 'You can't have any more yellow pills, there is nothing wrong with you. Dismiss. Next.' Much later they received a telegram from the Air Ministry.

The fly had been following these earlier events, it flew away to meet the others, but would never know of the telegram, it too was dead by then.

We'll now pause for more fun with another fly on yet another wall.

The third lad, resenting being expelled for merely kissing the girl, goes home and tells his step-mother and grandma that he has packed in schooling, he's had enough, and would stop learning and start earning. 'Oh, very good, give me a hand turning your grandma's mattress and then fetch some coal.' The toothless, deaf grandmother just stared at him, the step-mother quite content so long as he grafted around the house, and now he would be earning his keep.

He simply got a job with the man who delivers groceries to the school dining room. He is now back in the school once a week shouting to any old mates he chances upon and uses the boy's toilet every visit. One day the caretaker shops him to a passing master for smoking and not wearing a cap. 'You daft sods, I've left school.' This fly speeds merrily back to his mates.

Again we must pause to have more fun, aided by yet another fly on a different wall. The girl arrives around 11 am at her council house home perched on the hillside. Entering she notices the photograph on the mantelshelf of her father in uniform. He had now spent months in Alexandria exploring Egyptian brothels. 'The sods have expelled me, thrown me out – and I didn't have time to sell my hockey stick either.'

Her ever-loving mother, oblivious to the time, clumsily wrenched herself from the arms of the American Army Corporal on the couch. Turning her head, 'Oh, what the hell for? I scrimped and saved for that stick.' Her tone quite casual, she was much more intent on restoring her elaborate make-up.

Both got the good news, the girl just as casual. The American fell off the couch laughing, suddenly sobered by the thought of a magical three-some, chance would be a fine thing. Oh boy! What a tale to tell them back at Burtonwood.

'You stupid sod, we don't want the two of us pregnant, besides your Aunt Moira's only got one pram. Get down to Woolworths tomorrow, her on the cosmetics counter was knocked down by a bus last week and they'll be seeking somebody quick. You'll get cheap lipstick too.' The girl disappeared to the toilet, the shouted afterthought following her, 'Your cousin Mavis'll buy your hockey stick, I'll tell her mother at the club.'

Both settled back on the couch, the better to develop the US/UK cordiale, gin from the Post Exchange improving the cordial.

The fly moves up the wall, the better to see over the back of that couch, as it waits to swap notes with the other flies. The buzzing sound associated with flies is not really the noise of beating wings, they are just laughing at the antics of human beings.

Months later the whole morning assembly waited agog when warned the Head would again arrive late. Massed minds and imaginations in overdrive. How disgraceful would this be, would even a teacher be involved?

He soon strode to the lectern, the apology, the breathless silence, eleven hundred eyes stared at two lips. 'I have today expelled xxxxxx senior for smoking in the toilets.' Much breath was also expelled that day followed by groans and laughs from the rear ranks. Normal breathing once resumed, the revival meeting concluded and the Head led the exodus.

A total let down for all, never a mention of the lucrative trade over a few years, all the boys familiar with coughing youngsters, eyes streaming, at break and lunchtime, no detail given of the cunning formula: 1 penny in my pocket = 1 puff on 1 (stolen) cigarette (this order of play was mandatory) multiplied over two or three years equals success. The disappointment was soon forgotten, but the diabolical caretaker had struck once again.

Next time the Head was late we waited breathing normally but hardly interested, certainly not excited. How wrong we were. He duly appeared at the lectern. First the usual apology, then, his tone never changing 'I have this morning expelled the Head Boy and Head Girl as a result of a thoroughly disgraceful incident in Manchester over the weekend. I do not wish to see him again until he returns on leave from the Indian Army.'

The multitude sucked in one giant breath, the excited muttering and laughing grew intensely to include even the staff. The Head marched straight out, faint smile just showing. We had gone national, perhaps international. Would this hit *The Times*, the *Bombay English Language Daily*?

The staff, hymn abandoned, remained on stage. An intense circle formed around the Headmistress who, being one of only four in the know, was having her moment of glory. Even the pianist had her head in the circle, the rest of her perilously close to the edge of the stage, avoiding falling only by gripping the shoulder of the English literature spinster who never even noticed. The young English language teacher gave a sudden shriek of laughter putting us all on tenterhooks. Whatever this story was it had to be sensational. Eventually the merry staff left and we all drifted off. Towards the end of that abandoned period the caretaker patrolled the lower corridor, grabbing successive lads demanding to know what was going on. As ever, no one would tell.

From just two lines of script that day the Head had created an ever-expanding epoch of drama, laughter, pathos, love, even revenge via the anti-caretaker rule, with a cast of hundreds, not one single trained actor, no prompter, not even a rehearsal. It was all Shakespeare melded into one single play. No wonder the faint smile. The simple, infinitely beautiful story finally filtered down to us.

Seems that the Head Boy and Girl, long known to be partners who walked out of school each afternoon hand-in-hand, he carrying both satchels, had realised that the Indian and Japanese armies together could ruin their planned future. So, following the school motto 'we teach you not just for school but for life' they had decided that the 'life' bit should start, the sooner the better. On the Friday evening they went by train to Manchester, thence to a hotel. The delights of wartime Manchester proving irresistible despite the bombing, they returned to school the following Tuesday lunchtime, when the boy-now-man reported everything to the Headmaster. After all they were (now) both men of the world, of equal height and both wore moustaches. This time the caretaker had been kept right out of the loop.

Shortly after this, I had a fight with a lad at this school. I thumped his chest and he collapsed onto the ground. He was carted off in an ambulance and returned to school two days later, saying 'they' had discovered he had some slight heart problem. I was worried but we became the best of pals. He was the first lad in our class to have a Biro pen, at that time made to resemble a normal stubby fountain pen. We all had a go with it and were amazed, our first introduction to the mass technology yet to come.

Our next exposure to the Head's dramatic performance was on a more sombre occasion, when months later he announced that the expelled hero had been killed in Burma. There followed a subdued and fidgety one

81

minute silence, (muttered 'keep still' from prefect at the back) all four verses of a hymn and hurried who-can-say-it-fastest rendering of the Lord's Prayer. Finally from the Headmistress a solo prayer for the dead hero, his parents and for unknown and probably already dead comrades in a distant land including a 'keep your heads down' fierce whisper from the same prefect. Never a mention of the grieving beloved who after all was not dead but certainly pregnant and would therefore shortly be leaving her brief job at Boots Chemist.

The staff left quietly. Much subdued we shuffled away, the baffled first form newcomers nagging for an explanation. The caretaker would also be seeking enlightenment, the first formers couldn't tell him, the older ones wouldn't.

The dead lad was not only a hero to us before he joined the army, but also unique in causing the whole school to commence one period late, and this TWICE in one year.

Regarding the other teachers and subjects, some memories remain very strong, others rather faint, of the teacher and their methods of teaching and maintaining discipline. The most powerful memory of all spanned three years and involved a girl rather than teachers.

Commencing the second year in form 2a I used the desk second from the front row behind a then unknown girl. My immediate view was of shiny black hair ending in tight curls. Reaching forward with the end of my ruler I could tap the bottom of a curl and it bounced like a coiled spring. She tolerated this for a while until when the teacher wasn't looking she would suddenly swing her arm round to hit me with her ruler. Being a naturally clumsy action once or twice she connected with my head, mostly I drew back quickly after each tap at the 'springs'.

One day she managed to knock my glasses off, they flew past the nose of the lad to my left and landed on the next desk. This resulted in one bent side wing and a cut on my nose. She jumped up producing a delicate handkerchief from wherever girls keep these and started wiping away the blood, muttering 'I'm so sorry, I didn't mean to'. She spat on her hanky and dabbed some more as the teacher dashed across saying, 'Are you all right?'

'Yes miss, just a scratch, I was borrowing her ruler, somehow it slipped.'

Sniggers from the class.

'Both of you sit down, the rest be quiet.'

This was all rather thrilling, two females fussing over me together. I suddenly realised this girl had green eyes. I had never seen anyone with green eyes before, I have never seen anyone since, grey yes, rarely, but green never. One green eye winked, we both sat down and order was restored. I straightened the bent wing.

After this I ceased flicking her 'springs' and we developed a working relationship albeit limited to her doing my chemistry homework, I doing her maths. Daily, weekly, monthly I gazed at that shiny black hair, just longing to bury my face in it.

The 3a year started in yet another form room, she grabbed a front row desk just as another lad settled into the desk behind her. I bundled him out of it. All through the year the homework swaps continued, the longing increased, so did the shyness.

There was a similar pattern to the start of the fourth year. In yet another form room she grabbed the front desk. Some wit shouted 'Guess which desk Ainley will have.' I ignored him and settled as usual behind her. During the summer holidays, a party of older pupils with perhaps two teachers went off to harvest camps. School only re-opened when it was known what date they would return which was governed by the weather. I no longer took chemistry and only occasionally did her maths home-work when she asked me to if overloaded.

One afternoon during the first term of 4a we had all returned from some distant classroom after the last bell to collect our books for home-work. I became aware that the others had already packed their satchels and gone, we were alone for the very first time. For more than two years I had this girl on a pedestal, worshipping secretly my very own goddess, always spotless from shiny black hair to white ankle socks in ever-new sandals, never even a slight scuff mark on the latter, in contrast to the dried mud on my boots every morning, from taking a short cut through a swampy field on the paper round. Propinquity no doubt played a part yet I kissed my pillow every night when she was in bed three miles away. She had blooded me, even temporarily captured my DNA on her handkerchief, attacked my spinal column (more of this later), more than proved you only hurt the one you love. She had once even winked at me and mesmerised me constantly with green eyes. She still had some puppy fat, no other lad in the class even looked at her but to me she was simply perfect.

To hell with it, I'd been longing for long enough. I lunged round my desk and grabbed her round the waist. She tried to pivot away and my finger caught in a belt loop on her gymslip, partly torn it now hung away from the belt.

'Oh! My mother will be furious if she sees this, I will have to stitch it as soon as I get home. Whatever were you trying to do?' Her shout seemed so loud in an empty room, green eyes blazing from an angry face.

'I'm so sorry, it was an accident, I just wanted to kiss you, hug you, bury my face in that beautiful hair, I've wanted to for ages, will you come to the pictures on Saturday afternoon?' All this in a desperately subdued voice, it tumbled out in one single word as though I was speaking German.

Without realising it I had started by repeating her exact words from long ago. To my amazement her face softened, she smiled for the first time in over two years and whispered 'yes'. The most magical word I had ever heard, I could have jumped over Jupiter. We were alone, eyeball to green eyeball, our faces but three inches apart. The whisper continued 'provided you don't tear any more of my clothes and you come back to our house for tea afterwards.'

My world fell apart, Jupiter with it. She saw my face fall too, moved closer and gripped my hand. In her now normal voice in typical Yorkshire style she asked, 'What's up with you now?'

'I can't meet your parents, I'm far too scruffy.' This said very quietly.

'No matter, on Saturday you can wear your best clothes.'

I looked down at me then back up at her.

'These are my best clothes.'

She seemed to hold my hand for ages, there's no way I can describe her rapidly changing expression. Her grip slowly relaxed and finally her hand withdrew. Turning away she whispered 'I'm (sob) sorry.' Went to her desk, hoisted the satchel, stopping at the door said, voice normal again, 'See you tomorrow.' Frozen to the spot, totally shattered, unable to stutter even one word, I listened to her receding footsteps leaving a silent school, just a distant cleaner banging a bucket and a master outside starting his car.

I collected my books and savagely banged the desk lid shut, went out through the boys' entrance of the now empty school, out into my now very empty world. At the gate where she had turned left to return home to multiple electric lights I turned right uphill to the bus stop. A younger lad who I knew slightly started to chat but was cut off in mid-chat with a brusque 'shurrup'. Travelling not one but two stops too many I jumped off the bus to the shouted reprimand from the conductor and walked all the way back to the paper shop. Round completed I trudged home to my gas light, greeted as usual by my long suffering mother's 'Dear God, I thought you had been run over.'

From classroom to gas light I saw only green eyes, angry, amazed, happy, hurt and back to normal but dull. I kept repeating every word we had both said in the longest conversation we had ever had. That night I hugged the pillow hard, it was still wet next morning. I was in a weird state, I was in the real harsh world and I had no idea how to cope. Back at school next morning, I noticed a big crack in the desk lid.

At the end of 4a and through the 5a year, where I again by habit sat behind her, we rarely spoke. I remember one occasion when she dropped a rubber which bounced under my desk, passing it back our fingers briefly touched but our eyes never met as she muttered 'thanks'. I suddenly felt an intense longing to grasp that hand and beg her to forgive me. Grasping any part of this developing and now attractive female, puppy fat and white ankle socks long gone, was not part of courting, for me it would be courting disaster. The last term sped by, the homework increased as we approached the school certificate exams.

ICI would hardly appreciate my knowledge of chemistry. Potassium was shortened to K, lead to Pb from the Latin *plumbum*. I well remember the strong smell of hydrogen sulphide, and two acids which when poured on to copper granules turned them blue or green, vivid colours only seen on parrots; no recollection of any formulae. I do remember one lad putting some chemicals in a flask with a full roll of explosive 'caps' used in boys' wild west revolvers, then placing the flask over a Bunsen burner. Shortly after there was a loud crack, followed by a series of sharper cracks. Broken glass and blobs of still burning substance shot in all directions. The lad stamped his foot on the caps and left it there. The teacher rushed down the room, to pour water on the small flames. Protective goggles were unheard of in those days, it was amazing that no one was hurt. This lad was really risking it, for this teacher, having retired as assistant headmaster before the war, had returned in the same role.

This was the man who held the boy's shoulders over a chair back as the Head lashed out with the cane. You just did not tangle with this teacher. Curiously he had snow white hair but very bushy black eyebrows, in the distance he looked like a panda. He taught just the one subject and at the year end quietly said 'Ainley, you are not cut out for chemistry, but I know maths, physics and art are your strengths; keep them up.' 'Yes sir' was perhaps only the second time I ever spoke to him. Gases play an important role in chemistry, he never knew my close connection with one particular gas which lit the mantle needed to copy the ever-correct homework on winter nights.

A mousy drab spinster taught us English Literature for the first three years. She wore small round glasses and minced along with very small steps, age anywhere between 35 and 50, hard to tell, a dismal pouting eyesore in sagging mauve cardigan and flat heeled shoes.

The books we had to study were *Heidi,* some or all of Charles Lamb's *Essays* and endless reams of Shakespeare. Of Heidi, I remember she was a girl tending goats with bells, the scene a Swiss mountain. No other memory, but still I liked the gentle tale. Of the Lamb and his essays I remember nothing at all. Shakespeare however made a lasting impression. Wild thyme growing on grassy banks had little appeal to a 12 year old intent on running his own little war, plus survival, having to learn great chunks of his writing for homework was even less appealing. This process put me right off the world's best scribe, a classic master at very cleverly revealing every facet of human nature through strong characters. My loss.

On one occasion this teacher arranged a coach trip for us to see *Henry V* at a nearby cinema matinee, the boys no doubt intent on a rehearsal of Romeo and Juliet mixed with a midsummer's afternoon dream involving girls, all staged in darkness. I alone went home to chop firewood.

Against the classroom wall stood a large deep glass-fronted bookcase on a base cupboard with sliding doors, neither were in use. I had something with me to swap at break time, too large to go in my desk, so I put it in this cupboard. Came the second bell for break, climbing half inside to retrieve it, some lad pushed me further in and slid the door fully closed, jamming it with something. There I stayed, after break the whole class knew I was in there from the occasional snigger and my empty desk. The teacher too must have guessed, perhaps helped as I faintly heard some swine say 'Please Miss, where is Ainley?' Louder sniggers. I had plenty of musty air, I was not claustrophobic but I was fed up with the hard shelf and being unable to move or stretch in any direction. Also fed up with the irritating screech of chalk on blackboard, amplified by my sound box.

The bell went and I heard her voice very near 'Ainley, get the homework from one of your friends and report for 1 hour's detention tonight.' She slid the door open but didn't help me out. Instead I backed and fell out, dusty parts of me again re-united with hard planks. Loud laughter. Whatever had jammed the door she must have taken it with her to prevent a recurrence.

This time I was a quadruple loser. I had homework based on a lesson barely heard, detention with spin-off lateness and none of my porcine 'friends' as she called them would reveal who slid and jammed the door. To be on the receiving end of the Sicilian treatment of 'nobody knows, nobody talks' is very frustrating indeed, a process normally reserved for the caretaker. I was too proud to ask any girl. I was also the innocent party. Some days later we arrived to find bookcase and cupboard gone. It would have made good firewood. All that remained to record this incident was a lighter rectangle on the once-cream wall: no sign of where the cupboard had stood for many years as below window sill level the walls were tiled.

It could never happen again, but now fifteen swine had been added to prefects, staff and caretaker – hostiles all. The odds were worsening plus there were evil forces now at work to eliminate all trace of my very existence.

One day the boys traipsed back into our 3a form room for a French lesson. In five years we must have walked miles lugging books etc. round that school. We knew the girls would be late as usual after PT. The teacher was late too, very rare that this happened.

Each desk had a narrow fixed top, to which was hinged the lid, the top with a hole at the right-hand end for a white pot inkwell. Naturally, I was left-handed. With no teacher present one lad pushed upward on the loose inkwell which rose and tilted, wet ink running across the lid. I grabbed him, we brawled onto the floor when in walked the teacher. He was Austrian and started at the school at the same time as his maths-teaching colleague. He was a Doctor of something or other, his English much better, his punishment technique faster but just as painful. We knew what was in store, we had seen other victims. With a curt 'remove your glasses' to me his arm swung to slap me with his palm on one cheek, followed through and returned to clout the other lad with the back of the same hand on his opposite cheek, all Teutonic efficiency and no wasted motion. Stumbling into each other and the desk, with eyes smarting we were back on the floor again. 'Get up, clean up that ink, find another inkwell, sit down.' With any non-Austrian all this action would have resulted in a howl of laughter but the room was silent, they knew better.

A very efficient form of classroom law – 'you're guilty, therefore have to be punished, bang, go to your desk (if you can walk) sit down (if you can bear to)' designed to ensure maximum teaching time for the majority, the culprits were allowed to convalesce in their own time. Any other teacher finding us on the floor would have commenced the usual inquest 'What are you doing? Who started it? Are you hurt?' Sniggering round the room, 'The rest of you be quiet'. There would follow conflicting answers, argument, debate settled by 'one hour detention each' more sniggers. Result, half the period wasted.

I hated detention, spent writing the same sentence one or even two hundred times over. I was one hour late starting the paper round, one hour late for a warmed up tea after being greeted by 'Oh dear God, I thought you had been run over', one hour late starting homework and missed my favourite radio programme.

I very carefully cleaned the ink off desk lid and seat with an old sock I kept in my desk. The other lad put my nearly full inkwell in the desk in front. We sat down and the girls filed in with the usual 'Sorry to be late sir, we've been to gym.' One particular girl returned to the desk in front of mine. I wrote in pencil for the rest of that lesson but at break time smuggled a full inkwell from the next classroom. Next morning my tongue could wobble the loose tooth, I never gave him reason to hit me again.

This Austrian doctor of something, teaching French in an English school proved to have some good points. He managed to get me to master French grammar, he said we would speak French better if we first practised singing it, so some lessons he arrived with a mandolin on which he was quite competent. By the end of 3a a class full of young Yorkshire voices plus one cockney could have matched any Welsh choir, albeit with a limited repertoire. One girl asked him to play 'Nymphs and Shepherds'. He replied, 'If you sing it in French I'll try it'. Full stop, we continued with Frère Jacques, Lilli Marlene and some song involving a bridge in Avignon.

The headmaster's house in its own grounds was situated across the lane which was the school top field boundary. In the grounds was a small dam feeding a mill boiler lower down the hillside. The Austrian doctor had procured an RAF bomber type dinghy from somewhere. Perhaps he had been a spy but given up the trade. Instead, he gave up one lunch hour a week in the summer to teach lads from any form to swim. He could dive from one bank and swim right across under water. One day he really impressed by re-appearing clutching a rusty old bike.

Amongst the hybrid collection of older teachers was the Headmistress, who was well past retirement, taught Latin and no doubt other subjects. I remember very little of her and even less of the Latin, except that this near-skeletal crone was always to be seen in a voluminous black gown with a hood down the back. In the hood there appeared to be hanging a dead, or perhaps just hibernating, badger. She was occasionally stationed at the end of any one corridor shouting 'remember, do not run', providing the verbal emphasis for first formers with reading difficulties, the back-up to the notices on every staircase which carried this warning to kids hard of hearing. She was known as Sour Puss One or Acid Bag.

An even older crone in an advanced state of decay made a valiant effort to teach French plus whatever, her very gaunt features never smiled. Smelling of mothballs her hood cradled a moulting white rabbit or it may have been a cat. Her dusty gown was frequently opened and re-wrapped more tightly as though she longed to be a female flasher or was just feeling cold. At home each night the gown probably doubled as a blackout curtain or at any moment could be needed as a shroud. She could have taken the female lead in any horror film, her extended wracking cough adding a nice graveyard effect. She was Sour Puss Two or more often called The Witch. However witches are known to be quite crafty. Both spinsters would be drawing full pensions plus pay for their extended careers. I always remember them together, standing thus every morning in the Hall. I never tangled with either.

The geography teacher had previously taught here, retired and returned to help out. Due to some 1914–18 war experience he always spat when talking. If a lad in any front desk held out a light blue covered exercise book it became speckled with darker blue spots. Realising this, the teacher would shout 'cease' and clout the lad's head with the book. He always carried a globe in one hand and cane in the other but never used either. Perhaps shell-shock had left him with an identity crisis so he had to convince himself that he taught geography. He always hung the cane on the top edge of the blackboard. He used a corner of his gown to clean the board. I don't think he ever actually read any homework because there was never a tick, a cross or a word altered, just his final encouraging scribble 'map drawing and spelling must improve' and his automatic 7 out of 10. Everybody got the same mark. We never really had any problem with him.

The outside stone walls of the school were buttressed by evenly spaced pillars doubling the normal wall thickness to stiffen it. The elderly geography teacher had a small black Austin 7 which he always parked by the male teacher's common room. One day some sixth formers bodily lifted it to fit between two buttresses and returning to the library above, leaned out of the window waiting for him to go home. He came out and stared at the car. Driving forward would crunch the front wing, reversing would get the rear wing, he could not get in the driver's seat as the car was too close to the wall. He got help from other masters who smiled as they moved it, with raucous laughter from above.

Some of the other teachers ran a crafty system to lighten their work load. The sixth formers' self-study periods in their common room (where we others assumed they practised advanced mathematics by playing poker) were sometimes interrupted by some teacher dumping homework for them to mark. We always knew when this had happened because the returned book had more of their red ink than our original blue, still more red ink if the prefect who marked it recognised your name from a recent incident.

Everything was unusual about Religious Instruction, teacher, teaching method, even the classroom itself. Only 'taught' to first formers, for some reason the boys separated from the girls, the room had no desks, just chairs to seat the total of around 50 at once. Being war time, teachers were scarce as was everything else; of those retiring some stayed on, of those already retired some returned to help out.

This strange specimen may have been recruited from a list of unfrocked curates unfit for active service. He was small, with jet black hair smoothed away from a centre parting. He always wore a black jacket, black tie, grey striped trousers and suede shoes but no gown. Stick a black moustache on his lip, he was a Hitler, stick a flower in his lapel he was an hotel manager. An old adage warned, never trust a man with a centre parting. Another adage warned women of men in suede shoes. He always carried a Bible but never opened it.

Marching in like a brisk Ronnie Corbett without glasses, once at the front he started on the Ten Commandments, then elaborated each one.

He delivered all this in a non-stop high pitched whine, waving the Bible around. On one occasion the wrath of God was duly delivered to the head of a sleeping lad on the front row when the Bible accidentally flew out of his hand. He was never asked questions about the subject matter: it wasn't that he discouraged questions, he just ignored them. He ignored everything, chattering, arguments, thrown balls of paper or used chewing gum, even lads playing marbles at the rear of the class. At first boys would politely hold up their hand to ask to visit the toilet, ignored they just went. Later there might be up to five in the toilet reading comics, one in turn keeping watch for the caretaker. The teacher just rabbited on, and on and on, pre-programmed and paid by the word.

The school motto '*Non scholae sed vitae discimus*' means, as any kid wot has been learned proper will tell you, 'We teach not just for school but for life'. He concentrated on just Ten Commandments ignoring the five more useful ones in life:

11. Thou shalt not get caught.
12. Don't whine if you are caught, you have just been stupid.
13. Remember if it can go wrong it will do.
14. Remember also if it does go wrong it may be far worse than you expect.
15. Do unto others just before they do it to you.

The classroom itself was also unusual, in that pre-war it must have been used to teach mechanics or engineering principles. At the rear were parts of dismantled machinery, metal brackets on the walls, near the ceiling a shaft with a single flat pulley ran across the full width of the room. Half way along the room mounted in a similar position ran an I-beam carrying a block and tackle, its chain hanging against the wall. Before the teacher entered we found that one lad pushed by two others could grasp the chain and fly across the room above the chair backs, coming to an abrupt halt when his out-flung feet hit the opposite window sill. One day three lads pushed extra hard but the travelling lad, legs too high, hit the thin middle window frame. Three panes broke, some glass fell outside. The teacher never noticed anything amiss, later the care-taker definitely would, and definitely curse.

Amongst the scrap pile at the rear we rigged a lever supported by string, in such a way that a lad could lean back to cut the string with his penknife, creating a single loud 'bang'. Ever more ambitious we rigged up double levers of different lengths again held by a single string which when cut produced two separate 'bangs' each with a different tone. As usual the teacher ignored it. The girls reported that he was just the same with them, but without the bangs. He never set homework and there was no year-end exam. Bless you my son. Everyone's term reports read 'a most attentive pupil'. More programming.

In the first two years we suffered the useless teaching of one tall elderly man, again returned to help out after retirement. Some 1914–18 war experience left him with a curious impediment – often during and always at the end of a spoken sentence his lips formed a buzzing sound. Reading aloud from a text book he would carefully chalk each part of a theorem on the board. Any daft kid who asked a question buzz buzz got the inevitable answer 'We must press on buzz buzz.' Whether he meant we must press harder on our pencils, he must press harder on the chalk or that we must all progress together was never clear.

We sometimes used a nail to laboriously hollow out the end of a piece of chalk and with a blob of aero glue stuck a live match head in the recess. With luck it fired as he scratched chalk on the board, mostly it fell out and he might then tread on it, when it should fire up but mostly did not. We soon tired of this, he ignored it as he had to press on.

At the beginning of 3a things changed considerably with the arrival at the school of an Austrian refugee to teach arithmetic, algebra, geom-etry and trigonometry as separate subjects, one lesson for each. In art class I had laboriously and secretly painted a large black swastika on a foolscap sheet of paper which I stuck to the underside of my desk lid. With the desk lid open I had tried firing opened up paper clips into this target with an elastic band, a few stuck in, most ricocheted around the room causing howled threats.

One day this teacher must have come from behind down the aisle of desks and seen me open the desk lid. Spotting the swastika he growled something in German, tore the swastika into shreds, and grabbing my right ear he twisted it 90 degrees and pulled me to the front of the class. 'Stand zere, stay zere, keep kviet'. This was the perfect opportunity for the particular girl in the front desk, for reasons outlined elsewhere, to start a savage demolition job on my spine, repeatedly hitting the same vertebra with the end of her wooden ruler. I was a sitting duck, I must have soon cried out 'Pack it in'; the teacher hearing this leapt across the room, broke her ruler in half and grabbing the same ear dragged me forward to stand by the blackboard. 'Ven I say keep kviet I mean just zat!'

My ear ached for a fortnight, my back for a week. It all seemed unfair as I had used the swastika as a target. I was the first and only one to experience his punishment technique and discipline was firmly established for all. I, as usual, was the loser.

He began to make maths very interesting and soon proved to be a very good teacher. Out in the school field he showed us how to measure roughly the height of a distant mill chimney by using a trig formula, even though the base of the chimney was much higher than the school field. As time passed I found him to be the best teacher in the school.

By far my favourite subject, physics, was ably taught by a tall, no-nonsense, brisk, erect chap, always smart in rimless glasses and bow tie, very competent and well-liked who did his best to make a complex subject very interesting. He was perhaps ten years from retirement. I would have been quite happy had the lessons spanned two solid days per week. He never lashed out at any lad, instead lashed anyone slow, dim or stupid with a cryptic sarcastic tongue, often playing off one kid against the other, but always quietly spoken. Physics was his only subject and he loved it.

One day he surprised us by suddenly lighting a cigarette, followed by 'Don't anyone else light one'. This was to demonstrate some feature of how a warm compound grey gas rises yet on mixing with air the grey disappears. Amazing. He smoked the cigarette to the end. We eagerly awaited further tricks.

Woodwork was easy and enjoyable, one double period per week with the added benefit of no homework and no year-end exams. The instructor, somewhat deaf and perhaps 75, had been a skilled cabinet maker. He had never been a teacher and was lucky the woodwork room was on the ground floor as he had arthritis. He was a friendly old chap, never needed to chastise anyone and we regarded him quite differently from the rest of the staff. He once brought us a photograph of a large sideboard, dining-table and six chairs he had made for his son's wedding present. We were impressed – it was inlaid. His first name was Tom, naturally we referred to him as Timber but never in his hearing. He worked in an old brown smock and wore pince-nez spectacles. Being a pensioner and conscious of fountain pen ink economy, every lad's term report showed the single word 'good' plus half a treble clef, the latter his economy signature.

We started year one making basic joints, sometimes too much glue, sometimes too little, the wood becoming progressively dirtier and spotted in red, sometimes starting all over again as tight joints split when belted with an over-eager mallet. Fingers were cut, sometimes sandpapered, glue spilt, wood split and shavings swept up as every lesson just flew away.

During the third and last year each lad had to decide, with Tom's guidance, on what to build for a take home souvenir or present. 'Darky' (so named because of a profusion of black hair all over his body) was a very quiet lad, good at football, whose brother had been expelled for tobacco trading. He decided he wanted to carve a huge yacht from one solid chunk. Tom advised against it, but Darky insisted. When the wood arrived via a local joiner it seemed like half a railway sleeper. The lad duly produced a drawing of an ocean-going real yacht culled from some pre-war boating magazine, complete with hull sections. With Tom's help he scaled everything down, producing internal and external cardboard templates from old cornflake packets, each carefully numbered. By the fourth double lesson he started to hollow it out, banging away through the whole lesson. Each week Tom brought one of his own hollow wood-turning chisels for Darky to use. Tom insisted on sharpening this but let Darky turn the crank handle of the huge grinding wheel. Each week he steadily banged that chisel through two whole lessons. We had long since changed his nickname to Banger. Plank clamped to bench with hull upside down, it still looked like half a railway sleeper. He started on the external sculpting to leave a uniform wall half an inch thick to balance the whole hull, to be followed by endless sanding.

I decided on a low buffet with cane top. The buffet itself progressed very well but I messed up the woven cane seat. As there was no more cane, crafty Tom suggested two pieces of wood instead, screwed and glued with a broad gap left between for fingers to lift it. Finally varnished it was presentable. When I got it home my mother was pleasantly surprised as she thought I could only make firewood.

During the penultimate lesson whilst cutting the slot to take the keel insert, Banger misjudged one blow and the boat split in half down the grain, followed by his loud and anguished bellow. Undeterred, the patient Tom lit the gas under the iron glue pot. Banger proudly carried his yacht home having produced more wood chips and used more sandpaper than all the rest of us put together. There ended all three years of once-a-week therapy, very happy bunnies in a cosy warren lined with wood shavings – magic, with not a girl in sight.

At the beginning of my last year, now in 5a, a vision arrived in the form of a new English language teacher. Around 22, long brown hair, slight trace of some mysterious scent from a distant harem, a trim figure in tight clothes, high heels and always dead straight stocking seams. To us by now 15-year-olds, this was our very own Marilyn Monroe/Ava Gardner all-in-one package, which came with faultless BBC English. From day one she got from the boys rapt attention, full co-operation, the door opened for her, the board cleaned. The teacher's desk had a modesty panel to the front so we could never see those lovely legs. From the girls the boys got ribald comments: 'You've forgotten to clean her shoes', 'Are you just going to sit there while she lifts that heavy chalk?' etc.

Collecting the homework one lesson, she stopped at the London evacuee, who for some reason had never returned to London although the war was long over. He offered no homework, just leered at her saying, to the horror and amazement of the whole class, 'What are you doing on Saturday night?' No reaction, no response, instead she placed books already collected on the nearest desk and promptly slapped his face, so fiercely that he fell sideways into the next lad and thence onto the floor. In five years we had all contacted those hard school planks, but never in such dramatic circumstances. He picked himself up, blood trickling from his nose. 'Go and wash that off and return immediately' all crisp calm BBC, expression still unchanged. She picked up the books and continued, whilst the whole class clapped including the girls. She sat down with a faint Mona Lisa smile, perhaps appreciating the applause. The girls were clapping her, the boys were applauding the nerve of the absent lad. Somehow Londoners are different from Yorkshire folk. Had he put his hand on her knee instead of the Saturday night proposal she might well have thrown him through the window.

At twenty-two, this vision must have well known the effect she had on any male: even a three-year old boy would have wanted a big hug. Perhaps as well that the male staff were mostly elderly. Quite amazing not one as yet had suffered a heart attack just looking at her. She announced the homework as the bell rang, then to her victim: 'I want last week's, this week's and this extra by next lesson or you go straight to the Headmaster.' No mention of why as she passed him some scribbled instructions.

Via the lunch grapevine half the school was aware of the incident. By the last bell, which doubled as the fire alarm, the embellished version reached the remainder and staff. On his ground floor patrols, the exasperated caretaker was still trying to decipher frequent sniggering whispers, to no avail. Frustrated, he knew something juicy must have happened, but he had nothing to report to the cleaning women, one of whom had a sister who ran the dining room. She too had nothing to report to her crew.

The school dining room was a separate single storey block at the top end of the upper playground and built long after the school. The food was delivered on trolleys by canteen staff to the teachers and prefects who, sitting at the end of the long trestle tables, doled it onto plates to be passed right down the table. A simple system which worked perfectly. You could swap food with the kid either side of you but not across the table or this would be seen by the teacher.

The first formers were only allowed into the dining room last of all, they had to queue by the door guarded by a different teacher each day, who made them recite the multiplication tables parrot fashion. By the end of the first year you certainly knew these off by heart providing you survived pneumonia from queuing in the rain whilst the teacher remained snug and dry in the doorway.

In summer we had Spam and salad once per week, in winter it was Spam done in batter. We also had tripe, which I always left on the plate, but I liked the onions done in white sauce. Kids who went home for lunch missed out on all these treats. Alternatively, five minutes' walk away were two shops where beautiful haddock and chips were available for just over one old penny, scrap bits of over-fried batter were free.

Above the main road the school rented a farmer's field as a second football area, the lower slope of this was dug to provide a limited kitchen garden for the canteen, mainly cabbages, carrots and potatoes galore. Some teachers would allow working on this garden as an alternative to one hours detention or you could opt out of the Wednesday afternoon games periods and work instead as a slave on the plantation. If it started to rain this was a cute way of sneaking off home early.

My final experience of the Headmaster was personal, brief and formal, involving the whole staff and form 5 only, as some days after my final term ended, I received a letter demanding I return to the school hall the following Tuesday noon, this from no less than the Headmaster.

At the ceremony, my name beginning with 'A' meant I was first to walk up to the Headmaster and we shook hands as he gave me the Certificate, stiff card in white envelope.

'Well done Ainley, do keep in touch.'

'Yes Sir, thank you Sir.' The only time we spoke in five years.

As nearly a hundred were handed out, I moved away to open the envelope. Credits in art, maths, physics, English language, French. The sole reward for five years of graft, boredom, love, sorrow, adoration, irritation, a little blood, tears and . . . caretaker! Unlike today where one single O-level in Bee Keeping in the Arctic, Street Theatre or Social Studies will do, in my day it was a minimum of five passes or nothing at all.

Alone on the stage a girl commenced to play mood music on the piano. There followed cries of joy, anguish, hugs, the teachers dressed in their best clothes, all discreet scent and lavender, not a chalky gown in sight.

The 'film star' looked stunning. A happy, joyous, relaxed occasion, the turning point when the staff welcomed us into their adult world, a world extending even beyond Manchester.

The hovering clique of parents now mingled with the rest. To one side a trestle table held sherry, biscuits and cheese. In this suddenly adult world I could have walked boldly up to one special teacher, thanked her for everything and given her a peck on the cheek. She might even have returned the peck. Across a crowded room I could have leapt to one very special girl, hugged and kissed her full on the lips. No one would have even noticed. Conscious of the boots, I did neither, instead backed into the maths teacher who, hand on my shoulder to steady himself, said, 'Vell done Ainley, but remember, no more svastikas.'

Ignoring the laden table, I quietly edged out of the hall, and walked along the corridor noticing that one rather special girl, certificate held aloft, was hugging her mother. Down the stairs and out of the strangely empty school I went, giving the caretaker a two-finger salute, he just scowled. Outside was the geography teacher's car in the usual place, I imagined the long ladder nearby but saw only the bare wall.

True to the school motto the staff had taught me for school – their school – but when would the teaching for life begin? I now had a school certificate, a well practised knowledge of commandments 11 through 15, far more confidence than apprehension but as yet little idea of how best to deal with people. The polite but ambitious Headmaster subsequently moved on to an expensive boys-only boarding school, with three assistant heads, matron, nurse, army cadet force and three caretakers. He would cope well in his new role as Head, God and Field Marshal. We had both been through a baptism of fire quite unconnected with the war. This was a final definitive ending, there could never, ever be a next time.

I sped home, intent on buying a pair of black shoes. Tomorrow I needed a job as an apprentice draughtsman, in one of the nineteen local machine tool builders and one boiler maker, although I didn't fancy the latter.

Twenty-four years later, my wife and I visited three local senior schools, one of which our son would shortly attend on leaving junior school. At the boys-only school dating from the sixteenth century I asked the Headmaster if he would translate the school motto, the Latin spanning both huge main gates in welded steel letters.

'To be perfectly honest, I don't know, I am a science man myself.'

Twenty-five years later our son, now attending my old school, once arrived home to announce:

'All the kids in my class have Parker pens'.

'You might get one if your writing improves'

'It would improve if I had a Parker pen.'

Kids don't change, he must have been rehearsing this all the way home.

We went to our first parents' evening, each group of parents being shown round by a teacher, our group by the attractive school secretary. After all those years the smell was the same, that curious mix of bodies, floor polish and disinfectant. On the ground floor we reached what had been my 4a form room. I stopped, the rest moved slowly ahead, my wife with them. I opened the door, to find the old desks replaced with square formica-topped tables each with four chairs facing inwards. I could have sat opposite her and looked straight into those green eyes for hours every week. The old wooden blackboard and easel were now replaced with a roller board mounted on the wall. I stared at the spot where a gymslip loop had torn, even after all this time strong memories came flooding back.

Suddenly the school secretary was beside me. 'Do keep up, lots more to see yet.' She sounded just like a teacher. Climbing the stairs together she whispered, 'Why that particular classroom?' I laughed and replied, 'Don't even ask.'

Later on the tour I found the much extended Honours Board. There, in gilt letters, the magic name in full followed by MB, BSc Hons. (Chem.), her seven years recorded for posterity. Driving home thinking of Greeneyes, a following van driver gave a long blast on his horn, perhaps hinting that his van could do over 20 mph chance permitting. In my case not even a blue plaque on a preserved desk with a cracked lid to record I had ever been there. Nothing at all, I had been and gone like chalk wiped from a blackboard.

Days later I called at her by-now elderly father's shop for some light bulbs, mentioned my school visit and asked after his daughter.

'Oh, aye, she's a brain surgeon in Derby now.'

No pride, emotion or enthusiasm in his voice to emphasise the impressive performance of his only daughter. Spoken so casually, as one would say 'It looks like rain now' or 'My biro's run out', it was to him just a mundane occurrence.

12

Life in Halifax

The house my mother rented in Halifax was five minutes' walk from where she worked, ten minutes from all the bus routes and the main shopping areas. It was quite an improvement on the cottage, being a back to back terrace house with two rooms up, two rooms down and a cellar which in turn led into a large coal cellar. Electric lights were everywhere, even in the coal cellar but there were no sockets anywhere at all. Still no bathroom but a large zinc bath in the cellar, along with a cast iron coal range with built in hot water boiler, a stone slab sink and in one corner a square brick set-pot for the laundry with its own fire underneath.

A large communal stone flagged yard served five such houses, at each end were outside flushing toilets, the incoming water pipes thickly bound with sacking against winter frost. The toilet blocks were linked by a high stone wall with but a single entrance gate. Along the building face and the top of the wall were hooks for washing lines. All handy and private but not a blade of grass or tree in sight, it cost five shillings per week in rent which had to be taken every four weeks to an estate agent's office five minutes' walk away. Five steps onto a small, railed landing led up to the door. Under the landing, steps led down to the outside cellar door with a window beside it. As with my old pal Donald's house, where the wall had collapsed through the kitchen window, this cellar had a grating in the corner to empty the bath.

Upstairs was an identical iron range but with oven, kettle crane and hot water boiler, beside it full length cupboards hid a porcelain sink and a gas ring.

My mother bought a meat-safe, the frame and door of which were covered with perforated zinc. At last we were well organised and there was ample room for the huge ornate sideboard to stand directly against one wall. We now had a townhouse but the toilet was cold to use on winter nights.

When we moved to Halifax I started another paper round where I could use my old bike as the route was reasonably flat. I collected the papers from Bell Hall sub post office, then had to cross Saville Park Moor on the bus route to Copley village. Half way across was a small café owned by the council. Although called 'moor' it was actually many acres of mown grassland marked out as eight football or rugby pitches in winter. It was surrounded on three sides with expensive properties and the land was originally bequeathed to the townspeople by some rich merchant in Victorian days who stipulated that it should never be built upon.

The first house I delivered to belonged to the Mackintosh family of the 'Quality Street' firm, then came Richard Asquith, Albert Kitchen and Jim Butler who were all machine tool barons. Next call was the Gledhill family who made cash tills. Their house had a small private cinema in the grounds. On the bike the whole round took me about 45 minutes back to the post office. In a severe winter I had to walk round due to the deep and frozen snow and it took forever. The single decker bus to Copley village had been abandoned half way across the 'moor', blown snow had drifted up against the bus side, further snow froze each night until eventually I could walk right up the drift onto the bus roof.

Although the public were not allowed to ride in Post Office vans, the driver on his collection took me across to the first house on three or four nights. He used skid chains over the tyres, most light vehicles needed them in such conditions. That same winter a double decker bus to Wainstalls village remained abandoned for some weeks, this village being around 1000 feet above sea level. Beyond the village was just miles of barren moorland across to Keighley. At one point an RAF helicopter had to drop bread to the villagers. My mother's half-cousin died in this village and it was some weeks before the low-slung hearse could reach her cottage. She left my mother £250 which was a windfall to her, but not so to another half-cousin who lived in the Manor House at Pool-in-Wharfedale. She had already buried two rich Bradford mill-owner husbands. That Christmas the paper round yielded just over £5 in tips. I bought a 'Record' smoothing plane, which I still have to this day, and a second hand vice from a neighbour.

Just around the corner from our townhouse was a detached house, then used as 'The Irish Democratic Club'. In the eighteenth century, eight miles away at a remote farm on the edge of the moors, the cunning rogue David Hartley started filing dust evenly from the edge of solid gold guinea coins. He then returned these into circulation, and persisted to such an extent that banks and a few expensive shops, such as jewellers, bought apothecary's scales to weigh the guineas, if under weight they refused to accept them. These defiled coins began turning up as far away as Liverpool, Hull and London. The wrathful Treasury sent a customs officer named William Deighton to find the culprit, and whilst in Halifax he lodged in this very same house, the building at that time being run as a common doss house.

Deighton searched among the low life in the seedy taverns and disreputable ale houses and word of his quest soon passed through the underworld to David Hartley, who then bribed some character to shoot Deighton with a blunderbuss right outside this house. When news of this reached the Treasury in London, they were not best pleased and sent in the cavalry. Red coated troops 'persuaded' the local bandits to betray Hartley, and he was captured and hanged after being convicted at York Assizes, the charges being 'defacing coins of the realm' and the minor charge of conspiring to murder. His body was then mounted on a frame erected at the top of the hill overlooking Halifax as a warning to any other ambitious locals. At night he was secretly taken down and buried by his cronies in Heptonstall churchyard.

One of the old Halifax pubs was called 'The Saddle', a rough hostelry frequented by prostitutes and rogues, with regular police activity right up to the 1950s. The brewery owners refurbished the place and re-named it 'The William Deighton'. As a teenager living nearby I knew nothing of this history but learned much later that Halifax was known for savage justice; tramps used the prayer 'May the good lord preserve us from Hell, Hull and Halifax'. A man was once put to death on the town's gibbet for stealing one sheep. Today there is still Gibbet Street to remind drug dealers of the good old days.

No young children lived in our immediate vicinity, but a neighbour, Donald Acklam, persuaded me to join Holy Trinity Church Boy Scouts group and this was where I met two lads who were to become close friends for some years. One of them, Mick Rhodes (always called Jammy because his initials were JM) lived ten minutes' walk away in a stone built semi-detached house. He attended Heath Grammar School, a boys only school, where the school week included Saturday morning with Wednesday afternoon devoted to games. His father and his Uncle Jack owned an ironmongers shop nearby with a factory behind it making wire products – lampshade frames, bed spring units for mattresses, woven wire guards for machinery, in fact anything in wire. They also owned another wire products company in Keighley which still ran under their late father's name, Bethel Rhodes & Sons. In one corner of their Halifax works was a two storey shed rented by one Norman Seed, a cabinet maker and furniture restorer.

On one occasion Mick's father drove the whole family (Mick had a pouting younger sister called Marilyn) to Paris, then down to Monte Carlo for a week whilst their lounge was redecorated. Norman Seed then installed some new kitchen units he had made and somehow drove a steel spike straight through the single brick wall into the lounge. Rather than redecorate this wall yet again they hung on the spike a huge straw sombrero bought as a souvenir in the South of France. There it stayed as a wall decoration, with much moaning from Marilyn as she wanted to hang it in her bedroom.

Colin Archibald was another Trinity scout who also became a pal. He left Holy Trinity senior school and started work for a Mytholmroyd firm called Fisher Controls Limited. They made complex units for controlling varied timing and sequence programmes on large commercial laundry equipment, similar to the programme selector on a modern domestic machine. When Fisher died his wife managed the firm for some years, by then Colin was a service engineer covering the whole of the UK. When Mrs Fisher retired she sold the firm to a much larger company who ceased production of this equipment and instead changed to making coin-operated controls for car park barriers, altering the name to Fisher Karpark Limited. Colin was made redundant but realised that the countrywide customers, including many large hospitals, would need servicing and spares for years ahead. With a bank loan he continued in his old job but now self-employed. Later he rented a workshop and started to make a special valve used in the controllers instead of buying this in from Sweden. He moved to larger premises but a mile from the old Fisher Controls factory and thrived on this right through to retirement.

Barry Bairstow, a pal of Mick's, became an apprentice joiner with the maintenance department of Websters Brewery but he was not a boy scout.

Mick's father had waited ages to get a new Humber Hawk car, the best styled car of its time, in metallic grey. The waiting time for a new car in those days was so prolonged that he could have re-sold it immediately for £200 profit! When Mick passed his driving test he found some hilltop farmer advertising a pre-war Jowett van for sale at £9. We put in £3 each and the farmer towed it down into the wireworks yard. This old van had a rickety wooden frame clad with metal panels. Both chassis side members had cracked and been plated in the cracked position without prior straightening, so the van sagged in the middle. We stripped it right down and Mick's father paid for the two-cylinder, horizontally-opposed engine to be overhauled in the local Rootes main dealers who had supplied his Humber. Barry made a new wooden frame but we clad this with sheet metal on the inside so the outside then looked like a Morris Traveller. Mick's father taxed and insured it in his name and took it to a testing station in Bradford where it passed as roadworthy but was nearly 100 lbs heavier than the original van. It was always kept in the works yard where it was quite secure as the big gates were locked every night.

Barry was called up into the army and went to the war in Korea, Mick started at Leeds University and I was later conscripted into the RAF. Mick's father wrote to me in Tripoli and told me he had sold the vehicle to a window cleaner and had given my mother £22, my one third share of the profit! With a degree in chemistry, years later Mick Rhodes became technical director of Lancashire Tar Distillers at Irlam, Manchester.

After the war all manner of military surplus began to be available, both retail and at auction sites. Someone had bought a quantity of American army troop-carrying gliders and stored them in a flat field at Mytholmroyd. The wings had already been removed and the idea was to slice off the cockpit and the rear fuselage complete with fin and tailplane, retaining just the central portion to be converted into caravans or horseboxes. Mick's father obtained one of the cockpits, cut out the two curved re-inforced windows in front of each pilot and used them to cover his cold frame, thinking that the curved surfaces would magnify the rays of sunshine to increase the growth of his marrows. It did not work, so borrowing the Scout handcart Mick and I shifted the cockpit into our yard, using ropes to drag it over the wall as it would not go through the gate. The pilot's seats and control columns were still in position, as was the central lever with the big red knob to release the line from the towing aircraft. Pulleys with ball races were fitted to guide the cables to move the flaps but the cables had already been removed. It was the first time I had seen the name 'Formica', moulded in raised letters on the side of each pulley. It sat there in the corner of the yard for months, and delivery men and visitors to the neighbours all peered at it, for the older people it was perhaps the closest they came to the recent war. My mother's only comment was, 'Whatever are you going to do with that thing?' Eventually I persuaded the local scrap dealer to bring a rope and shift it back over the wall. 'It's no good for scrap, I'll dump it in my sister's garden, her kids can play in it. Here's two shillings.'

Across the main road a cobbled street ran through to the next road, on each side terraced houses, with the usual steps up, steps down, the cellar drop protected by spiked railings interrupted by spiked gates to each house. I learnt from a witness that a loud backfire from a truck had caused a horse to bolt along this street, the cart had collided obliquely with a lamp post swinging the horse across the pavement to impale itself on the railings. Three of the spikes were deeply buried in its neck. When I arrived the street was littered with scrap metal with steam rising from the gutter awash with blood. The horse was dead. A young girl stood there sobbing, slowly stroking the horse's tail, surrounded by silent onlookers, but no sign of the Irish scrap-man. The local newspaper reporter had only five minutes' walk to get his front page story and picture for the next day's edition. The day after, all that remained were scratch marks on the lamp post, slightly buckled railings and the forlorn cart parked at the kerb with one broken shaft. It was the same cart used to haul my glider cockpit.

As time passed, coincidences began to emerge in my weird lifestyle. I had twice attended infants schools where I had only to cross a road to reach school. Although penniless and homeless I had been driven each morning to two other schools, despite petrol rationing and cars being a rarity. Years later I was a manager at two of these schools where I was the only one of twelve managers who had actually attended both schools as a child.

Over the years the house where I was born had been demolished and replaced with a block of six luxury flats. Two houses I had lived in were later condemned as unfit and were also demolished. A German aircrew had attempted to demolish me and the house where I lived for only three weeks. As one single bomber dropped one single bomb at least three miles from the usual target, perhaps this had been intended for me.

On two occasions I had seen what spikes could do to living flesh. Of the two horses I had known, one after doing its best to make me rich had been shot, the other died a horrible death one hundred yards from my home. Even my old school desk with the cracked lid had been scrapped. It seemed as though some unknown force was at work intent on eliminating all trace of my very existence.

When the war ended my mother ceased to assemble detonators as the contract ran down and the firm reverted to making their traditional cash tills. She was switched to building small sub-assemblies for these and eventually retired. A man who had previously worked at this firm was posted to the far east during the war and became a prisoner of the Japanese, made to do forced labour on the notorious Burma railway. He survived and after recuperation back in some army hospital in England returned to work. When he landed back in England he weighed just seventy pounds! I saw him just once, thin, gaunt and subject to recurring bouts of malaria.

Eventually the British Government obtained cash reparations from Japan – he must have been so grateful for his £15 share. He worked on the same sub-assemblies as my mother.

Just before she retired my mother received a letter from the National Insurance office asking her to attend their Halifax office to sign an application for her state pension. One question on the form asked her to state whether married, single, divorced or widowed. The indifferent young male clerk told her unless she could answer correctly whether widowed or not she would forgo the meagre pension. 'Next please.' She was in tears when I got home and she told me the story. As these offices then opened on Saturday mornings, we both went and I stormed straight past the queue to the counter, demanding loudly to see the manager and the clerk. After some argument the manager appeared, took us into his office and told the clerk to produce three cups of tea. My mother, in tears once again and clutching the form, gave him the story of my missing father. He was most apologetic, castigated the clerk and promised to speak to him later. He took the form and scribbled on it saying it would be sent straight to Leeds area office and she would be sent a pension book immediately. This actually happened. He guided my mother right out to the street with more apologies. Some man in the long suffering queue, probably well used to being treated like dirt, shouted, 'You did right lad.' As we walked home I suddenly realised that no one in the queue had made any objection when I barged straight to the front.

Sometime during this period I developed a boil on my neck, then yet another, and they continued to appear. I went to my mother's doctor, a dour old Scotsman who told me to apply hot kaolin poultices to draw out the infection. I got some from the local chemist but it did not stop more forming, always in awkward places, sometimes I had two festering at once. On calling for some more kaolin (I think this was basically Cornish clay used for pottery), the chemist pointed out that it was doing no good, I should instead try an old remedy. I should get some baker's yeast, drop a thimbleful in a cup of warm water and drink it. 'The badness in your blood will be eaten up by the living yeast.' I didn't grasp what he meant but thanked him and dashed across to the baker's shop. The baker knew well enough. The existing boil dried up and I never had another.

At one point I got a tiny sliver of chromium plate in my thumb, it came from the peeling plating on an old machine tool handle. It quickly went septic, within a week the thumb was badly swollen and where the metal entered was by now a small area of tight yellow skin. I again went to the same doctor who told me to bathe it in the hottest water I could stand containing dissolved boracic powder. I regularly did this, but nothing happened. One night I could not sleep because my elbow and armpit were throbbing so I got up and walked to the nearby Halifax Infirmary. The night porter found a doctor who looked at it and just said, 'Lie on that trolley, I'll have to slit this immediately, another day and you might have lost your thumb, have you been to your own doctor?' I told him the result. He did some telephoning and a nurse appeared wheeling a gas cylinder on a trolley. I didn't quite count to ten, next thing I knew was waking up to see a huge bandage round my thumb. The nurse got me a cup of tea and a sling. In this infirmary you didn't have to wait for hours. 'Have you far to go home, the ambulance is out at the moment but will run you home if you wait, I'll write to your doctor with a complaint, keep the bandage on for four days then get your chemist to remove it, he'll advise you.'

'Thanks very much, I only live ten minutes away, the throbbing has stopped already.' I walked home, managed to sleep, got to work an hour late when the sarcastic foreman asked, 'Have you been fighting the police again?'

'No, just a septic thumb and anyway I'm left handed.'

I went to the early evening surgery, walked straight into the doctor's room. Ignoring the patient sitting with him I shouted, 'You are totally bloody useless, get back to Scotland!' The woman patient looked amazed as I just walked straight out again.

Back home I told my mother that she should change her doctor, but she wouldn't. Apart from first registering with him she had never had to suffer his total incompetence. To this day there is clearly visible on my right thumb a scar two inches long and another near it one inch long.

A pleasant chap called Frank Sutcliffe lived with his wife in the end cottage of a terrace across the street from our yard. He worked at a small local mill owned by an elderly widow. He looked after the mill boiler and occasionally chauffeured her around in an immaculate Wolseley limousine with a glass division behind the front seats and a speaking tube. Two jump seats swung down facing backwards. Mounted on the roof was a spot-lamp swivelled from inside by a lever above the driver's head. When she died the mill closed down and he was out of a job so started to help his brother who owned two taxis. She left him the Wolseley in her will so they used it for weddings and funerals, but he kept it on the street at his home. When washed and polished, the dark blue body-work, gleaming chrome, with beige interior and two white satin ribbons stretching to the windscreen, he decked out in his chauffeur's uniform with white gloves and loose white top on his peaked cap, the whole rig was fit for any princess and must have featured on Halifax wedding photographs for many years.

One Saturday morning he showed me round the mill and eventually the boardroom, which was actually part of the old lady's house, built on to the mill. In this room was a huge polished table that would open to allow extra leaves to be inserted to extend it. The winding handle was hidden in a recess underneath. Against the window wall were ten matching chairs. Against the opposite wall was a huge matching sideboard. No carpet, just highly polished wooden floorboards. The sideboard appeared to have doors and drawers but all were fake. Instead a door opened at the end to reveal a hollow box lined with green baize and with fitted wooden bars. The six extra table leaves slid into these grooves when not in use.

Two streets away from ours were the premises of Ernest Gutsell, ophthalmic surgeon and part owner of Halifax Optical Company. This firm made spectacles for other opticians in the area. I had recently seen a picture of Glenn Miller wearing rimless glasses and rather fancied a pair. I went to see Mr Gutsell and of the few examples he had, most of the lens profiles had too many curves for my liking. When I showed him the picture he said, 'Why not design your own shape like those? Whatever the shape we can make it and they will still cost £4. Whatever your preferred lens profile, it will be no problem as we do not have to frame them.' After the eye test he wrote down the maximum height and width I could work to in millimetres. At home I used some graph paper from a school exercise book to draw the exact shape and returned with it. The graph paper was printed all over in one millimetre squares. 'They will take around two weeks, we will send you a post card when they are ready.' When I tried them on he adjusted the fit and once outside I looked at my reflection in his window – they hardly showed on my face. Back home, my mother who had known nothing of this transaction, just said, 'What have you done to your glasses?'

I didn't realise it at the time but drilling holes at each top corner of a glass lens made for a very fragile assembly. At the slightest bump the corner broke away. Twice I had to have new lenses made at £2 a time and they had to be cleaned with extra care. I kept them for special occasions and reverted to using my old pair. When I first wore them at school I got the same question, 'What happened to your specs?' I didn't mind, I looked like Glenn Miller. This would be around 1946.

In sharp contrast in 2005 I bought a new pair for reading costing £220 and a second pair for distance vision and driving costing £208. Both are amazingly lightweight with very small, thin, plastic lenses fully framed in springy titanium. The eye test cost me nothing, tax payers footing the bill, yet I too pay taxes. Waiting for them to be made, having worked with titanium in the aircraft industry I knew that such a minute amount in wire form would have a maximum material cost of well under £1. Corning produce the optically pure plastic material, Kodak market it under their name to lens manufacturers, the wire is supplied to frame manufacturers, the independent opticians worked as a concession from a branded chain of shops and a French designer of the most stupid looking clothes for women gets his cut for allowing the use of his international name so they are then called 'designer' frames. Seven lots of profit on one pair of spectacles. Progress!

One day when going out of our yard I opened the tall wooden door and a young local lad let fly with an air pistol from about four feet away, hitting me on the cheek, very close to my new left lens. I grabbed him and gave him a right earful. Turning to close the door I noticed a target pinned to it and gave him another loud earful. The pellet really stung but left no lasting mark.

I next saw Barry, now out of the army and back working at Websters on pub refurbishment, when I came home on leave from Tripoli. We went for a drink at a Halifax pub on a corner site with its main entrance on one street and a side door on the branch street sloping down to the station. Due to the slope three steps rose from pavement level to this side door. We went in, down a short passage and into the bar lined with drinkers. We got two pints and found a table close to the bar, so close that one man sitting on a bar stool kept leaning round to flick his cigarette into the ashtray on our table. Needing to stub the cigarette out, he leaned over once again just as another man squeezed past him and put him off balance. He missed the ashtray and stubbed it out on the back of my hand with his full weight on it. I let out a scream and shot round the bar counter to get my hand under a water tap. The landlord, who was across the pub collecting glasses, must have thought I was robbing his till and hurtled back shouting 'What the hell are you doing?' The stranger who did it was most apologetic, 'It was an accident, I was pushed.' All eyes were now on the huge blister that was developing under the stream of tap water as the landlady came downstairs, saw it and said, 'Don't touch it, I'll be back in a minute.' She returned with a needle, striking a match she put the sharp end in the flame and with the needle flat on my skin slid the point straight into the base of the blister. Murky water poured out and the blister began to deflate but slowly. 'Don't put anything on it at all, new skin will grow under it and don't pick at it.' We sat down again, the bloke still apologising bought us each a pint and promptly left the pub.

Eventually we also left, going along the short passage just as two blokes came in up the steps. I leaned back against the wall to let them pass, opposite me Barry did the same but without knowing he had leaned on the unfastened door leading straight down stone steps into the pub cellar. He disappeared backwards with a loud cry. The two blokes and I stared down at him in a heap at the bottom as the landlord once again dashed up beside me.

'You two again, you're barred!'

Barry recovered and rubbing his back climbed very slowly up the steps. 'You don't need to bar us, we'll never set foot in this pub again. I was a bloody sight safer in the Korean war.'

Barry went to Canada to work as a joiner on new houses for some years. Returning he bought the site of the long demolished Siddal Hall and built himself a new detached house with integral garage. His old home where his mother still lived was but a few minutes' walk away and he stayed with her whilst he built it. When finished he got married and liked to be known locally as the new Squire of Siddal. Carved into one gatepost was the word Siddal, the other read Hall.

13

Apprenticeship

Little is known of the William Asquith who as a young man went off to seek his fortune in the Californian gold rush but whilst there he became interested in developing shakers driven by a water wheel to 'pan' the gold much faster than panning by hand. To build these he needed to drill holes in metal. He eventually returned to Halifax, and obtaining rented premises he commenced to make a belt-driven radial drilling machine similar to one shown in a lithograph in the US Government Census of Industry and Manufacturing published in 1875. Now run by his two sons the firm had grown and it was here that I was apprenticed in 1947.

This area of the Pennines had perhaps the largest concentration of machine tool manufacturing in the world, although a similar pattern existed in towns within Connecticut, USA. In Halifax the larger firms had their own sales agents abroad, the smaller firms often obtaining export business via the Crown Agents for the Colonies, together sending a huge tonnage into machine shops world-wide. Some were massive machines – the transit of but a single Asquith horizontal borer to Liverpool docks could involve up to four Pickfords low-loaders plus a police escort at front and rear. All this activity generated massive overtime, night shifts, Saturday morning and Sunday working, but Saturday afternoon was sacrosanct for Rugby League matches. It also caused heavy work-loads for local ancillary suppliers such as Pratt Chucks, Halifax Rack and Screw Company, Crowthers (telescopic slideway guards), Harrison & Allott (chrome plating and engraving), Hope Bros. (heat treatment) and Dargue Bros. (drafting machines). Everyone in these firms clocked in and out on Gledhill-Brook Time Recorders also made in nearby Huddersfield. Keighley Laboratories provided metallurgical testing facilities and heat treatment. The more distant ball bearing manufacturers also gained as ball races gradually replaced brass bushes. Of the foundries then in action Asquiths' own was called Modern Foundries Limited, the smaller Hargreaves foundry and Baldwins who cast only in aluminium.

The 1945–1970 era was boom-time for this industry, so great the need for skilled fitters that Asquiths once 'imported' six from a Scottish shipyard, each arriving with their only tool – a four-pound hammer. They did not last long, being more used to rusty steel plates rather than precision work.

Writing this brings back memories of a more personal nature. 'Tis often said that school years are the happiest, yet for me five years apprenticeship far outweighed anything that school had to offer. For someone with a mechanical bent how can Shakespeare, French verbs or Palmerston's foreign policy compete with sculpting great chunks of cast iron built to run for fifty years in all corners of the globe? As a schoolboy I had delivered newspapers to the homes of Albert Kitchen, Richard Asquith and Jim Butler, the top local men in this industry, never imagining that years later Richard Asquith and I would be fellow magistrates.

Sometime in the 1920s Asquiths had completed a giant plano-miller for a South American customer who could not pay. The financial problem this caused was solved by a rich solicitor named Rhodes who invested and became chairman. Asquiths had to retain this machine for their own use and it was still on constant night and day production work in 1955. I also remember the steam driven hammer and steam crane on railway tracks in the yard, both in daily use. I still have hand scrapers made on the steam hammer from old flat files.

Occasionally a huge Dutch man called Smit (who wore a white suit and was the other half of Smit-Asquith) would be shown round the works by Robert Asquith, each smoking a fat cigar. Slyly following them would be a labourer pretending to brush the floor but waiting to retrieve the cigar butts which he later smoked in his pipe. Smit-Asquith Diamond Industries Ltd made machines for grinding diamonds on the same site.

One time an apprentice decided to take up weight-lifting. Steel disks were duly cut off in the stores, drilled and smuggled out wrapped in his overalls, but to get the five-foot-long lifting bar home was more of a problem. This he concealed by wearing his overalls with the top of the bar up the side of his head and covered by his duffle coat hood. The bottom of the bar rested on his foot. This lad lurched to the bus stop amid ribald shouts of 'Frankenstein's made another'. The lower deck being full he prised himself upstairs, only to find he could not sit down. He then descended backwards, and stood for the rest of the journey on the platform. He had to repeat this process on a second bus to reach home. This acquisition of the necessary steel was known locally as 'government work', in Lancashire always called 'foreigners', and was rewarded with the usual twenty cigarettes.

One employee, a production planning engineer, decided that Asquiths would make for him a small bench lathe. He prepared the drawings, machining sequence cards with times allowed, ordered patterns and castings all on a phoney works number. It was duly made and inspected; the scam came to light when the sales department could find no trace of customer or order. He was fired and went to work at Butlers as a fitter on the night shift. The lathe was donated to the technical college.

Conscription into the armed forces continued long after the end of the war in 1945, normally at the age of 18 but deferred to 21 to allow apprenticeships to be completed, on condition that night school courses were continued during that time (the assumed rule but perhaps not the law of the land). One Asquith apprentice followed this rule but never passed the exams, repeating the easiest first year course every year hoping conscription would end before he reached 21. It didn't but he missed conscription anyway as he was an Austrian national.

A nightshift fitter was once discovered building a caravan chassis, the parts always hidden by morning under rarely used patterns out in the yard. He was switched back to the day shift losing his 25 per cent extra night pay.

Amongst the 800 plus there were quite a few examples of father and son(s) working together in Asquiths, and the men who ran the firm stood out as rugged individuals who made decisions without endless meetings and committees. Among these was George Hoyle, who had travelled the world as a service engineer for the firm and was then made chief engineer. He had a glass eye, having lost the real one in a grinding wheel accident, as did Stanley Walker, a fitter, but he wore a black eye patch like a pirate. Stanley Walker was born in Akron, Ohio and ultimately returned to the States to start his own company reconditioning turret lathes. His brother, Donald Walker, was then chief draughtsman at Kitchen & Wade Limited. The chief inspector at Asquiths was a dour Scotsman called McGlashan whose word was law, although he spoke little and mostly in Gaelic grunts. Everyone agreed with his decisions as few could understand him. I remember also John Holmes, the well respected tool room superintendent. Norman Booth and his successor Ronnie Brothwell were both very effective works managers, whilst the chief draughtsman, Alf Johnson and his jig and tool design counterpart Arnold Ridley were gods in their respective domains. The checker in the tool office was one Tom Blakelock, a genius on gear design seconded to Asquiths from David Browns in Huddersfield to organise the design and manufacture of tank gearboxes during the war. He remained at Asquiths until he retired when his draughtsmen presented him with the latest edition of 'Machinery Handbook'! Two thousand pages of technical reference work – what use in retirement I cannot imagine (not guilty as I was then in the RAF in North Africa).

Ken Kershaw, whose step daughter years later married my brother-in-law, was home sales manager, his brother was chief metallurgist in Modern Foundries. Helping Ken Kershaw was Drummond-Asquith (Sales) Ltd, based in Birmingham. Drummond was the same Guildford firm who made the little old treadle lathe so beloved of model engineers, but at this time produced very modern 'Maxicut' high speed gear shaving machines.

Of those running the firm few, if any, had an engineering degree, yet their collective talent was a formidable back up to the commercial thrust of the Asquith brothers, as evidenced when they bid for and took over Kitchen & Wade Ltd (including Ormerod Shapers) whilst Albert Kitchen was on a sales trip to South Africa. In this they eliminated a lower-priced competitor and gained extra machining capacity, yet no jobs were lost. Undeterred, Albert Kitchen made his chief draughtsman, Donald Walker, a partner in A. Kitchen–D. Walker Limited, and in rented premises started building the South African orders.

Asquith radial drills for UK delivery were left fully assembled and sheeted over on a truck. Occasionally a British Road Services driver would return one to the works with the elevating gear box at the top of the pillar shattered after impacting a low bridge – Asquiths' own drivers were much more careful. At the peak of war time production around sixty radial drills left Asquiths per month, an ancient thermometer type gadget remained on one wall of a fitting bay to record this even when I worked there. Near this gadget another device from pre-war was a long clothes drying rack similar to old ones seen in kitchens, but fitted with hooks for hanging top-coats. The system in those days was, as you clocked in you hung your coat on a hook and right on starting time the foreman wound the rack up into the air. If you didn't get your coat on the rack you were sent home for the morning, thereby losing half a day's pay. A system the union wouldn't tolerate for a moment today.

Despite cash betting on horses being illegal in those days, most factories had a bookie's runner but Asquiths had their own bookmaker who drove an overhead crane, transactions being via an old paint tin lowered on a rope.

On the Wednesday morning after leaving school, in stiff new shoes, I walked up the long street past various machine tool makers and the boiler works. I had selected Butlers as Jim Butler had given me a good tip on my paper round at Christmas. I marched into the separate office block with the drawing office above, I could see drawing boards through the lighted windows.

'I have just left school and would like to be apprenticed as a draughtsman please.'

The receptionist replied, 'Sit down, I'll get Mr Butler to come down and see you.'

He came down the stairs, I rose and he suddenly stopped, 'I seem to know your face, lad.'

'I've been delivering your evening newspaper for the last two years.'

'You're too late, we've just set another lad on. Here in Butlers they don't go through the works, they just start straight in the office. Go further up the road to Asquiths, the last firm on the right. They are much bigger and have lots of apprentices, you'll soon learn up there and you'll have to go to night school. Just tell them I sent you.'

I went up the hill past the barracks and found the oval neon sign on the front office block, the sign was left switched on night and day, two red Bentley cars parked under it at the roadside. It was a sign I came to know so well over a period of years. I found the main works entrance with the two commissionaires. I repeated my story to one of them who replied, 'Do you know Jim Butler then?'

'Yes.'

'Right, I'll take you over to see Eric Northend the personnel bloke, just let this truck get out first.'

I looked round. Crawling slowly along the loading bay was a huge Pickfords low-loader, on it some massive object painted grey and with the same oval name picked out in blue and cream on the side, at the end of it the much smaller words 'WM. ASQUITH LTD MAKERS HALIFAX ENGLAND'. A large card was strapped to the machine, on it the name of some shipyard in Rotterdam and Huskisson Dock, Liverpool. An overhead crane startled me as it trundled past. Everything seemed so big. I knew what a machine was and I knew what a tool was but I wasn't quite certain just what a machine tool could be. Eric Northend explained that my father would have to come to sign the apprenticeship papers with the directors.

'I haven't got a father.'

'Have you got a mother?'

'Yes.'

'Well your mother will have to sign, both of you come back tomorrow, any time will do in the afternoon. You will go through the works for four years, final year in the drawing office. You will go to the tech every Wednesday and two nights a week for the first two years, three nights for the last two to get your Ordinary and Higher National Certificates in mechanical engineering. You can't do overtime until you are 18, that's

122

a union rule, they will want you to join but you are not forced to as an apprentice.'

He then outlined the meagre pay for each year, also agreed with the union. He showed me out, back to the loading bay. As I left the works I could just see the quarry on the skyline where we kids had found ammunition. I walked home and outlined to my mother everything that had occurred.

'You once won a prize for drawing, we'll go down now to Milletts to get you some overalls.' Amongst their ex-government military surplus was a pair of brown ex-army ones, which with the legs turned up would fit me.

Next day we returned to Asquiths. Eric Northend took us to the boardroom to meet Robert (cigar) and Richard (pipe) Asquith. All three signed, shook hands and I was told to report the following Monday at 7.40 am to the commissionaire's gate, and to call at the technical college to enrol.

It was my first brief experience of the two Bentley-driving kings of Halifax machine tool building. Richard's wife had given me a Christmas tip on the paper round. Theirs was the very first house near Birdcage Lane, the millionaires' row of Halifax. That afternoon I told the paper shop owner that I would finish on Saturday night as I was starting work. He promptly put a notice in both windows.

I was met at the gate by a foreman on Monday morning. The brown overalls puzzled him, as he told me the firm provided three pairs for everyone on the shop floor and had one pair per week laundered. When we got to his office he rang the personnel manager and played hell about the overalls, and also the fact that I had not been told that each Wednesday I had to clock in at 7.40, hang about and then catch a bus back to town to reach the tech by 9 o'clock, this pattern reversed at 4.30, then hang about at work until clocking out at 5.30. The foreman's own son was already an apprentice. On the first Wednesday after tea at home I then walked up to the tech for 7 pm, finished at 9 pm, walked home and went to bed. A longish day, the very first week I condemned it as a totally stupid system.

The man at the tech who taught engineering drawing sold secondhand drawing instruments on a pay-by-instalments basis, so I got a small compass and T-square this way. The firm provided basic tools but you had to buy a twelve-inch steel rule, a long narrow pocket was stitched down the side of the overall to take this. At home in the cellar I made a wooden tool box with shallow drawers and a locking hinged lid, a copy of many such in the works.

I soon began to know other apprentices and although still amazed by the size of everything, began to enjoy it. Cast iron dust became engrained in the palms of your hands and the only time they were really clean again was at the end of the one week annual holiday, then you promptly got them black again.

I spent an interesting and enjoyable three months on the final assembly line for radial drills, although I learnt nothing I didn't already know about the job, working with Stanley Walker (with eye patch) and his long term buddy Ronnie Mosey. Both had done this one job since before the war, Ronnie with a break in the army. They worked until 7.30 five evenings, Saturday mornings and Sundays until 4 pm, earning then over twenty pounds per week, paid in old white fivers. They were the highest paid fitters, not just in Asquiths, but the whole Halifax area and inveterate gamblers on horses. Every morning they would select favourites and second favourites and would devise complicated doubles, trebles and each way back to back bets from their deliberations in the foreman's office using the foreman's newspaper. It was then my job to take these bets written on old cigarette packets to the bookie and return with yesterday's winnings if any. For this they paid me five shillings per week. Many the time I brought back a rolled up bundle of white fivers, some-times over fifty pounds. On my birthday I asked them to pick me a winning horse for one shilling.

'Don't start betting, it's a mug's game.'

I persisted, pointing out that it was birthday money.

'It will have to be an outsider.'

They picked one called Squander Bug, showed me how to write the simple 'one shilling win 2.30 Uttoxeter Donald' and I went merrily off to the bookie. When he saw my bet in his paint tin he shouted down, 'Who's Donald?'

I pointed to my chest.

'Don't start betting, it's a mug's game.'

'Its my birthday.'

'Right, but if it loses I'll give you the shilling back but think on, no more!' All this in semi-Gaelic, barely heard above the background din.

This bookie brought sandwiches every day and a flask so he could stay in the cab throughout the lunch break to take bets from different parts of the works as clients went to and from their lunch break. His flask was filled from the tea trolley which a woman trundled round from the canteen, the urn kept warm by sacking tied round it. For the ten o'clock tea break every single day she delivered 1 inch thick onion pasty cut into 3 inch squares. They were very tasty indeed. This Scottish crane driver, known as Big Mac, had an enormous waist, if in the distance you saw him climbing up the wall ladder to get into his cab he looked like a circus clown on his way to the high wire.

Squander Bug won at 33/1, including the returned stake money I had two shillings more than my week's wage. As I could not blatantly sit in the foreman's office poring over his newspaper, instead I took it into the toilet desperately seeking the next race for Squander Bug. I backed it on five more occasions, each time the odds shortened, but I always bet only to win. I was now nearly six pounds in profit. On the sixth race at Redcar it fell and was shot. It certainly is a mug's game – I have never backed a horse since.

Stanley and Ronnie teamed up with George Siddal, one of the spray painters, who said he could read the tick-tack signals providing he remembered to take his spectacles, to start weekend bookmaking at local Yorkshire tracks. They promised to take me with them if in return I made them a collapsible stand and painted a sign for it headed 'Honest Bob Rawden, Halifax' (Bob Rawden was the name of the dead and therefore now untraceable uncle of Ronnie's wife). I was asked to find a bag for the money so I used my mother's old red leather Gladstone bag and painted 'Honest Bob Rawden' on this too. They also wanted a taxi arranging to take us to the racecourse at Ripon on Saturday morning; I was to tell the driver that he would be bought a meal after the races in return for a cheap fare. Ronnie had some tickets printed in the name of 'Honest Bob Rawden, Halifax'.

Armed with a twenty cigarette bribe I went to the maintenance shed, mentioning that this 'government work' was for Stanley Walker. All work was abandoned while two men cut angle iron, welded it and welded iron spikes to stick in the grass and within an hour I was back. George promptly sprayed it with metallic grey cellulose, this normally reserved for exhibition machines. We stood the stand up on the shop floor and there were murmurs of approval, then the foreman appeared.

'What the hell is that, you'd better shift it under the bench, Bob Asquith's due in with some customers.'

I was given two pounds to get some plywood, chalk and blackboard paint on my way home from the tech. I painted the board that night, carefully adding 'Honest Bob Rawden, Halifax' in white writing at the top of the board. The collapsible stand was taken to my house in Ronnie's car, a bright red Austin Atlantic drop head coupe, bought secondhand from the chief buyer at Asquiths. The cylinder block for the engine in this car was completely machined on an Asquith transfer machine, the four cylinders bored and finish-bored on a special Asquith four-spindle borer.

On the Saturday morning I carried the collapsed stand, with the board now screwed in place, to the taxi office. We picked up the three others at the Odeon cinema and off we went to the races in brilliant sunshine. To my surprise all three were wearing trilby hats which I found to be standard headgear for the racing fraternity. We got to the races a little late as the driver, one Cyril Brown, got lost when negotiating Harrogate and we had stopped for a pint in Ripon market place. Here Stanley spotted Prince Monolulu in his long brown raincoat selling his tips in brown envelopes. I had seen him on newsreels at Epsom; face blackened and dolled up in full African chief's regalia with the Prince of Wales feathers on his head. In Ripon he just looked drab but he did have a very penetrating voice. Ronnie gave me two shillings and six pence and told me to go buy a tip. When it was opened he laughed and said, 'That one's only fit for the knacker's yard.' In the pub with the taxi driver we stood at the bar, I at the end of the row, and Stanley ordered five pints. The barman pulled four then looked at me and said, 'How old is he?' Stanley's reply 'He's with us' produced the extra pint. If you want results, be six foot tall and wear a black eye patch. I sipped about an inch, didn't like it. George supped the rest and bought me an orange juice.

When we arrived at the track we were the last in a long line of bookies, much too far away from the crowd. Stanley was far from happy with this so found a shifty-looking steward, and slipped him two pounds to get us a better position. The steward went half way along the line to a small seedy bookie in a flat cap: 'You were barred last month.' Seedy rapidly folded his gear and hurried away along the line, the steward pointing to the gap. I folded our gear and we moved to a much better position. As today's estate agents always stress, 'location, location, location'!

After each race a small cripple shuffled along the row of bookies with a bucket of water. For two shillings he sponged the boards clean ready for the next race.

I went to the toilet, a corrugated iron shed with no roof, no door and no stalls. Inside were three beefy looking characters inviting punters to have a go at the three card trick on their green baize folding table, or else! They ignored me. For some reason one kept stroking his cut throat razor, although he never opened it. Outside was a fourth one perma-nently on watch.

After the last race and the exchange of many pound notes, there was still some profit left in the Gladstone bag. We all went back to a hotel in Ripon and enjoyed a duck dinner. Some pints later we set off home, Ronnie still reckoning up the book on which he had furiously scribbled all afternoon whilst balancing it on George's back. Because we couldn't rely on George's tick-tack readings with or without his glasses it was simpler to keep a constant check on the bookies' prices either side of us.

Before we got back into Halifax Ronnie reckoned we had a profit of £48 after paying for drinks, dinner for five, £2 to the steward, 12 shillings to the sponge man and we still had to pay £9 for the taxi. Stanley told the taxi driver that I would arrange the next trip and he dropped us off at each individual house.

This was the big time; this was the real world of hard bitten orange juice drinkers and big time gambling. Another memorable day ended with my mother's 'I began to think you had crashed, nasty people go to race tracks.'

One three month period was spent building portable universal radial drills, fitted with a forged loop at the top of the column so a crane could move it around, and wheels and jacks on the base. It could be used to drill holes up to two inches diameter through solid steel, at any angle, even upwards and also at compound angles. It was a very complex machine with a flat leather belt driving the spindle. Rhodes Wireworks made the woven wire guards for these machines.

They were much used in shipyards, lowered by crane into successive compartments of a ship's hull and left outdoors in all weathers before the deck was added. Occasionally when returned to Asquiths for recon- ditioning, they would arrive in a horrible state; rusty, handwheels cracked, levers bent or even missing and the wire guard buckled. It was hard to believe that anyone could treat a machine tool in this manner, yet when repaired they looked like new again. For shipyard use it was quite point- less chromium plating the handwheels and locking levers that stuck out in all directions: equally filler and paint were wasted, a liberal overall coating of grease would have been much better. Asquiths used three of these versatile machines around their own works and they were kept spotless for demonstrations to customers.

Time flew past as I spent three months in each department, endlessly learning to sculpt metal into machine tools that were dispatched world wide to sculpt more metal into finished products. I soon learnt to read engineering drawings and envied the draughtsmen who started at 8.30 and were always clean. The most interesting period was six months spent in the calm of the toolroom, everything clean and precise, most jigs and fixtures carefully made to an accuracy of one-ten-thousandth of an inch. No bonus payments here but enhanced wages for these highly skilled men, which meant enhanced overtime rates and precision machining other than jig boring was done by both day and night shifts. This area was run by John Holmes, his title superintendent rather than foreman and he was the only man on the whole shop floor to wear a white smock – around the works the foremen all wore brown. His son was also an apprentice.

At the far end of the toolroom was a floor to roof glass partition with an airlock double entrance to maintain the 62-degree constant temperature required to ensure the accuracy of the single Swiss and two American built Pratt & Witney jig borers and a Swiss jig grinder, all worked by elderly highly experienced men who had to teach the apprentices very thoroughly. The art was in learning how best to clamp the work piece to the machine table and how to set the vernier scales and dials to control table and spindle motions in three axes, with two more as the table could be revolved or tilted to provide compound angles. The drawing would show the finished angle of the axis of the hole, intermediate setting angles you had to work out by trig tables. It was one of the jig borers who showed me the cunning way to create a new temporary measuring datum by simply clamping an angle plate to the machine table, and it was he who first told me that to solve any problem, first identify it clearly, then isolate it and only then try to solve it. Equally cunning but in later years I only ever seemed to use this when juggling money. No overhead crane ran in the toolroom, just three quiet electric hoists swung out over the machines and benches, with a separate one to serve the jig borers.

This six months was the best period of the whole apprenticeship. It was a pleasure going to work and a nuisance spending Wednesday at the tech. My pay had started at £1–5s–0d. per week, I was now getting just over £5 and fast approaching the move upstairs into the drawing office.

Staff were paid an annual bonus each November based on the firm's profit in the last financial year and directly related to their individual pay rate. The quite different system for the shop floor was that workers were set individual times per job, each hour saved against the rate fixer's time generated cash paid with the following week's wages. The rate fixers used very flexible and often generous formulae for assembly times on special purpose machines, often one of a kind, then being built for the motor industry.

I did one three month period working in the heavy erection bay where they assembled the massive boring machines. In this area three fitters and an apprentice would toil for three months to hand scrape all mating surfaces truly flat and square, frequent crane work was necessary and space was at a premium. They would then start to fully assemble the machine. After inspection and testing a further week would be required to strip down the machine for packing and loading, the waiting trucks taking up cven more space. During the tests the machine was simply used to manufacture other Asquith parts. Delivery to the customer could easily be two years after placing the order for a big horizontal boring machine.

The fitters on these jobs resented the fact that they only received a bonus payment three times a year and they could easily miss out on extra cash at Christmas depending on when they started building a particular machine. The union became involved and a strike threatened. Asquiths had its own boxing club – twice a year the canteen tables were cleared and a ring erected with the canteen chairs around it. At a hastily arranged lunchtime meeting the Asquith brothers climbed into the ring to announce that it had been a year of heavy expenditure. They had purchased both a new eight wheel and a four wheel Leyland truck, a new Cole's mobile yard crane (both these firms were customers) part of the foundry was being re-roofed and new fume extractor plant fitted. A new Ceruti Italian precision boring machine had been purchased at a European exhibition (already installed on the shop floor but as yet not in use as no one was found who could master the metric sizes). They had also had to replace both Bentleys, the new ones costing over £4000 each. No one present objected to the Bentleys as Robert was always off round the world chasing orders with a recent very large one from Russia, when the *Yorkshire Post* and *Halifax Courier* carried a front page spread showing him stepping off an aircraft at Yeadon wearing a Russian fur hat. Not long before he had even sold a radial drill to a Texan rancher whilst on a flight across America, whilst Richard was grafting in the offices every day of the week, sometimes even Saturdays or Sundays.

To solve the problem they had devised a scheme whereby an interim estimated weekly bonus would be paid in the heavy side, starting next week, with a final balancing bonus when the machine was shipped. The shop steward led the clapping and all dispersed back to work.

Huge cotton lifting ropes around three inches diameter were used. After numerous six monthly inspections they were eventually condemned by the weights and measures official who had to witness the rope being cut in half by the slinger who used them, they were then scrap. A labourer cut a one foot length off a scrapped rope, took it home and tied it to his worn bristle brush. It worked perfectly, so he sketched this and put it into the suggestion box as an idea to save the firm constantly buying new brush heads, which didn't last long when in contact with sharp steel swarf and cast iron granules pushed over concrete floors. Some days afterwards an office girl, ignoring all the whistles, delivered an envelope to the foreman. The labourer gleefully went round everybody showing the letter of thanks and £2 in notes. The foreman stuck the letter facing outwards on the window of his office; this was the same labourer who took his bets across to the bookie so it was wise to indulge him a little.

'Money for old rope' said the grinning labourer.

These wooden suggestion boxes were dotted around the works, a typed notice on them stated that any idea was welcome but all technical suggestions would be vetted by the chief engineer who would decide the level of cash reward. All suggestions must include name, clock number and department. This seemed to me to be a good way of increasing my meagre pay, so the foreman ordered for me an extra sheet of one drawing of the huge casting I was then working with. By re-arranging holes feeding oil to one brass bearing, the result was two holes to drill, one plugged, instead of five to drill and two plugged. I marked the drawing with a red crayon, identified myself and put it in the suggestion box. The foreman thought this 'a good idea, they'll pay you for this'. Up to then these small holes had always been a problem to drill with an electric hand drill, especially if the drill hit some sand. On large complex castings this was quite frequent, as the sheer weight of flowing hot liquid metal would often move some moulding sand from a core, this sand then remained embedded but hidden in the finished casting. Sometimes the hot metal flowed too quickly and small air pockets would be trapped, again hidden but leaving a possible weak area.

Asquiths were then selling an increasing number of machine tools to Russia. When one was ready for testing two Russian inspectors would arrive with a curious device like an old fashioned wooden box camera. They would fully scan with this gadget every machined surface and if any blown holes had been plugged with cast iron, even though invisible to the naked eye after scraping or surface grinding, this amazing device showed the plug as a black spot on a grey surface. If it showed the Russians would insist on a new casting and returned to their London embassy. The engraved instruction plates on the first machine would be changed for English language versions and the machine switched to a home market customer. The Russians would then be summoned to return and inspect a different brand new machine. This meant some juggling in the sales department and played havoc with the fitters' bonus, they hated the sight of 'those communist bastards'.

Some days later the foreman waved me into his office. 'George Hoyle wants to see you, get washed, you go up the second stairs above the drawing office.'

I did so, eventually coming to a polished wooden door with the simple sign 'George Hoyle. Chief Engineer. Keep Out'. I knocked and a woman's voice shouted 'Come in.' I did.

I was amazed to step onto a thick dark blue carpet, on it a huge leather-topped desk with typewriter and beautiful desk lamp, behind the desk the elegant young woman I knew by sight and vaguely remembered from the sixth form in school. Against one wall a row of neat grey steel filing cabinets, two of the walls appeared to be covered in black glass. Most of the ceiling was glazed and I could see the sky above. I suddenly realised that we were higher than the overhead crane tracks and thought I must be in some sort of nightclub. On one corner table stood an electric kettle and gold edged tea service, on another a vase of flowers.

'Donald Ainley? His bark is worse than his bite, go straight through.'

'Thank you Miss.'

I was about to come face to face with a far higher god than the school headmaster. I had already seen this George Hoyle in action on the shop floor, and remembered one such encounter, which I saw from a distance. Three fitters had hit some problem with part of a huge transfer machine being built for Austin Motor Company. Their foreman was called over, he in turn called an inspector, five men now stared into the machine, the motionless overhead crane parked above them with a casting swinging gently on a rope over their heads. Muttering 'that bloody drawing office again', the foreman went to his phone to get the machining superintendent, the inspector then used it to summon the chief inspector, who in turn rang Johnson, the chief designer. It was the fifth time on this machine, and it was still perhaps only one-third built. I just stood and watched, the crane driver just sat watching. The machining superintendent was first to arrive with his usual greeting, 'Morning, what have you buggered up now?' The elderly chief inspector plodded in with his deputy, flashing dour looks all round. Johnson shortly arrived, followed in single file by a section leader and two of his draughtsmen each clutching rolled up drawings. Twelve heads now peered into this casting, twelve different opinions were advanced and promptly rejected by the other eleven and the foreman was instructed to 'get George Hoyle'. The three fitters went across to the foreman's office.

It was some while before the wicket gate by the roller shutter door opened. In walked a small man with both hands in his pockets as though he had forgotten his braces, cigarette dangling from his mouth and followed by the clicking heels of his secretary carrying a large notebook. No one whistled at her, not with her boss present, but all eyes followed her every step.

They passed me and reached the inquest. Directly facing Johnson he spat out, 'What's your bunch of bloody clowns done now?' There was little love lost between these two as around the shop floor Johnson always liked to create the impression that he personally had designed their world-beating, best-selling radial drill, Hoyle knew of this and also knew it to be rubbish as he had personally known the pre-war chief designer, one George Feather, whose brainchild this had been. In a spare moment Feather had also designed the oval nameplate.

Johnson duly explained the problem, Hoyle too peered into the casting and there was a long pause, everyone silent. He then looked more closely inside it and announced his verdict: 'Strip it down, bush it and re-bore it on the correct centre.' His secretary duly scribbled the date and main drawing number on her pad and made a note of what he said, grinning at the foreman. Hoyle turned and walked out, secretary following, both hands had never left his pockets, the now short cigarette had never left his lips. Everyone dispersed and the three fitters emerged from the foreman's office where they had filled in 'waiting time cards' to record the time lost so that this should not affect their bonus.

133

The foreman suddenly shouted to me, 'Donald, get down to the tech.' As I went towards the toilets to wash I too peered into this casting but was no wiser, one of the fitters saying, 'You got a better idea?' A shout came from the patient crane man. 'Where the 'ell do you want this?'

Travelling down on the bus I thought about this little man, somehow *he* knew how to deal with people. What I didn't realise at the time was that he had quickly decided the fastest and cheapest way of solving the problem based on years of practical experience of installing Asquiths machines world wide – and now for the first time I was to meet this god.

I went straight in. More black glass, glass ceiling and same thick blue carpet, an even larger desk with my drawing laid open on it and a nearly full ashtray. Through the glass partition at the end I looked into a further office with a single drawing board, filing cabinets, with text books in a shelf unit and an angle lamp on a wheeled table. No black glass or thick carpet in here, just brown linoleum on the floor with a single bare fluorescent tube hanging on long chains from the peak of the glazed roof.

'Donald, sit down, you've done some good thinking here lad. I've told Johnson to get the drawings altered before they start building the next one, there's five pounds, think up some more.'

I signed for it, thanked him and going out the grinning secretary said, 'How did you do?'

'He's going to use it, I've got five pounds.'

'That's to encourage you.'

I went gleefully back and told the foreman.

'Good lad, better than that rope idea. That labourer spends more time picking swarf out of his brush than he does sweeping.'

Shortly after this the Halifax Ford main dealers laid on a trip to visit the Ford plant at Dagenham. I learned of this from a lad I knew at the tech who was an apprentice with this garage. Anyone was welcome, so I called there and booked my place. We left Halifax around 5 am on the Saturday by special train to London, then by coaches across London and down the Thames on waterbuses to Fords, alighting at their delivery quay. That Saturday the assembly line was finishing Zephyr cars, some fawn, others green. What seemed strange to me was one man wearing a yoke over his shoulders holding hub caps in two huge wicker baskets. Most English cars in those days had bulbous chrome plated hub caps, these had the outer edge sprayed fawn or green. Staggering slowly along at the speed of the track his job was to hold a cap by hand against the wheel notches and kick it on with his foot. I thought they could have trained a big gorilla to do this on three bananas a day, but the union wouldn't have been too happy.

At some point in this tour I saw for the very first time air-driven socket spanners used to tighten nuts. I also saw the hot rolling of steel bar to make half-shafts, these when machined became the final drive shaft to each rear wheel. It was rather exciting to see it all live although I had seen this kind of thing in films. We were not shown round the foundry but saw the conveyor with hooks mounted on it which came out of the building, rose at an angle to roof height and continued round all three sides of the building and then across a road to disappear into a machine shop providing a non-stop stream of small castings. The guide said the conveyor system allowed these to cool after leaving the moulds.

On the boat back we bought some sandwiches and tea, then were coached to a London theatre to see Jimmy Edwards in 'Take it from Us', the stage version of the radio show 'Take it from Here'.

On the way back by train I kept thinking about those air-driven tools and the assembly of radial drills. High-pressure compressed air was fed round all areas of our shop floor. After a very long day we reached Halifax at 4 am.

I got up late on Sunday and that day wrote and carefully re-wrote my next suggestion. Monday lunchtime I went into the newsagents shop by the works entrance and bought a small box of chocolates, then straight into the typing pool to bribe a girl to type this out and find me an envelope. It looked very professional with my name, clock number and department at the top. I sealed the envelope and slid it in the nearest suggestion box.

Some days later the foreman waved again. 'Hoyle wants to see you again, what have you done this time?'

'It's a secret, I'll tell you if I win anything.'

Hands washed, I climbed both sets of stairs, this time more confident and prepared to argue my case if necessary.

I knocked and she smiled, 'You're soon back, go through.' I knocked again, this time the nightclub décor seemed less impressive.

'Sit down Donald. This is very good but the fitters on final assembly make so much bonus already that we would have to reduce the times allowed for each job. They wouldn't like that and next thing you know the union would be muttering about a bloody strike'.

I noticed the envelope on his desk.

'But it shows you are doing the thinking and this time you've found something right outside the firm and applied it to our machines and you can write in plain English, better than some of the bloody scribble I get out of that suggestion box.' He laughed so I laughed too. 'There's a fiver in there, next time pick something we *can* use.'

As I went out Molly (I don't know how I came to know her name but I knew her older brother, Colin Barratt by sight, he worked in the main drawing office) smiled and said, 'He seems to like you. When I showed it him he grunted "we'll have a bloody strike". I got the fiver from the company secretary this morning.'

As she was so friendly I told her about the letter I had received from school inviting me to an old students' Christmas reunion dance, which stressed that I had to bring a partner, would she like to go?

'Sorry but I'm engaged to be married, otherwise I would have loved to come. I've never been back since I left and I've never had one of these letters, why not ask one of the office girls?'

'I will.'

I went back down the double staircase, waited for another Pickfords low loader to crawl past and found the girl who had typed the suggestion. 'I've got five pounds for the suggestion, thanks for the typing, would you like to go to a school reunion dance at Christmas?' It came out as all one word, the shyness still there as at school.

She pointed to one finger. 'Can't, you fathead, I'm married. If that's how much you got, next time fetch a bigger box of chocolates!'

A negative but quite logical rejection, somehow it didn't bother me in the slightest, nor did the female sniggers as I left. I must be going up the learning curve, I never went to the school reunion and that didn't bother me either.

Over a period I entered two further suggestions, one for using a small hand-steered electric fork truck in the steel stores, where two men normally lifted heavy bars to feed the giant saws. I had seen one of these machines advertised recently in an engineering magazine. Hoyle paid me two pounds for this, said it was a very good idea, they would get one. Some while after as I walked through the steel stores I felt rather proud as I saw the new bright red machine. The labourer using it grinned at me saying, 'What do you think of this then?'

'Good idea' I said.

For the other suggestion Hoyle gave me two pounds for doing the thinking, but condemned it as there was some other firm's patent involved which I had known nothing about, but he didn't elaborate any further.

The name 'horizontal borer' is perhaps somewhat misleading as even though the spindle was horizontal and could be up to twelve inches in diameter by sixteen feet long, the whole spindle assembly within its slide carrying gearbox, drive system, fifty horse power motor and railed platform for the operator all moved vertically up a column which could be up to twenty-four feet high, the column alone could weigh up to seventy tons. All this assembly could travel along a wide bed up to twenty-four feet long and fastened to this bed would be a massive slotted table to hold the work piece to be machined. Sometimes an optional intermediate revolving table would be fitted between base table and work piece. The sheer size of the finished product was really impressive and the floor space needed to build one was always a major problem.

To machine both sides of the column it had to be turned end on end, a risky operation which meant clearing the shop floor of all personnel except the two slingers handling the casting and the use of both fifty ton overhead cranes acting together. As the casting was raised and passed its fulcrum point to tilt over, the weight actually dragged one crane towards the other. A present day health and safety inspector would have gone white watching this and promptly closed the whole place down prior to starting an immediate prosecution. Had he known that the process demanded releasing the overwind safety trips on both crane cable drums to get the hooks high enough he would have had a heart attack.

Asquiths had done this without accident for years and the four men involved were cautious but well practised in this manoeuvre; the thick wire lifting hawsers and spliced links were examined and stamped every six months by a weights and measures inspector when he came to check the huge weighbridge in the loading bay.

Later there was a demand from customers for borers with even taller columns. To build these Asquiths applied for planning permission to raise the crane tracks and the part-glazed roof. This was refused as when viewed from adjacent hills the existing roof was on the skyline and brightly lit five nights a week. As these hills were up to six miles away in line of sight, what difference could it make were the roof to be raised by eight feet? I'm sure not a single individual objected to the proposal but the planners were totally against it. Instead Asquiths dug down into solid rock, creating havoc in that erection bay with dust, tipper trucks, rock drills hammering all day long, then lined the huge hole in the shop floor with concrete and surrounded it with protective steel railings with two steel ladders leading to the bottom. It was a massive internal quarry next to a machine shop, but it solved the problem without requiring planning approval, nor did the safety trips need ever again to be removed from the crane drums. It was completed whilst I was away in the RAF but I saw the partial hole when I came home on leave.

At the end of a three month period in this heavy erection bay I saw Norman Wood, the assistant works manager, approach the foreman's office, then both came across to me. Norman said, 'Your four years with us are up on Friday, the vacancy is in the jig and tool drawing office, go up and see Tom Blakelock now, he will sort you out for next Monday.'

I washed my hands and climbed the stairs, turned and then up two more steps, along a short corridor and down two steps and passed three glass cabins into the office with thirteen draughtsmen, one empty board and at the far end an old fashioned printing machine. The whole floor was a long narrow triangle, its point beyond the printing machine. The windows overlooked Bob Lane, the public road that ran at a slight angle through the works (hence the triangular drawing office). Immediately under the office was a lift which led to the tunnel under Bob Lane, providing access into the 92 machine shop, so called because during the 1914–18 war 9.2 inch diameter naval shells had been produced in there.

In one glass office was Jack Ridley, the boss. Jack Parratt, the estimator, had the next office and the third office with drawing board housed one Eric Buckley who did all the building design alterations and particularly structural steel work changes for the foundry. At the entrance to the office Tom Blakelock had his large table, he was the section leader and checked and signed all the drawings. Jack Ridley being a widower, rather unusually lived permanently in a hotel in Halifax. His son-in-law was one of the senior designers in his office.

Overall the office was generally grubby, one fluorescent bulb had a constant flicker and the floor was covered with old brown worn linoleum. I knew Tom Blakelock as I had seen him occasionally when I worked in the tool room. We shook hands and went to the empty board.

'You'll need to give it a good clean on Monday, give Maureen in the time office your signature as she will need it for the time clock. Heinz will show you how to use it. Have you got some drawing instruments?'

'Yes.'

'Have you got any relatives in Huddersfield?'

'Not that I know of.'

He walked across to Heinz and said, 'This is Donald Ainley, he will be starting on Monday, sort him out.' Heinz nodded to me.

No longer wearing overalls, on the Monday morning I got to the time clock early, when a draughtsman I knew by sight from the main drawing office arrived. He showed me how to sign the paper ribbon and then pressed the long lever which caused the machine to stamp the time beside my name and in the same motion fed the ribbon along ready for the next signature, more Gledhill-Brook wizardry. A notice on the machine warned that you were allowed to be late a maximum of five minutes in any one week but did not state any penalty if this was exceeded. I went up to the office and removing the dust cover and old backing paper I started to clean the board with some screwed up scrap paper I found in a basket. Tom walked in carrying his lunch box, saying that my first job each morning was to sharpen three HB and two red pencils for him. He would leave them on his desk every night.

The rest came in and as they passed us he introduced me. Heinz Sharmatz worked on a board directly across from mine, Tom said he would show me everything. He was Austrian, dreading being conscripted into the British forces as the RAF had killed his grandmother in a bombing raid. He had permanent bad breath.

One job he showed me was to use a little machine clamped to a table. This folded sticky masking tape along the edges of new drawings to protect them when handled and when stowed away in the large shallow drawers of the filing cabinets against the wall.

The only woman in this office was one Glenys Turner who was secretary and typist for Jack Ridley. She shared Eric Buckley's office and for some reason also worked the machine for printing drawings. This machine had a large revolving drum, the drawing to be copied and paper from the roll in the trough were fed into it together, with the drawing underneath. The drum was housed in a huge glass cylinder, inside the drum on a track were two acetylene arc lamps, which moved back and forth as the paper revolved. As the drawing disappeared you had to cleanly slice the paper from the roll with the kitchen knife which was retained on a string, to leave the minimum waste. When the current was switched on it took about fifteen minutes before the lamps were fully bright, the carbon rods gradually burnt away and replacing them was somewhat tricky. As the print came out of the back of the machine it appeared to be blank, you then had to feed it through rollers with a third running in a trough of developer, quite unlike a modern copier. Glenys showed me how to do all this as part of my job was to help her when she was overloaded. She was a pleasant woman, engaged to one of the design office estimators, but couldn't stand Heinz or his bad breath.

Another job was to empty the three fire buckets and position them along the aisle to catch drips from the roof when it rained, empty and reposition them before leaving at night and if it rained overnight I had to mop the floor. Of the thirteen draughtsmen, the eight more senior were engaged on designing complex tooling which was built into the special purpose machine tools for the motor industry, where all the holes in say a tractor engine cylinder block or cylinder head are drilled and tapped etc. on the one machine. That is all the machine could be used for and they took many hours of design and build time and included an enormous amount of electrical circuits. Reams of drawings were issued to the shop floor, one alone could take six months to build and the five or six fitters were paid interim bonuses each week as in the heavy side. The other five draughtsmen designed all the tools required for making Asquiths' own standard machines. One benefit of working in this office was that I went to the tech and home again each Wednesday without having to come to work twice a day, but at the end of each term I had to produce an attendance record for the time clerks.

For the first few weeks I followed Tom's instructions to 'work with Heinz, he'll show you the ropes'. He did but with little enthusiasm, his sole ambition was to marry a rich English woman and head back to Austria. I noticed he always put a bar across the figure 7. He just dodged the question when asked why I had never previously seen him working on the shop floor.

Tom owned a row of terrace houses in Huddersfield which he rented out. He frequently brought bits from these for repair, and the tool room superintendent was his particular mate so I had to take these to John Holmes to get them mended. He always brought the bits wrapped in brown paper, once a cast iron oven door with a broken hinge, rusted gutter brackets, anything might arrive. John Holmes would redirect me into the maintenance crew with 'Tell 'em it's for me.' Once there Tom's usual twenty cigarettes produced the response 'It'll be ready Friday.'

I was the general office boy, dogsbody and odd job man. Sometimes Heinz would start designing a jig and I would start doing sheet 2 of the same drawing. Sometimes we argued over the content and I began to realise that he had spent little if any time on an engineering shop floor. His father had a carpet shop in Todmorden and on Saturdays Heinz made his spending cash by stitching carpets together. He had to catch three buses to work and three home again, perhaps totalling three hours a day just travelling – no wonder he was seeking a rich wife.

For six months we had an eighteen-year-old Finnish lad working with us following Tom's instruction 'You two show him the ropes.' His father's engineering firm in Helsinki had to supply Russia with sixty per cent of their production as a result of reparations after the Russian/Finnish war. His father had bought a radial drill through Asquiths' Scandinavian agents and had arranged for him to get some work experience, via these agents. We had never seen a Finn before, he spoke passable English, said all Finns hated Russians, there were 52,000 lakes in Finland and much of the north was just tundra. He spent lots of time chatting to Glenys and she showed him how to print the drawings, and Heinz or I would occasionally take him to see the shop floor.

Heinz and I did our homework at work. Tom didn't mind and allowed us to use his calculator but only for homework. This was a purely mechanical version with only four functions, add/subtract, multiply/divide but would produce an answer to thirteen places past the decimal point! Only Tom was allowed to use this on Asquiths work to speed up the checking of drawings and they were also only used by the main drawing office checkers. All the draughtsmen had to do calculations the hard way.

During this final year, now nearly ended, I had been taught very little, certainly far less than the six months spent in the tool room. I didn't relish call up into the forces, nor did I fancy the options of jail or working down the pit for two years. The draughtsman aged around 30 who worked on the board behind mine, one Selby Rushworth, was married with a son of around eight and a daughter. His son developed an ear infection, which his doctor said needed an operation. The specialist said it would mean a six month wait but he could have it done privately within a week. We all thought this was disgusting as the lad had constant earache. Selby once saved up to buy a Rolex watch costing over £60, expensive to him as his pay at that time would be around £12 per week. He proudly showed it to us but no one was impressed by the insulting six month guarantee.

Some weeks before my twenty-first birthday I received the call up papers and chose the RAF which was later confirmed.

Then one day George Hoyle suddenly came into the jig and tool office. He spotted me on the first board and came straight over, hands in pockets, cigarette drooping as usual.

'Hello Donald, didn't know you worked in this dump.'

The whole room gradually quietened, all eyes on my board. For some strange reason I told him of the now pending call up into the RAF.

'Bloody nuisance, never mind you'll soon be back, if you'd only one eye they wouldn't take you! Think on, come up and see me before you go.' With a loud laugh, dropping ash, he stalked into Ridley's office and closed the door. No doubt another inquest starting, probably about the cost of excessive overtime in this office, whatever the problem it would be held behind a closed door and would involve Ridley just listening and then promptly obeying the chief engineer.

Heinz leapt over to me. 'That was George Hoyle!'

'I know, he's a mate of mine'.

Then Selby leaned round his board. 'Didn't know you were well in with him, lying sod'.

'Yes, his wife gives me a cup of tea with biscuits when I mow his lawn and clean his car on Sunday mornings.'

'Lying sod.'

'Didn't know you were well in with the wife'.

'Oh, yes'.

'Lying sod'. With that he stared at the Rolex, shook his wrist and glanced at the wall clock. He was getting worried, it was two weeks since the guarantee ran out.

On my last Thursday in the jig and tool drawing office I got my week's pay of £7–7s–0d., and did no work. I went on the shop floor to say goodbye to my old racing pals. Ronnie, who had been in the army during the war, said, 'Don't volunteer for anything.' The foreman came across. 'Look us up when you come on leave.' Many hands were shaken, then I went to the tool room to talk with the men who had taught me so much on the jig borers and John Holmes, whose son was already in the army in Scotland.

I used John Holmes' telephone to ring Molly.

'He told me he'd seen you, hang on I'll tell him.' After a short pause 'He says come up now.'

I dodged into a toilet block to remove the oil from shaking so many hands and got to the endless stairs. I knocked as usual and went in. He was standing at Molly's desk.

'Come on in to my office, both of you'. We did, he offered me a ciga-rette, took one himself, lit both and we all sat down. (I had started smoking and drinking in the last year.)

'The forces have a habit of trying to kill you off even when there's no war on, so watch yourself. Come in and see us when you are on leave.'

I promised I would and shook hands with both of them. Going through her office, at the top of the stairs Molly shook hands with me again and pecked me on the cheek muttering 'Take care'. I pecked her back and answered 'You too, it's been nice knowing you. I hope you have a great wedding.' At the bottom of the stairs I turned for one last look up at the nightclub – to my surprise she was still there and waved and disappeared before I could return the wave. I stepped into the loading bay and jumped straight back, three inches away from one more low-loader crawling towards me. I'd be safer in the RAF – if I had his job I'd have an office on the ground floor, over at the far side of the works.

On the Friday I just loafed around, in the afternoon finally shook hands with every person in the office and was the first to punch the clock. At the end of the loading bay I ducked into the commissionaire's cabin and told the commissionaires, both wearing medal ribbons, that I was going into the RAF. With the usual 'Don't volunteer for anything' and 'You'll be all right with the Brylcreem boys but don't walk into a propeller', more hands were shaken.

Outside I glanced at the sign in orange neon. I would miss that now so familiar oval shape and the smells of hot oil, coolant, the sharp stench of cellulose, petrol fumes from trucks, coal burning in the steam crane on a frosty morning and newly sawn timber in the packing areas. I had known and grown to respect a variety of highly skilled people who had nudged me ever further up the learning curve. If I could stay clear of propellers I might work with them again but it would never be back in that damned drawing office. Next week I would be in a different world, the RAF.

I caught the bus home.

14

RAF Dishforth, N. Yorkshire

It was a beautiful June morning when using the rail warrant supplied I travelled to RAF Padgate via Manchester. On the run into the city I thought of the head boy and girl on a much pleasanter mission. Norman Stansfield, a friend from schooldays, had already arrived and we started the rigmarole known as 'square-bashing'. Most of it was boring and repetitive but I enjoyed firing a Bren gun. The training was too limited, the practice firing far too brief, the instructor stressing that this Czechoslovakian gun was a superb weapon but could jam in five different ways. He never outlined why or the action required to clear the jams. He hadn't time to go into such details, this simply meant either he did not know or did not know how to explain it clearly. I had a good look at the breech and could appreciate the intricate machined parts forming this mechanism.

On the only practice at the butts I found it very comfortable as some of the exploded gas was diverted into a cylinder to counterbalance each recoil such that on automatic firing the butt did not bruise my shoulder. Lying prone on the concrete pads with the gun balanced on its two legs we were each firing short bursts when the lad next to me suddenly gave a scream and still firing the gun whipped off his tin hat to rub his cheek. The gun swivelled to fire at the next target but one. The sergeant behind us gave a bellow and leaning over moved the safety catch to stop the gun. 'Stand up, stand to attention, what the hell are you doing you stupid sod?' A spent case had hit the concrete and ricocheted back to lodge itself between the strap of his tin hat and his right cheek, burning the flesh.

In contrast, firing the old fashioned Lee Enfield rifle was awkward for me as the bolt action is designed for right-handed users and I am left-handed.

Later on the Medical Officer gave us a long lecture, with enlargements, on his slide show of the harmful effects of venereal diseases. We had to be particularly careful if posted abroad and if we caught anything we had to report this immediately. Any second occurrence would result in punishment. From the photographs it seemed to me that the punishment had already been inflicted. Various dramatic posters on this same subject were pinned on the toilet walls. For some reason the Padre sat beside him all through this session but never spoke, though at the end it was he who asked for questions. No one responded.

Contrary to all the good advice given when I left work, one day at the morning parade a wing commander needed a volunteer to paint his caravan. I marched forward and spent a very relaxing week rubbing it down, painting it dark blue gloss up to waist level and all cream above. Morning and afternoon his wife produced tea and biscuits and the sun shone all week. Each lunchtime I discarded the overalls he had borrowed from the hangar and walked to the airman's mess, where the food was a surprisingly good three course meal. It seemed strange that both Saturday and Sunday tea was just jam and bread and all the tea you could drink. I varnished some areas of plywood on the inside and once finished he gave me a five pound note. We were only allowed out of this camp after six weeks and I then went to Padgate post office to send my mother a postal order for five pounds.

One morning I was told to report to the Padre's office in the headquarters building. En route some distant corporal shouted 'You do not walk across a parade ground, you march round it!' I went in and saluted this elderly squadron leader with grey hair and dog collar.

'At ease, take your cap off, sit down.' He glanced at an open file on his desk. 'I understand that your mother is a widow.' I explained about the disappearing father. 'In that case she will be regarded as a widow.

146

You are therefore entitled to claim a cash grant for her and you will also have to contribute from your pay. The pay office will deduct this fortnightly. If you fill in this form I will put it straight through the system, her grant will be backdated from when you joined, your deduction will only start next pay day. She will be sent an order each week to cash at any post office.' I filled it in and signed, thanking him, back at attention saluted and marched out.

Near the end of the training, Norman's fat envelope contained a fortnight's leave pass, and rail warrants to get home along with others to reach Lyneham, Wiltshire. There he would 'emplane' for RAF Changi in the Far East. He was due to marry Evelyn Green, a girl I vaguely remembered from school, and spend one week on honeymoon at Blackpool.

My fat envelope held a leave pass for one week, rail warrants home and a further warrant from Halifax to Ripon, with orders to report to RAF Dishforth, near that ancient city. I was given the guardroom telephone number and RAF transport would collect me from the station.

On the final Friday came the passing out parade. For some reason we had to be lined up beside the parade ground by 0700 hours, the saluting officer and his side kick with gold ribbons and tassels appeared at 0950 hours. In the boring interval I heard the clump of rifles hitting tarmac as two men passed out prematurely and slumped to the ground. Some trucks arrived with an RAF band. During the parade we all learned that marching to music is far easier than just marching.

Norman and I piled into the RAF coaches and 'entrained' for Warrington, Manchester and Halifax. We shook hands on the station platform – circumstances and timing rather than any distant enemy would ensure that we were never to meet again.

I lugged the heavy kit bag home, up the hill from the station, eager to get out of the sweaty uniform. I was tanned and fit and my mother hugged me with the usual 'Oh dear God, I'm so glad you are back safe.' I showed her the orders and said I would be going to Dishforth, near Ripon, and should be able to get home quite easily. I was to be an air movements clerk. I had visions of working in a control tower, leaning out of the window firing green flares, a frequent shot I remembered from war-time films.

On the Monday morning, wearing the uniform, I got the bus up to the works. The commissionaires both gave mock salutes.

'You look very brown, you been to Egypt?'

'No Warrington.'

'Carry on but let us know when you come out.'

'Yes Sergeant,' returning my mock American salute.

I ignored both drawing offices and went to see Stanley and Ronnie in the REEMA building.

'Still going racing?'

'No, we got warned off when George thumped a queer steward in the toilets at Ripon.'

I went to the toolroom where I had been so happy. Later in the canteen I found the food had improved. Finally I was back with the commissionaires. 'Good luck lad.' Nothing had changed but things felt different, somehow I had changed in just a few weeks.

On the Sunday I got trains to Ripon station, rang the guardroom and after an hour one 5-ton Bedford truck arrived to collect one airman. We crossed the junction with the A1, just one lone tree, otherwise open fields and the extreme corner of Dishforth airfield. In the distance were the huge camouflaged hangars, and parked around were 2 and 4-engined aircraft painted silver overall but white on top of the fuselage. From the guardroom an RAF policeman took me to a 2-storey brick barrack block, in through a central door to a room with a door marked 'watch-keepers – do not disturb'. Inside was a corporal's partitioned bunk and 22 beds, identical to those at Padgate. One lad was in bed snoring, another sprawled on his bed reading. 'New lad for air movements, sort him out will you?' He stood up to shake hands, in perfect BBC English said, 'Ex Cadet Pilot Officer Cyril Washburn, now condemned to humping drums of sand on and off aircraft night and day.'

'I thought air movements would be working in the control tower.'

'If only it were.'

'Why ex-cadet?'

'At Cranwell they thought I was unsuitable as officer material, too irresponsible they said. I thought they were a bunch of pompous idiots. Air movements Dishforth simply put dummy loads on and off aircraft.'

148

'Why?'

'Training ex-bomber pilots to fly transport planes.'

He showed me the bed linen store at the end of the room. 'Two blankets, two sheets, one pillow case, laundered every week, dirty ones in that wicker basket. Pick any empty bed space. Leave it for now, we can go to tea, 4 pm on Saturday and Sunday, jam and bread.' We ate and once back I sorted out the bed and unpacked. 'You mentioned nights, do we work eight to four etc.?'

'Yes, but if night flying finishes early we toss up, one stays in the section with the corporal, rest go to bed.' He used two extra empty tall lockers, there were civvy suits in one and to my surprise a dinner suit in the other. His third held RAF kit. He told me he had been called up from Millfield school. His mother, divorced, retained their London flat, which he used some weekends, but she now lived in France, working as an interpreter at SHAPE HQ. His father had returned to the USA to run a radio station. His grandfather owned a chromium mine in Turkey. 'He's the money bags!' It took some believing, yet I had seen the dinner suit.

I found Dishforth ran 24 hours but flying ceased at weekends. Air movements was run by a Sgt Pettit on days only, with eight hour shifts of a corporal and six men. The camp was base for 242 Operational Conversion Unit, training ex-bomber crews to fly transport aircraft at differing load weights. The dummy cargo was simply old 'Tee-pol' drums, filled with sand and the top welded in place. When competent they did a one-week trip to the Middle East to become familiar with engine settings for hot climates. Sgt Pettit got me some overalls and chrome leather gauntlet gloves. 'Leave them in here after each shift, what are you like at maths?' I explained about the five years at the tech and work. 'Working out the aircraft balance will come easy then, good. Learn the air movements manual and you can take the exam for Leading Aircraftman, you'll get propeller badges to stitch on your uniform and two shillings a week rise.'

'How wonderful.'

He spent some time showing me the compartments in both a Hastings and Valletta, each clearly marked with the maximum weight and lower limits, mounting floor points for seats or lashing cargo with S-hook, chains and turnbuckles to tighten the chain. 'All seats face backwards on these, safer in a crash. These Hastings were flogged to death on the Berlin Airlift. The Jerries called it their *Luftbrüke*! We moved butter, flour and ton after ton of coal! Polish crews flatly refused to help keep the Germans alive, not surprising.'

I soon mastered it, passed the exam and was promoted to LAC. To qualify to go on the overseas trips you had to first turn over a 12-man bomber dinghy floating inverted on the water in Ripon public baths. Here the training was very thorough, with an instructor, two men treading water and another on the side with a lifebuoy. It took me three attempts to break the suction. How it could be done at sea with eight-foot waves I don't know, but each Hastings wing had a dinghy under the top surface, deflated and retained by a lid held with spring clips. A valve in the cockpit released compressed air which inflated the dinghies which in turn pushed off the lid. Having removed an escape window you were expected to be standing on the wing to grab the rope mounted in clips all round the dinghy side wall. In Ripon you had to put your feet in the loops, throw yourself over the dinghy inverted floor and grab two opposite loops. You swung upwards and backwards using body weight to break the suction. The dinghy then fell onto you pushing you underwater. It was as near drowning as you can get. All this was done in a spare pair of underpants or swimming trunks, then you dried off using the pool's towel provided.

Cyril and I were walking past the parade ground one day to the mess. Approaching us were two young WRAF officers. No one else was in sight round the square. As they drew nearer, I was ready to salute when one of them suddenly gave a cry, ran up to Cyril and embraced him. 'You disappeared, what happened?'

'They slung me out, promoted me to loading bloody aircraft.' Her pal and I just stood there grinning, but I noticed she was looking round the square to see who might be watching. 'I'm in admin., ring me.'

'Will do ma'am.' Only then did she release him.

'Who is the ma'am?'

'Pamela, she was at Cranwell, we had a few dates, a very active wench. Dishforth has suddenly improved no end. Don't mention it to anyone.'

'Course not, lucky you.'

His status went rocketing up and every one in the section finally believed him when the phone rang one afternoon. Cyril was wanted at the guardroom. He took off his overalls and went. He drove back in a brand new dark green MG sports car! 'It's my twenty-first birthday tomorrow. My mother wrote to say she couldn't post my present but she didn't say what. A salesman brought it from a Harrogate dealer. She's craftily registered it in her name to avoid purchase tax! Pamela will love this! I've arranged to keep it in the MT yard, can't park on camp roads.'

That evening we went for a ride into Ripon, a perfect winding road to try it out. We had a drink in an old pub at the corner of the square. The bar and downstairs rooms were full of pongos, then a nickname for anyone in khaki, so we found a quieter room upstairs, just a group of older blokes in one corner, all in civvy clothes, some wearing blazers. One left the group, and as he came across we recognised the squadron leader from the hangar.

'This room is reserved for officers.'

The portly red-faced landlord caught this as he reached the top of the stairs with our drinks. 'My customers sup anywhere they like in my pub, more talk like that you'll fetch your own drinks up them stairs.'

They ignored us from then on. Cyril only drank whisky and soda, and insisted on buying my pint, always. His name was Washburn, he was awash with money to burn. As we left the pub the officers stared at the new MG. Everything about us could not be more different, background, cash flow and accent, yet we became good pals.

'I'm going to Wetherby tonight to see if there is a hotel, have a weekend with Pamela. Boroughbridge is too near the camp, otherwise it'll be Harrogate. Come for the ride, I'll open it up on the A1.' We went and found an old coaching inn with arch leading into a courtyard. They had seven bedrooms and he'd better ring first to book. We had a drink and went back to camp. 'Tomorrow I'll ring her from the MT section.'

When the next 48-hour weekend came round they stayed in Wetherby. When I got back on Sunday evening he reported, 'Marvellous time, four-poster bed too. Now we're planning a week's leave in London at the flat!'

'You didn't drive out of the camp together, surely?'

'Course not, she got the bus to Ripon, train to Harrogate. I picked her up at the Old Swan, we spent the afternoon there, then drove to Wetherby, same coming back. Her parents live in Virginia Water, her mother is part of the Courtaulds textile family. Make rayon for tyres. Pamela looks smashing in civvy clothes.'

Both Hastings and Valletta aircraft had a smaller door which could be removed from one of the larger freight loading doors. With this removed and laid on the floor inside the aircraft, we had a go at supply dropping. The army brought wicker panniers from Catterick. With one of us harnessed to the door frame and the other guiding them down the temporary roller track fitted to the floor, the object was to hit a huge fabric cross pegged to the grass triangle between the runways. The army lads on the ground collected the panniers in the truck and were waiting, ready to reload when we landed and taxied round. We repeated it using larger panniers each fitted with a parachute which we clipped to the static line along the roof. When the pilot switched on the green light by the door our function was to get them out in a continuous flow so they would land close together. It was interesting, we avoided loading drums, but a howling gale came in through the door so when we tried it at night we wore greatcoats and the leather gloves. The cross was lit with two torches laid on the fabric.

On one occasion the station warrant officer used all our shift to guard a crashed Meteor in a farm field outside Boroughbridge. When we got there our corporal had to sign for one torch, one radio and one loaded sten gun. 'SWO's instructions. Ring the guardroom every hour, on the hour. Anybody comes, threaten 'em.'

'Who's likely to come?'

'SWO says gypsies or scrap metal gangs.' We unloaded more coke for the brazier, they piled in and went. I managed to get a turbine blade off the engine and kept it as a paperweight souvenir for years.

Dishforth camp ran an RAF bus to Leeds and return five nights a week for recreation. I signed on for a course run by the Institute of Production Engineers in the chemical engineering block at the university. That winter's session was 'The impact of tungsten carbide tooling on modern machining methods'. The RAF paid the £8 fee, I had to provide a record of attendance to the education officer when it finished at Easter. I looked forward to it each week and avoided loading drums for one evening shift every third week.

We were out loading a Hastings one evening in a freezing gale, everything, including the drums, covered with frost. A sudden gust caught the forward freight door which swung round, knocking the lad guiding it from the back of a truck onto the tarmac. The door catch didn't open fully, instead buried itself into the aircraft skin about an inch above the aperture it should have entered automatically. The corporal ran into the hangar to return with the tech. sgt. 'Ambulance is coming for him, damaging an aircraft is a court martial offence.'

Cyril asked 'Will they kick us out of the RAF?'

'You're an optimist, lad. Where's the hole?' He examined it, climbed inside. 'Clean puncture, no pipes or cables anywhere near it, we'll patch it but I'll have to log it. Come in the hangar, I need your details for the Wingco., you too driver.'

Next day we all had to report to Wingco. Flying. 'I've seen your handiwork on my aircraft, it's a very serious offence to damage one. Tell me in your own words just what happened, keep it short.' The squadron leader we had crossed in the Ripon pub gave me a very hostile stare.

I described events, then added 'The driver was not involved sir, just sits in the cab with his window down to hear us as we guide him back up to the aircraft door sir.'

He made a note. 'Right, send in the next one.'

Next day Sgt Pettit said 'The Wingco. rang, he's not charging you, just said be more careful working in strong winds.'

Christmas approached, the station notice board proclaimed that the camp would stand down for four days except for a skeleton staff. On leaving the camp all personnel would collect a form at the guard room A sample form was pinned beside this. Personal details and address over Christmas had to be filled in and the form handed to the nearest police station. They would contact and inform of any recall in an emergency.

On the Thursday of the next dayshift, before we went out to unload, Sgt Pettit announced: 'You're on a mission tonight, report to the Wingco. at 1800 prompt with greatcoats and leather gloves, it'll be very cold.

RAF Waterbeach in Cambridgeshire is in danger of being flooded and it must stay operational. You'll be shifting sandbags!'

'Where from, Scotland?'

'No Zurich.'

'Christ, surely they've some sand around Cambridge?'

'Perhaps, no time to bag it, these were left from war-time. Our night shift will stay on 'til 1000 so you get some sleep, because it gets better but colder, next night it's Oslo. You'll have sandwiches and flasks of coffee aboard, you serve the crew. Full meal in the mess when you're back.'

Cyril said, 'I don't deserve this.'

'Join the RAF and see the world' laughed the sergeant.

We doled out the food and coffee and finally landed at Zurich. At the end of the runway a van pulled ahead of us. An illuminated sign read 'follow me', repeated in French, German and Italian. We were guided to the extreme far side of the airport, to find a group of Swiss air force blokes with a lieutenant in charge. They had a fork truck with a big board across the prongs already loaded with sandbags. We soon had it balanced with as much weight as we could take. Flt Lt McWicker, one of the training captains, checked it. The 'follow me' van appeared guiding our second Hastings to the pile. He then guided us back to the runway and we left. It was the first time I had ever been in a foreign country and a civilian airport, albeit for less than two hours. I saw nothing except acres of tarmac with a light dusting of snow, a distant airport and sand-bags galore.

After more sandwiches and coffee we landed at Waterbeach. Here the turn-round was even quicker, a gang of RAF lads came on board and we all threw the sandbags into a large RAF truck. We ran back to Dishforth to a good meal and were in bed by 0320. Next night was identical but with Norwegian air force blokes, again a fork truck speeded the process, the crisp air distinctly colder.

The miserable pay per week was becoming a real irritant by now, so I went to the pay sergeant. The options he outlined had no appeal. I could re-muster to a technical trade but would not rise above corporal tech. in the eight year mandatory engagement, or I could re-muster to air quartermaster with corporal's pay during training, promotion to sergeant after one year and with flying pay, again minimum eight year term only. The only alternative was to stay in air movements but sign for one extra year, backdated to when I first joined, i.e. three years in total. I would get seven shillings more per week as a regular and would very likely be posted abroad. This would get me a further but slight pay increase and cheap cigarettes. I decided on the last as the only way out, was sent all the way to Cardington in Bedfordshire just to sign on, have another medical and swear allegiance to a distant rich King who didn't give a damn about me. His government cared even less.

Back at Dishforth I volunteered for the next overseas trip, a week away from loading drums, but I would miss one lecture in Leeds. My function throughout the trip was to close and secure the parachuting door, check that the escape windows were secured, check all freight lashings and the weight/balance sheet. During the flight I had to serve the coffee or orange juice from the huge aircraft flasks. Our night shift had fitted three seats in the back. Cyril gave me a fiver to get him some cigarettes. We left at 0500 for Lyneham, Wiltshire. Civvies loaded freight for Fayid whilst we had breakfast in the transit hotel. We were driven to the tower to check the weather to Idris. I did all the checks and reported this, then sat with the two trainee pilots, a flying officer and a flight sergeant. 'Should be around eight hours, diversions Luqa or Tunis civil.'

We stayed in the transit hotel at Idris, an RAF unit based on Tripoli civil airport. The evening meal and breakfast were very good. Next morning we left for Fayid. This leg the sandwiches were just corned beef, from Lyneham they were salmon or corned beef, both with salad. We crossed the Bay of Sirte, over Benghazi and Benina airport. The trainee came down to the toilet, then said, 'Captain says you can ride up front if you want.' I went and climbed into the seat, he showed me how to fasten the four-strap harness and its quick release centre button. I looked out, we were simply following the coast. 'Have a go.'

'I've never flown an aircraft sir, I haven't even got a driving licence.'

'Not to worry, have a go. I'll take the auto-pilot out. The nose dips, just pull the stick gently back, watch the little aircraft on that dial.' He moved a knob on the console between us, the nose dipped and I pulled the column towards me, far too suddenly, causing the aircraft to climb. He pushed the throttles forward a little. 'Too much, push it slowly away, watch the dial.' I did, very gently, the plane gradually centred itself on the bubble. 'Try again.' I was rigid in the seat. Sweat dropped from my forehead onto my glasses. It was warm in the cockpit but this was fear. Each time he re-engaged the auto-pilot. After five or six attempts I mastered it. 'There's a little pause before anything happens. Control cable must have stretched with age. They all do. OK go back and relax. Don't tell anyone!' I climbed out, wet with sweat, after an experience never to be forgotten.

Eventually we started to descend. I could see the pyramids, the sprawl of Cairo and the Nile. We turned to land at Fayid, near the Suez Canal with big ships barely moving. The base was littered with aircraft and had a huge air movements section. Again we ate and slept in the transit hotel, the first time I had used a mosquito net over the bed. Next morning we found the aircraft re-loaded with freight for Nicosia, Cyprus, with three army passengers going on leave. After a wash and meal we returned to take six army blokes back in an otherwise empty aircraft. Next day we left at 0500 for Habbaniya, Iraq, this time mostly freight, but including two RAF flying officers and a WRAF corporal. The latter explained about the twin runways, one higher as the lower one flooded in winter and how it was the only RAF camp in MEAF to have WRAF personnel, but she didn't know why. Once again we had mosquito nets. Next day we returned empty to Fayid. The following day we left for Khartoum, droning our way south over the Numibian desert in the Sudan, hauling freight.

When we landed and left the aircraft the heat was like a furnace, I had never known such a temperature, the nearest I have ever been to the equator! In all directions sky merged with the land in a constantly shim-mering haze. As the crew bus approached the buildings I noticed a railway which ran along by some hangars. Skinny blue-black Sudanese were unloading sacks of something into road trucks, the whole gang chanting some sort of song. I was drenched in sweat just watching them, thankful I wasn't loading aircraft in this climate. The shower in the transit hotel was marvellous but tepid. That night after a cold meal we went to the camp cinema to watch one of the new films we had delivered.

Next day our only load back to Fayid was two radar tubes and six army officers, one of them a colonel. I spent most of the time in the crew bunk up front and once again the landing was perfectly smooth.

Finally Flt Lt Hanrahan announced 'That's it, back to Idris tomorrow and home.' In the morning we were delayed two hours while the army brought a teleprinter for urgent repair in the UK, otherwise the aircraft was empty. In Idris I bought 200 cigarettes for myself and 400 for Cyril in the transit hotel bar. After we ate I ambled round the now quiet camp. A lone BOAC Argonaut was parked at the far end of the hangars. We had a surprise in the morning, two cars were loaded on the aircraft, a Morris Minor and an Austin. I checked the lashings under each. When we landed, the civvies just rolled them backwards in neutral in no time.

We landed back at Dishforth in the early evening. I gave Cyril the cigarettes and his change, 10 shillings for 200 Senior Service. I told him about the whole trip, the brief visits to Cyprus, Iraq and the Sudan, 'No loading or unloading, all done for you. You ought to go sometime. All those transit hotels have single rooms and the food is good too!'

Some days later a strange Valletta landed. It was met by the Group Captain, our CO. Two women descended the steps and got into the rear of a chauffeur driven Rolls. The crew were all officers, including a squadron leader pilot. Between them they handed four suitcases into the boot and the car purred away. We stood at a distance, looking at the small pennant hanging from a stick clipped to the open cockpit side window, the top of the aircraft painted the usual white, every other surface was just polished bare aluminium. Huge chrome-plated spinners were fitted to each propeller hub. There was a crest below the cockpit and the neat wording 'Royal Flight'. Two days later the aircraft had departed. None of us recognised either woman, perhaps one was a minor royal.

Days later we were parked, sitting on the drum-loaded truck waiting to pass whilst a Meteor prepared to leave. The pilot revved one engine to turn before the lad retrieving the wheel chock had got clear. The jet blast blew him backwards a foot clear of the ground and he landed with a scream. We heard later his kneecap was so badly damaged he would have a permanent limp and be invalided out of the RAF. The pilot was unaware and continued to taxi away.

The following morning Sgt Pettit put down his phone. 'Don, go see the Adj. You're posted to the Middle East, It'll be Luqa, Idris, Fayid or Habbaniya. If it's Idris you'll be laughing.'

The Adj. said, 'You're wanted in the Middle East for air movements. This is the drill: You have one week embarkation leave, here's your leave pass, travel authority, rail warrants Ripon-Leeds-Halifax and Halifax-Leeds-London. RAF police at Kings Cross will direct you to transport for Stansted. You go out on a civvy charter flight to Fayid. There you wait for your final posting. Sign here for two weeks advance pay. Get this clearance chit signed by whatever sections apply and return it to me promptly.'

'Will do sir.' I took it to Sgt Pettit, who signed it and I took it back to the Adj. 'Thanks and good luck.'

That night Cyril and I went for a farewell drink in the Ripon pub. As he ordered drinks he told the landlord 'His last night, he's been posted to the Middle East.'

'Right, yours is on the house lad, and good luck.'

We had another drink and Cyril said he and Pamela had enjoyed another weekend in Wetherby whilst I was away. He had been a good pal and a generous one too. Back at the camp I finished packing. Once again a five ton truck took me to Ripon station. I got home and told my mother the situation. 'I've done a year, two to go. I'll come home on leave if I'm able half way through.' We went on a few bus rides and with a promise to write every week, a hug and a kiss, I left.

From boarding the train in Halifax to stepping on the aircraft at Stansted everything was as the Adj. predicted. We stopped at Malta for a meal in the transit hotel, then a different crew took us on to Fayid. On the civilian charter flight we were served a snack meal and coffee on both legs. At Fayid we were bussed to the transit hotel. There a sergeant wearing a red armband printed 'Air Movements' shouted 'You'll be called at 0500, shower, eat, line up outside here in number two dress at 0600 prompt, I'll be back to sort you out.' I'd been travelling for 14 hours non-stop and slept like a log.

15

RAF Fayid, Egypt

The sergeant was outside the Transit Hotel at 0600 hours. We piled onto trucks and were taken to acres of tents, strange because they were large ridge tents mounted on three foot concrete block walls. Each contained six beds, and you could walk upright anywhere inside. To enter you climbed over the wall. 'Right, make a note of the row and tent number so you find your way back. Now, the strict rules – do not drink the water in the shower block at the end of the tents, drink only from the coolers in the mess. You'll be given two salt tablets with each breakfast, swill them straight down with water before you eat, otherwise you'll be sick, stops you dehydrating from heat. Final rule, those mosquito nets at each end of the tents must be dropped during hours of darkness. The sheets are in the wicker basket. Dump your gear, make your beds up sharpish.' We did and he shouted, 'Any aircraft or truck mechanics, air movements or cooks back on the trucks. All the others rest up, mess is open 11.30 to 13.30, that's that big block by the hangar. You'll be collected by RAF police truck at 1900 for guarding the wire.'

He dropped me at the massive air movements sheds next to the transport section. I went in and found a squadron leader. '576 LAC Ainley in transit from Dishforth, sir'

'Good, Cpl Pettit still there?'

'Sergeant now sir, his son started school just before I left, good boss.'

159

'He worked with us on the Berlin Airlift, he'll well remember the freezing sleet and coal dust.'

'He's mentioned it sir.'

'Right, you'll be loading aircraft, you're allowed to work in just vest and trousers because of the heat. Permanent days for you but we run three shifts seven days a week. You'll also be on some armed truck guards to Port Said docks.'

I walked to the nearest Hastings being unloaded and started to graft, dumping my jacket, shirt and tie on the wing. It was intensely hot with high humidity and not a breath of air. After a while a corporal said, 'You're working too quickly, slow down or you'll be knackered by the end of the shift, move more slowly.' In the evening I found the NAAFI, had a bottle of very gassy Tennants beer, bought a post card of the pyramids and sent it off to my mother. There was a handy post box built into the NAAFI wall outside. Then I just found the tent and went to bed.

This continued for nine consecutive days. On day ten the sergeant said, 'Your turn for truck guarding, a quick ambulance run to the docks. A seaman badly injured on a fleet oiler, the RAF will fly him home for treatment.' I climbed into the cab with the driver, a lad from Preston called Vickers. He drove to the armoury. I was handed a rifle. 'It's loaded, sign here, don't fire unless they fire at you.' Vickers put the headlights on and shot off the camp, soon to join a dual carriageway, and we passed the huge statue of De Lesseps, who had cleverly sliced Africa from Asia to open a fast sea route from Europe to the Far East.

'This thing is governed to 60 max.' We were hurtling along, horn blasting continuously and with both windows down we were getting a welcome wind through the cab. 'It's about 50 miles, we go through a deep rock cutting, the bastards are hidden above us in the rocks. They fire down with machine guns, they want to stop the truck to nick the wheels. You're supposed to open that flap in the roof and poke your gun out. Don't think about it, it's suicide.'

Eventually I saw the cutting through the heat haze. We started through it and heard five tinny thuds somewhere on the big box body behind us. 'You all right?'

'Yes.' We hurtled on and eventually pulled through a huge army compound of trucks, then onto the dock side. An army redcap stopped us, 'Come for the seaman?'

'Yes'

'That building opposite the second ship.' Vickers weaved between crane hooks and fork trucks. Two ships were unloading, the whole place a hive of activity. Two merchant seamen lifted the stretcher onto the ambulance floor, two Wren nurses climbed in with suitcases. An army redcap wandered up. 'If you had been going a bit slower that first one would have been through the door into your guts. Even spacing, heavier than a Bren.' A sobering thought – I remembered George Hoyle's ominous words in what was fast becoming a distant world. We went back at the same pace, I was dreading the cutting. We ran into the approaches and right through. Nothing happened. Back at the aircraft the sergeant had already fitted the vertical tube frame to take the stretcher, two seats fitted beside it for the nurses and more seats at the back for the slip crew. He said they would stop at Idris for fuel and more food, the slip crew would then take it straight to Lyneham. This was Transport Command showing off to the Navy.

The squadron leader ran his own pay parade and for the first time I got the one shilling per day increase for being abroad. It seems pathetic now, but at that time it would buy 20 Senior Service cigarettes in the NAAFI at Fayid.

Day 17 brought the second call to arms. A docks run. I collected the rifle and we set off in a 'Queen Mary' artic. In the cutting we heard the twang of bullets bouncing off the girder frame behind us and we were through. En route Vickers pointed to a crashed car dumped beside the road. 'This is where they faked a crash to block the road. My mate rolled up in one of these trucks and stopped. Four of 'em came from the back of a pickup, one held a sten on him, the others jacked up his truck and nicked every wheel, threw 'em in the pickup and hopped it. The army shifted it back to Fayid on a tank transporter.'

We finally pulled through the army transport compound onto the docks proper. 'We'll be queuing for ages now.' I watched as a Bren gun carrier was swung smoothly from the deck on a four-wire sling onto the dock-side.

We just sat smoking. Some of the deck cranes were massive. I could have watched for hours. We moved forward and eventually an English civvy with a clip board approached 'Eight boxes and two propellers for you. You're next, the last ship.' We were loaded quite quickly and Vickers lashed the propeller cradles to the girders with some rope. We pulled along to the end of the dock to park. 'We can get some grub in that army mess, we just sign for it.'

As we ate exactly the same food as at Fayid, he said, 'Remember that young pay clerk in the NAAFI last night? Your lot's flying him home today in a coffin.'

'How come?'

'The guard corporal forgot to warn him not to touch anything on the fence. He saw a piece of rag flapping and must have pulled it off, a butterfly bomb blew his face off. The corporal will get a court-martial, be kicked out and two years in Colchester for that, the stupid sod!'

We set off back. En route Vickers ran his own one-man war. Passing a fat Egyptian driving a tiny donkey pulling a cart piled high with some sort of vegetables, he threw his lighted cigarette at the Egyptian. It landed somewhere in his voluminous night shirt. In Ismallia we pulled up at a small grubby bar which he had discovered on a previous visit. 'Bring the rifle with you.'

It was narrow, a steel roller shutter served as a front door and the single room was very long, a stage at the far end with curtains drawn, just visible through the cigarette smoke. The customers were all pongos. We each got a bottle of Tennants and sat down.

Suddenly a drum beat started up, the curtains parted and a very fat Egyptian belly dancer began her routine. As each flimsy layer came off the drumming became more frenzied. When she was finally just clad in a G-string and tassels on her nipples the curtains closed to desultory clapping in the bar.

Soon afterwards with another drum roll the curtains parted to reveal a small donkey with enormous ears on centre stage, four young Egyptian boys crouched each holding a leg. A fifth boy crawled between its hind legs and arranged himself on the floor with his back uppermost. To another blast on the hidden drum the belly dancer reappeared and arranged herself

162

upside down, back to back, on top of this young lad with her head towards the donkey's front legs. She then commenced to masturbate the donkey, the donkey either liking the idea, or perhaps desperate to escape commenced to lurched forwards a little, dragging the Arab kids with it. They dragged it back and the woman put the donkey's penis between her thighs, the whole audience by now clapping like mad and roaring with laughter. At that point the donkey suddenly began to bray and the curtains swished down.

Vickers and I lurched out of the bar holding each other up and weak with laughter. My guts ached. I have never seen anything so funny in my whole life. This earthy, unsophisticated entertainment was just perfect for troops far away from home. An Arab was standing outside the bar holding the reins of a camel, and without me realising the camel swung its head to a point just behind my shoulder and suddenly belched. The stench was unbelievable, I would never again get close to a camel's head. We were still laughing when we got back to Fayid. Vickers mentioned that the last time he went into this bar a male juggler was throwing dolls up into the air, but from where he sat they looked very much like real babies. We were back in time for a shower and tea. In the evening Vickers mentioned he had a 'soft' run to Kasfereet the next afternoon. If I could get time off we could go for a swim in the Great Bitter Lake. 'You just can't sink, full of salt.'

The next morning the squadron leader called me. 'You've been very lucky, you're posted to Idris. Go to the clothing stores behind this building to draw your khaki uniform. You're booked on the Valletta, leaves 0700.' I asked about visiting Kasfereet, 'I could come back after tea to make up the time.'

'You've been grafting since you got here, so have the afternoon off, don't bother about coming back afterwards. Here's your signed clearance chit and your other records, give them to the Adj. at Idris. Good luck.'

'Thank you sir.' I found the clothing stores and got three pairs each of khaki slacks and shorts, three tunic shirts and six propeller badges which I would have to stitch onto the shirt sleeves. These propellers were embroidered in red on the tan backcloth, as were the bird logos already stitched on the shirt shoulders.

I worked all morning, found Vickers in the mess and told him the good news. 'What time you going to Kasfereet?'

'When I've eaten, it's already loaded.'

We reached Kasfereet, booked in at the guardroom and drove to a hangar. Inside he found a corporal technician. 'Brought some spare bits for your planes, owt to go back dump it on, we're going swimming.'

He unhitched the trailer and we drove to the lake. I could see some parked Meteors and another was just landing. The lake shore was one boundary of the otherwise barren airfield. A bold sign on the bank read 'Swim within yellow buoys. Sail within red buoys. By order O.C.'

We stripped nude and walked in. It was lovely to be fully immersed after the stifling heat. Further out in deeper water I found you could stand upright, or lie motionless on the surface – you just could not sink. We swam along the yellow buoys and eventually walked out, soon to dry in the sun, and then brushed all the salt away. As we dressed I spotted a huge ship moving north very slowly, slight bow wave and smudge of smoke from the funnel. It looked like a ghost ship in the distant haze, but we could just detect the slow throb of the engine.

We hitched up the trailer and took just two radar tubes back to Fayid. We had some tea and showered to get rid of any salt residue. I got the number one uniform out of the kitbag and wore it for a final drink with Vickers in the NAAFI. Providing he survived the cutting he was due for demob in seven months. He was intent on getting a PSV or heavy goods licence back home.

I never knew his first name and I never saw him again.

164

16

RAF Idris – Tripoli Airport, Libya

I soon settled into the easy life at Idris and made some good friends. Harry Lidgett had been an apprentice maintenance mechanic in a Sheffield steel works where his father worked a rolling mill. With such similar backgrounds we became close friends. We worked on freight only, which meant no fixed shifts and we had little to do. Some weeks we might only load a few bags of army surface mail onto a Hastings returning to Lyneham, sometimes in contrast we would spend most of the night loading a car belonging to an army bloke due to return to the UK, very infrequently as rarely was space or weight available.

Three other lads became close pals, all worked the early, late or night shifts in our section. Ken Leach had worked in his father's ironmongers shop in Warrington, Les McDowell for Thomas Cook travel agents in Liverpool and was intent on starting his own when demobbed. He was convinced that air travel was the future and would soon replace passenger liners. Doug Harrison had worked in 'that bloody boring council office' in Twickenham, his father was a draughtsman at Hawker Aircraft in Kingston-upon-Thames. He was amazingly good looking, a younger version of Clark Gable without the moustache. He had one surprising talent – he could cleverly imitate a woman's voice of any age group. I first experienced this when we went into the army cinema in Tripoli one afternoon. At a tense moment in the drama, as the struggling woman reached for the kitchen knife, a woman's voice beside us pleaded 'Help – help, I'm being raped – I hope!' The audience roared with laughter, which must have really puzzled the projectionist. The timing, the change of tone from desperation to anticipation was so real it could have been part of the film.

Any two or more of us spent many off-duty hours sitting outside the village bars or exploring Tripoli modern city or the fascinating original walled city by the harbour. The compact civil airport was used by the RAF simply as a staging post. Every section was within easy walking distance, the total RAF personnel around 90. We had a NAAFI and a cinema, a NAAFI shop which was out of bounds to ranks below sergeant as it sold liquor, but our sergeant would buy for us writing materials, stamps, chewing gum or orange cordial. We also had a swimming pool and a camp laundry which did uniforms. Civvy shirts were best washed in the shower and taken there to be ironed, otherwise they were rigid with too much starch. There was no charge but we left a tip.

It was the first foreign country I had lived in. Harry summed it up as we stood in front of a map of Libya in the HQ building. 'That King Idris is a crafty old sod. He has a deal going with the British, allows them to keep up to five thousand troops in Libya, the RN and USN patrol the Med, his only coastline, he has a USAF base here with atomic bombers and jet fighters and the French Foreign Legion based in Chad police the barren south, the Fezzan province. That means he doesn't have to pay for an army, navy or air force. Brits run air traffic, the power station, water and sewage works and run the postal sorting office. He also gets the whole of this airport maintained by air ministry works. He owns the only cigarette factory "Gefara" and only brewery "OEA", that gassy bottled beer we drink. He's on a right good racket.'

Insects here were larger than at home. Black hornets, twice the size of wasps, hovered round the cookhouse door but never stung. Huge dragonflies skimmed insects from just above the pool surface at dusk; black or green scorpions did their precise courting dance only on sand, the same captured on film in Walt Disney's 'Living Desert'. Small lithe lizards scurried to hide as they saw approaching feet. Most interesting were the chameleons with their amazing ability to change colour to blend in with the background; beady little eyes on swivelling cones, the rapid-action suckered long tongue shot out to catch a fly in the space of a blink. They had suckers on each foot, would stay on a wall or ceiling for hours and never responded when picked up. This marvellous evolution looked like a miniature pre-historic monster. Harry said one once walked into the freight shed and sucked the leg off a cockroach quick as a flash.

The civil end of the airport had regular flights going through, BOAC to Nairobi and South Africa, BEA to London-Malta-Cairo, Sabena ran from Brussels to the Belgian Congo and a French airline with the long-winded name 'Union de Transport Airiennes' painted along the whole fuselage flew Paris-French West Africa. BEA used the twin-engined Vikings, the civil version of the RAF Valletta transports. Sabena and UTA used Lockheed Constellations. All this was run by an ebullient Greek, Andreas Papadopoulis, better known as 'Andy'. He spoke four languages and was line manager for BOAC and BEA and handling agent for the others. I asked Andy about the weird plane which came through weekly, strange because it was some sort of US wartime cargo plane, a fat tubby shape with no glazing in the windows down each side, painted in olive drab with no markings except a registration number. As it taxied past I once heard pigs squealing inside. 'It's an old English pilot, runs a one-man airline, pays cash for his fuel, but his landing fees are paid by cheque direct from a Lebanon bank. His call sign is "Levant Lifter".'

I asked about the other odd aircraft, a modern single-engined all white Cessna which always parked outside HQ for the night. The pilot in a white suit was met and driven away by the CO

'He's Swedish, Count von Rosen, married to an English woman related to a Lord. He's a director of a Belgian mining firm in the Congo. He comes through every few months, flies himself.' Andy's company car was a huge seven-seater Studebaker shooting brake, which he used for taking crews to the tower. Passengers and crew were then taken to the luxury Uaddan hotel in Tripoli by BOAC coaches.

Italians and Arabs were employed by the RAF but only Italian men by BOAC. The RAF paid BOAC to keep one of their cafeteria cooks on late so that any of us working nights could go there at midnight for fried egg in toast sandwiches and cups of coffee, as many of each as we liked. This saved running the airmen's mess kitchen all night for just a few men, the hangar mechanics, air movements and the signal cabin lads. We had no parades, no inspections of the barrack blocks, no RAF police, no parade ground and no bullshit.

The RAF ran scheduled regular flights through every month just like an airline. The two engined Vallettas, known as 'flying pigs' ran twice a week Lyneham-Istres (French air force base to refuel), night stop Luqa (Malta)-Idris-El Adem (near Tobruk)-night stop Fayid (Egypt) and return by the same route. The four-engined Hastings all ran Lyneham to Idris (night stop). Two a week then went direct to Fayid, night stopped and return. Two more each month continued Idris-Habbaniya (Iraq)-Negombo (Ceylon)-Changi (Singapore) night stopping at each place, then return. Once a month one Hastings went on to Mallala in Australia (taking mostly scientists to the Woomera test ranges) and return, whilst another went from Changi to Japan, returning with war wounded from Korea. The whole aircraft was taken up with stretchers fitted to tubular frames and an army doctor with two nurses. Ambulances took them all to the military hospital in Tripoli overnight and the ambulance crews carried them down the ramp.

No doubt transport command ran similar flights into Germany and to keep track of where every aircraft was each base sent a signal to all the others on that route showing ATD and weight available for loading at the immediate next stop. How much was actually available depended on the volume of cargo and the uplift of fuel for the next leg. The Dishforth trainers came through on random dates, sometimes one a month or even two. Every few months six Royal Australian air force Vampire fighters came with a Dakota carrying a servicing crew, to stay for a week on rocket firing exercises at the US range down south. They all stayed in the transit hotel, condemned the NAAFI, the swimming pool and bemoaned 'the lack of Sheilas on this dump'. They played poker for cash but worked any hours to keep those jets flying. We got the clear impression that in any situation they would be best on our side. We also had occasional visits by Canberra bombers from RAF Wyton, bound for exercises in the Middle East.

168

We once watched as a BOAC Argonaut took off for London. It rolled normally, lifted and we saw the wheels go up. Very suddenly, as though a huge invisible weight had been dropped on the nose, it dived steeply into the orange grove. Flames started to rise, there was a huge explosion and thick black smoke rose and increased against the vivid blue sky.

Top BOAC brass and accident investigators arrived late afternoon on another Argonaut but we never did learn why around 50 people flew one minute and died horribly the next. The fuel tanks would be full and there would be young stewardesses on board, possibly a few young children amongst the passengers. A BOAC pilot told us later that all that remained was a large black hole surrounded by burnt trees and four engines with bent propellers and undercarriage legs. 'Aluminium burns, it doesn't just melt.'

Another incident could have wrecked an Argonaut and an Auster army spotter plane. This aircraft was kept in the first RAF hangar and flown by a captain in the Army Air Corps. He would start his take off from inside the hangar and lift off the taxi-track at right angles to the runway, for exercises with various army units. He wore a white silk scarf and suede desert boots. He always carried spare fuel in jerry cans. Rumour had it that he had been a glider pilot in the Normandy landings and was banned from over-flying Wheelus Field at any height. He took off in his usual fashion but today shot right underneath an Argonaut just about to touch down, banked and headed north. The Argonaut landed normally but taxied round to BOAC far faster than normal. There, both pilots came off the aircraft before the passengers and demanded Andy take them straight to the tower. Andy said they cursed the madman and both controllers, promising to report all of them. Some weeks later mad Captain Milligan went home but was not replaced. The Auster never flew again but the Adj. ran the engine every week. The other aircraft in there was an RAF Avro Anson, which the CO and Adj. took up for an hour every month. Both were old wartime planes partly covered in fabric.

On one occasion a Hastings freighter for Fayid landed with one engine shut down. The hangar gang fiddled around and ran it up repeatedly, until they were satisfied. The Captain was called and wanted it unloaded for an air test. We emptied it and Harry and I rode as ballast in the back, as when empty they flew nose heavy. An hour cruising over the sea at various power settings and on landing the pilot turned off the runway a shade too early, causing one main wheel to sink in the soft sandy soil. Five hours later, using the combined pulling power of both the RAF and BOAC tractors and the lifting cable taken off the old crane, it was finally towed to the hangar for undercarriage and tyre tests. The runway was now clear for the first BOAC departure.

We'd just finished reloading the Hastings when Myers pulled up at 7 am. He opened his passenger door and out stepped a woman of around 40. 'This is Miss Nairn Bennett from the Air Ministry, here to investigate why it takes so long to load and unload transport aircraft in the MEAF. This lady has the equivalent rank of Wing Commander so you address her as ma'am.'

It seemed a strange name for a woman until we saw the gilt lettering on her brief case. 'Miss S. A. Nairn-Bennett OBE, BA'. She was neat, trim and all BBC English.

'What equipment do you have available?' I left it to Harry.

'One piece of rope, that sack cart and three useless Arabs on each shift ma'am.'

She scribbled on the clipboard. 'That cart is not RAF issue.'

'No ma'am, the AMWD bloke gave it to us.' More scribble.

'I see you've got a crane.'

I answered this time. 'That's useless too, the clutch on the winding drum is worn out, ma'am.'

'What do you do if you need a crane then, say for an engine change or heavy cargo?'

'Borrow one from the Yanks.'

'Which Americans?'

'Big airbase near Tripoli, they've special cranes for everything, ma'am.' Prolonged scribbling. Myers, still at rigid attention and perhaps feeling out of the loop, said, 'The Americans are most co-operative ma'am, and the Arabs are very competent at unloading passenger baggage.'

'This is most unsatisfactory, would you please take me back to the CO's house.'

170

'Right away ma'am.' Again he held the car door, then they sped off.

Far more unsatisfactory was our missing breakfast and a shower, only switched on for an hour at 6 am and 6 pm and tepid too. We went to BOAC to scrounge coffees, then to bed. 'I wish they'd post that Myers bastard to the Air Ministry, he'd be just right greasing round that bunch.'

My first Christmas at Idris was a surprise. The officers continued the old tradition by serving the men. The meal was perfect, probably because it was organised by two corporal cooks from some army unit. Flying Officer Francis had invited us to his married quarter for 'drinks and a nibble' on Christmas Day evening. Together we bought him a bottle of whisky. His wife was a natural, friendly Yorkshire woman. At some point Les announced, 'Mr Douglas Harrison will now entertain you good folk.'

'I can't do it with people watching me.'

'Go behind that door then.'

We heard him clear his throat a few times, then a young girl started to nag her father. Next a young woman bemoaned the price of cosmetics. Another pause then an old woman moaned about her gas bill. He reappeared to applause. Mrs Francis was enthusiastic, 'What amazing talent, you ought to get on radio, you'd be famous.' We'd never heard him do variations. Finally, after handshakes all round and mutual good wishes for the New Year we left for bed. 'Grand Yorkshire folk' said Harry.

As I paid some cash into my savings account the Adj. passed me a signal. 'That any interest to you?' The army wanted two RAF personnel to help search for an imaginary aircraft crash site in the barren south. Two vehicles would collect us at HQ at 0500 hours tomorrow morning. Greatcoats and mugs must be carried. Basic food and fresh water would be on board. 'I'll have a go sir, I'll ask our lads.' Harry would have nothing to do with pongos and Doug thought there would be snakes and buzzards in the desert. Ken was quite happy and went to the Adj. When he came back we told Myers, omitting any mention of volunteering, Ken just said, 'The Adj. has put us two on a desert rescue exercise with the army, a mock aircraft crash down south of here, sir.'

'When are you due back?'

'Don't know sir.'

'Right, don't let the Royal Air Force down in front of the army.'

171

'No sir.'

It was just beginning to get light when dead on 0500 two tracked Bren gun carriers clattered to a stop, the Bren guns missing. 'Right lads, jump on sharpish, we need to move while it's still cool, one of you in each.'

'I thought they'd have Land Rovers.'

We clattered out of camp, through the village and turned south towards Gharian. Running on each side of the road was much quieter. Each vehicle had a corporal in charge, the driver and one other pongo in the back. As the sun rose I could see the trailer full of fuel cans and some jerry cans marked 'drinking water'. There was a compass fitted in the dashboard and the corporal had a wrist compass, a map with just a cross and six figures beside it, on the otherwise empty area.

We crawled through Gharian, avoiding donkey carts and battered pick-ups, not an Italian in sight. A cattle market was being held on the fringe, a few camels, donkeys and goats, feral pyards (wild desert dogs) watched from a distance. A lone Shell tanker and trailer passed north as we continued to Misrah. We stopped to top up the fuel. They produced primus stoves and we had a brew. The corporals daubed face cream on all our chins and noses against the fierce sun. Ken and I had a quick look at all the equipment they carried. Coiled under the cans was a spare track, each vehicle had a rack holding binoculars, a winch mounted front and rear and shovels clipped on the outside. Inside was a big fitted radio with a high whip aerial, red and green flares with a pistol in a rack. Three mounting points on the floor must be for the Bren swivel. 'What's in the rolled up sacking on the floor?'

'Sten guns with spare clips, corp. has a pistol under his seat too.'

'What about the rolled up overalls, they're wet through.'

'Keeps our sandwiches soft.'

'Final daft question – what is that piece of stainless steel for?'

'Vital if we broke down, prop it against the track at night, full of drinking water in the morning, cold air condensing on the metal. In daylight we can use it for signalling in morse.' It was about 18 inches square with one edge rolled to form a trough. 'You certainly are well organised.'

'All these ideas come from the long range desert group operating a long way east of here during the war, our Lieutenant's father was in that mob. Sometimes we carry tinned food and tents, stay out for a week. The whole rig is over 7 tons, with a 6 litre Rolls engine. Right, lets move.'

We clattered through dusty Misrah, a sand-blown dump with one petrol pump and pressed on. 'In twelve miles we enter the rough.'

We turned onto 244°, running on hard shale, the tracks throwing loose bits to rattle on the trailer. We started to detour round low rocky outcrops, running on blown sand with occasional low dunes. Each time we came back on 244°, but when we reached the theoretical spot we could be due north or south of it with no way of telling. I shouted to the corporal, 'Any minefields down here?'

'Not known, they're further east, right to the Egyptian border.' We came to more extensive dunes, our speed at times down to 5 mph and wallowing around, the four tracks hurling masses of sand over the trailers.

We stopped, 'By my reckoning this is it. Get the primus stove going, we'll eat. The Sabrejet is due at 1200 and again at 1300. It's now 1220.' He loaded a green flare in the squat pistol.

We had a pee, munched corned beef sandwiches, apples and oranges, drank tea and smoked. The corporal issued a salt tablet to everyone.

Right on 1300 came the blast of sound from the north. The corporal fired the flare, the pilot responded with a brief burst of gunfire and disappeared. He came back low and slow about a mile to the east, something dropped from the aircraft, hit the ground and yellow smoke poured from it. He waggled the wings and roared north, climbing. The corporal was straight on the radio. 'Our ATA 1220 sir, 1300 rendezvous complete, the Yank's just left.' Pause. 'Yes, sir, the RAF lads are fine, very impressed with our tackle.' Pause with static. 'Right sir, plenty reserves, heading back, over and out.'

I had a quick, last look round with the binoculars, nothing at all round the full horizon, just a ring of shimmering heat. We were mere specks on the barren surface, no more significant than grains of sand. We set off on the 64° reciprocal, our original tracks already obliterated by blown sand. We got back to the blacktop and turned northerly. Near Gharian we stopped for a smoke, drank water, re-fuelled and went back to HQ Idris. 'Thank your lieutenant for the invitation, that was a damned good ride.' They clattered away with a wave, we went to bed. Next day the Adj. said, 'The lieutenant rang to say the pilot reckoned you were within a mile. How far did you go?'

'137 miles.' Naturally Myers condemned our effort: 'Within a mile is not much use to a badly injured pilot.'

My mother forwarded a letter from Selby Rushworth at Asquiths. He said the rest of the office had chipped in my share to buy a retirement present for Tom Blakelock. It was the latest issue of *Machinery Handbook*, 2000 pages of complex engineering data always known as the 'Engineer's Bible'. What good to him in retirement I couldn't guess. Perhaps it was their Halifax sense of humour, knowing that he couldn't refuse it.

One day, as we worked on a Hastings, an army Land Rover with a triangular pennant on the front bumper drew up close to the aircraft. A corporal jumped out and opened the passenger door. Out stepped a weird figure from a comic opera in the full dress uniform of a colonel in the Hussars, complete with brass chainmail epaulettes, ornate belt, sword and spurs. He marched briskly to the aircraft steps. Harry and I were in the doorway above him.

'Need you chaps to move our polo ponies home.'

The Arabs, fascinated by the spurs, moved close behind him to peer at them. Sensing their approach he turned to shout 'Imshi, you bloody heathens.' They looked angry but moved back a pace. Harry said 'No can do, sir, against regulations, no livestock in RAF transport planes, their urine will corrode the aluminium.'

'Rubbish, they fly racehorses round England regularly.' I had to think fast.

'They'll use stainless steel sheet with drains in the floor and stalls built into the inside sir.'

'Get me your officer.'

'Right away sir.' We went and knocked on Myers' door. 'There's a man in fancy dress at the aircraft, wants us to fly some mules home, sir.'

'Mules – mules? Don't be ridiculous, send him packing!'

174

'He insists on talking to you sir, I didn't want to argue, he's got a sword, sir.'

'My God, we've a madman on camp, I'll sort him out, ring the armoury.' He jumped up, jammed his peaked cap further onto his head and shot out. Harry and I followed him.

On sight of the colonel his stride changed to marching, he came to a noisy halt and the exaggerated salute caused his fingers to push his cap askew. 'Good day to you Colonel, how may I help you sir?'

The request was repeated, the request denied and regulations quoted. 'Regulations my foot, I'll take this higher up, much higher. Corporal, get me back to base right away.'

Our other two officers and the sergeant were in the office doorway grinning, Pooley was at the window laughing. Myers then realised just how close the Land Rover was to the aircraft wing and berated the corporal, 'Move it immediately!' He then set off back to the section, the grinning figures disappeared inside, Pooley moved away from the window.

The corporal, perhaps dreading an irate colonel for the rest of the day and resenting being bawled out by a mere lieutenant without medals, leapt aboard, slammed it into reverse and put his foot hard down. The Land Rover shot off the tarmac onto the sand, the thick ribbed rear tyre flattened the Arabs' only cooking bowl and one of the old tin cans they used to make tea. A branch pierced the canvas rear cover, the corporal jumped on the brake and stalled the engine. The tyre had disturbed the dying embers of their fire, fanned by the breeze, small but growing flames now licked the tyre.

Harry shouted 'Corp., your van's on fire.' The corporal leapt out, unclipped a fire extinguisher to spray the tyre, the fire and cooking bowl debris with white powder.

'Corporal, you're on a bloody charge, move it.' Both climbed in, the vehicle shot forward onto the tarmac, the flattened bowl was hurled out from under the tyre to hit Basribi on the leg. He wailed and the jabbering increased. The violent swerve caused the tall whip aerial at the back to hit the trim tab on the rear of the larger wing flap (used for fine-tuning flight to allow for drift), the aerial snapped and trailed on the tarmac beside the broken branch, still impaled in the canvas. The Land Rover sped off.

The tech. sergeant, who had been leaning on the hangar door watching, now ran across, moved the aircraft steps to the wing to inspect the trim tab. 'Lucky, not even a paint scratch. He should be court-martialled for that, the stupid sod, by the time they reach Tripoli that aerial will be worn away, bloody pongos.'

We'd watched a Marx brothers film compressed into five minutes. In the freight shed Jerry said, 'That bit about the mules was a scream.'

'You missed the best bit.' As we told it, the more he laughed. The tale must have spread through the camp for the next day a corporal walked into the mess shouting 'I've gotta hoss!'

I got a flight home on leave, right through to Dishforth, from there a quick lift in an army Land Rover to Wetherby, then a lift in a quiet but fast Daimler hearse, with the back empty, right to City Station in Leeds, had a pie with a cup of tea and finally the train home. There I had a pleasant surprise. My mother showed me a letter from some Leeds solicitors in Park Square, the same spot where we had been bombed but survived. Her cousin, the late Mrs Alicia Turnbull of the Manor House, Pool-in-Wharfedale, had left her £250. Aunt Laura had received the same. Clipped to it was a cheque. 'It only came Tuesday, I've never had so much money in my life.' I gave her 400 Senior Service cigarettes from the 600 I'd brought home. 'I've never seen so many.'

On the Monday we went into Halifax Building Society and got a simple savings account organised. She would have to wait a week for the cheque to clear, after that she could pay in or draw out any time with a passbook. They would add the interest each year.

I took my mother on lots of bus rides into the surrounding country-side and three times to the genteel Collinson's café for lunch. On other days she cooked my favourite meals, followed by tined fruit and cream, another favourite. I went over all the postcards she had saved and explained where each one was, using my old school atlas. One was a picture of the airport: 'The sky is actually darker blue than that print.' I stressed just how secure we were and that the local Arabs were friendly and worked with us. I explained the hows and ways of the whole airport as

176

my mother had never been on an airport, but I never mentioned scorpions, atomic bombs or the air crash, no point in worrying her.

On the final Friday we went to the Building Society and tried the system. She was given £10 cash and the counter clerk entered it and wrote in the new balance of £240. All was well. 'When the winter stock comes into Marks get yourself a good quality coat, but don't spend anything on the house. Soon as I'm home we must look for a better one with a bathroom.'

'That would be nice, and a toilet indoors.'

I kept one full packet of the cigarettes, left her the rest, caught trains to Leeds and then London to doze the night away in the waiting room at Victoria coach station with other khaki, dark and light blue clad figures and one stinking tramp on the floor. I caught the first coach to London Airport, to be told that the aircraft was unserviceable. I explained I would be late back from leave so was switched to the BEA flight, night stopping Luqa, Malta. I would still be late by a few hours. I was rushed through the crowds out to the people boarding a Viking. In the aircraft doorway a stewardess looked at the BOAC ticket. 'Oh, a transferee, last seat at the back.' Her haughty tone suggested I was a leper.

We refuelled at Istres, finally landed at Malta. Ignoring the passengers boarding the coach I dashed across to air movements and was directed to the signals office. There a corporal sent a signal to the Adj. at Idris. 'That keeps you in the clear, they won't charge you with being AWOL'

'Thanks a lot.' I ate in the airport and slept in the transit hotel.

I was standing at the aircraft steps next morning when the coach pulled up. The same blonde stewardess was first off. 'Where were you last night, you should have been in the Phoenicia Hotel with the rest of us.'

'I can't afford posh hotels on RAF pay.'

'It's included in the ticket price.'

'You saw my BOAC ticket, you should have told me, stupid woman.' I was the only one to alight at Tripoli and, in a loud voice, told her, 'The RAF take more care of passengers than you lot do!'

I went to the Adj.

'Ah, you made it, I got your signal, did you get right through to Dishforth?'

'Yes, sir, then a lift home in a hearse running empty.' I gave him the unused rail warrants and the leave pass. 'It was nice to see summer rain falling on green fields, drink English beer and eat fish and chips.'

'Sounds good.'

I went to the section and Myers shot out of his office 'LAC Ainley, you're absent without leave, report to the Adjutant, he'll charge you.'

'I've just come from the Adj. sir, he didn't charge me, I sent him a signal from Luqa last night.'

'Whatever for, you should never use signals for personal matters.'

I explained. Wilson listened intently, pipe going well. 'What else could he do? It wasn't his fault.' It was only then I noticed he'd been promoted to Flight Lieutenant whilst I'd been at home. 'The next time I go home, sir, I won't come back at all, I'll be demobbed.'

'You should be signing on, it's a man's life in the Royal Air Force.'

'I seem to remember a woman from the air ministry saying it was most unsatisfactory, sir. When I'm back home I'll probably be earning more than a colonel in the Hussars.'

Wilson roared with laughter. 'I well remember the mules.' Myers glared at me, turned into his office and shut the door.

It suddenly dawned on me – I had never called at Asquiths!

With no RAF planes due in that day I changed into civvies. Harry was lolling on his bed reading my latest copy of *Industrial Equipment News* which my mother posted each month. 'You're late back.' 'I'll tell you about the flight up at Andy's.' I did, Andy was not at all happy. 'I'll get you compensation for this, I'll have her disciplined, she'll get moved onto London-Belfast routes for six months. The Phoenicia is the highlight of the flight, a very classy place. I knew one was transferred but I was on the phone when the aircraft landed. What was her name?'

'I don't know, but she was blonde, the other was black haired.'

'Ah, that's Janet Hennessy, good.' He typed three copies, rubber stamped 'Line Manager, Idris', and signed all three, so did I. He was claiming £20! 'When I get the cheque, I'll ring you. This will go internal mail with the captain, could be two weeks.' It duly came with a long letter of waffling apology and a hope that I would fly with them again. I took it to Jerry Francis to cash it in the shop and explained. 'They say beware of Greeks bearing gifts, but he did you a damned good turn.'

'I know, I've given him 400 cigarettes.'

The CO walked into the section one day, the sergeant shouted 'Officer present.'

'At ease, I wonder if anyone could paint a large sign, big bold letters but needs to be very neat?' The last time a wing commander wanted something painted I got a week off square-bashing and £5. Naturally I volunteered immediately. He wanted 'Transit Hotel' painted on the building front so passengers saw it as they left the aircraft door. With paint, brushes, rags, turps and a 6 inch nail from Alf's compound, the trestle platform towed down from the hangar and our very own piece of rope we scratched two arcs concentric with the arch, then the letters. Harry started with 'T', I at the other end with 'L'. The paint dried as soon as it touched the warm wall. With a break for lunch we'd finished before dark and cleared everything away. From a Hastings door height the dark blue letters showed up bold and clear against the faded cream cement.

In the dockside offices of an Italian shipping company Les had found a leaflet and map showing the route to the ancient city-port of Leptis Magna, to the east of Tripoli. It had been built by the Romans to ship locally grown grain to Rome by wooden barges with a sail and company of slaves rowing. A car could be hired from Gandolfo's garage in the eastern suburbs, as the bus to Benghazi ran too far inland from Leptis. Ken swapped shifts and with Les and Harry we found the garage, Les flashed a blue card at the old Italian mechanic who muttered 'Si, si, benzina OK.' We squeezed into the baby Fiat and with Ken navigating and Les driving set off. En route I asked Les about the blue card. He passed it back. I asked him how he got a membership card for the Khartoum Yacht Club. 'Found it in the transit hotel.' It would take pages to describe what is today a much restored world heritage sight. We finally left the Arab guide with a tip and a lasting impression of just how clever the Romans were in the building trade.

On, or just after every pay-day, we went to Tripoli to an unusual Ristoranti di Roma, perhaps so named because it was on the top floor of the Banco di Roma. Unusual because the otherwise Italian menu offered just one English dish – an excellent mixed grill including a piece of veal. I'm certain the full platter would not be bettered anywhere at home. It included half-carafes of red and white Italian wine, a waiter ambling from table to table playing a scratchy violin, and any amount of coffee.

As we waited to be served one day, Les was leaning out of the open window by the table. 'Hey, quick, look at this!' We all looked down on a battered pick-up, two Arabs sitting in the back amongst land mines on a bed of straw. They were being hauled through the main street, Sharia Istiklal, previously known as Via Vittorio Emanuel II. It was a street with expensive Italian shops, three banks and the old Italian government offices. At the southern end it opened out into a palm lined circle with the ornate mini-cathedral in pinkish stone, at the other an Arab point duty policeman controlled the T-junction with another shopping street. He waved the traffic forward, as the pick-up drew level he must have seen the mines from his high vantage point on the concrete plinth, for he gave a shout and pulling his pistol fired up in the air. With a cloud of dark exhaust the pick-up shot forward through the smoke into the rabbit-warren of narrow streets in the old city.

An army corporal waiting in air movements to go on leave had once told us that Arabs down south dug the mines up when the wind exposed them, and sold them to fishermen. They in turn took them out to sea, fitted floats and exploded them by rifle fire from a distance. All sizes of fish were killed by the blast, killing the young ones was illegal.

Whilst in Idris we saw four odd things involving just Arabs. During my first February in Idris an Arab lad appeared with a flock of goats to graze the young grass between the runways. Next day another arrived, we heard shouts and a scuffle developed. One lad slumped to the grass and remained there, quite still. The other lad herded the panicking goats away through the orange grove. We had been peering at this through the shimmering heat rising from the main runway, but the controllers in the high tower would have a much clearer view. Andy drove down, lifted the lad into his 'brake and took him off camp. He said later the lad was dead, the knife still in his chest. He had taken the body to the village police sergeant and banned future grazing.

On one occasion we were walking back from the village towards the main gate, along the Azizzia Road. Beyond the cacti and thorn hedge we heard a baby cry. Peering through the hedge we could see an Arab woman wiping blood from a newborn baby with the hem of her long skirt, just sitting on the bare earth. No midwife, not even a bowl of hot water. She was sitting in front of a large packing case with the end missing. Presumably her home in the corner of a field of growing vegetables. 'Probably happened like that for centuries round these parts.' Doug started singing 'Away in a manger'.

Djuma once invited us to an Arab wedding reception to be held surprisingly outside the police station on the hard packed sand, and to start at 8 pm. Doug borrowed the tech. sergeant's RAF bike and went down earlier for a drink. When we got there we found a crowd of Arabs, all adult men only. Two played bongo drums, we were handed highly spiced kebabs and shallow, two handled glasses of strong and very sweet shi, the Arab tea poured on burnt peanuts. At some point an upstairs shutter flew open and someone's arm dropped a white sheet with a large stain on it. The crowd muttered and clapped. Seems like the bride's father had kept his part of the bargain. The drummers stopped and they all melted away in the dark. The only light in the village was the single bulb under the arch of the police station door. Doug retrieved the bike from against the wall, mounted and rode just a few yards towards us, then with a shout he fell off. A figure, who must have been sleeping on the sand, rose up and dashed through the police station wicket gate, returning with the sergeant waving a pistol. After much broken English it was established the injured party needed compensating, partly for being run over, but mainly for his dream with Mohammed being ruined. Doug passed a handful of small coins. The Arab looked and said 'Much quoise.'

'He wants more.'

'I have no more, give him summat, my leg's bleeding.' Les gave the sergeant a large coin. 'Five pounds English sterling' and held up five fingers in the lamplight. We caught the word 'kumsah' in the translation. 'Quoise' said the Arab, who grinned and promptly lay down on the sand.

'Let's get out of here, it's still bleeding.'

Walking back I asked Les what he'd given the Arab. 'Half-a-crown, found it in the transit hotel.'

The other curious experience also came as an invitation from Djuma. The function was unclear, with Djuma trying to explain. After various attempts the message was mimed with his hand held out at 3 feet he said 'Boy no zig-zig.' The hand rose to about 5 feet, 'Boy zig-zig.' The hand rose to a man's height 'Man plenty zig-zig.' Eager to help Ali said 'Quoise.' Ken laughed 'I get it, man rapes boy, it's a poofters' convention.' Doug: 'This we gotta see.' Les: 'Don't bring that bloody bike. I think it's boy reaches manhood, reaches puberty, then he can breed, like Jews have Bar Mitzvah, it's just a ceremony.'

When we got there, flat scrubland at the edge of the village, we found flickering rushlights and two bongo drummers. A strip of burning char-coal about the length of a cricket pitch by 2 feet wide was kept glowing by Arabs using bellows. The crowd was again all male Arabs. At one end two men held a lad wearing just a loin cloth, repeatedly forcing his head over smoke rising from something burning in a bucket. One repeat-edly sprinkled some powder into the bucket. The heat was intense, the smoke sickly. Three more lads in loin cloths awaited their turn. We spotted Djuma at the other end. The bongo thumping increased as the lad suddenly ran along the charcoal path. He was grabbed at the other end by two Arabs, a third plunged what looked like a wooden meat skewer through one cheek and out the other, and immediately withdrew it. Djuma wiped soot from the lad's foot. 'Shufti.' He pointed to the lad's cheeks – no sign of blood, barely a mark, no sign of blisters on the foot. Puzzling. We each gave Djuma some cigarettes. 'Quoise, boy sleep now one day, one night.' As we left the second lad ran the gauntlet. Harry said, 'I bet that was some kind of dope in that bucket, drug him up so he wouldn't feel any pain.' Doug's comment 'I'll remember that, it's like some jungle film.' Les: 'It would be a good stunt for tourists, bloody voodoo!' It would have been a tradition amongst this Senussi tribe for generations.

One day a Valletta arrived from Luca bound for El Adem. The whole interior was empty except for one large packing case stencilled 'The Pelham Silent Toilet'. It was a corporal, going on leave from that desert strip, who weeks later told us the purpose of this weird plumbing. The then Princess Elizabeth was holidaying at 'Tree Tops' in a Kenyan game reserve. Her leisurely intended route home was Nairobi-Khartoum-El Adem by VIP Hastings, thence by Royal Yacht to London river. Her father died and this was abruptly changed to flights by BOAC to London. The silent 'throne' had been for her sole privacy whilst staying just one night in El Adem Officers' Mess!

Harry and I managed a weekend in Malta, scrounging lifts on the Valletta. We stopped in the transit hotel for 5 pence per night for a bed each among 16 in a Nissen hut with a shower block at the end. We ate in various scruffy cafes but at least it was basic English food. On the main street I found a branch of Gieves Military Tailors and ordered a blazer badge in gold wire. The assistant showed me a sample of a typical army version. It would be posted to me from their London workshop. The cost, delivered, was £4! Outside I told Harry I could get a blazer at home for £2. We also found the Church of the Knights Templar on the main street of Valletta. Sir Richard Aneley would have called on his way east many centuries earlier, during the Crusades. We went on bus rides in the most ramshackle buses I have ever ridden on. We met two sailors in a bar who took us over their submarine, parked in Sliema Creek with two others, all tied to a depot ship. As we climbed out of the diesel stench Harry asked the usual question about wide bottoms on the sailors' trouser legs. His version was 'Gerrem off quick if the ship sinks, quicker still if a tart winks.'

Christmas came and again the meal was excellent, two army cooks supervising everything. From 1st January 1955 I started to mark off the days on my diary calendar. Flt Lt Wilson completed his tour and went home. An ex-navy test pilot, Mike Lithgow came and captured the world airspeed record over a measured kilometre on the Azizzia Road with a Swift fighter, only to lose it just weeks later to an American in California.

Six more Canberra bombers dropped in. Next morning five left, one stayed with the port engine unstartable, despite using four cartridges. The crew and our tech. officer finally decided on an engine change. A Rolls Avon replacement was flown out with a five man fitting team from Wyton, the Canberra base. Help was requested in the way of a special crane from

Wheelus Field. The hangar officer instructed us to 'remove the seats, but don't put the ramp up. This crane goes through the aircraft doorway.'

With so much technical talent around Harry and I just sat around to watch as the unusual jib was manouvred right inside the aircraft door, swivelled at the hinge half way along the jib and the hook finally brought over the engine's lifting sling built onto the skid mounted cradle, by using both steerable axles. The master sergeant engaged the hook and signalled for some lift. Two corporals were in the crane cab moving hydraulic valves. Crane men know the term 'inch the winch', this engineering marvel could move a quarter of an inch at a time. More and more people came to watch, including the CO and Andy, who said, 'We'll need to borrow this if we need to change a Comet engine.'

'What Comet?'

'UTA are replacing Constellations, starting in two weeks time.'

Eventually the dud engine was put in the Hastings and we lashed it down. The crane had drawn to one side and the fitters were fastening the engine covers back on the Canberra. The m/sgt was by the crane watching. We ambled over to look at this machine. 'This is quite a machine you've got here Sarge.'

'We got all sorts of 'em at Wheelus, special cranes and fork lifts for different loads.'

'Any chance of us seeing them?'

'Sure, best come Saturday around 1900. I'll show you round then we can go into the NCO's club – we have a band flown down from Germany every week. Show your ID at the gate.' He wrote 'M/Sgt Vernon Humbolt, Motor Pool Extn. 319' on a diary page. 'I'll come collect you. Don't bring any cameras.'

'This Saturday OK?'

'Sure, an airforce bus runs a shuttle from the Old City Gate in Tripoli 1900 to 2000.'

We spent the day around Tripoli and caught the bus, along with lots of Italian women smelling of cheap scent. At the main gate manned by huge armed Negro air police was a floodlit bill-board. Bold letters proclaimed:

USAF Wheelus Field
OC Col. Roland B. Anthis
123 Heavy Bomb Wing
321 Fighter Squadron

Beneath in a wavy scroll the motto 'We Deliver'. Considering what similar aircraft had delivered to Japan the two simple words were ominous yet somehow reassuring.

He showed us around a whole fleet of varied cranes, tractors and trucks etc. being serviced. 'You can't go on the flight line, but you can look over a bomber.'

As we drove along we caught sight of the massed ranks of B29s and Supersabres, all bare dural reflected the massive arc lamps. After showing our ID to a major and captain we climbed up into a bomber. It appeared massive but was cramped inside. Cables and pipes ran everywhere. It was strange to think that the floor we stood on could have an atomic bomb fitted underneath. Eventually we thanked the two officers and Vernon drove us to the club. Inside we could not buy anything as only 'scrip' money was used on the base. I experienced my very first hamburger, ham not beef, including a fried egg buried within three layers of bread and what the world now knows, MacDonald's tasty sauce. Twenty men played the Big Band sound with lots of jive and Glen Miller tunes. Italian women swirled around with airmen. Negros gave marvellous demonstrations of jitterbugging. The band leader announced 'Now folks, a special treat, the one and only Bob Hope' to tumultuous applause. He strode briskly across the stage and for about forty minutes gave us the crisp, non-stop humour, far better live than in film scripts. There was more prolonged applause. The dancing continued, finally the leader announced 'Now, regretfully, the one you all know.' The Star-Spangled Banner was played in waltz time.

Vernon drove us back to the main gate. 'How many men have you at Wheelus?'

'Around seven thousand, many of 'em aircrews. Eight colonels run it, Anthis is the boss.'

'You must use most of the Tripoli power and water supply.'

185

'Glad you came tonight, I'm about through here, rotate stateside next week.' We shook hands

'Thanks for everything, best night I've ever had in my life.'

'Me too.'

With the Italian women we caught the bus back to the City Gate, then walked to the Uaddan Hotel, lounged around in luxury until we could get a lift on the BOAC coach to Idris, then a shower, breakfast and to bed.

My promotion to Senior Aircraftman came just 10 weeks before demob, with a 10% pay increase to sixty three shillings per week gross and new badges to stitch on the uniform, but I didn't bother with the blue ones.

Harry went home in March. We had a farewell drink in the transit hotel with Alf Pemberton. Harry had been a good friend for so many months, and we had had lots of laughs.

One curious thing occurred. We first got warning in a signal from Khartoum. 'They' were massing in the Yemen, then a further signal reported 'they' were moving north easterly but still well south of Khartoum. Varied sightings then came from civil aircraft, and finally it was established 'they' were on a direct track for Idris. Two Sabrejets left Wheelus to scout for 'them'.

The sky dulled to the south-east, the overcast increased until the sun was blocked out completely. The airport closed down and a Sabena flight was diverted to Malta. They began to fall out of the sky to cover the whole airport, runways, even the orange groves. 'They' were adult locusts, seeking a coastal area to breed but once, then die. The chameleons and perhaps some of the lizards would have a bonanza. A Super Sabre came over low and slow for a looksee. Alf started to skim the runway clear with his mechanical shovel. Idris reopened at 1800 and the diverted Constellation landed from Malta. Whether they slept on the wing like migrating birds or why they should pass over two coastlines to seek another 1700 miles away we never knew. It was the most impressive example of the natural world I have ever seen.

My turn finally came. I was described on the signal from Habbaniya as 'uplift one half two pax ex Idris stop.' It was the returning Australian aircraft. I was called to the CO for a final interview. 'This is quite informal, you can drop the 'sir' business.' He poured two glasses of sherry. 'I am supposed to ask if you're considering signing on but I assume that's rather pointless?'

'Quite pointless, I am going back to start earning real money in engineering – it's what I trained for.'

'What do you think of Idris?'

'You ex-bomber aircrew run it smoothly, without the bawling, shouting, bullshit with pomp and circumstance of an English camp, yet everything gets done and the aircraft leave on schedule. I appreciate it and I'm certain all the lads do too.'

'Nice to hear that. During the war we depended on you lads to keep the aircraft flying and we had a lot of corporals as air gunners, many of them didn't come back.'

He passed me the 'Certificate of Service' booklet. 'I shall be leaving the service myself in two months, going to settle in New Zealand, my wife was born there.' I shook hands with a straightforward, competent Englishman who would soon be clear of the bureaucrats in the Air Ministry. In the evening I bought 600 cigarettes in the NAAFI, moved into the transit hotel for my last night, had a meal and changed my Libyan cash. In the bar full of civvies back from Australia I had a farewell drink with Reg Pooley and Alf Pemberton.

We took off at 0800, I sat right at the back with the air quartermaster sergeant. We were perhaps 30 minutes over the sea when a pilot came and whispered 'Radio message, Wheelus Field have just gone to Yellow Alert, heavy Russian naval units moving through the Bosphorus into the Med, don't tell the pax.'

I was demobbed at Upavon, given rail warrants to Halifax with a voucher for one night's stay in the 'Union Jack Club', a stopover for other ranks en route through London. I was also paid up to 2nd June and received a complete set of civilian clothes, including a grey suit, trilby and raincoat, and a note forbidding civilian employment until 3rd June. On the train from Swindon, glancing round the passengers I realised none would know of the Yellow Alert, or what may portend if it changed to Red.

As when leaving Asquith's, I had known some good people, including the only Greek I have ever known and the very first American. In future

I needed to avoid anything called 'Royal', any contact with British government systems and irritants like Myers. Much more pressing was the need to start earning real money and find a better house.

17

Back From the Sand

A money order for just over £92 arrived, along with a statement showing my RAF savings account now fully withdrawn and closed. I cashed this in the main post office and went across Commercial Street to the Midland Bank. Here I closed the child's savings account I had first opened when ten years old, adding the £3 from this to the £92, I opened a current account. The clerk entered the total into a passbook, adding 'this passbook remains the property of the bank and after six months satisfactory operation of the account you will be able to apply for a cheque book.' His tone implied that this was a special concession for me personally. With my leave pay, for the first time in my life I had over £100.

I went to Sam Stocks and bought an RAF tie, at the Fifty Shilling Tailors I bought a black blazer and a pair of mid-grey slacks. My mother had a problem trying to stitch the gold wire badge onto the blazer pocket so I asked her to stitch right through, sealing up the pocket I would never use. I could now go for a quiet pint looking neat as anyone with the deep tan even more obvious against a white shirt. The gleam was developing as every morning I polished the black demob shoes.

Next morning, in RAF uniform, I caught the bus to Asquiths, telling the commissionaire I wanted to see Eric Northend in Personnel.

'You've finished then, looks like you saw some sand?'

'Yes, Egypt and Libya.'

He made out a pass.

'You know where to go? Hand it back when you leave.'

'Yes, thanks.'

Eric shook hands. 'We've given up advertising for men, can't get 'em for love or money. Only people we can get are office girls and labourers and we don't need any more. Asquiths took over Kitchen and Wade whilst you were away. We lost two fitters last week – went to ADA, the bonus is better.'

'What's ADA?'

'It's what was Ajax Machine Tools, now called Ajax Domestic Appliances – ADA, get it? Old man Carter has started up making washing machines, they're selling like hot cakes.'

An office girl came in and dumped a file on his desk, leaving the door open on her way out. Footsteps passed the door, slowed and stopped, then came back. I turned to face George Hoyle, hands in pockets, cigarette drooping as ever. 'Just the man I want, have you finished with that damned air force yet?' I explained that until June 3rd I was on leave and not allowed to work. 'Come up to my office.' Not 'would you please', or, 'I will explain in private', just 'come up to my office'. He would never change, but I was glad to see him and 'just the man I want' was intriguing.

We plodded up the endless steel stairs, Molly jumped up, shook hands and laughed 'You have caught the sun.' I noticed the vase of flowers, but somehow the offices were not quite the Uaddan Hotel.

'Sit down, will you make some tea, Molly?' said Hoyle. 'What I'm going to tell you must remain confidential, in the air force you'd probably call it "top secret". It's something I've discussed with the Asquiths for some weeks now and we are agreed we must pursue it. For years now we have been giving customers machines which they can use for thirty years to make their profits, but we don't make enough profit on any of them. In fact I'm damned certain that we make a loss on some of the specials. It is natural for a salesman to get every order possible, but if he is unwittingly selling machines which generate little profit it is a useless activity which needs to be curbed. Our best selling machine is the O.D.1 radial drill, but it was designed twenty years ago, in 1935.

190

Except for the rubber drive coupling, nobody has looked at the design since because it continues to sell. Every big machine shop in the world has this machine. During the war we built 60 a month. Nowadays, we tart 'em up with filler, rub it down and spray it, like we were making a car for some fool to polish every Sunday morning. Everything is chrome plated to make it look smart, yet is it only a tool to work with to make holes in metal, and the men using it are only rated as semi-skilled in a machine shop. We fit engraved and chromed instruction plates to tell 'em what speed to run for a particular hole size, but these guys always run faster to make more bonus. Johnson's clowns carry all these ideas into the latest machines and never think of the cost of it all. Your job will be to break the mould, starting with the six-foot O.D.1, looking for any way we can cut the cost without compromising the function of the machine. We may finish up with a lot of small changes or even a major change with small ones. We'll then start looking at other machines. It's a job with a future for you, and it could be a big help in the long term future of the company.'

'If it has to stay secret where would I work?'

He pointed to the unoccupied office next door. 'I'll get that place done up before you start.'

'What sort of pay will I get?'

'I was thinking of half as much again as the draftsmen get, that would be over £24 per week and as much overtime as you like, after six months we will review it. We always keep this place locked, Molly will give you a spare key. Are you happy about the job?'

'Yes, definitely, and thanks for the offer.' We shook hands.

'Right, that's settled then, when can you start?'

'Third of June, I finish with the RAF on 2nd June.'

'I was talking with a Yank last year at the German Exhibition, he was from Pratt and Witney and said their designers have brainstorming sessions.'

'What's that?'

'They bounce ideas off each other to see who can come up with the best solutions to a problem. That's what you and me will be doing. Don't forget, not a word to anybody. If someone asks just tell 'em you're doing a special project for me. It's just you, me, Molly and the Asquith brothers. Molly will keep a record of everything we do. She won't tell anyone, she's my niece! I'll tell Eric Northend what we've arranged, see you on June 3rd.'

Passing out through Molly's office, she jumped up from the desk. 'I heard all that, I am surprised.'

'Me too, start on 3rd June, my birthday.'

'Good, you'd be a fool not to, don't let him down.'

'I won't, and I won't let myself down either. I didn't know he was your uncle.'

'Keep that a secret too.'

'Will do, see you on the third. It'll be nice to be back.'

I clomped down the steel stairs, somewhat dazed. Looking over the rail the whole place seemed smaller. Going out past the commission-aire's cabin I banged into Selby, on his way home for lunch.

'Hello Donald, you're back then. You'll be going on Harold Wiley's board, he's now the checker since Tom retired.'

'I won't, I'll be working on a special project for George Hoyle, I told you I was well in with him.'

'Lying sod.'

'You wait and see,' I burst out laughing.

'Lying sod.'

I told the commissionaire I was going to the canteen and would have a look round afterwards. 'Right, the food's got better.'

I spent three hours that afternoon, wandering round waving the RAF cap at familiar faces in the distance, 'I'm starting on 3rd June, to endless people who admired my sun tan. Finally I went into the REEMA building, the final assembly line for O.D.1 radial drills. Hammers banging benches responded to my mock bow. One radial drill was being masked ready for spraying. I went along the line and found Ronnie Mosey.

'Stanley, we've got a visitor from overseas.'

Stanley was on the floor rooting under a bench for a small drill he'd dropped. He came upright.

'By gum, it's Donald. I could do with that sun tan, when are you going to get demobbed?'

'I've finished, I'm on leave and starting back here June 3rd. That's my birthday, remember "Squander Bug", you picked that for my birthday.' Both foremen had joined us, then Arthur Raine ambled across the line. ''Av you seen 'em racing camels in t'desert?'

'No, but they seem to take five minutes to get up off their knees, let alone race.' Everybody laughed, then Raine added 'I don't need to back horses, I knock out two LDRs every week and make enough bonus so I don't work Sundays and I've got the wife out working since her mother died.'

The LDR was a lighter duty machine, the initials stood for 'light drilling radial'. It was only built with a 54 inch arm to drill up to 2 inch diameter holes in solid steel.

'Have you brought any Arab girls home? You can marry four of them out there.'

'Just two, I'm going to get them working for me down in "The Saddle"!'

In those days this downtown pub was notorious for brawls, frequent police raids and general mayhem. It was the haunt of con-men, drunks, petty thieves and the just-out-of-jail town dregs who slept in the local working brick-kiln, or had done until one had been found dead in the morning, having suffocated from furnace fumes. It was also the base for the town's few prostitutes, the best known of these was one 'Diamond Lil'. Winter or summer she wore a full length fur coat over her bus conductress uniform; she conducted the bus on the early shift, then conducted her early afternoon trade in the stinking toilet yard behind the pub. When the pub closed at 2 pm she could be found in Woolworths or Marks & Spencers, engaged in advanced shop lifting which involved the voluminous fur coat. When the pub re-opened at 5.30 she would continue in action, alternating between bar and back yard, to cease at closing time or a police raid, whichever occurred first. Some wit had presented her with printed business cards bearing the legend 'Diamond Lil', the pub address and phone number and the word 'Therapist'. When the landlord saw the cards he told her to put up her prices as she was lowering the tone of the place. She had never been known to be prosecuted for any offence. Most pubs sold beer, crisps and elderly meat pies, here in the back yard one could purchase bundles of brand new copper pipes or the odd roll of sheet lead, and even arrange for a late-at-night delivery of a new washing machine, still warm from the production line. For some strange reason the pious landlord had always banned card-playing.

After many years trading a startling event triggered a change. A Polish man (quite a few settled in Halifax after the war and were known as hard working and equally hard drinking) knifed a man in the pub yard. He survived but the Pole was jailed. As a result landlord, brewery, town council, magistrates and the Women's Luncheon Club finally called time. 'The Saddle' was closed, gutted, refurbished and re-opened as 'The William Deighton', named after a London customs officer who had been shot in the town years before.

Stanley asked, 'Are you going back into jig and tool?'

'No, I'm starting a new project for George Hoyle.'

'George Hoyle, bloody hell, he's the top man in Asquiths. You've done well to get working for him.' I didn't enlighten them further. 'I'm off now, before the buses get crowded.'

I handed in the pass, went home in beautiful sunshine and told my mother of the new job. 'Oh, good, you've always been good at drawing, you once won a prize for drawing.' I didn't explain that right now I was much more intent on drawing good wages, instead I mentioned that as soon as possible we must find a far better house and modern furniture. 'It would be nice if we had a bathroom.'

'That's what I had in mind, and a toilet indoors.'

I dashed round to Ernest Gutsell, the optician, he booked me for an eye-test on Saturday morning, and said rimless were now £5 and they could be ready in under a week.

Early that evening my mother was knitting as I sat drinking tea, staring into the empty fire grate. I thought back to the brief interview with Hoyle. Perhaps the vague promise of a pay review really meant that I was merely on six months' probation and if I could not perform I would be discarded. The pressing demand country-wide for engineers at all levels meant that even if I failed it would not matter. I had survived twenty years of poverty in unpleasant and sometimes risky situations. In contrast this job held no risk and would enable us to move quickly to a much better home. I would also be working for an extremely practical and powerful boss, a vast improvement on Flight Lieutenant Myers.

That evening I went into the town for a pint, as so often happens in any English pub, I got talking with a total stranger at the bar. He was French-Canadian by birth, working for Geo. Cohen's 600 Group on demolition jobs. They had just bought the scrap metal contents of Turner's Grease Works in Copley, outside Halifax. Old man Turner had been buying small quantities of crude oil from Persia, but after kicking out the Shah the new prime minister, Dr Mossadeq, had cut off all oil supplies to the west, so Turner decided to close down and retire. He had only employed his unmarried daughter and one labourer. Turner and his daughter lived in the old house by the works. Cohens had bought all the valuable, but now scrap copper pipes, copper still, brass valves and lead linings from the huge wooden vats.

I told him my background and the RAF leave period. Over one more pint it was agreed that I would help him for two weeks as he could find no one from the labour exchange. The pay was £12 a week, plus £2 'dirt money' plus £2.10/- lodging allowance, all as casual labour. We left the pub and he ran me home in Cohen's pick-up, so that he knew where to collect me. 'Eight o'clock, bring some sandwiches and old clothes, there's some overalls in the pick-up.' He wrote Pierre Fournier on a beer mat. 'It's pronounced 'Fourneay'.'

We stopped in Copley village where he used the phone box to ring Stanningley. Back in the cab he said 'That's done, you're on the pay roll, the wages man comes Friday morning from Stanningley, but he calls in Huddersfield first. We have a gang of ten men ripping a boiler out of an old mill. It's not scrap, they've sold the boiler to a brewery in Belgium.'

We drove to Turner's dump, where ramshackle sheds appeared to lean on each other. In one corner of the sloping field next to the works a single strand of barbed wire on drunken posts guarded a triangular pool of what appeared to be liquid tar. A dead rabbit floated on the sunlit surface. This was presumably the works dump containing the final sticky residue after processing. Perhaps it was the dead rabbit which prompted a mental flashback to a much smaller black pool in a sunlit school yard. In the largest building was a huge dome, the insulating double brickwork encasing this was partly removed to reveal the discoloured copper below. Copper pipes ran from this in both directions, fitted with large brass valves. At the end of this shed was a water tank made from flanged cast iron plates bolted together, the nuts rusted years ago. In one corner were some brand new red-painted 40 gallon drums, stencilled on each the name of a well-known cosmetic firm in America. I rocked one, they were empty. 'That's a funny thing to see in a dump like this.'

'The old man's daughter told me they made a grease here from the oil which is later refined and used as the base for women's face cream.' I thought of the corporal in the half-track in Libya, with his wife's little jar. Bits of my life seemed to be linked together. The oil had come from a desert region where I had been, the face cream sent to another desert area. My parents had both worked in Canada, now I was working with a French-Canadian. Both links had come from my casual meeting with one man in a pub.

He taught me to use a shearing hammer, the size of the largest sledge hammer, but with one end of the steel head formed to a slight wedge shape, but the cutting edge was not sharp. The technique was to swing this edge accurately and with the maximum force at the point where nut touched washer: the edge 'sliced' through the three-quarter-inch diameter bolt and the nut shot along the room. It took me five or six attempts before I mastered this.

'OK, you start dismantling the cast iron tank, I'll get more bricks off the copper.' We worked till 12, then he opened up the padlocked lids on the pick-up cargo box to produce tea, sugar, powdered milk and an electric kettle. I knocked on the kitchen door and we went in to brew. Turner's daughter, who could have been around forty, found us mugs and spoons. We ate in the long abandoned greenhouse. It was there that I learnt that Pierre's divorced wife lived in Montreal, he now had no actual home but lived in lodgings wherever the job took him and had now worked for Cohens for seven years. They were the best firm he had ever worked for. He had been a foreman for three years and was looking forward to

196

starting to demolish the Liverpool Overhead Railway, this could last two or three years and the bonus would be good with a higher lodging allowance.

'There are no cranes in these sheds, how are we going to move the metal out?'

'I've got chains in the pick-up, we'll drag each piece behind the truck down the dirt road onto the tarmac at the end of the bridge. Cohens will send a truck and a crane for it.' He seemed to be very well organised but I couldn't help feeling he must live a very lonely life. I suddenly realised he was homeless just as I had been years before. Another link.

On Friday when we arrived at the dump he produced a book of time sheets with carbon paper from the cab. 'Fill them in before you get mucky.' I filled in one for each of us, the hours per day, a total of 40. Then my name, address and age, and rather ominously, the address of 'next of kin'. His address was 'c/o The Foundry Man Inn, Goal Lane, Halifax'. He passed me an envelope showing his ex-wife's address in Lonqueuil, Quebec. The place name rang a bell, I wasn't certain but thought Pratt & Whitney had a factory there.

The wages chap arrived, I passed him the time sheets. 'By gum, that's the neatest I've ever seen, you an artist?'

'No, a draftsman, don't forget to tell the wages office I am only working one more week, then I start back on a drawing board at my old firm.' He passed us the wage packets, the one corner cut away so the notes could be counted in his presence to avoid any subsequent dispute. 'If you need owt, just ring, see you next week.'

As we munched sandwiches I opened the packet, the wage slip showed tax – nil, NI – nil, a rubber stamp had left across the slip the words 'temp.casual'. The amount was exactly right. 'Another week of the same and I would be well on the way to the first £200.

The following week we started to earn the 'muck money'. It was greasy, slippery and it stunk. Wearing the firm's Wellingtons we slid around in one inch of oily sludge residue on the floor of the first vat. We finally cut out the last piece of lead, but the lead covering the floor of each vat we left under sludge. On Friday we were dragging bits of metal to the large doorway when the wages arrived. Time sheets were exchanged for wages. 'Get a truck and crane over on Monday morning.'

He dropped me off at home, we shook hands. 'Thanks for the job. I'll be in the Plummet Line Hotel tonight if you fancy a pint.'

'Right, see you there around eight.'

I got the boiler going, had some tea, then a bath in the zinc coffin in the cellar. At eight I entered the 'Plummet' to be greeted by a blackboard announcing 'Live entertainment, tonight only'. I joined Pierre at the bar. In the corner a blonde finished her song and went. The pianist then played some popular tunes and later introduced 'Len Jackson, Bradford's finest comedian.' Jackson appeared wearing a string tie.

'You look like the best audience I've seen for ages'. He then launched into his repertoire, stale, boring and even mentioned the Italian tank with one forward gear! He got gentle groans, some boos and a burst of applause when he announced we had been a lovely audience and he would have to dash as he was booked for Las Vegas next week. As he left some wit asked the barman 'What time does the stripper come on?' With deadpan expression the barman replied 'I thought they'd only booked one comedian tonight.'

I looked at Pierre.

'That's as good as it gets in Halifax.'

'It's even worse in the Montreal Music Hall and they're professionals!' At closing time we shook hands, never to meet again.

Next morning I collected my new rimless glasses, Gutsell adjusted the fit and they were perfect for reading small print. I was finally ready to go back to work. From there I went down to the Fifty Shilling Tailors and got measured for a grey suit. 'Ready in two weeks,' the man said. I would wear this and the demob suit on alternate weeks. Next stop was the barber's shop.

On Monday morning I caught the bus to Asquiths. We had no full length mirror at home, but I saw my reflections in shop windows approaching the bus stop. I looked smarter than I had ever done. One unusual thing about this route was that the driver's wife was the conductress. They had worked the route together from when I first started as an apprentice.

Queuing at the time clock, I nodded to some familiar faces and there would be puzzled stares as I continued alone up the second flight of steel stairs. Molly had already arrived. 'Good morning, Donald, welcome back, many happy returns.' She handed me a white envelope. 'I'll get you a key before I forget. George has called in the sales department to get some brochures and price lists.'

We went through George's office and I got the first shock, a plate on 'my' door proclaimed 'D W Ainley, New Projects'. I opened the door and was amazed. The whole floor had been covered with carpet matching the other two offices. There was a corner table with reading lamp, two new fluorescent lamps hung from the high glass ceiling, each fitted with shrouds hiding the tube, the room still smelt of fresh paint. There was a three drawer filing cabinet and bookshelf, both in grey steel, a huge desk, upholstered chair, waste bin and a huge calendar courtesy of Hoffmann Bearings hung on one wall, showing June. The real shock came when I saw that the old desk top drawing board standing on the wooden base cabinet full of wide shallow drawers had gone. In its place stood a brand new German pantograph drafting machine with an angle lamp mounted on the counterbalance weight. I went over to examine it. A lever locked the large AO size board at any angle and it could be raised by pumping a foot pedal at the cast base. There must be a hydraulic cylinder buried inside. One side of each rule was graduated in imperial, the other in metric, both very clearly marked on white plastic. It was a draftsman's dream machine.

'Well, what do you think?'

'I'm just amazed.' I opened the card, inside was written 'Double congratulations. From Molly.'

'Thanks, that was very nice of you.' I stood it on the desk beside the new scribbling pad on a clip-board and container with three pencils and a biro pen.

George came in. 'Morning, Donald, you're looking very smart. I've got you some sales stuff, the instruction book and a blank inspection form, all for the 12-speed 6 foot O.D.1. That pile of drawings on the floor covers every single piece of the machine with a parts list and list of all the drawing numbers. I think for the rest of today you'd best look through all this so you get to know the machine. I've got to go sort out another mess made by Johnson's clowns, grab your pad Molly.'

'What if somebody rings up?'

'If it's the Asquiths secretary, tell her I'm in the REEMA Building, tell anybody else to ring back in an hour.'

Molly explained that I should answer her phone because mine and George's had first to be switched through from hers. They went out and I was alone in surroundings far removed from cutting lead out of a greasy wooden vat. I unwrapped my drawing instruments and put them in the top drawer of the desk. I went over to the board and set the adjustable seat as I wanted it. Seat and back were covered in soft padded fabric, below the seat a tubular steel ring footrest was fitted above the legs, the seat swivelled and would rise and you climbed on to it rather than sat in it. The bottom of the board was cut away for knee clearance. It was the most comfortable seat I had ever used. A plastic wallet held some Allen keys and a special tool for removing the rules, along with an instruction book in six languages. I checked the rulers for squareness but they had already been adjusted by whoever delivered it, then brought the board to horizontal and dumped the whole file of drawings on to the desk, then sat at the board to look through the sales brochures.

The well laid out photographs and full specifications showed a wide range of sizes of radial drilling machines, the smallest with just three spindle speeds, the larger ones up to twelve. One mid-sized version was portable with iron wheels and jacks. It could drill at any angle, even vertically upwards. The last few pages showed the optional extras – various tables on which to clamp the workpiece, speed increasers for very small holes, automatic drill ejectors, coolant pumps and a threading attachment, known as a tapper. In a lifetime spent juggling with nuts and bolts I have never known why the tool used to cut an internal thread, as in a nut, is called a 'tap'. In the world outside engineering the same word is used to describe a valve on a domestic water pipe or to 'lightly hit something'. Similarly the device used to cut external threads, as on a bolt, is termed a 'die', the same word being used to describe the lower part of a press tool. It is much more familiar to the public as the oppo-site to 'live' and in the term 'straight as a die'. The basic benefit of a radial drilling machine as distinct from any other drilling machine is the facility to move the spindle to drill holes over a wide area without having to re-clamp the workpiece to reach a remote hole position.

It was an impressive range of high quality drilling machines to satisfy the whole world's increasing need to make holes in metal. It had evolved over many years and was the firm's speciality range but it didn't make sufficient profits. My job was to improve the situation by design or manu-facturing changes. I had no idea where to start but I expected a lot of opposition. Looking through the whole book again I realised I had helped build all these machines except the smallest. With the book and my scribble pad I went to George. 'Is it all right if I go on the O.D.1 line?'

'Course it is, if you need any help down there tell 'em I sent you, but don't tell 'em what you're doing.'

With the machines in front of me the ideas started to emerge and that soon prompted other ideas. I began to compile the first of what was to become many lists, ultimately typed by Molly, with three carbon copies.

Back in the office I was doodling with another idea when George called me in. 'Have you ever seen one of these?' A photograph on his desk showed a special two-spindle machine to drill and ream 'king-pin' holes in each end of a Leyland truck front axle.

'I'd forgotten about that, I once worked on one.'

He passed me an enquiry from Ford Motor Company with a drawing attached. This was a similar steel forging but smaller. Scribbled on the drawing in red 'locate in pre-drilled holes' from which arrows pointed to the extended areas where the springs were to be mounted. 'I've come up with a different way to do it, you have a go and we'll compare notes.'

'Now?'

'Yes, then we can get rid of it.' I doodled repeatedly, by the time I'd had half a basket of screwed up paper I was happy. I borrowed George's steel tape measure and went down to the drilling section and showed the foreman the sketch. He got the idea and held the tape to represent half the axle, I mentioned it was for George Hoyle and I'd proved it could be done on a standard vertical drill. Back upstairs I called in the drawing

201

office and had a word with the electrical section leader. I made a final neat sketch and took it to George.

'What's up, have you got stuck?'

'No, finished it.'

'Bloody hell, let's have a look.'

'That vertical line is the slideway of our standard vertical drill, that's the table locked permanently in its lowest position. The only special bit is this fixture-cum-jig which positions one end of the axle under the drill at a three-degree angle. The combined lock and plunger has to be fully closed to work the microswitch before the spindle motor can run, ensuring that the driller locks it fully every time, unlocks it, swings it round and does the other end. He'll then repeat this to ream each end. That's quicker than drill and ream one end at once. The electrical section leader told me it's simple, just a bit of conduit clipped down the column and into the fixture and a standard relay added inside the contactor panel. They've done it before. What did you come up with?'

'I just can't think at your speed, I must have been four hours, you do it better in one hour. I must be getting past it.' He showed me his version using a radial drill and a much larger special fixture involving a casting and therefore a pattern to make, which would only ever be used once. 'I'll give your version to Johnson, anyway it's proven one thing.'

'What's that?'

He didn't answer, just screwed up his version, aimed it at the already full basket and went.

I went to the canteen with a stream of draftsmen and office girls, using the area where greasy overalls were barred. I sat with two of the tracers, Eunice and Brenda. Eunice had attended the senior school but was in the form below me, and I'd known them slightly through five years as an apprentice. We ate and chatted like old pals. I told them snippets of what I had seen abroad but Hoyle's secret remained intact. 'Some new project, I'm only on it temporarily.' Whatever I said would almost certainly be passed on. The canteen food had definitely improved.

That afternoon, as I was compiling a list of what I would investigate on the machine George came in. 'We've a meeting at 2 pm tomorrow with the Asquiths, in the board room. I forgot to tell you about that drafting machine. It's on three months loan from the importers, they're hoping we'll replace all our boards with these, eighty odd, there's no chance of that, but we'll buy yours.' I thought of the two red Bentleys parked outside. The cost of doing up my office was peanuts to a firm this size, the only outside labour would have been a carpet fitter from some downtown shop, and he'd even scrounged the drafting machine. I was learning fast.

One idea was a very radical change which would certainly save a lot of money but I was expecting some massive opposition. I needed to do a lot of calculations and knew nothing about the strength of rubber. When Hoyle returned I went to his desk. 'Would it be possible for us to have a calculator in here, like the checkers use?'

'Course you can, I'll order one. I should have told you when you started, any tackle you need, just ask.'

It arrived next day from King's Stationers in Halifax, I used it for the calculations and once again had to stop at the rubber coupling. I went in and told him, having to explain the whole idea fully.

'My God, you're beginning to worry me now. If you're convinced there is a saving we'll pursue it right through. I'll get the rubber firm's rep to come in – he'll design it for us, he did the present one.'

'Even if we retain the existing coupling we can still save cash on the motor mounting, it's far too strong at present for a motor that only weighs sixty-seven pounds.'

'Good, something to fall back on at least.'

The rubber firm's sales engineer arrived some days later and proved to be extremely competent after we explained what we intended to do and our total ignorance of rubber. He looked at my sketches and promptly condemned the square rubber block. 'The optimum shape is always an equal cross, no problem, you'll just need mating slots across each flange. Could I borrow a calculator?' I brought mine.

'I'll show you how it works.'

'It's OK, I've got the same one, I work from home in Leeds.' He passed George a file marked 'Asquith' with the part number of our present coupling. 'You might like to browse through that while I do some figuring.'

203

Moving my chair next to George, we started to read a full report of the original tests they had done on our coupling. There were frequent mentions of temperature and some graphs, also a dynamometer setting for 8 horse power. George muttered 'Our motor is only 5 horse power, we'll ask him about that later.'

Alan Parker's visitor's badge entitled him to a free lunch in the canteen, well before then the whole job was finished. I had the exact sizes I needed to draw it full size, and was looking forward to using the new drafting machine. Alan explained that running temperature was critical because it could affect the plasticiser in the rubber, the 8 horse power gave a huge safety factor which could be reduced if space for the coupling was tight. He stressed the rubber must not be squeezed on assembly as this could affect the life of the material. His suggestion of one-thirty-second to one-sixteenth clearance would give us very easy machining tolerances. He would organise three samples for their tests, three more for us and as we were existing customers there would be no charge for the new mould.

As they shook hands George said, 'You've done a right good job for us. Thanks for coming quickly, we're very grateful. Would you get us a quote for the new version, it will be nice for us to put an exact figure on the total cost saving.'

'Certainly, same quantity as you're taking now. I'll get everything in motion this afternoon. Goodbye Mr Hoyle.'

'If we leave now there's time to show you the present design being built before we go to the canteen.'

'Good, I always like to get on the shop floor.'

When he saw it and heard what I proposed changing, he just commented, 'That design is crying out for a flanged motor, it's a good idea, glad to help.' Perhaps he was being polite. We hurried to the canteen to avoid the queue.

As we started to eat Eunice and Brenda joined us and I introduced Alan. During the meal he told me he was born in Holbeck, Leeds, but sent to live with an aunt in Skipton for two years during the war to avoid the bombing. On return he was apprenticed at the Royal Ordnance factory at Crossgates, learning machining and fitting army tanks. He was called up into the army and maintained tanks in Germany. There he met and married a German girl and they now lived in Bramhope. He worked from home using a spare bedroom as an office and covered all the northern counties with a Riley company car. His mother-in-law lived in a Bavarian village, being wheel-chair bound and scared of flying, she had never visited Bramhope but they had taken her lots of photographs of their house, and the Yorkshire countryside. They now visited Bavaria every Christmas and each summer. His wife Erika had never known her father as he was killed in Castel Benito, Libya when the Africa corps were fighting New Zealanders just after she was born.

'What a funny coincidence, I lived for only three weeks in a house in Leeds which was bombed and I was stationed at Castel Benito in the RAF. It's now called Idris after the Libyan king. It's the civil airport for Tripoli, but the RAF use it, that's where I was based.'

The two young women had listened intently, now Eunice said, 'We should have gone in the forces Brenda, they get sent all over the place, we could have got sun tans like Donald when he came back.'

'Not on your life, I'm not wearing daft caps and those thick stockings.'

Walking back from the canteen Alan said, 'I forgot to tell you this upstairs, the formula for the rubber was stolen from some German firm after the war by the Control Commission, but our managing director invented the formula for the mixture we use when bonding to steel. He owns the patent on that. Ring me if you have any further problems and thanks for the lunch.' We shook hands, I was never to see him again, but we spoke on the phone when he reported their test results – everything normal, the design was proven.

I vaguely knew of the Control Commission, searching Germany for any clever developments which could be of use to British industry, particularly those with military applications, just as the Americans and Russians had found rocket scientists and promptly put them to work in their respective countries. I was not to know then that within three years I would be working in a different firm for another boss who himself had been seconded to the Control Commission whilst still in the army and on

205

demobilisation had continued to search Germany, by then back working for his pre-war employers, the Plessey Company.

I drew the whole coupling out full size and its individual flanges. Next day George went through the whole twelve proposals, spotted one where he suggested a further improvement and approved the remainder. He then rang to arrange a meeting with the Asquith brothers.

That night I told my mother I would start working overtime every night until seven and Saturday mornings until 12. 'The canteen food's very good so I'll just have a snack when I get home each night.'

When I arrived back from lunch next day Hoyle was waiting. 'We'll have visitors in a few weeks, two Americans from Pratt and Whitney – they want to discuss special purpose machines, lots of them. Bob Asquith will be talking about this. Bring your scribble pad, we'll go downstairs.'

In the boardroom Bob Asquith outlined what George Hoyle had first told me about trying to cut manufacturing costs, but there was another area which might prove well worth looking into. He passed me a two page letter headed 'Pratt & Whitney, Gas Turbine Division, Hartford, Conn.' Clipped to it were two photographs with a business card stapled to each. The letter confirmed prior arrangements and they would be in Yeadon Airport Monday at 10.30 am.

'Normally these people would talk with Alf Johnson and Ken Kershaw, our sales manager. Between them they would sort out enough details to quote, then we might get an order, but in the past this has involved one special purpose machine at once. These Americans are talking around nearly fifty separate components, so we need to explore whether we can supply any standard machines with special tooling attached, or multi-drill heads on standard machines. On this job, and just as an experiment, we would like you and George to vet the whole thing before it ever goes near the drawing office and hopefully we'll start making some money from these machines.'

Richard chipped in: 'From now on our whole philosophy must be based on (a) we're in business to make money, (b) we make and sell machine tools to achieve this.' I wasn't quite sure about the word 'philosophy' but no doubt Molly had a dictionary.

206

He continued 'The two from Pratt and Whitney will be quite familiar with our machines, they have bought nineteen O.D.1s since the war, and in 1951 a 2 inch horizontal borer.'

Next morning I called into the papershop to collect a magazine for my mother. The usual national dailies were spread on the counter along with the *Yorkshire Post* and *Keighley Advertiser*. The latter paper carried a front page headline complaint that pending roadworks would cause havoc in the town centre. Below a smaller headline ran 'Dan Mitchell's Closing Down'. The text stated that the firm had first started making textile machinery in 1887 and later concentrated on lathes. Orders for these had dwindled in the last few years and the present owner, Joseph Mitchell, son of Dan, now wished to retire. Sixteen men would be out of work. The reporter, who probably didn't know the difference between a lathe and a tin-opener, had concluded with the then oft-used comment 'manufacturing today has to modernise or go under, as with one local cotton mill which closed last year with the loss of 130 jobs'. I paid for the magazine and the paper.

I clocked in and went to the sales department, asking for sales figures of all radials in the last financial year, home, export and all those via the Drummond-Asquith Sales Organisation Ltd. in Birmingham. This had been established to rationalise a group of member companies into making specific types of machine, i.e. Asquiths would concentrate on drilling and boring machines, other firms would make only milling machines, still other firms would specialise in grinding machines etc. It was a very loose arrangement, particularly as all Asquith borers were also horizontal milling machines and Asquiths had later bought out Norton Grinders from the American parent company. This firm would be a constant money spinner as they also made grinding wheels used on any make of cylindrical or surface grinders and these were constantly replaced as they wore away in use. In addition Smit-Asquith machines were built for grinding diamonds. 'I need these figures for George Hoyle as soon as possible please.'

'We have them but I'll have to dig them out, can you give me an hour? Where do you work?'

'With George Hoyle.'

'Oh, right, I'll bring them up to you.'

I went up to the office and showed George the newspaper. 'I've never heard of Dan Mitchell's Lathes.'

'There'll be some skilled men and a machine shop available, why don't you tell Bob Asquith? He might be able to buy it for a song as it's shutting down.'

'Why don't you tell him yourself, he'll think you're a genius.'

'What happened when they took over Kitchen & Wade, are their machines still made?'

'No, we delivered the machines on order, since then we just use it as a machine shop and for some fitting of sub-assemblies, and we store all the foundry patterns there under cover.'

Molly rang the Asquiths secretary, asking her if I could see him for five minutes. 'Yes, go on down, now.' I grabbed the newspaper. In his office he said 'Good morning Donald, have you and George got an argument you want me to settle?'

'No, nothing like that.' Showing him the newspaper I explained. 'They'll have skilled men available and a machine shop, you might be able to use it, being only about ten miles away.'

He read the article through. 'I've never head of Dan Mitchell's'

'Neither have I or George. It might be a small place you could buy for a song.'

'That was quick thinking on your part, leave it with me and I'll let you know how we go on.'

Back up in the office I found the girl had brought the sales figures I needed. She was chatting to Molly and had left them on my desk, so she would have read my name and 'New Projects' on my door, and she had seen the 'Night Club' posh offices. All this would be common knowledge round the sales staff in no time. I looked at the sales figures and was surprised at how few O.D.2, 3 and 4 machines had sold in one whole year. I had asked for these figures because it seemed strange to me to offer an identical O.D.1 with four different arm lengths ranging from three feet six inches to six feet. Many products, particularly machine tools, have in common the fact that a large one will do everything a small one can do, but not vice versa. It had seemed sensible to me to offer only the four foot six and six foot. I promptly scrapped this idea as the chart showed sales of all four sizes to be quite robust:

Type of Radial	Qty sold last 12 months
Cunliffe & Croom small radial	54
LDR	88
Portable radial	16
'Girder' Radial	34
O.D.1 42" arm	31
O.D.1 54" arm	63
O.D.1 60" arm	51
O.D.1 72" arm	87
O.D.2 72" arm	11
O.D.3 72" arm	4
O.D.3 96" arm	1
O.D.4 96" arm	0
O.D.4 120" arm	1

The sales office, perhaps embarrassed by the last three low figures had added a note: First ever O.D.4 ordered five years ago, another three years ago and one currently on order for delivery next February. Customer for all three is Canadair, Montreal. This is an aircraft manufacturer, not an airline.

George always went to have a pint and steak pie in the pub opposite the office block with his crony John Holmes, the toolroom superintendent. Molly ate in the canteen with the Asquiths' secretary and I ate there with the two tracers. Back from lunch, Molly's phone rang. I heard the single ring as she switched the call to George (two rings for mine) and saw him pick it up. He listened, nodded, muttered something, put it down and came into my office. 'Robert thinks us two should have a break from all this grafting and have an afternoon in Keighley.'

'Doing what?'

'We're going with him to look over Dan Mitchell's.'

'Are we going in his car? I've never been in a Bentley.'

209

'It's very quiet but in winter those leather seats are cold and it's a swine to park.'

'When are we going?'

'Now, put your jacket back on.'

We went downstairs and out through the main entrance. I climbed in the back, George in the front. As we crawled out of Halifax onto the Keighley road Bob Asquith told us of his talk with Joe Mitchell. 'He seemed to jump at the idea of keeping the place going and particularly glad we might keep his workers in a job.' We soon entered back streets and he stopped the car for me to dive into a corner shop to ask directions. We found it, one more grubby back street and half way down was Mitchell's. It was built between two rows of terrace houses, their front doors opened straight onto the pavement, opposite was a continuous row of similar houses. Mitchell's frontage had a large roller shutter on which faded, peeling letters proclaimed 'Dan Mitchell, Engineers 1887'. Some kids had chalked wickets on the bottom of the shutter. Beside it another door with peeling paint bore a dull brass plate which told the neighbours it was 'Dan Mitchell. Lathe Manufacturers, est. 1887'.

We went in to find a drab brown painted corridor, in the wall a square recess. I rang the bell beside it. A sliding door opened to reveal a girl's head.

'Yes, what can I do for you?'

I told her Robert Asquith and party had an appointment with Joe Mitchell. The girl's head moved, to be replaced with an elderly man's face which announced 'Good afternoon, gentlemen, come right through.' We went into a gloomy office with two old desks, one a roll top, a phone, typewriter, an old wooden filing cabinet and Joe Mitchell wearing overalls. Bob said, 'We need to have a good look round the whole place and before we leave I hope we can agree a price so we can take over by the end of the month.'

We went through a door straight onto the shop floor. The whole place was just one long shed, grimy roof windows above tracks carrying a five ton crane which could traverse the full length of the building. Down one side were a variety of machine tools, all manned and a bench

210

with a few fitters ran down the other side. Two other fitters were starting to build one small centre lathe. Some machines were driven from a line shaft with the usual leather belts. One of their old-fashioned simple centre lathes was finished and had been painted in grey undercoat. A man was starting to apply the final grey gloss with a two inch paint brush.

'Why don't you spray them with cellulose, it's far quicker?' asked George.

'We had a look in a local car repair shop and we thought it would stink the place out, so we stick to brushing. It's good paint, from Wadsworths in Halifax.'

I asked him if he knew their salesman, Cecil Grenshaw.

'Yes, known him for years, he's Australian.'

'I used to play out with his son Christopher when I was a lad.'

Robert and Joe disappeared back into the office to talk money, George and I ambled round. The place was amazingly neat because so little production was going through at once. 'You'll notice they don't use filler, George.'

'Yes, I'd noticed, it certainly keeps the place cleaner, and quieter without the hand grinders and sparks.'

Eventually they came out of the office, all smiles. Joe said, 'The deal's done, I can retire and play some golf with my old cronies. Our office girl has already got herself a job at Woolworths.'

Bob said, 'We want everyone to stay on, we'll be building sub-assemblies, and we will feed across all the machining you can handle. We have an individual bonus system and all the overtime you can manage.' We all shook hands. 'Our lawyers will be in touch very soon.'

We piled into the car and purring back to Halifax, lolling back in luxury, I suddenly wondered what Harry Lidgett in Tripoli would think if he could see me now, or even Myers.

Robert said, 'He's happy, we're happy and it was very sharp thinking on your part, Donald, which made it happen. It will not be forgotten. Eric Northend will be happy too – sixteen skilled men recruited in one afternoon.'

I asked him, 'What happened to Ormerod Shapers in Hebden Bridge?'

This small firm had belonged to Kitchen & Wade at the time Asquiths had taken over the latter.

'We closed it down, some of their machines we moved to Kitchen & Wade, scrapped the rest and sold the town centre site at auction to some development company in Manchester, it was a very valuable site.'

As we parked at the main entrance and got out, Selby Rushworth was passing on his way home. He stared at me, walked further on and turned to stare again as I followed them indoors. He'd have a tale to spread through the jig and tool office next morning and he would have to stop calling me 'a lying sod'. I'd learnt one clear thing that afternoon. If you've got money it is not difficult to make more money and quickly too, but you have to spot the opportunity and move fast.

George and I climbed back upstairs. Molly had her coat on waiting with some letters for him to sign. 'I've started your list, it's on your desk.'

'Thanks, goodnight.' They went home and I sat to concentrate on the sales figures. The largest machines were very disappointing to put it mildly. I decided I needed some further figures for every standard machine they made to see just what else hardly sold. It was not within my present remit but cutting out dead wood was.

On Saturday afternoon I took my mother for a late lunch in Collinson's café, an up-market ever-so eatery much favoured by affluent elderly women of the area, where everything was over-priced but daintily presented. We then went to collect the suit, which fitted perfectly. I would wear this next week.

Bob Asquith collected the two Americans from Yeadon airport and George and I met them in the board room. They were booked into the White Swan hotel for the night. This was the only four-star local hotel and run by Trusthouse. It was a pricey establishment which still served full à la carte meals in a dining room staffed by mature waiters in tails, no part time school girls in this august area. There was even a gold-braided commissionaire guarding the revolving front door, highly polished brass everywhere but no match for the Uaddan in Tripoli. Being right in the town centre, very near the over-ornate town hall which some Victorian gentry decided must have a tall spire like a church, the hotel had not a single overnight parking space. Guests left their cars in the street along the hotel frontage.

Eugene (call me Gene) Speers was vice president for tool procurement, his colleague Byron (call me Ronnie) Murchison was machining superintendent. Each had a second briefcase bulging with drawings.

The four of us climbed to the nightclub, Molly was introduced, then we settled in George's office and they produced the drawings. Gene outlined what they needed to do and the tight time-scale available. 'We've just received the biggest single order for jet engines ever placed by the air force, two-thousand-four-hundred and eighty copies plus spare engines. We won this against General Electric but a condition built into the contract is that we have to sub-contract some to G.E. if we fail on delivery times. Naturally we want to avoid this. The total have to be delivered within four years. Outside Hartford is a small textile town called Manchester, one of the mills is closing down with around one hundred and fifty females available and all used to using machines. We're buying the whole mill and will set it up as a machine shop, that's where we'll need your machines shipped. Incidentally, we're not seeking other quotes at this stage. If you can come up with proposals to meet our timescale we'll order against firm prices as soon as you can supply these.'

Ronnie took over, 'This is a four year programme, six-hundred and twenty bombers with four engines on each plus spares, so we've decided to fully tool up, if necessary one machine to do just one job.' He unloaded his drawings onto George's desk. 'Every part is steel, some mild, some tough alloy steel, so we'll need coolant on every machine. Some parts are just drilled/countersunk, some drilled/countersunk and tapped, some drilled for reaming, some parts have a combination of some, or all, these operations. Our design people are working on a version of this same engine with increased thrust for a new twin-engined fighter but many of these parts will be common. The air force reckon they'll need twelve hundred, the marine corps also want a fighter bomber version and the navy want more still but with beefed up undercarriages for carrier operations. This is due in service within two years. If we get it we may re-order some of these machines with identical tooling as the orders will overlap in years 3 and 4, so can you keep the drawings?'

213

'We always keep tool drawings indefinitely, we store them in the loft over the jig and tool drawing office.'

Molly knocked and said, 'Lunch-time, gentlemen.' The four of us went across to the pub for a drink and the homemade steak and kidney pie, served with gravy, in a soup bowl. John Holmes arrived and George introduced him. During the meal the Americans praised the pie and John praised their jigborers. Gene said, 'We're hoping you can get the first finished machines ready for shipping in four to five months with the total ready in eight months.'

George lowered his knife and fork, 'Four to five months is totally impossible, believe me. We'll have to pull out all the stops to produce the first in eight months. We are already overloaded, we can't get skilled men for love nor money, we always have around thirty apprentices under training for five years, as soon as they could be of some use to us the government whips them away for military service. Donald's only been back a few weeks. It's a vicious circle and we have to tolerate idiotic government ministers telling us we must invest and modernise.'

We went back up to the office and ploughed through more of their components, by half past five we had completed 29. So far this totalled 17 standard Cunliffe radials, 9 used the standard vertical drill with the rise and fall table and 3 O.D.1 42 inch radials, each with its own unique tooling. Some jigs would need foolproofing so the part could only be placed in position in one specific way, other symmetrical parts didn't need this feature.

George and Molly left, they would drop the Americans at the White Swan hotel. I decided to carry on alone so we could be well ahead next morning. I opened the window in each office to try and get rid of the cigar smoke. The remaining drawings, as with the previous ones would be all standard machines and special tools. I began to jot down my conclusions, and the more I thought about it the stranger it became. Gene was vice president of a huge American company, right up next to the president. Why do a six thousand miles round trip when Ronnie could have done it on his own? Surely no buyer would ever say 'We are not looking for competitive quotes'? To ask for first deliveries in four and a half months for special purpose machine tools was ridiculous, yet they had continued the process when George insisted it couldn't possibly be less than eight months. The story about the fighter engine might be just a red herring to urge us to greater efforts – having missed out on the bomber engine General Electric would fight tooth and nail to get the fighter. Another point that stood out was that Ron Murchison would know full well that apart from the tapping, all these holes could be done on a battered old bench drill in a back street garage. They could have even contacted their own retired machinists around Hartford, provided them with a machine, new or old, from any tool dealer, and got them sub-contracting. Surely there were enough tool making firms around Connecticut to make the simple drill jigs. I put out the desk lamp, locked up and went home.

On the bus I realised that four minds had been applied to the problem yet Ronnie and I had done most of the talking. George had contributed very little but gradually filled his ashtray, whilst Gene, after his initial speech, had simply filled the room with cigar smoke.

When I arrived next morning Molly was standing with her back against the wall behind her chair and looking a bit worried. 'What's up?'

'There's a bird in your office, you left the windows open.' I went in, so the bird flew into George's office. I asked Molly to open the door and moved into George's office whereupon the bird shot through the door and disappeared. Molly shut the door, I shut the windows.

The Americans came back in with George and we went through the remainder of the drawings. George said, 'We'll get our tool estimator straight on to this and a quote in the post as fast as possible.

The brothers took them for a slap-up lunch in the White Swan, George went to the pub and en route to the canteen Molly asked, 'How's it going?'

'Finished, thank God.'

In the afternoon the brothers, George and I took them for a brief tour of the works. They were impressed by the 50 ton cranes and the huge castings and as we neared the filling and fettling area I took Gene across and pointed out that if we didn't put filler on their machines it would speed up delivery, particularly as the stuff had to harden overnight and it was applied to every single casting on each machine.

215

'What is it for? Is it anything to do with the function of the machine?'

'Not at all, it just provides a smooth base for spray painting.'

'If it speeds the job up, leave it off ours. We need drilling machines, not works of art.' Eventually we came to the toolroom, always a must for visitors, where they met John Holmes once again, this time wearing his white smock, and it was here they saw 'their' jigborers. Ronnie said, 'We use around a dozen of our own jigborers on production work, particularly on accurate milling of some jet engine parts.'

We then went to the board room where Olive, the brothers' secretary, delivered coffees. Robert said, 'You'll get the airmail quote as soon as we possibly can. We'll do our very best to get the first machines into Liverpool docks in eight months.' Outside we all shook hands and Gene said, 'If you're ever near Connecticut look us up, be glad to show you around our machine shops.' Dick then purred them away to Yeadon Airport.

Back in the office I added the final conclusion to my report – strange for a top buyer not to ask for some price reduction for not using the filler. First thing next morning I asked Molly to type four copies.

Next morning Dick rang for us to go down and give them a de-briefing. George ran through all we had done, stressing that we would need standard machines throughout, just the tooling was special, and very simple drill jigs too. Robert asked me, 'What was that all about in the fettling area when you were talking to Gene?'

'I told him it would save time if we just sprayed grey cellulose, he agreed and said they wanted drilling machines, not works of art. You may remember they didn't use filler in Keighley.'

Robert said, 'Mention of Keighley reminds me of something – are you still quite happy doing this job, Donald?'

'Yes, it's getting more interesting every day.'

'Right, ignoring that promise we made of a pay review after six months, which we shall of course honour, Dick and I have decided that your pay should be increased immediately to twice draftsman's rate, effective this week. That is for your quick thinking about Keighley.'

'Thank you very much indeed.'

Dick said, 'There's another point Donald, when I brought those

Americans upstairs the board on your door said you were a graduate. You are now in a management job and therefore should be an associate member, Robert and I are full members and will sponsor you. I'll get that organised.'

'Once again, thanks very much indeed. I've come to some weird conclusions about this visit.' I gave them a copy each and there was intense silence for a while, pipe and cigar glowing. George whispered, 'A pound says they won't agree to fifty per cent.'

'Right, you're on.'

Robert was the first one to speak, 'It is a bit unusual, in fact it is very unusual.'

George said, 'I didn't think of any of this, my mind was bogged down with drill jigs.'

Robert continued, 'My final conclusion is that we are simply helping them out and this will cause us a great deal of inconvenience. We don't know yet whether Cunliffes can cope with the overload, even our sales department will have to write to fifty odd customers to delay their deliveries of standard machines, perhaps by two months or more. I think, therefore, that we should add fifty per cent to all the machine prices and one hundred per cent to every tool.'

George gasped, with a look of horror, 'Christ!' Dick said, 'This business of our helping them out reminds me of some years back when we paid right through the nose to get a 50 ton crane mended over the weekend. I remember we had to pay double, double time for six or eight fitters to work in relays through Friday and Saturday night but by Sunday afternoon the crane was running again. We'd to pay air fares from Belfast and accommodation down town. It was a horrendous price, but the crane firm dropped everything to help us out. I'm beginning to think he's right. Lets gamble. If we don't get the order it'll save us a lot of inconvenience. I think, Donald, you've read the situation precisely.'

Robert just grinned. 'I well remember that crane, I think we should go ahead but lets go to sixty per cent on the machines, gives us more margin to haggle. We taught you jig and tool design, seems like you are becoming quite a business man.'

217

George, still in shock said, 'He's got a right devious mind, comes from mixing with Arabs.' He passed me a pound note.

George and I went back upstairs and I slumped in a chair in George's office.

'I'm knackered, that was the hardest concentrated thinking I have ever done, two days solid.'

'I'm knackered too, just trying to keep up with you.' Molly brought him two letters to sign. 'Have they gone?'

'Yes, back to America. I can't wait to see the end result of all this – it totals 19 vertical drills, 33 Cunliffe radials and 4 O.D.1s.'

The changes were tearing apart the best thinking of the old chief draftsman in 1935. Times change, costs escalate; there would have to be changes and quickly too. It mattered little to me just what the changes were so long as they provided a manufacturing improvement and delivered cost savings.

'We are supposed to be bouncing ideas off each other, when do I get to hear your ideas?'

'So far I'm still absorbing yours and I haven't got your imagination.' He seemed to find this amusing.

When Molly brought my next pay packet it showed just over £43 but still no tax taken off. Once tax was deducted I could reduce the overtime. I suddenly realised that the crafty Yorkshire brothers had made any move on my part to their shop floor pointless as I could never make the same pay, in fact nowhere near it. I could now only move down south which I certainly didn't want to do.

My daily life became ever more hectic. I was working in a rare situation, in reality working alone but with the direct backing of the three most powerful men in the company. The mere mention of 'George Hoyle needs ...' got me instant co-operation. All I had to do from this was find and prove some cost saving. I was going rapidly up the learning curve, learning to deal with people as I learnt from them. It was a path that could lead to pitfalls but I was not to know that until later. I was deep in the most concentrated thinking process I had ever known, far harder than swotting for exams, yet I was enjoying it.

On the Saturday morning I left at 10 am, caught the bus downtown to the estate agent's office of Crossley, Crosland and Uttley. This was the firm to which my mother paid our rent every week. I asked if they had a much better house to rent, anywhere near Asquiths. 'We have a very nice two bedroom terrace at Newstead, small garden at front and back with a bathroom. It's just come empty a week ago but it's 18 shillings a week paid four weeks in advance. The last tenants have just emigrated to Australia so there is a lot of stuff left in the house.' I took the keys, promising that if my mother was happy with it she would call in with a month's rent on Monday morning and agreed further payments every fourth Friday.

I went with my mother in the afternoon, finding it exactly as described. Number 17 Newstead Terrace was off Gibbet Street, in a pleasant area of parallel streets spaced well apart. There were three steps up to a small, lawned front garden, a larger one at the back with a clothes post, a small stone shed at the back wall which had a recess outside with a dustbin. Three cellars were under the house, each with electric light. There was a gas cooker and surprisingly an 'Ada' washing machine. A carpet square and three piece suite had been left in the lounge along with lampshades and curtains in every room.

The rear windows looked out onto some allotments, beyond these the huge assembly shed of Butler Machine Tools, but well away from the terrace. Three closely spaced bus stops up Gibbet Street would get me to work in five minutes if raining, or I could walk it if fine. One short bus ride would get my mother down Gibbet Street to the junction with Queen's Road and masses of shops including a Co-op and an 'Economic Stores'.

Beside the front door was a coal grate. The door badly needed a coat of paint and had a small oval stained glass window. The lounge had a modern tiled fireplace, the rear kitchen had a huge iron range with oven one side, water boiler the other and the usual crane for a kettle. The bathroom had a white enamelled bath with stains below each tap, toilet and washbasin with mirror above.

At work Molly got me the estate agents on the phone. 'The house is fine, can I re-paint the front door, and could I post you a cheque every fourth Thursday?'

'You can do any painting and decorating you like but don't do any structural alterations. With your mother's record of paying rent, she's never missed for years, a cheque will be fine, we'll post the marked book back to you each time.'

Molly then got me Hamilton Bell's Removals. The earliest time I could get a truck would be Wednesday and yes, Keith would be the driver, I could pay him and he would give me a receipt.

I told George I needed the day off. 'Right, some problem?'

'Moving house to Newstead Terrace.'

'The Queen's Road shops'll be handy and you can walk to work.'

In the evening I went next door to see Mrs Holdsworth. 'Do you still have an instruction book for your Ada washer?' She got it and I told her about the pending move.

'It's Ronnie's day off on Wednesday, I'll get him to help you. You must keep in touch, your mother's always welcome.'

Wednesday came and I heard the truck rattle on the cobbles, a blast on the horn and Keith appeared dragging two old tea chests full of newspapers. Ronnie came and four of us wrapped crockery. We were soon loaded. 'Keith, have you any coal sacks on the truck?'

'No, we can use a rolled up tarpaulin.' Next to last we loaded my little bench with the vice, then the coal and wood. Ronnie and I climbed into the back of the truck, Keith latched the tailboard and my mother rode in the cab with him for the brief ride uptown. All was unloaded by 11.30. My mother put the kettle on the gas ring in the kitchen, I walked into Gibbet Street and we all had our first meal in the new home – fish and chips and a buttered teacake each. I thanked Ronnie, paid Keith and promised to find him in Friendly Club for a drink on Saturday night. He left, to drop Ronnie at home. I got both fires lit, then went to talk to the elderly couple next door, who had watched our activity from their window. I explained that I was working at Asquith's and I had no father.

'I was a moulder in Modern Foundries for thirty six years. If you're working overtime you won't have time to run your allotment.'

'What allotment?'

'Each house has one at the back, if you don't use yours I'd like to use some of it.'

'You're welcome, my mother will probably want to grow just a few flowers.'

'Being on't pension I grow as many vegetables as I can, there'll be plenty for your mother.'

'I need to order some coal.'

'He's due next week, get the best as the other stuff is rubbish. There's a wet fish man calls Friday mornings and a greengrocer who sells mucky eggs straight from t'farm Wednesday. There's a rag and bone man comes on here once a flood, he sells bags of horse manure and firewood. There's loads of shops on Queen's Road. If you ever need owt shifting my son has a Morris van.'

I tried both new keys, then my mother got a surprise as we explored the allotment. It had a very small greenhouse with a lean-to shed, inside a rusty spade and even rustier lawnmower. A few good kicks and some oil should get this working again.

Next morning I told Molly and George of the successful move 'and I get an allotment at the back of the house with a view of Butler's too.'

On Friday, after lunch, Molly came with my pay packet, surprisingly followed by the two brothers, who stopped at George's desk. Robert waved me in as he passed George some papers. George read through them, his only comment, 'Bloody hell!' as he passed them to me. Both Asquiths were grinning. It was an order from Pratt & Witney and appeared to be an exact copy of our quote, each machine and its tooling priced, finally one basic machine of each type without tools, every machine to be fitted with coolant equipment. Total price £53,821 sterling f.o.b Liverpool. I asked, 'What's f.o.b. mean?'

'It means we pay delivery into Liverpool docks, the Yanks organise and pay for the onward shipping.'

'Is that what we quoted?'

Dick replied 'The exact figure, they've never queried the price. Donald, I think you should take up poker, you'd be rather good at it.' The letter attached, from Eugene, said their surveyors had insisted the second floor of the Manchester mill would have to be reinforced from below so they could not move machines into the ground floor for some time. Delivery of the first machines in ten months with completion in twelve months would seem more sensible and he hoped this would be of some help. 'Nice letter from a practical bloke, it will be useful but we'll still have to pull all the stops out!'

On two occasions I found possible cost savings quite unrelated to the precise task I had been set. The first came about through once again having to dodge the Pickford's low-loader crawling in reverse along the loading bay. I walked to the end of the bay, where the truck was now parked, the driver leaning against the front mudguard enjoying his pipe, his mate sitting on the trailer swinging his legs.

'Hell of a truck you've got.'

'Aye, very powerful. As usual we're stuck waiting for t'crane.'

'Spend a lot of time waiting?'

'Regular, same at foundry, much rather be on long distance up to Glasgow.'

'Right, I better be off, my boss doesn't believe in waiting, be good.'

Back in the office I wondered what best to do. If Asquiths bought their own they could use it seven days a week and also for dock runs when available. It might be worth looking into so I made a note of it.

The second thing was very simple and would cost nothing. The idea was prompted by casually browsing through an instruction manual for a drill-sharpening grinder made in north Wales by a firm called Z. Brierley. This book carried various sectioned views but the usual diagonal section lines were omitted. I thought back to the RAF servicing manuals in the hangar in Tripoli, they had many sectional views of cut away engines but again no section lines. Instead in both books each sketch was clearly entitled 'Section A-B' etc. With nearly 80 draftsmen here plus tracers, a few more in Colne and more still in Nortons the time saved by dropping this habit must add up considerably over a year. I made a note and then traced a small component section of an O.D.1 part, with section lines, then repeated it without section lines on a separate piece of paper, but both entitled 'Section A-B'. Just for fun I showed them both to George but he couldn't spot the difference. I explained that you didn't really need the section lines, the title underneath told you it was a sectional view and omitting all these lines would save endless drawing office and tracing time. He said, 'Let's try it on that bright bugger Johnson.' Johnson's reaction was, 'Is this one of those kids' trick questions?' He couldn't spot the difference but his section leader did, immediately. George instructed, 'From now on stop scribbling all these daft lines and you'll save a hell of a lot of drawing office time. Tell Jack Ridley to do the same.' He picked up Johnson's phone and got through to Norton Grinders. Eventually he said, 'Nortons work to the original American drawings, special tooling they get done out by a contract design office in Birmingham, so we can forget them.'

On Saturday afternoon I went downtown to a second-hand furniture shop by North Bridge, the beginning of the road leading out to Leeds and Bradford. He hadn't a rocking chair but I found two old, scratched bentwood chairs and for £1 the shopkeeper agreed to deliver when he closed at 6 pm. We would keep them in the greenhouse for my mother to sit outside in the sunshine. She could sit reading a magazine lulled by the nearby melody of Butler's trundling cranes. I carried on clearing up the allotment, adding dead stuff to the existing compost heap. In the middle of tea the chap arrived with the chairs and I explained why I had got them. I put them in the greenhouse and went back to finish tea.

After a shave and a bath I walked on Queen's Road to catch a bus to 'Friendly Working Men's Club' for a few pints with Keith. He said he had two mates who drank Saturdays 'down t'Foot in t'Weavers Arms'. Next Saturday we could meet at the club a bit earlier, have a pint then go down there. They had a pianist who also played an accordion.

'Down t'Foot' meant the next village along the main road out of Halifax to Burnley. Its unusual, but quite logical name Luddenden Foot came from its location at the foot of the side valley where the river Ludd (merely a stream) joined the river Calder. A mile up this valley was the far older but much smaller compact village of Luddenden. With an extra 'L' in front it could be a Welsh name.

On the Sunday I wrote to cancel my subscription to *Production Engineer*, asking for a refund, there was no point in buying it as George had a variety of such books delivered each month. I had been deliber- ately changing five pound notes and now gave my mother a reserve of twenty one-pound notes. 'Where can you keep this hidden? Tell me whenever it drops to ten pounds and I'll top it up, that way you've always cash for shopping or anything else.'

'I know, I'll keep it in the little drawer in the sewing machine, no burglar would look there.'

Monday morning Molly brought me a white envelope containing a stiff card printed in gilt – an invitation to bring a guest to the Asquith Senior Staff Christmas Dinner at the White Swan Hotel, Black Tie. George came in holding his card. 'Seems to come round quicker every year. Have you got a dinner jacket?'

'No.'

'Don't think of buying one, you can hire them at Sam Stocks. Get a single breasted one, not tails, those are for waiters, and get a tie on an elastic band, the elastic slips under your collar. The ones you have to tie yourself are a menace. White shirt, black shoes. Nip into Stocks this Saturday afternoon, they'll measure you and reserve a suit for you.'

'Right, thanks George. By the way, what does all this cost?'

'No idea, under a tenner for certain, take this card with you.'

Saturday came, I flashed the card in the shop, was measured carefully, again measured and all was duly noted on an order form. He ticked 'single breasted' as I mentioned the elastic tie. 'I would recommend the latest version sir.' From a glass fronted cabinet he brought one with metal clips behind it. 'Very strong spring clips, simply snaps behind the collar wings. It sits a little lower on your neck so your chin is not rubbing on it and it's not disturbed when you move your head.'

I tried the clips, admiring the powerful buried springs. 'Right, how much is the tie?'

'It comes with the suit sir, the hire charge is seven pounds.' I tried to pay him and he said 'No, sir, pay when you collect the suit. It will be ready on the Friday before. Could I suggest a new white shirt to go with the suit?' He produced a luxury package. 'Van Heusen, finest London tailoring.' Once again he went through the measuring process. He was just as thorough as the men on our shop floor, always double check! He found the right size and just as he was about to open the package I stopped him.

'How much are these?

'Seven guineas sir'.

Hiding the shock I said, 'Fine, let's have a look.'

Once out of the elaborate packaging, he pointed to the immaculate collar. 'That retains the stiffness through repeated washing. May I suggest your wife washes and irons it before wearing – gets rid of the packing creases and it's more comfortable. Always best with a new shirt.'

'These cuffs look too long, why no buttons?

'They fold back and you secure them with cuff links.' He demonstrated how all four slots were aligned.

'Right I'll have it, I've got some cuff links.' I paid and he opened the door. 'Good afternoon sir, I look forward to seeing you again.'

All this time an elderly man had been trying on bowlers, trilbys, sporting flat caps and was still at it, another assistant hovering round him. A third, younger, assistant leaned on a counter staring at two young women walking past the windows.

I got a bus home, still in a state of shock, and announced 'I've got a new shirt.' Together we examined the box. Below the celluloid window was a printed coat of arms with the fine print 'By appointment, shirt makers to H.R.H. The Duke of Edinburgh'. Below this a more flamboyant crest with the discreet wording 'By appointment, shirt makers to H.R.H. Prince Rainier of Monaco'. Below this 'Bespoke Shirt Manufacturers'. The end of the lid showed the neck size and proclaimed 'Finest London Tailoring'. We spread it out on my bed. My mother said, 'Careful of the pins, they hide them all over, I'll wash it for you, my, how white!'

I showed her the long cuffs. 'I'll use the cuff links I got with my demob suit.'

The daylight was really diminishing as the days sped by to Christmas. Icy blasts from Keighley Moor brought horizontal hail, occasional rain, the weather hardened and we got the usual winter frosts, then it softened to bring fog and snow. I was going back and forth on the bus now in the demob raincoat, gloves and scarf. It was barely light when I left home and dark long before I returned. There was nothing to do in our garden or the allotment, the ground rock hard, but one Sunday I saw the old man, well wrapped up, turning over his compost as steam rose from the rotting pile. He later crossed over to turn my pile, releasing more steam.

I got my black shoes from the wardrobe, the rubber heels were wearing away so I asked my mother to drop them into the cobblers shop on Queen's Road, 'Ask him just to fit new rubber heels.'

'What's all the shiny bits stuck on the bottom?'

'Steel swarf, pick it up from the shop floor at work.'

The vital Saturday came, I took my mother for a late lunch at Collinson's Café, then went to Stocks to collect the suit. The same rotund man waddled to meet us. 'Mr Ainley, I remember, dinner suit hire, I'll get it. There's a dressing room behind that curtain, do try it on.'

He passed the suit on the highly polished beech hanger. It seemed to fit perfectly but he was not satisfied. 'Trousers just hanging a shade low, if you'll remove the jacket I'll adjust the braces.' He fiddled around and finally announced 'Just right.' I paid and said. 'This is my mother, I'll be at work Monday morning so she will return them.' As he lowered the suit into a large paper bag clearly printed on both sides 'Sam Stocks, Bespoke Tailors' he passed me a black bow tie. I checked the spring clips and put it in his small paper bag, then into my jacket pocket. He held open the shop door for my mother, saying he knew the head waiter in the Swan. 'Asquith's is the most posh of all their winter functions, no expense spared, you'll look as smart as anyone there, sir. I know you'll enjoy it. Goodbye, Mrs Ainley.'

Back home I polished yet again the already shining and repaired shoes, had a bath then dressed. Against the total blackness of shoes, socks, suit and tie the spotless shirt was a pristine white. Looking me over my mother said, 'The last time I saw men wearing dinner suits was in Canada, The Bullocks always wore them every evening, winter and summer, with red cummerbunds round their waist. This "do" must be for bosses, I thought you worked in the drawing office.'

'No, I work for the Chief Engineer, but I have my own drawing board in my own office and I share his beautiful secretary.'

'I've wondered why you're always awash with money. At least your collars don't get black now. I used to have a devil of a time scrubbing them when you were an apprentice.'

The dressing table mirror was no use, so I stood on a chair, but still no good. I went next door. 'Have you got a full length mirror anywhere?'

'Come in out o't'cold, by gum you do look rich. Mavis, look who's come.'

She rose from her rocking chair, 'By gum, you are posh tonight. Take him upstairs, we've one fastened on t'wardrobe door.' We climbed up and he switched on the overhead light, then both bedside lamps. I looked at myself from all angles as he said, 'Looks very good from the back an'all.' I looked like a penguin. We went downstairs. 'I'm going to Asquith's Christmas Dinner, got to dash as a bloke is giving me a lift.'

'Is it in t'canteen? Don't wake us up when you come back drunk.'

'No, the White Swan. I won't. Thanks for the mirror, good night.' Back indoors I grabbed some loose change and two white fivers, my raincoat and told my mother not to wait up, I might be late, and I had my key.

The card said 7.00 for 7.30. I was waiting in Gibbet Street by 6.45 pm. George pulled up within minutes and as he braked he skidded the last few inches. Being a bus route the street had been salted but was still treacherous.

I climbed in beside George, Molly and her husband were in the back. 'Thanks for the lift.' Molly introduced Eric. Outside the hotel were two red Bentleys, beside each a loose sign on a pole said 'Reserved'. We piled out to leave George to find a parking space, went through the revolving door into the warmth to wait for him. Our coats and Molly's curious long cape with a huge collar were dumped with the cloakroom attendant and we followed signs to a very sumptuous room with two chandeliers. Plaster cherubs watched us from each corner of the ornate ceiling. Five circular tables were laid for dinner, sparkling glasses, gleaming cutlery, cleverly folded white linen napkins surrounded a large central vase of flowers. Lighted candles were spaced around the flowers. A simple but very large Christmas decoration hung on each wall. In one corner, on a raised dais, three men were arranging their seats and instruments; they switched on small lights above each music stand and went out. Along one side wall was first a table with a huge glass bowl, with floating slices of orange and lemon. George nudged us towards this and the hovering waiter ladled some into a glass. 'Punch, that'll warm us up. Donald, this stuff is liquid dynamite, just sip it, don't gulp it like a pint.' Next, also with a waiter on guard, was a long sideboard loaded with bottles of spirits, in the centre, propped on a bed of holly, a hand printed card advised that 'the Manager and staff of the White Swan Hotel wished the guests from Wm. Asquith Ltd a Merry Christmas and happy and prosperous new year.'

Further along was a large Christmas tree with coloured lights. We ambled around, meeting strangers and eventually reached the brothers, of the two ladies with them I recognised their secretary. Dick introduced his wife to Eric and me. 'Do you remember Donald?'

She peered at me 'Can't say I do, should I?'

'He delivered our *Evening Courier* when he was a schoolboy.'

'You daft thing, how could I remember, he's a grown man now!'

We ambled around the room and looked at the printed menu on an easel. John Holmes joined us, introducing his wife, Alice. The menu showed a starter choice of two different soups or melon fan, then paté with toast, traditional full Christmas Dinner, rich Christmas pudding with brandy sauce, followed by mince pies, coffee with petit fours and a liqueur. We were also informed that with the main course red or white wine was available, both the wines with very long-winded French names and specially selected from a 1950 vintage. I whispered to Molly 'What's this French paté stuff?'

'I think it's made in Belgium, you just spread it on the toast. It's very rich and tastes of liver – you'll love it!' We moved around the tables, our chance to find our names on the place cards. Beside each woman's name was a beautifully wrapped present. I saw that Molly, Eric, George and I were to sit with John Holmes and his wife. That was a nice thought on someone's part.

We came to the Company Secretary with his wife. He said to me 'You spend all your time saving money, but this is the one night in the year when Asquiths lash out spending it!'

At some point I got talking to the brothers' elderly secretary. 'You must have been to lots of these "do's".'

'Oh yes, I remember the first, well before the war, when William was alive. He started these and he had a huge photograph propped up against that wall. Hugh Greaves had made it and stuck it onto a plywood sheet. When William rose he toasted the King, the Company and the photo of the new boring machine, the biggest they had ever made. It's that photo hanging in the board room. Of course there were far fewer of us here then.'

Eventually the head waiter banged a gong. 'Ladies and Gentlemen, will you now take your places please.' Frock coated waiters scurried round offering wine. Robert rose, we all followed. 'Welcome everyone, please raise your glasses to the Queen, the Country and the Company'. He got muttered responses, all slurped and sat down, when waiters again swung into action.

We gradually got through a sumptuous meal. Looking round the room I realised Molly, Eric and I were by far the youngest present, even most of the waiters were much older. This pleasant atmosphere, amongst civilised people, cocooned from the raw winter night reminded me of the last day at school, but there were no cries of delight from a hundred teenagers in this room.

I wondered what Harry Lidgett in Tripoli would have thought if he had poked his head in the door and seen me in all this luxury. In Ripon Cyril Washburn, smooth as ever, would no doubt have taken all this in his stride, he had a dinner suit of his own.

We ploughed our way through the rich Christmas pudding. The flock of waiters had never stopped. There was a break before coffee was served so people moved around to chat to others, for some perhaps the only time they met in the whole year. George said to me, 'Who's that chap on the next table, next to the woman in blue?'

'Don't know, lets ask him.'

We ambled across. 'Hello, I don't know your face, I'm George Hoyle, Chief Engineer. This is Donald Ainley, he works for me on new projects.'

He stood to shake hands. He was Ed Wilkinson, the General Manager at Colne, that was why we'd never met. 'We've 4 inches of snow still on the side roads over there, so we came earlier by train. Didn't fancy getting stuck. We're booked in here for the night. There is more snow forecast.'

The waiters were now serving coffee and pouring some liqueur into glasses the size of egg cups. They were delivering warm mince pies piled high on silver salvers and plates with small squares of cheese on cocktail sticks. This wasn't the sort of place where you got one pie each. I sipped the hot coffee and had a mouthful of mince pie as a hand fell on my shoulder. It was Dick, Robert with him. 'A word in private, Donald.' I gulped the mince pie and walked over to a quiet spot by the tree. 'Your six months probation is up in a few days, we've decided to up your pay to 3 times that of draftsmen. You'll get the first rise just in time for Christmas. Don't tell anyone, although George already knows.'

'Thank you both very much, that's a great Christmas present.'

'You're doing a damned good job.' They returned to their table as I spotted a clean knife on the side table. Using it as a mirror I could see that the bow tie had never moved. I had asked Molly earlier on but she said it was perfect. Back at the table she opened her present – a fine gold necklace chain. 'I got some tiny earrings last year, this will match them perfectly.' George produced his wallet and slid a white fiver under his saucer. 'That tip's from all of us on this table.'

The three musicians stopped to considerable applause, even the waiters clapped. They had played smooth mood music right through the meal, except for a short break, although few had danced. One, alternating on saxophone and clarinet, had done a few solos including tunes from the Glenn Miller film score. A waiter switched half the chandelier bulbs back on. He'd switched them off along with half of each double wall light as we started the first course, which made the candles and the tree lights seem brighter. Presents were carefully gathered and people started to drift towards the cloakroom girl.

Eventually, hands were shaken with many exchanges of 'Happy Christmas', 'all the best', 'see you next year'. Ed Wilkinson said they would have a nightcap in the cocktail bar before going up. Our little crew walked the one block to George's car. He pulled the damp corrugated cardboard from under the windscreen wipers, rooting in the glove box he passed me a shaped piece of wood. 'Will you scrape the back window?' He dropped me off at the end of Newstead Terrace.

'Good night all, thanks for the lift, see you on Monday. See you next year, Eric.'

I found my mother still up, nodding in front of the nearly dead fire. 'Did you have a good time? Do you want a sandwich?'

'Marvellous, I'm full up, just some tea please.'

I sat smoking and sipping tea, staring alone into the fire, the house and the whole terrace silent, occasionally a faint glow showed amongst the ash as a slight down-draft stirred in the chimney. I thought back through that wonderful evening, my first sight of how the other half lived. I wondered how long it would take me to save up for a Bentley, mine would be sprayed metallic grey, no better still, black up to waist level, with metallic grey roof. I had moved from 63 shillings to £48 per week in just six months, plus increased overtime pay as well. On that pleasant thought I went to bed. Of those present on that wonderful evening none would imagine that a perfectly natural event would occur in the months ahead which would lead to a cascade of disasters for the company as we knew it, which in turn would make this the penultimate dinner dance.

On Sunday morning I checked all the pockets and carefully repacked the dinner suit, putting the tie in an inside pocket.

Immediately before the Christmas break (in Halifax in those days only banks had a New Year's Day holiday) we had another prolonged session with the brothers. The suggestions I made included an extensive re-work of the Cunliffe radial and the already approved O.D.1 changes (except the coupling drive) extended to the O.D.2 and 3 radials. This was readily agreed, as was the provision of a calculator for each draftsman as they could see a quite rapid payback time.

They were surprised when I told them the use of the Pickfords low-loader, available for only the first three days of each week, was costing £105 per day. They got a greater shock when I suggested buying our own to use every day in the week. Robert's quick response was, 'My God, around £15,000 per year, we'll look into this immediately.'

Prompted by the Americans' visit, my suggestion to do away with the filler on every machine prolonged this session, as did the built-in problem of what to do with the men who would be out of a job. All I could think of was re-training them. As a result the four of us went on a careful tour of the full length of the longest heavy machining bay in the works. It was the only one where cranes were needed at both ends for unloading trucks, neither end could be extended as the Pickfords loading bay was built on to the main office block and the roller shutter at the other end opened directly onto the public road, without footpaths, known as Bob Lane. I was once told that its earlier name was Bobbin Lane when it was still a dirt road, long before William Asquith returned from California.

In this bay waiting for a crane was the order of the day, yet installing a third crane would merely restrict the travel of the two existing cranes, each of which could lift 25 tons. Space was at a premium and each gap between the huge machines was used for temporarily dumping castings, sometimes two deep. It was only the crane driver's care and the slinger's skill which avoided any accident in this overloaded shambles. The problem was further exacerbated as the full length of aisle needed to be kept clear as it was a through route for the Lister petrol-driven tugs and hand pallet carts moving boxes of small parts around the whole works. My doing away with the filling process would help but slightly as it would free up space concentrated only at the Bob Lane end, and would mean less use of one crane only.

The result back in the board room was (a) they agreed to do away with filler and change to the metallic grey cellulose, even though it cost four times the normal grey, as they knew how attractive it could look on exhibition machines. (b) The lack of space needed further thought by everyone. (c) The idea of re-training their own men would be explored fully, the two brothers would deal with the men and the union, meanwhile not a word to anyone.

George finally mentioned doing away with section lines on drawings. It had been entirely my idea and he'd already actioned this to save hours of drawing office time. Naturally he added that Johnson and Ridley should have done this years ago. It had been the longest session so far.

Over a period we had decided to stop producing the largest radial drills, both key seaters and the horizontal plain milling machine. The sales performance for the latter was hopeless – one recently dispatched to a mine maintenance facility in Sierra Leone was the only one ordered since a batch of twenty built for the Ministry of Supply during the war! There was massive competition world wide for this type of machine, the basic concept of which dated from perhaps 1895. In any shop which cuts key blanks you will find a very simple light milling machine using a shaped cutter with multiple teeth to produce a profile.

We needed to build up the portfolio and look to the future, and for weeks I had been doodling with the idea of Asquiths making a low-cost limited jig borer for smallish components. The idea sprang from the Americans' comment that Pratt & Whitney used around 12 of their own jig borers on routine production work, producing precision jet engine parts including the light milling of accurate contours.

The essential feature of any jig borer was precise control of both sideways and rearward table motions and spindle depth position to within .0001 of an inch. To ensure prolonged accuracy they were operated in rooms where the ambient temperature was maintained at 62°F. Main castings were left to mature naturally for up to twelve months to allow cooling stresses to dissipate gradually throughout the metal. Thin portions cool more quickly than thick and the difference could even cause cracking in extreme cases, thus this was avoided in the careful design.

Very few firms specialised in making these machines, the best known, and the originator in 1921, was Societie Genevoise S.A. who first developed miniature versions for the Swiss watch industry. A lesser-known Swiss firm, Henri Hauser et Cie later made larger versions. The German firm Deckel made an equivalent type with a highly complex swivel-any-whichway table to hold the workpiece, but mainly intended for tool-room milling operations. In the UK the sole manufacturer was the Newall Co. in Peterborough who used a totally different measuring system from the others, it was cheaper but it worked perfectly albeit slower to set up. North Americans would use Pratt & Witney machines. The market had to endure extremely long delivery dates and very high prices.

The repeated doodles, sometimes even at home, began to evolve into firm ideas. Using as many standard Asquith parts as possible, I settled on a new-version O.D.1 with a four foot six arm and twelve speeds, which provided twenty-four power feeds to the spindle. Drilling can

233

tolerate a coarse feed, boring needs a fine feed to remove just a slight ribbon of steel to reach the final size in a pre-drilled hole.

A split, lockable bracket could be bolted to the end of the arm, an identical one bolted to the extreme end of the baseplate. These secured a ground steel tubular tie bar to prevent any swing motion of the arm, which therefore could only rise to accommodate high workpieces. A standard box table would be fitted on the baseplate.

I abandoned the idea of vertical spindle control to within .0001 of an inch as it would mean involved and expensive changes to the slide – the two-axis motion of the special sub-table would suffice. There was an odd spin-off from the whole arrangement – by releasing the tube tiebar from the baseplate, raising it and locking it to the arm and then removing the boring table meant that the machine reverted to a normal radial drill. It was not intentional, it just happened. It might just be a sales gimmick, but it did provide versatility.

So far around 80 per cent of the machine was standard parts already in production which sold well and would therefore continue. Only the tube, brackets and boring table would be special. I was going far beyond my original remit and decided to stop to discuss it with George. I showed him the sketches and explained what I was aiming at and why, stressing the use of standard components.

He listened carefully and studied the sketches. To my surprise he said, 'It's an unusual approach but you might have discovered a niche in the market. We must study the market ahead and customers' future needs, and target our products in that direction. It could be a world first, the industry will be amazed and so will the brothers.'

'I've been thinking that we could get the first table made by John Holmes, then install one in our own toolroom for testing, do all the minor simple jobs on it. If it's OK, once we we've tooled up to make the table parts perhaps it could be made in Keighley or Tierney Street.'

The result was a boardroom session at which George backed me up enthusiastically. He must have given it some thought overnight. When the brothers had digested the whole idea Robert commented, 'We must constantly study the market ahead and the idea of re-arranging standard items is clever and must be profitable. I think we should install two in the toolroom, they'd be useful as demonstrators. We'd just need to extend the airlock. If you draw the exact table details we can cost the whole machine before we cut any metal. Do it in your overtime so as not to interrupt the other work.'

George's final contribution was, 'Perhaps we should offer two or three sizes of boring bar with it, we always make our own but customers who can't will have to buy them somewhere.'

'Good idea, the whole thing could be an eye-opener for the industry.' Naturally George's response was, 'For Johnson too!'

There followed some enjoyable time on the drafting machine, in peace and quiet. The drum micrometers and length bars, ground and lapped to exact lengths of .5000, 1.0000, 2.0000 inches etc. were standard items made by various micrometer firms and there were of course metric equivalents. They had been available for years and regularly used in our gauge room. The simple yet very accurate drum was engraved on its outside rim with 200 divisions, the buried 50 fine threads per inch provided the .0001-inch reading on the fixed housing. This was fastened to the machine, the loose length bars rested in vee-grooves machined in the table base, concentric with the micrometer spindle, which only moved from 0 to .5000 inches.

The table had no winding mechanism in either direction, the operator just slid it along and a separate lock secured each motion. I drew two eye-bolts screwed into the table slideway base to lift it on or off the plain box table.

Once the costing was complete, the brothers ordered patterns and two sets of castings to be made and delivered to John Holmes. Each was around 20 inches square by 6 inches high and would weigh around 500 lb, the height was necessary for adequate rigidity for the table. It was hardly a major production for a firm this size.

18

We Deliver

In mid-December I asked my mother to order a turkey and a gammon joint at the butchers on Queen's Road. I wouldn't be working overtime on the last night before Christmas so I could collect them before he closed.

'We've never had a turkey before, I made a Christmas pudding last week but I've still got to ice the cake.'

I went next door. 'Where did you get your telly?'

'Radio Rentals downtown, they're very good, they send a bloke to fix the aerial on the chimney.'

'I'm going to order one next week, how do you pay?'

'We go shopping every Saturday afternoon.'

'If my mother gives you the money every week will you pay ours?'

'Sure, no point your mother traipsing down specially. The wife likes to browse round the market, while I have a cup of tea. Radio Rentals will give you a payment book.'

'Many thanks.'

On the last day I skipped the canteen and went to the pub with George. John joined us and we ploughed through the steak pie. The first pint was 'on the house, we must be mad' said the landlady. John got three more pints and said 'I thought the O.D.1 was supposed to be the bee's knees, how the hell can you improve it?'

'The performance of the machine will not be affected at all. Donald's been looking for ways to cut down the number of parts to reduce manufacturing costs.'

We got back and Molly said 'You're late, we got a free mince pie and free tea in the canteen!'

'George kept me talking shop, we got a free pint at the pub.'

I finally put the dust cover over the drawing board. It seemed strange to clock out at 5.30. Christmas day being Sunday meant the streams pouring out of work could use Saturday for last minute shopping. All the Halifax pubs had a half-hour extension until 10.30! The town centre would be littered with drunks by 10.45.

I collected the turkey and gammon. After tea I found the nearest pub to collect some bottles of Guinness for my mother, and Ramsdens' Stone Trough Ale for myself.

The weather stayed crisp through the holiday. Late on Christmas day faint snow flakes started to show against the street lamps and lighted trees in some front windows across the street. The temperature change left fog, which lingered through Boxing day. No traffic moved in Gibbet Street. I hadn't seen a bird moving for some days but heard the distant warning whistle of a train entering Halifax station.

I sprawled in front of the roaring fire, with eyes closed. I thought of the even fatter wage packet last Friday, the culmination of six months endless hard thinking. My mother was playing patience with the same pack of cards I had piled up end on end as a youngster in short pants.

I thought of the lads I'd known in Tripoli, most would be back in the UK now. A new lot would be passing time doing the same mundane jobs in the scruffy uniform. It was just seven months since I'd left but it seemed so long ago. I thought again of the wage packet. Once back at work I'd curb the increasing income tax by stopping two evenings at time and a quarter, just do three nights and the Saturday mornings at time and a half. The brothers' shrewdness was rubbing off. I would also start working more slowly and much more carefully. I woke with a start as my mother nudged me. 'It's half past ten, you've work tomorrow, I'm off to bed. Goodnight.' I'd been asleep for over three hours.

* * *

The bus was late due to fog and back at work I casually mentioned to George that in all the time I'd worked there I'd never once been in the diamond grinding department.

'I haven't been in myself for ages, we might find something we can improve.' Walking across he told me of one Leslie Harkness, who ran the place. 'He has a degree in engineering, far as I know the only other is Trevor Kershaw in the foundry, he has a degree in metallurgy. Harkness was at Norton's when we bought it, his father is a director there, one of Robert's pals. Geoff Toothill also makes his tappers in here. He was a draftsman working for Johnson when he invented a machine tapper, in his own time. Asquiths patented it jointly with him'.

We went in, to be greeted by what sounded like a very brief burst of machine gun fire. It came from the far end of the room where a man with his back to us was testing a machine tapper on an Asquith vertical drill. The noise was the clutch slipping as the tap reached the bottom of a blind hole; it sounded like something breaking but was quite normal on tappers. We went into Leslie's glass office and George introduced me. Leslie was tall, quietly spoken with no trace of a northern accent, and wearing a neat suit. On his desk, under an inverted small glass dome, was what appeared to be a huge diamond, the size of a plum stone and set in black velvet. Only half showed above the velvet. He switched on an angle lamp, the close light caught the facets sending off sharp spikes of intense brilliance. He turned the dome slightly from side to side to give a dazzling effect.

'That must be worth a fortune!'

'No, it's worthless glass, but it's optically pure, the same as used for spectacles, binoculars, microscopes and bomb-sights. It's free from flaws and minute air bubbles. Around the works people think we keep real diamonds in here. A few years ago someone broke in at night, came through that window at the far end. All they took was this from my desk. They'd get a shock when they tried to sell it to a jeweller. I had to go to Horsfalls Jewellers in town to buy a new stand and dome. All the grooves in a cut-glass vase are ground, not cut. In the diamond trade for some reason they call it polishing, not grinding, although diamonds are polished after grinding.'

239

He took us to where two fitters were assembling two machines. Taped to the wall were drawings of a most complicated assembly. It seemed you could present the blank diamond to the wheel at any angle and revolve it to any compound angle up to one hundred positions. All this was made up from small pieces of steel. 'What's this black finish? Reminds me of guns,' I asked.

'It is gun black, it's put on with a heated chemical compound containing selenium. We use the grade for ferrous metals but there are various mixes for other metals. Ours won't cover stainless steel because of the nickel and chrome content.'

'How thick is the finish?'

'I honestly don't know, well under .0001 inches, probably a few microns.'

'Will it go on cast iron?'

'Would think so, anything ferrous.'

'Where do you get it done?'

'We do our own in here.' He took us across the room to a chap lowering a wire basket into a vat. He was wearing large rubber gauntlet gloves, goggles and a long rubber apron. Above the vat was a stainless steel hood with an extractor fan humming away, above the hood a stainless pipe went out through the roof. I'd seen the outside tube many a time and assumed it was a chimney from a heating boiler. A large sign on the hood warned 'DANGER – trichlorethyline, not to be in contact with bare skin'.

Reading the sign George asked, 'Is this some sort of acid?'

'Alkaline, I believe, it certainly shifts grease and oil.'

I thought of the huge cranes trundling heavy castings around, the low loader to be dodged frequently, a battered old steam crane in the yard constantly dropping a huge steel ball on to scrap metal (although anyone passing was well protected from the shrapnel by the high three-sided wall of old railway sleepers), screaming circular saws in the joiners and pattern shops, hot molten iron flowing round the foundry night and day, a cyanide salt bath in the heat-treatment department and now a tank full of acid. It was indeed a dodgy place for humans, yet in my previous five years I only remember one fatality. Not an Asquith employee, but a poor chap working with others one Sunday. High up on scaffolding planks, they were contractors repainting girders forming the roof structure. He fell perhaps 60 feet onto a machine and was killed instantly, the only witness to see the hurtling body being Big Mac, the bookie, up in his crane cab. He had to have a day off to attend the inquest. All painting stopped until a Board of Trade inspector had checked the scaffolding and pronounced it safe.

I saw one incident from quite a distance one day in the heavy fitting bay. A borer bed casting was starting to be lifted on a sling of four thick wire ropes. The slinger would have warned any fitters to move well back, this always repeated by the crane man banging his bell, so no one was at risk except the slinger. There was a sudden sharp screech and a loud 'ping' as one wire strand fractured and sprang out from the rope. Others started to break and the slinger frantically signalled the crane man to lower off, then ran down the shop. The eagle eyed crane driver had already acted on the first 'ping', stopped and reversed the winding drum to lower the huge casting back onto the floor. It had only risen two feet. The whole sling was promptly condemned and taken to the scrap pile in the yard. While I had been away in the RAF little Joe, the labourer who invented the 'money-for-old-rope' brush, had foolishly been trying to brush cast iron swarf from a planer with the table moving. His long brush handle had jammed between the workpiece and the tool, which had sliced through most of his wrist before the machine was stopped. Halifax Infirmary had amputated the arm above the elbow. Joe was still working in the same area, pushing his brush with one hand, with one overall sleeve safety-pinned to the shoulder.

Leslie took us to Geoff Toothill, introduced us and Geoff outlined details of his tapper. 'We make around thirty per week, most go overseas to Asquith agents and others. They keep them in stock all the time. We keep them in stock here too.' We walked back to his fitter's bench. I looked at the knurled ring which adjusted the spring compression for different sizes of tap, each of five marks at increasing intervals were engraved onto the ring. 'Where do you get these engraved?'

'Over there, that chap in the wheelchair.' The phone rang in Leslie's office.

'Excuse me.' He went and George remained chatting to Geoff.

I walked across to a man whose head, shoulders and wheelchair were nearly hiding a Taylor & Hobson engraving machine. Hanging on a nail in the wall behind the machine were stencils of upper and lower case alphabets and numbers. As he finished one cut I asked him to stop the machine. There was a platen mounted at the side of the machine to clamp the stencils or a copying template. The operator moved a pin against the profile to be copied and the cutter repeated the profile in the workpiece, working through a pantograph similar to my drafting machine. 'These levers are adjustable, right?'

'Yes, you can cut letters far bigger or a little smaller than the stencils, you just change the pantograph arms to whatever enlargement you want.'

'Have you got cutters which will cut right through, like if you wanted to cut a shape out of metal?'

He pulled open a drawer and held up some very small end mills. It was the sight of the mahogany drawer which made me realise somebody had cunningly mounted this engraver on a standard Smit grinder base cabinet.

'OK, thanks very much.'

'You're lucky to catch me at it, I only come in one day a fortnight to do these rings.'

I joined George and we went back into Leslie's office. Leslie said, 'That Smit fellow must be a very clever chap. He also owns a patent on bonding diamond dust onto steel discs. He has a factory making these diamond grinding wheels, and he also makes engraving machines for glass, again using a diamond tipped cutter. His sister-in-law has a string of expensive shops in South African cities. She's related to the Oppenheimer family, big in diamond or gold mining. He once told me his only hobby is sailing and he has an ocean-going yacht based at Cape Town!'

George replied 'He's a hell of a big bloke, it sounds like he has a hell of a big bank balance too!'

We thanked Leslie for the tour and went outside. George looked at his watch, 'Bloody hell, we've been in there two and a half hours. What the hell's a micron?'

'It might be time well spent, I've never heard of a micron. I'll look it up.'

'Why did you ask him about putting that black stuff on cast iron?'

'I wondered if we could do the handwheel rims on the slide, instead of chroming the whole lot, remember, chrome plating is charged by the weight of the whole part! This would apply to lots of other machines. There are five handwheels on the portable machines, they are on the borers, the verticals, even on the small tilting tables! We must be chroming upwards of a thousand handwheels a year, think of all this weight, most of any handwheel is sprayed afterwards. Painting chrome is absolutely mad.'

We moved off the concrete path to let a labourer trundle past with a cartload of parts for the REEMA building. Hearing the 'absolutely mad' and seeing our serious faces he would have thought we were having an argument.

'What were you talking about to the cripple?'

'He works an engraving machine, but only part-time – just one day a fortnight!'

'So?'

'So, we're paying eight pounds to Harrison & Allott's plating shop for each engraved speed chart, yet we have our own engraver standing idle most of the year!'

'Bloody hell!'

'It gets worse. I've just remembered, there are more feed/speed plates on every borer too. That man could cut the letters out on the name plates for our two test machines, using a small diameter end mill. He's got some in his drawer, smallest I've ever seen. I'll get the plate drawings back from John. A tiny milling cutter will give us a very neat little radius in the corners of each letter, save a lot of laborious filing.'

Back in the office Molly announced, 'Another Christmas present has come for you.' I ripped it open, Ed had sent two of each of three sizes of sheet metal plates, sandwiched between thick plywood sheets to stop them getting bent in the Colne parcels office. A 'with compliments' slip advised 'If you need any more it's just scrap. Ed'. Molly saw the sheets. 'That looks fascinating, what are you going to do with it?'

'Can't say, everything we do is secret.'

'I don't know how you stand the excitement!'

I rang Ed to thank him.

In the canteen Eunice announced, 'Brenda and me are leaving next week, going to Pratt's Chucks for a pound a week more.'

'What, both of you?'

'Yes, you'll have to find some other girls to eat with.'

'Don't know any, anyway they all think I'm a management spy.'

One day towards the end of January, George once again cradled his phone and shouted, 'Board room for us Donald.'

'I hope it's not more Yanks coming.'

'He just said they'd something to show us.'

Down in the boardroom Dick started with, 'Don't look so worried Donald, we thought it time to put you two in the picture regarding how we're progressing.

'First, Cunliffes can handle the extra American machines and Harold Brown will design and build all the tools over the next twelve months. Jack Croom has offered us a 49 per cent shareholding and will use the cash to extend their building, the local council have agreed to lease the vacant derelict land and the whole area is zoned for future industrial use. They will continue to build the power guillotine they make for a printing machinery firm in Birmingham and are free to take on any other sub-contracts. Jack Croom will retire shortly but Eric Cunliffe and his son will continue as directors.'

It was now Robert's turn. 'Secondly, regarding the considerable changes to the O.D.1 and Cunliffe machines. We've decided to build one each to the new designs, assemble and install them at Tierney Street to test them on normal production work. We've found four men to run them on days and nights. John Holmes will make all parts necessary in the toolroom. Will you therefore, Donald, do simple drawings for these as soon as you're back upstairs, and get the prints down to John. Kershaw has written to two more long-suffering customers delaying their delivery so we'll transfer it part-built from the O.D.1 line, same with Cunliffe who will use the American spare machine. Our heavy gang are down there today installing rag bolts in the concrete at Tierney Street. If we are completely happy with them we will spray them metallic and get photos for the eventual new catalogue and price lists.

'The next thing has been in discussion for six months or more, we have now concluded an agreement to sell two sizes of Warner Swasey American chucking automatics in the UK, Europe and the old "Empire" countries. If sales are sufficient we will make them here but through a joint company. You two will not be involved, just the sales department.'

It was now Dick's turn as Olive arrived with coffee. 'We've had amazing luck with your idea about the low-loader. Scammell advised they could not deliver a new one for at least 18 months as they were tied up making a batch of tank transporters for the army. However, a Scottish shipyard has just installed a railway track for a shunting engine, and have asked Scammell to find a buyer for their low-mileage tractor with 100-ton trailer. It's on route to Pickfords, Leeds, who will recondition the tractor and paint the whole rig metallic grey for us. Pickfords, Leeds are the Scammell sales and service agents for northern England. The cost, including one week's training for a driver and mate, is £21,400. Signwriting is also included. The plan is for our eight-wheeler Leyland driver to go for this training, the four-wheeler Leyland chap will drive the eight-wheeler and with luck we'll poach a new driver from British Road Services.'

'The next item is the filler, or lack of it.' He passed us each a list:

14 Filler/Fettlers at present working days/nights about

1   Leaving next week to go on the buses as a conductor, later to train as a driver. His brother is a driver
1   Started an apprenticeship pre-war with a Bradford textile machine makers. Got his O.N.C. before he packed it in to join the army. Keen to retrain as an inspector and will start in the gauge room
4   Will retrain at Tierney Street as radial drillers and will stay there doing nights about on our two new machines
2   Will re-train as a progress chasers
4   Will continue fettling only as large castings have blemishes and surface imperfections. All small castings will go straight into machining

245

1   Will re-train on spray painting but will continue to fill only the base cabinet for the diamond grinders, which he will do in the REEMA spray shop
1   Two years to retire, will move to labouring

Eric Northend – Personnel to be informed for his records later.

'Next time Smit visits we'll ask him if he'll change to metallic. Don't do anything about cost saving on this machine. Smit has the patent and we only make it for him. It's the most profitable machine we'll ever make, pity we only make a dozen a year.'

'We set up a meeting with the fettlers, in the canteen, one evening when the shifts changed, our shop steward brought the full time union chap in from Leeds and we laid on tea and sandwiches and paid all the men. The surprising thing was that these men were only too glad to get rid of the masks and goggles and the stink of filler on their clothes. One man said his wife insisted he change in the garden shed before he stepped indoors. Another said he wore the goggles when he rode home on his motorbike! I told him to get a new pair from the stores and keep them just for travelling. In the space of one hour everyone was satisfied, the Leeds union chap shook hands and said "a very fair outcome, it's a pity other employers don't approach necessary change in the same way."'

Robert then continued, 'We've bought the calculators and one of the section leaders says the difference is already showing, drawings are getting to the checkers much more quickly.'

Dick glanced at their agenda and continued, 'Going back to fettling, we will create more space at that end for storing castings, but I thought of perhaps a better idea to gain even more space and reduce the "waiting for a crane time". If we stop using and padlock the roller shutter, we can dump castings in the yard and unload with the Coles mobile. At the pre-machining stage a drop of rain won't harm them. This in turn led me to the next stage. Jack Crump, the steam crane driver, retires next month so we cut up the crane and melt it down as foundry scrap. I've got Eric Buckley involved, he's clued up on steelwork and concrete. We lift the rails only and re-lay them across the yard, setting them directly into concrete paths, the rails being flush with the yard surface for traffic to pass over them. He found that the side roller shutter door in the machine shop and the one directly opposite into the REEMA building are dead in line. He is now designing a flat steel truck with a geared axle so one labourer can wind about eight tons of castings by himself. One of the local building firms who do our foundry alterations will start this as soon as the frosts have gone.'

Robert, grinning, said, 'Not bad for a few weeks work and a hell of a lot of phone calls, eh?'

George replied, 'Amazingly so, and in double quick time. The fettler problem was solved very neatly too, I'm very glad of that, it worried me.'

Dick Asquith was the more approachable of the two brothers, ever polite but more relaxed, whereas his younger brother was equally polite but somewhat reserved, more formal yet in no way aloof. Their joint, elderly secretary would never find two better bosses. Looking at the list I thought of the motto on the sign at Wheelus Field in Tripoli – 'We Deliver' – it wasn't only the Yanks who could do this.

Going back up the stairs George said, 'Get those drawings dead right for John Holmes, I don't want him teasing me in the pub.'

After doodling for an hour, desperately trying to remember a similar mechanism I had once seen on an aircraft door, I had managed to include a cunning 'open the guard and release the belt tension' device using a single lever. The following day I took the prints round to John Holmes, who told me a new 5 horse power flange motor had already been delivered to the toolroom and that Dick had earlier briefed him about the whole exercise. 'Those two foremen down at Tierney Street are pretty well organised considering they worked for Albert Kitchen.'

We now just needed to wait for the next six foot O.D.1 to come off the line. Some weeks passed and George took John Holmes and me down to see the two machines installed and wired up. Some weeks later, after constant night and day use by the now retrained fettlers, the four of us together with John Holmes, Johnson and his section leader and the works manager piled into both Bentleys and went again, this time to see the machines resplendent in metallic grey paint. There were some baffled stares. The works manager was the first to recover, 'Are we going to make that welded gadget ourselves?' pointing to the coupling cowl.

'No it will be cast as an integral part of the slide, it's just a mock up to get the machine running without doing pattern changes.'

The section leader then asked 'How the hell do you assemble the coupling?'

I pointed out the big access hole underneath the cowl. 'That will be cored out of the casting.'

He put the gear lever into neutral and felt inside the hole. 'The rubber coupling's changed, it now seems to be a cross shape.'

'That's right.'

Dick said, 'After all these years it's going to be strange seeing radial drills without an arm end bracket.'

Robert said, 'I now see what you mean about the much bolder name-plate. The letters stand out black and yet there's nothing there, you're just looking through at the background. Perhaps for an exhibition machine we should put a little lamp in there!'

The section leader said, 'The whole machine certainly looks much neater.'

Robert's final comment before we drove back, 'The O.D.2 and 3 machines will be the same from now on. Any more questions gentlemen?' There were none so we left the drillers to make yet more holes and bonus. The brief trip must have been an eye-opener to five of those present.

Gradual changes occurred in the diamond grinding department as a result of our original long visit. I told George that he would hardly see a micron = 1 millionth of a metre = .000003937 of an inch. Inside the building extra degreasing and blackening tanks had been installed, along with a second identical Taylor Hobson engraver, a used one bought unseen from the Fattorini jewellery and heraldic regalia manufacturers in Birmingham. Two men and a woman now blackened all the machined cast iron handwheels instead of the expensive chroming process, and dipped masses of small bare steel parts using wire baskets.

Peter in the wheelchair now worked full time and overtime. Arthur Hill, the one-time foreman over portable radial assembly who could no longer work following a severe stroke, had now recovered sufficiently to walk with one crutch. He was brought back to work the second engraver. The metal instruction plates riveted onto every machine, including the 'gates' for gearbox levers were now slotted and engraved here, all made from shapes in sheet metal supplied by our Colne works. The whole sheet was now matt black instead of polished chrome, the letters and numbers were neatly filled with contrasting white gloss paint by a middle-aged woman with a speech impediment, helped by another woman.

The window where the burglar had entered had been enlarged to a doorway and an airlock built externally to accommodate a Lister petrol tug and trailer. This was to avoid rain, snow or dust blowing inside. It was here where the letters in 'Asquith' were cut out on the engraver, again in sheet metal, but later sprayed metallic grey after assembly. All Asquith machines were now finished matt black, white and metallic grey, the only colour the red knob on the electrical control lever. By the end of the year Geoff Toothill ran the whole department, as Leslie Harkness had been made Managing Director of the newly created 'Warner-Swasey-Asquith Ltd'. Sales of these lathes must have flourished because this was now starting to function in a factory in down-town Halifax, vacated by the Wadkin Woodworking Machinery firm. Fortunately this factory had a 10-ton overhead crane already in place.

At the time George and I put my suggestions about blackening and engraving to the brothers I mentioned the young man in the wheelchair who had lost both legs in a motorcycle accident, now just working half a day per week. 'I've seen him about, I assumed it was a war injury, he can't make much money, we should help such people whenever we can,' was Dick's response.

We had been in the office but ten minutes when Molly switched a call to George, who listened intently, then gave an anguished shout, 'Bloody hell, *Bloodee hell!*' Molly and I went to his desk. 'What's up, has a 50 ton crane run off the tracks?' In a weird voice he replied, 'That was Dick. Robert died in his sleep, the housekeeper found him, bloody hell fire!'

Her arm on his shoulder, Molly gulped out, 'Oh God, how horrible . . . absolutely awful.'

He then did a very strange thing, he stubbed out his half-smoked cigarette. Jumping up, he said, 'I'm off to see my old buddy, better ring Hepplethwaite and the works manager, oh, and tell the foundry boss too.'

'What about Mr Johnson?'

'Bugger him.' He shot out of the office.

As I cradled his phone I noticed he'd left cigarettes and lighter on his desk. The latest idea I had been working on and eager to show him now seemed so trivial. We would never again see the immaculate suit, the small diamond tie pin and fat cigar or share Robert's quiet competent judgement. I put the kettle on, lit a cigarette and without thinking offered Molly one.

Next morning I noticed the Union Jack was half way up the flagpole and the neon sign had been switched off. Inside the whole works hummed as usual but everyone was very subdued. The only raised voices were the slingers shouting up to the crane drivers to emphasise the frequent hand signals.

The local paper carried a bold headline announcing Robert's death, with a potted history of the firm he had helped to build. He was only 56.

On the day of the funeral, Colne, Keighley, Tierney Street and the main works were all closed. George picked me up, I was wearing my old black RAF tie, and we went to the church in a soft drizzle. Most of the packed congregation were people from the works. Dick read a lesson from the pulpit, speaking slowly but clearly to the silent crowd. The vicar then started his melancholy dirge, going on endlessly as they often do. Eventually we were out in the drizzle; George pointed to two elderly men standing beside Dick, one wearing a trilby, the other a black bowler hat. As we scurried to the car he said, 'Those two are main board directors from London, there should be a third one somewhere around. I can never tell which is which but one's an accountant, one's a stockbroker and the other a lawyer. They're directors of lots of other companies too. The one in the bowler is the chairman. I'm not going to the graveside, that's for family. Anyway we'd get wet through.'

He dropped me at my door. 'I see what you mean by the view of Butler's, we could do with a shed like that.'

'I spotted Jim Butler in church. Thanks for the ride, 'bye Molly.'

I dashed indoors and switched on the electric fire in the hearth.

'Funerals are always sad affairs, I remember Mrs Bullock's – the huge church was packed, there were people right out in the churchyard. Your father and I were right at the front with the family.'

'I hope you had better weather.'

We were fast approaching the Halifax one-week annual holiday, known as 'Wakes Week'. Hilda Gledhill, a woman my mother had nursed through a severe haemorrhage during the war, had always kept in touch, and when Bert Gledhill retired from the Midland Bank they moved to Eastbourne. Their younger daughter, Caroline, had married Gerald Mitchell, he was a year older than I, but I knew him slightly from the senior school. He got a degree in dentistry at Leeds University and was now a partner in a thriving practice in Sunbury-on-Thames. The older, unmarried daughter, Marjorie, still lived with her parents and was a school teacher.

The Gledhills had arranged to collect my mother to stay with them in Eastbourne for Wakes Week, and would bring her back en route to their holiday in Scotland. I had arranged to move into the 'General Rawden' Hotel in Luddenden Foot for the week. The 'hotel' was actually a large Victorian pub with three letting bedrooms.

Dick told us that the three London directors were to recruit a replacement for Robert as soon as possible, to ease his load. The chap they had finally selected duly arrived, strangely bringing with him a male secretary. We learnt that the new bloke's name was Ralph Lennox and he had previously been a divisional director in charge of the Fordson Tractor plant. The secretary was one Julian Bland. Arriving the week before 'wakes', Lennox called a meeting of all department heads in the board room. Dick introduced us one after the other. The handshake was firm, the smile flashed on and off but his eyes didn't smile at all. The secretary didn't impress anyone either, standing silent with his centre-parted, greased down black hair and spotted bow tie. There had been a slight suggestion of cockney in the repeated 'good mornings' from Lennox. Bland was the only one present giving off a faint whiff of cologne or aftershave. He looked out of place standing in front of a huge photograph of an ancient boring machine, next to it a picture of the new O.D.1, and further along the wall a group of men posed outside the new Cunliffe extension, the roof in place but wall cladding still to be added. In the centre of this group was one man wearing a mayoral chain, flanked by Dick, Robert, Eric Cunliffe and Jack Croom. The remaining younger man was presumably Eric's son.

Lennox announced briskly, 'I'm confident, gentlemen, that in the months ahead we'll soon get this place kicked into shape, right, let's all get on with it.' Dick frowned at George who gave a slight shrug. The company secretary looked surprised. The rest just responded with hostile stares. It wasn't the best choice of words to aim at perhaps the most experienced group of machine-tool designers and builders in the country.

The company secretary I only knew by sight, although he fully knew my function. His name was Andrew Hebblethwaite, according to his office door he had two accountancy qualifications, was a director of Wm. Asquith Ltd and ran the wages office, while no doubt keeping a sharp eye on the purchasing office, sales figures and the Birmingham reps' expenses. He looked at George and just shook his head.

Moving out into the loading bay George muttered to John, 'I don't like the look of that bugger.'

'Me too neither.' Climbing up the stairs he said 'I bet they're a pair of cockney poofters, who the hell has a male secretary? Don't tell Molly about poofters, she was a Sunday school teacher before she got married. There's all sorts of funny buggers in London.'

I began to get occasional phone calls from the section leader handling the new machine changes. He was very keen on what we were trying to achieve. He was moving the job along at a good pace, Johnson keeping well aloof. Each query they had, either George or I went carefully over it with each individual draftsman. On one visit George had a useful idea – to make a note on each drawing, to add below the part title 'Post July 1956' – to be stamped also on the new or altered pattern. 'Concentrate on all the casting drawings first so we can get the pattern shop moving.' Pattern alterations would give us the desired changes to the casting shapes.

At Wakes Week I moved into the hotel, and after an early breakfast each day I set off by bus to explore the valley towns and hill top villages through to Todmorden. The July weather was warm and only spoilt by a brief thunderstorm one evening. I was back on the Sunday morning in good time to greet my mother, behind the door just a gas bill and a card from a dentist to confirm my mother's appointment. The Gledhills didn't linger, they needed to get back onto the A1 to stay one night in Newcastle en route to Edinburgh. Mother had caught the sun in Eastbourne, my desert tan had long gone. The weather had been sweltering and most days they had taken her out into the Sussex villages. Marjorie, home for the school holidays, had gone with them a few times. It had been a nice break for both of us. Mother soon settled back into afternoon tea in the allotment, the neighbour knitting, her husband busy with his hoe and my mother reading. It was a time of gentle retirement for all three.

Back at work the section leader rang to say all the new casting drawings were complete. George and I went down and carefully checked each one against my original sketches. 'Right, you've done a good job here but next time do it quicker.' It was just George's idea of a compliment.

The highly skilled pattern makers worked with the machined casting drawing only. It was they who increased all surfaces indicated by a machining mark, generally an 'F' across the line. Some firms used a small triangle pointing to the surface. These talented sculptors in wood also decided the 'draft' angles, slight tapers to enable the wood shape to be removed more easily from the sand. Skilful core makers created shapes in sand, each grain of which was coated with a chemical. This was then accurately positioned in the moulding box. When the poured metal had cooled this core was broken up and removed for crushing and used again but with limited life as the repeated heat ruined the bonding agent. It was then dumped, in Asquith's case into an abandoned quarry. This same quarry was the site of my mis-spent younger years searching for bullets. When the core was removed a hollow casting was created, the liquid metal only able to flow into the recess left in the sand round the core. Small bits of shaped steel, known as 'chaplets' held the core in place and these were left in the castings.

Robert's death had a very strange effect on George: he didn't have a stroke, his hair hadn't gone white, nothing like that. He simply stopped smoking. When I queried this after some days he gave me his lighter, carefully hand-crafted years before by Joe Price, the radial drill tester. It was now smooth and shiny but still worked perfectly.

Once again Christmas was approaching and the weather got worse. One day I was browsing through *Production Engineering* magazine when I spotted a write up on a new product with the curious name of 'thread whirler'. The photograph was unclear as it had been taken with the unit running, the action hidden by three jets of cutting oil. It was made by a local lathe manufacturer in nearby Brighouse. It was for milling threads and the interesting boast was that it would cut any thread form five times faster than conventional thread millers. I went in and showed it to George. 'We ought to see that.'

'Five times faster, I don't believe it!' He rang them and arranged for us to see one in action the following morning.

Because of who we were and where we came from we got the red carpet treatment. The director who had designed it explained just how it worked, then we saw one actually running, on the shop floor. The cutting speed was impressive. Being lathe manufacturers, their standard unit was designed to mount on the cross slide of a lathe where the tool is normally positioned. They were waiting for catalogues to be printed, so instead he got us a copy of the assembly drawing.

Going back in the car I said, 'That was a really clever design, just shows there is always room for some improvement. We might be able to fit one of those onto one of our thread millers, instead of tying up a centre lathe. We could do with that chap working with us.'

'You're right, we'll look into our Holroyd millers. He's certainly a bright bloke.'

None of us knew at the time that screw thread production would evolve further with the introduction of thread rolling, where the object to be threaded rolls along between a fixed and moving die, squeezing the thread into shape but without actually cutting any metal! It was limited to vee-threads on screws of all shapes. A similar technique was used to produce limited threads on an item commonplace in all domestic kitchens – a screw-on lid for a jam-jar for instance.

The next transfer machine for a Ford cylinder head needed seventeen slides, each requiring the present design of cast and machined aluminium dust cover, which cost £38 each just for the casting alone. The present design included 'Wm Asquith Ltd' cast into each side of seventeen base slides, and the name 'Asquith' in the hand painted oval was cast into each side of every dust cover. The name was also engraved on the huge push-button control panel. Sixty-nine times on the one machine, who in Fords would care so long as it churned out accurate cylinder heads? I proposed changing the dust cover to a welded sheet metal cover, supplied by Colne at £15 each, with the cut out letters on panels mounted to only the first and last dust cover. This went on the list.

The next idea was for the long steel ladder fitted to all 4, 6 and 8 inch heavy horizontal borers to allow the operator to climb up to the operating platform. It was laboriously made from two long steel bars drilled to take the rungs, each of which was reduced at both ends to protrude through the bar. The surplus had to be hammered over and then filed and polished flush with the bar. Naturally it was the apprentice who always did this, I had built just one and one was more than enough. The whole thing was too long to hold in a vice as it would preclude fitters using adjacent vices on the bench so you made it on the floor sitting on a big wooden block. You banged away all week and your arm ached for a fortnight. I changed it to welded steel tube bent in at the bottom end and fastened directly to the machine column. The top end had to pass through a manhole in the platform so was fitted with two extra tubes using screwed elbows. This also did away with two cast brackets and the machined surfaces necessary to mount them. It could be sent out for galvanising when completed. This too went on the list.

The final idea for all the borers involved the back of the huge borer column. This surface had a very deep integrally cast rim protruding outwards to mount the massive electrical cabinet. It could not be buried inside the hollow column as this space was required to take a heavy weight which counterbalanced the slide. Once again the rim surface was needlessly machined flat just to bolt a 'tin' box to it. This required the very dodgy operation to turn the column right over involving the use of two 50 ton cranes working in tandem. Naturally this went on the list. I began to realise that doing things the hard way had long been a habit in this place.

I began to look at the variety of drill tables offered. The simplest were two sizes of plain hollow box with top and one side machined and tee-slotted to fasten a workpiece. Sales levels of both were very good and having determined from George that the foundry just could not cast a tee-slot, I decided the only cost saving was to cast a staggered pattern of through slots in top and side. This was added to the list.

The three tilting and one rotary table showed hopeless sales, the worst being the rotary and the largest tilt table, only two of each sold in the last twelve months. My first reaction was to stop making all of them, then I had another idea, perhaps a second opinion might help.

Personnel said that four of our current apprentices were down for training as draftsmen and none attended the tech on Fridays. George agreed it might be a good exercise for them, just a focused extension of the suggestion scheme. Molly rang their respective foremen asking that they report to the Chief Engineer at 9 am on Friday. I got together 4 sets of prints and she typed out the sales figures.

They duly arrived looking worried, each perhaps wondering what they had done wrong.

George started the process. 'Morning lads, we have a little competition for you. The best answer gets ten pounds from the suggestion scheme.' Rapt attention replaced worried looks.

Pointing to the drawings I carried on, 'You have a totally free hand to scrap all or any one of these or re-design them to save manufacturing costs, preferably the latter. Here's some clues – steel parts can be welded more cheaply than bolted together, we can cast awkward shapes in iron at less cost than machining steel and pay particular attention to the worm wheels. Sketch your ideas on the back of the drawings. Don't confer with each other, don't ask parents, tech teachers or foremen for help. You have one month – any questions?'

No one answered, perhaps overawed by the surroundings, with interested glances at the drafting machine and Molly they started to file out.

'It might help if you took the drawings with you.' George laughed to soften the sarcasm and wished them good luck. One lad grinned, muttering 'sorry' as he rolled up his drawings.

When they had gone George said, 'God knows what we'll get back.' They returned within a fortnight with varied but meagre results. One lad's improvement was in the right direction but would add to the cost. None had realised that full diameter worm wheels and 360° engraving was pointless if the table could only tilt 90°.

George summed up. 'You were given some easy clues, there's no outright winner so I'm giving you five pounds each for trying, don't be discouraged, the suggestion boxes are all round the works.'

When they had gone I said, 'I doubt I'd have done any better at their age.'

'Nor me, we might have planted a seed for their future.'

I then had a go at the middle size only, cast slots through each table surface, improved locking and the best gain was changing the pivot to cast iron, with an integral quadrant for the 90° of gear teeth, 90° of engraving and of course no filler or chrome in sight. George reviewed this and approved everything. 'Those lads will get a shock when they see this on the shop floor.'

'We need this for the new Cunliffe, it can be made in Manchester, we'll just do the engraved bit and the pointer.'

As I had previously done away with the rise and fall table, its expensive slideway and worm geared raising mechanism the Cunliffe machine had to have either a box or tilting table on the base plate.

We then had a further session with Dick who approved everything calmly and quietly, and appreciated the idea of no longer turning over the huge columns. Relaxing over coffee, it seemed strange without Robert present, but he was watching our progress. His photo now hung on the end wall next to his father.

George asked if we'd ever heard of the heavy side fitter on nights, who was building a caravan chassis out in the yard. 'He kept it hidden under patterns. When we moved the patterns to Tierney Street he said he'd only stored it there as he had no room at home. Frank McManus shifted him on to permanent days so he lost his 25 per cent extra night pay. It's amazing what goes on in our works. One chap's run a bookie's business from his crane cab for years!'

Dick said he'd once overheard Molly described as George's 'fancy woman'!' I told them about Selby calling me a 'lying sod' and why he had stopped. 'When we arrived back from Keighley he was passing on his way home. When he saw me get out of the back he must have thought Robert was chauffeuring me around!' We all laughed as George said, 'He'd have a right tale to tell next morning in jig and tool.' At that point we left, George to gleefully inflict the latest changes on Johnson.

We were not to know that our next visit to the boardroom would be rather different, to end in chaos, leaving me surrounded by snakes and not one welded tubular ladder in sight.

Back upstairs I continued to struggle with changing one of our thread millers to fit the 'whirler' device. It could be done, the problem was the length of time the miller would be out of action during the conversion. We needed both running to provide the continuous supply of all sizes of leadscrews and worms. The alternative of laboriously cutting threads on a lathe with a slow-motion single-point tool was far too slow. It was becoming ever more apparent that we would have to mount the 'whirler' on a long centre lathe, denying us the use of a vital machine.

Back up in the office Molly handed out invitations to the Christmas 'do' at the White Swan.

The following morning I got off the bus to find a huge spanking new low-loader, parked on the Golden Lion car park, facing the works. On each side of the deep trailer beams bold white letters with black borders proclaimed 'LEADERS IN MACHINE TOOLS.' On each cab door similar smaller letters announced 'WM. ASQUITH LTD., HALIFAX' and a phone number. Spanning the full width of the cab a large board repeated the single word 'ASQUITH' in the scaled-up capitals I had laboriously cut from cardboard long ago.

Just then a red Bentley pulled up, Lennox got out of the rear door, Julian left the driving seat. Lennox peered across through the falling rain at the monster, then marched into the offices. Julian must also be his chauffeur. Since his arrival and badly-received threat 'to kick this place into shape' I had had no contact with him or the strange Julian. A second bus pulled up, more people stared then shot across to clock in. Dick pulled up to park behind the other Bentley, and came across. 'Very resplendent, eh?'

'Yes, let's get across, we're getting very wet.' From now on we would be dodging round our very own truck in the loading bay.

I booked the dinner suit at Sam Stocks. On the Saturday night George picked me up at our door. In the opulent room all was the same as last year. I spotted Ed Wilkinson from Colne. 'The weather's cold but clear over there so we drove this time, but we're staying overnight again. We're chopping up your steel bits.'

With glasses filled and the first course being served, Dick rose, banging a soup spoon on his side plate. 'Welcome, ladies and gentlemen. First, Mr Lennox and Ken Kershaw cannot be with us tonight, they are in Holland finalising an order for an 8 inch boring machine. Now please raise your glasses to the Queen, the Country and the Company.'

With the usual muttered responses we sat to start the superb meal. As last year we four sat with Mrs Holmes and John, who said, 'Pity about Ken Kershaw.' George and I laughed, John just grinned. Unlike a year ago, Dick never even mentioned a pay rise; either my value to the company had peaked or he perhaps felt he would never get Lennox to agree.

Back at home after another enjoyable night, I made some tea and sprawled gazing into the dying fire. I thought back over a hectic year. Already we were seeing new parts coming in as castings and progressing through the works, soon to be assembled into the first new style machines. The new truck was in action daily but no start had yet been made on the railway. Since Jack Crump retired the steam crane had remained forlorn and derelict at the end of the line, the battered chimney would never belch smoke again. In the distance it looked like some slain prehistoric monster with its trunk horizontal. Joe Price was now offering his lighters emblazoned with his customer's name, I knew exactly where he was getting them engraved!

I must have fallen asleep in the chair for it was the clock chiming three which woke me, the fire long dead.

On Christmas day we got a taxi down to join Ronnie Holdsworth and his wife for lunch. They had some unusual news. He was retiring from the police force and arranging to buy his cousin's small farm at Rishworth, a hamlet six miles out of town on the Oldham Road, as the crow flies over those hills, perhaps a mile from the farm where I had briefly lived in the pre-war days when I was chauffeured to school.

Back at work things progressed, the weather softened in late March so the builders swung into action on the rail tracks.

One day George said, 'That was Eric Buckley, he wants us at the railway.'

'Why, what's wrong?'

'Nothing, it's finished, he's rung Dick.' We met Eric in the yard. He was standing by the new cart. Four cast O.D.1 arms were loaded on the cart. We all had a go at winding it along the track – it took no effort at all to wind and as soon as you stopped winding the cart stopped, there was no over-run and you did not have to slow it down, due to the worm gear. The castings and cart would weigh around eight tons yet you could move it with one hand at walking pace. Eric proudly said, 'We've ordered a tarpaulin for it.'

The builders were just hitching their concrete mixer to their battered old tipper. Dick shouted, 'You've done an excellent job, thanks for doing it so quickly too.' The foreman shouted from the cab, 'Any time Mr Asquith, see you Eric.' They trundled away. In the distance two of the maintenance gang were creating showers of sparks, cutting up the remains of the steam crane for melting down. It looked even more forlorn, just the rusty vertical boiler remained on the heavy chassis.

Any neighbours in the council house bedroom windows overlooking the yard would think they had now seen the end of the steam age at Asquiths, yet they'd be wrong, for inside, but hidden from their view, the blacksmith still used his steam hammer. His high pressure steam was piped direct from the works boiler house as was the supply to the canteen hot plates.

We now had one continuous rail track stretching from the back wall of the REEMA spray booth, set in concrete to the doorway, then right across the yard into the machine shop to bring the cart under the over-head cranes.

The lists Molly had typed, re-typed and increased, were now filled with ticks showing changes approved and put into use, so I gave the 'yard railway' two ticks.

The Wakes Week holiday came and, apart from one day of constant drizzle, I took my mother on bus rides out into the countryside. She particularly wanted to visit Haworth Parsonage in the Bronte country. One day we went by train into Leeds and found the house in Park Square where the Luftwaffe had tried to bomb us. All three floors were now occupied by a firm of accountants. From so long ago it was hard to imagine the pile of bricks on the pavement.

Back at work one day George shouted, 'Bring your pad, Dick wants us in the boardroom.'

'Why, what's happened, has that O.D.1 coupling shattered?'

'Don't know, it can't be that or he'd have said, anyway that coupling was properly designed. It can't break.'

'Perhaps the pattern shop's burnt down?'

He didn't respond.

19

Battle Ground

Morning sun shone through the three identical boardroom windows, diffused by the frosted glass in the large lower panes and stained glass patterns in the smaller ones above. On the panelled long wall opposite the windows was the huge photograph of the old boring machine, next to it a smaller view of the new steel frame added to Cunliffe's building, with a row of men in front of it. In the centre was one elderly man wearing frock coat and mayoral chain, flanked by Robert, Richard, three more of varying ages were presumably Jack Croom, Eric Cunliffe and his son. Next were twin photographs of the latest O.D.1 and Cunliffe radial drills. The whole room was polished wood, panelled walls, floor, long table and comfortable chairs. The short end wall carried an old full length picture of the very late William Asquith, next to it a head and shoulder photograph of his late son, Robert.

It was a room in which I had spent many hours over the last two years, where a team of four, later to be three, had heard proposals, debated them, reached conclusions generating action, often involving others, and subsequently we had delivered. Never once had a voice been raised in anger or any personal dispute created. Today was to prove far more dramatic.

We filed in behind Dick, to find three elderly, well dressed men sitting at the end of one long side of the table; all looking very serious. Opposite them was Andrew Hebblethwaite, our company secretary, also looking glum. Across the end sat a relaxed Ralph Lennox, beside him was his sidekick, Julian, staring down the room at the photos of dead men, appearing a little nervous and endlessly turning his pencil end over point to tap his scribble pad.

Beside Andrew, Dick remained standing, so we did. He was the first to speak. 'Introductions are necessary I think. This is Mr Carruthers, an accountant and chairman, Mr Roy Merrow, senior partner in Merrow & Co., London stockbrokers, and the third is Michael Alwoody, a London solicitor. These three and myself form the board of the Asquith Machine Tool Corporation, quoted on the London stock exchange as the holding company for the subsidiaries, along with 49 per cent of Cunliffe Croom Ltd., and 50 per cent of Warner-Swasey-Asquith Ltd. These gentlemen are also directors of many other companies. This is George Hoyle, our chief engineer and Donald Ainley, in charge of new projects and cost reduction.' Good mornings were exchanged.

He then sat down, so did we. There was something strange about the huge table, suddenly it dawned on me – there were no drawings spread out on it. Just the scribble pads of Julian, Andrew and myself.

Lennox: 'Mr Chairman, before we start, may I ask why these two are present? They are not directors and this is a board meeting.'

Dick: 'They are here for a very good reason.' He didn't elaborate, instead continued, 'I would remind Mr Lennox a third person is present, also not a director.'

Lennox: 'He's my secretary.'

Carruthers: 'That's settled then, let's get on with it. Mr Hebblethwaite, will you record the minutes of this meeting?' A look and a nod was all the reply he got. 'Dick, you called this meeting, the floor is yours.'

Dick: 'I called this extraordinary meeting as a result of the recent diabolical activities of Mr Lennox. He has quite secretly, and I believe quite illegally, sold Norton Grinding Machines back to the American Norton Company, and has commenced talks with Contactor Switchgear Ltd with a view to selling Asquith Electrics (Colne) Ltd. In both cases he has breached the articles of association of

Wm. Asquith Ltd and the Corporation. The moment you three were told of this you should have sacked him, initiated immediate action to sue him and started police proceedings to have him charged under the Companies Acts. However, I can see why you wouldn't wish to do this.' It was no longer the polite, fluent tones of the Dick I knew, more the crisp, decisive voice of a Lieut. Colonel running a court-martial. Alwoody, the solicitor, frowned at Lennox.

Lennox shrugging: 'Everyone knows full well that such commercial negotiations must remain entirely confidential until concluded.' His calm voice suggested he was talking to backward children.

Dick: 'He seems intent on ruining what my father, brother and I have spent three lifetimes carefully building, always with due regard to the welfare of that band of skilled men out there, without which we have no company. We survived through the 1930s depression, even when one South American customer welshed on an order for the largest machine we have ever made. It's still running night and day. God knows how much money we've made from it. We have never paid high dividends but always built up our reserves, yet we have never borrowed one penny from a bank over all the years.'

There came a bang as the stockbroker, Merrow, brought his fist down on the table.

'Young man, STOP fidgeting with that damned pencil!' The shocked Julian brought it down too hard, breaking the lead. 'Sorry, very sorry.' His face went red.

Lennox still looked bored. Dick took a sip of water, then continued 'We have carefully and prudently grown to become known world-wide for quality machine tools. The reason young Donald is here today is very simple. He has spent two years plus massive overtime trying to increase our leadership in the industry. He was trained here, and on return from the RAF George recruited him for a specific job – to reduce our manufacturing costs wherever possible. He's been very successful in this, even improved the general appearance of our machines. He'd only been on the job a week when his quick thinking enabled us to buy additional machining capacity and 16 skilled men, all achieved in one afternoon and only ten miles away. This, and other things since which have no connection with the job he was tasked with. He has very sharp business acumen for his age and is set for a great future in this firm. Mr Lennox has put this in jeopardy.' He sipped some more water.

The three from London had listened politely, occasionally casting glances my way, perhaps amazed at the boy wonder in their midst, but when Dick paused the Chairman seized his chance.

'The time has come for the question we all need answered. Mr Lennox, exactly what was your intent in trying to sell off two self-contained and individually profitable parts of the corporation holdings?'

Lennox (relaxed): 'Perfectly simple, we need a cash pile to buy into, or buy outright, an engineering company or companies which sell more mass-produced products with far less labour content, thus generating far higher profit margins than can ever be made building machine tools.'

It was Alwoody's turn to bang the table, this time with both hands, total disbelief on his face.

'You had no authority, you're not even a director of the corporation, only Dick and we three are, man. What the hell will those American directors think? If they were so keen on buying they'll insist we can't cancel. The more I think about it the worse it gets.'

Merrow (table banged): 'We'll be a laughing stock.' In all my previous meetings the beautiful table had never suffered once, but these were worried men – worried about their image amongst cronies in London.
Carruthers: 'All you had to do was discuss it first with Dick and then the rest of us. We could have considered it and simply made a "rights" issue.'

George and I exchanged puzzled glances, I held up my hand like a schoolboy. 'Mister Chairman, may I ask what is a "rights" issue?' The table was again assaulted, gently this time by Merrow dropping both arms with a resigned 'Oh! For God's sake.'

266

Carruthers said, 'Hang on Roy, he's been trained as an engineer, you can't expect him to know company finance. Mr Ainley, it's very simple: the company offers the existing shareholders the chance to buy further shares, generally pitched slightly below the current price as an inducement. They are also offered on the open market but existing shareholders are guaranteed to get all they apply for, hence the term "rights", i.e. the right to buy. The benefit to the company is (a) it avoids paying interest on a bank loan, (b) it does not have to provide collateral to secure a loan and (c) the company avoids the chance of the bank calling in the loan at what may be a very inopportune moment. The cash for the new shares is then used for whatever new project is involved. It's a very common practice with quoted companies. Remember it well, young man, the way you're going on you may need it in future.'

'Right, thank you.' I remembered the ride back from Keighley two years ago. If you've got money, it's so easy to make some more.

There was a sudden knock on the door 'Coffee everyone?'

'Please Olive, good idea.' She brought it, Dick and Merrow lit pipes, Lennox and I lit cigarettes and Alwoody got a small cigar going. We all started to sip the hot coffee.

Lennox (leaning forward to look at Dick) said, 'The fact that you've had to make improvements, led by this, no doubt, very bright young man, surely shows that they were long overdue. However, there is one corner of the machine shop that is so quaint it looks like a film set, the area doing the thread milling: it's like a Gracie Fields cotton mill scene. A visitor must get an impression of a dark satanic mill. The chap working there actually wears clogs, he puts sawdust on the floor to mop up oil leaking from the machines. He's surrounded by dangerous flapping leather belts going right up to some weird system in the roof.'

George silently mouthed the words to me, 'Bob Sheldrake.'

I had listened to the sarcastic cockney long enough. 'It's the most efficient area of the whole works!'

Lennox said, 'How the hell can it be efficient? It's a museum.'

My reply (just beating George) was, 'Just one single electric motor drives five machines through the line shafts above. There's miles of that line shafting running in textile mills all over Lancashire and the

267

West Riding, even down in Worcestershire, spinning carpet yarn. It's a fit and forget system, just needs oiling every week, and it'll run fifty years. Our chap in clogs doesn't have to climb a long ladder to do this, just pulls the lever of a one-shot oiling system on the wall, pumping oil into all the oiling troughs up above – simple efficiency. He wears clogs because cutting oil rots normal footwear – he's walking on three-quarter inch thick wood soles clad with irons. The oil on the floor doesn't leak from the machines, it just drips from the parts taken from the machines. The sawdust is scrap from our joiners shop making packing cases. Every morning the labourer brings a new barrowful, sweeps up yesterday's and takes it to the blacksmith to light his forge fire.'

Roy Merrow had been leaning forward, obviously quite fascinated. 'Do you by any chance use steam power up here?'

'We did, but we scrapped the crane, melted it down in the foundry.'

George (adding to the excitement), said, 'Mr Lennox should take visitors to see the blacksmith working the steam hammer and his forge, clouds of steam and showers of sparks.'

Roy (still eager), replied, 'So you do still use steam then, don't tell me you still use horses to drag things round these works?'

George said, 'We have no horses, we need hot forged steel parts for machine tools – far cheaper and quicker than buying them from Sheffield!' Merrow, either a glutton for punishment or quite naïve, now tried something no-one in these works would ever dream of doing, trying to make George look foolish by a sarcastic question. 'Do you by any chance have any machinery here driven by a waterwheel?'

'No, we haven't got a stream running through the works. Anyway, how the hell would we get sufficient head of water? We're situated on top of a bloody hill.'

Dick joined in, 'Well put George!'

Merrow (defeated, now petulant) said, 'Then we must be thankful for one small mercy at least.'

I decided it was time to direct more firepower at Lennox. 'All the sawdust goes up in smoke so we don't have to pay for it being tipped. A few miles from here, just over the Lancashire border is another machine shop, working on very expensive precision parts for jet engines, they wear clogs too, yet their inspectors are all issued with white cotton gloves.'

Carruthers interrupted, 'Damned funny place for a Lodge Meeting.'

'They are not Freemasons, it's Rolls Royce at Barnoldswick. Our chap in clogs would take a dim view of Mr Lennox calling it a dark satanic mill. He's well known for very carefully teaching apprentices, setting those cams on that old four-spindle automatic is a work of art, believe me. He only works overtime to get his daughter through university medical school and on Sundays he's a Methodist lay preacher! That chap in clogs runs five machines on his own, you would not get that level of efficiency in Fords, the union wouldn't stand for it.'

Eight pairs of eyes stared at the 'boy wonder'. There was nothing wonderful about it – any one of them could have read the same article on Rolls Royce as I had read in an engineering magazine.

Carruthers said, 'I'm blowing the final whistle, Ainley and Hoyle United four, Lennox and Merrow, Nil. We must press on.'

Merrow asked, 'How do you get four?'

'They scored two good goals, you scored two own goals.'

It was Dick, however, who decided to press on. He now put some real pressure on, his firepower directed straight at Lennox, and the three Londoners. He switched back to the lieutenant colonel voice: 'Whilst I appreciated then your excellent work at the time of the public offering, I feel that you three have now let us down badly. You didn't sack Lennox when you first knew of his stupid act, through all this meeting you still haven't done so. I can never work with him again, there has to be the same trust in a boardroom as on a battlefield. I am somewhat overdue for it so I will retire, as of today, I shall be out of this firm by the end of the week.'

There was a bang, Carruthers' chair crashed over as he rose. 'Dick, I really must ask you to seriously reconsid . . .' That was as far as he got.

'There's nothing to reconsider. I will next see you three at the Annual General Meeting and I shall expect to see some drastic changes before-hand. I would remind you that my own shares, those of my wife along with the substantial block left to my son by my late brother, for which I am trustee and hold proxy, collectively amount to just under 29 per cent of the issued capital.'

That said, he rose, walked to the door and paused, turning. 'Any cash pile you develop, along with a great deal more, will be needed to completely rebuild the heavy line in the foundry. Could well top a million at today's prices.' He turned and went, closing the door quietly. It was not his style to bang doors, anger shows an enemy you're rattled.

Carruthers retrieved his chair. He and his team now looking very worried started muttering to each other. I caught the whispered 'million!' Lennox, who only moments before had sensed victory, now looked daggers at the two dead men on the wall, ambitions and cash pile demolished by Dick calling up his final salvo.

George muttered to Andrew and me, 'Bloody hell, he said on the phone it was urgent, he didn't say owt about this bloody mess.'

Andrew (also whispering) replied, 'What he said about the foundry worries me, we spent a packet in there only last year on some massive reinforcements.'

George said, 'Mr Chairman, I'm more than a year beyond my retirement date, there is no way I can work for Lennox so I'll retire too, I'll go at the end of this week.' He started to rise but I restrained him

'Hang on a minute, George. Mr Lennox, will I be working directly for you from now on?'

Lennox (puzzled) asked, 'What? Er . . . no, I'll handle any new projects in future, Julian can sort them out for me.'

'So what do I do then?' The three opposite were now standing against the wall, I just caught the whispered words 'Later train.'

'What did you do before new projects?'

'Jig and tool drawing office.'

'Well, er . . . go back in there.'

'Oh, when?'

'Er . . . well, whenever, just finish off whatever you're doing now.'

'Right.'

The beautiful long suffering table now got further abuse, this time from George, 'That's it, I've heard enough, come on!'

He rose, I followed as Andrew muttered 'So sorry to see this happen to you, Donald.'

'I survived bullets in Egypt, I'll manage this, but not in jig and tool,

270

definitely not there!' As I followed George, I slowed by Julian. 'Your bow tie's been crooked all morning, we do have certain standards in this board room.'

Lennox laughed saying 'You could have fooled me.' Julian looked daggers at me, clutching his throat.

Had Harry Lidgett been sitting there he'd probably have condemned the whole as a bunch of bloody idiots. Flt Lt 'Pomposity' Myers would have simply repeated 'Your attitude is all wrong.'

We went straight into Dick's office, where he was just pouring a whisky. He reached into the filing cabinet for two more glasses, as George announced his retirement.

Dick said, 'Soon as I got in here I realised I had left you two out on a limb, now it's even worse, we've both left Donald at the mercy of Lennox. He'll have his knife in Donald, from now on.'

Olive, Dick's secretary walked in with some letters to sign. 'My, that was a long meeting, what are you celebrating? I kept hearing bangs, I thought you were all fighting!'

Dick said, 'George and I have retired, time to make room for new blood, give younger ones a chance.' He got a glass, poured a little whisky, adding a good squirt from the soda siphon and passed it to her. I gave her my seat, glad to stand after the prolonged board room session.

Olive said, 'I've stayed on just because you did, so I might as well retire too, I'll go at the end of the week too. Cheers everyone.' We clinked glasses. Looking at me she said, 'So they're leaving you to hold the fort?'

'It's more like they've left me in no-man's land, surrounded by a mine-field, fighting off four useless bloody Londoners.'

'I've never heard you swear before!'

'You weren't in that meeting!'

Without realising, I had left the door slightly ajar – we then heard four sets of rapid footsteps approach and a barked command from Alwoody, 'Young man, we need to be in Leeds station rather rapidly, so put your foot down.' A bow tie with brief case below it shot past the gap. Julian was porter and chauffeur for this trip.

George said, 'Bloody good riddance, pity Lennox wasn't with 'em.'

Once again we have to resort to help from a fly on the wall, so easy

271

for a writer but a technique to be used sparingly. We have to assume that three angry men (nothing worse than a rich man's anger) would leave Julian without a word of thanks for the fast ride, not even a brusque 'goodbye', to rush to the Leeds station ticket office to buy first-class seats on the London train due in ten minutes, and due out 17 minutes later on a very tight schedule. They took seats. When the waiter announced 'Ladies and Gentlemen, first sitting for dinner' they promptly gathered three brief-cases from the rack and moved into the dining car. It was the sight of a briefcase hurtling towards him which made our fly retreat from its regular spot on the cord mesh of the luggage rack, straight up to the carriage roof, then back to settle on one briefcase, as the men seated themselves and arranged napkins. Our fly had been a minute egg deposited in a sticky white cocoon on a ledge where a rear support was bolted to the carriage wall. Despite its ability to move so fast in the blink of a human eye, it flew perhaps but ten yards a day, yet clocked up some 4,000 miles a week. It had never been tangled in a web nor even seen a spider. It had but once seen another fly when one of its kind had settled on the outside of the grimy window to stare at the goodies within. That was when the train was parked in Waverley Station, Edinburgh, it was the same day when our fly had been surprised and puzzled to see a weird object drunkenly ambling along the dining car making a peculiar buzzing sound. This sound stopped abruptly at the swift flick of a waiter's napkin, said napkin having destroyed a brilliant natural design which defeated the laws of aerodynamics.

Our fly would have picked up various snippets as the inquest continued, three different growls giving forth such gems as 'We need to find two quickly, then we dump that liability Lennox:' 'No more companies with foundries or chief engineers:' 'That chap made an idiot of you and your waterwheel: it was all that damned nonsense which has delayed us, and we missed a good lunch at that White Swan place too!'

During coffee our fly could have noted the fierce growl 'bloody northern peasants' but he had no mates to whom he could relay all this. Meanwhile he was willing them to talk less and eat faster. As the first course ended he was faced with a choice: mulligatawny residue, butter dish and crumbs from warm bread rolls. When Carruthers rose, excusing himself to go to the toilet, our fly swooped to the butter dish, gorged on it, demolished a crumb and fled three tables down the carriage. There, with a few quick hops he wiped his feet on a moquette seat cover and sped back to safety on the briefcase.

He managed a quick slurp of gravy from the main course and custard from a dessert, but had to forgo the coffee dregs as the waiter approached when he wisely fled up to the ceiling. He knew there would be a second sitting yet to come. His lifestyle was as good as any fly in the country: a warm domain, wide choice from the residue of three full meals a day, with second helpings every evening, no competition and not a predator anywhere near him. He well deserved this if only for being so useful to any budding writer. All he had to do was avoid the waiter's napkin and he would survive to clock up 4,000 miles the following week.

Other flies watched as the three irate men alighted at King's Cross. Merrow dived into a taxi with the brusque command, 'Claremont Gardens, Hampstead.' Not even a 'please'. Carruthers, with a muttered, 'Phone me tomorrow 'bout this mess.' used the next taxi.

Alwoody, spotting a vacant phone box, started to berate some incompetent member of his household who was having difficulty locating his chauffeur. He ultimately purred out to Swiss Cottage in the Rolls. Some foundry up north was a minor problem compared with missing his lodge meeting, where after the mysterious rituals were completed he would continue his running battle on the billiard table with Evelyn Box QC, whose cousin happened to be the Solicitor General. In the city it always paid to keep well in with the opinion-formers. He remembered Box showing him a new business card with the QC replacing KC after the princess had succeeded her father, inconsiderately causing senior members of the legal profession to incur printing costs. By this time our fly was asleep.

Up in the land of muck and brass we could only reiterate George's so appropriate words 'Bloody good riddance!'

'Bloody hell, I'VE MISSED THE PUB!!'

'I'm hungry, I'm going up to the canteen,' I said.

'You'll get nowt, it's shut long ago.'

'They'll be making sandwiches for the nightshift.'

Dick added, 'Good idea, we'll all go.' As we walked up Bob Lane he continued, 'First thing in the morning I'll ring the area factory inspector, and warn the foundry manager. The whole heavy line will have to be shut down, there'll be lay-offs, some of those men have worked here for years but I'd rather see them on the dole than horribly burnt, or more likely in a morgue.'

We went to the canteen, and sure enough found three women making overtime sandwiches, a fourth packing them into grease-proof paper bags. We went to the counter, Dick explained we'd been delayed in a long meeting and missed lunch. He gave her a fiver, 'Could you make us a sandwich apiece and a pot of tea please?'

'We've got corned beef, cheese slice with pickle or cheese with onion and pickle.'

'One of each, please.'

She turned, 'Nellie, put the kettle on.' She gave him his change. 'The last time I saw you in here, Mr Asquith, you and your brother, it was so sad about him, you climbed into the boxing ring and stopped the strike. That was quite some years back.'

We went to a table well away from the counter.

Dick said, 'I think that your best course, Donald, is to leave the firm. I know all the local machine tool bosses and I'll do my damnest to get you into the best job I can but you won't get anywhere near the pay you get now.'

George added, 'John'll want you in the toolroom, quick as a flash.'

'It's actually far worse.' I said. 'Even with maximum overtime I can't make the same money anywhere on the shop floor. But if I could I'd always be branded as a management man and a failed one at that. Whatever I said they'd always assume I'd been chucked out of the job. Leaving is the only option, so I'll leave.'

'It's perhaps your best move. What a hell of a mess. By the way I didn't know that Bob Shelldrake had a daughter, nor that he was a lay-preacher.'

'Neither did I, just made it up to make out Lennox to be a worse bastard!'

Dick chipped in, 'I liked the bit about the horses and the waterwheel, really funny and they never knew you were making fun of them. Tonight I'll put together a really good reference, you do the same George, Donald may well need them.'

'Right, it's the least we can do, I've never written one for anybody in my life, I'll get Molly to kick it into good English.'

As we approached the loading bay I left them, saying I was going to nip into the paper shop to get some cigs. I asked if he had a copy of last Thursday's *Courier*. 'The wife might have one upstairs, browses through 'em for days.' He went into the back of the shop, shouted 'Elsie ...' She must have found it and thrown it down the stairs for he deftly caught it and returned.

In the classified small ads both Halifax and firms as far afield as Bradford, Keighley, Leeds, Huddersfield and Burnley pleaded in vain for help with turning, boring, grinding, planing etc., offering nights, days, bonus, overtime and travelling expenses. There were but two adverts for drawing office work. One was a contract drawing office in Weybridge, desperately seeking jig and tool designers. The other was local. F. Pratt & Co Ltd. urgently needed a drawing office checker. Apply Mr A Haigh, Ch. Draftsman. I scribbled down the phone number, gave the paper back and shot out to the phone box on the corner of the narrow street where the engraver lived. 'Yes, the vacancy is still open, in fact you're the first to respond.' We agreed to meet at 10 am on Friday. It was now Wednesday.

Back up the steps I found the office locked, George and Molly had gone home where no doubt she would get the full story, blow by blow.

Next morning Molly clattered the typewriter to produce six copies of a wonderful reference, crisp English, on Asquith letterheading, ending with George Hoyle, Chief Engineer. The only words underlined were 'To whom it may concern'. She explained 'I put this together, his best contribution was "tell 'em he's a bloody good bloke". Keep each one in those envelopes, stops the paper fading.' I was standing behind her, watching the blur of rapid fingers, she never even looked at the machine, her eyes fixed on the copy, it was like a television close-up of a pianist playing a fast passage. When the last one was done I just gripped her shoulders and kissed her hair. 'I'm very grateful.'

'That's what friends are for, I glad you've been up here, you and George have a lot in common but you're much nearer my age.'

I took them into George to sign, when the ink dried put each into its envelope and popped them in my desk. George announced he was going to see John Holmes. 'He's on the committee of a local bowling club, my hobby from now on. If Lennox wants me, tell him to bugger off.'

He went and Molly said, 'You know he's my uncle, but there's more to it. When I was eight and Colin eleven, our parents were killed in a bad car crash in thick fog on Keighley Moor. A cattle wagon hit them head on. We lived in Warley, not far from George; his wife couldn't have children so they kind of adopted us, we grew up with them. His wife was just like a mother to us. He sold our house and put the money in trust for us until we were twenty-one. When Colin married he used his as a big deposit on a new house at Shibden Park. After George's wife died, when Eric and I got married George simply said why not live with him. Eric jumped at the idea as we didn't have to get a mortgage. George altered his will so I get the house when he dies. We didn't see much of him when we were young as he was abroad a lot on long trips installing Asquith borers, all over the world. He was an apprentice here, he's worked for them ever since. He'd already left for South America when that customer went bust, so he had to come all the way back for nothing. I wasn't even born then, he was only a young fitter, working for a foreman.'

'That's a hell of a story, what did your father do?'

'He was assistant chief cashier at Halifax Building Society, trained as an accountant, went straight there when he qualified.'

The phone rang. 'It's Olive, she's done you more references.'

I collected them, thanked her, 'Did you put this together?'

'No, he gave it to me this morning.'

'George's contribution was "tell 'em he's a bloody good bloke".'

'That wouldn't worry Molly, she's very competent with words.' I read through Dick's tribute, longer than George's, the crisp wordage half-way between a 'mention in dispatches' and a 'recommendation for a medal'. He'd outlined but one instance of 'action above and beyond the call of duty' – the new low-loader saving an impressive £15,000 per year for an outlay of £22,000. She passed me six large envelopes 'Keep them clean.'

I went through into Dick's office to ask a favour.

'Fire away.'

'Could I have the two boardroom photos of the new O.D.1 and the Cunliffe as souvenirs?'

'I don't see why not, if it hadn't been for you they wouldn't be there, help yourself, although it's little to show for all the work you've done.'

'I'll hang them in my bedroom, they'll be my constant link with the good old days, thanks very much.'

With the references trapped between the photographs I carted them carefully upstairs, added the other six references and wrapped the lot in three of the original O.D.1 drawings, then sealed them with masking tape.

George: 'What have you got there?'

'The photos of the O.D.1 and Cunliffe from the boardroom, Dick's given them to me as a souvenir. That's his reference.'

He read it. 'Very good.'

'I'm grateful to both of you.'

I started to work on the thread whirler, went down to Bob Sheldrake, told him I was trying to modernise both thread millers. I needed to measure the exact centre height, and agreed to go back around 11.20 when the bar then being cut would be finished. En route I signed out on temporary loan a test bar and Vernier height gauge from the gauge room. Approaching the corner, it did suggest a somewhat dark satanic mill, but to me it was just some machines, cutting metal to make money. I measured it, passed it to Bob, 'You try.' We both came up with the same 5.691 inches plus the test bar radius of .5000. 'Right, that's all I need, thanks, be seeing you.'

'Aye, tek care.' They were a wonderful bunch of blokes on the shop floor and I was certainly going to miss the place.

I called in to the drawing office toilets to wash my hands and went upstairs. I put a clean sheet on the machine and laid it out. I knew exactly what was required, the tricky interesting part was finding the best practical way of doing it such that the machine was out of action for the minimum time.

At home I dug out the School Certificate, the signed apprenticeship papers, Ordinary and Higher National Certificates, RAF discharge book, the scroll recording Graduate Membership of the Institute of Production Engineers and the more ornate scroll proving I was an Associate Member, then adding one of each reference I stuffed the lot into one of Molly's envelopes. A mere cluster of papers recording ten years of my life, one dangerous, the last two just hectic.

In the morning I clocked in, doodled with the sketches, left in good time with the envelope and entered Pratt's office door ten minutes early. A girl led me through machine shops, power chucking department, tool room and then a lift shaft. We went up to the fourth floor of what had been an old mill block. Another block was built on at right angles to it. The lift served each floor of this but the floor levels were staggered so some wooden steps led up to the drawing office double doors. Once inside, the first person I saw on an old fashioned roller board was Brian Laycock, who had been one year above me at the senior school.

'Morning Brian, long time no see.'

'How do, have you come for the checker's job?'

'Yes.'

'Where are you working?'

'Asquiths.'

'You'll get it, they're desperate!'

With a 'there's his office' the girl disappeared. I walked down the room as Eunice shouted, 'Hey Brenda, we've got a visitor.'

'Hello, you two, nice to see you again.' I shook hands with Arthur Haigh. He looked around 50 with quiet voice, dark hair and a Hitler moustache.

'I'll start by telling you what we need. Four of our draftsmen are young and haven't much experience, one is still an apprentice. Ronnie Baxter used to build drawing boards at Dargue Bros., Brian Laycock came from a firm making woodworking machinery.' He pointed to the adjacent office, 'Lewis Murgatroyd and I were apprentices at Butlers, then fitters there.' For some reason both wore long white smocks. Strange? 'You'll be working for Lewis, he has his hands full sorting out the work-load. Far too many drawings are going out on the shop floor with errors, so we need a checker, particularly for jigs and tools. None of us is really clued up on those. We have an endless stream of enquiries for special chuck jaws to hold all manner of things. I do all the estimating for quotes. We work 8.30 to 5.30, one hour for lunch, overtime 'til 7 pm, and Saturday mornings.'

'Have you got a canteen?'

'Yes, a director's dining room, senior staff dining room where I go (Lewis goes home) staff canteen which you'll use and the works canteen. We've also a canteen at Bankfield Works, but that's just a machine-shop we have in Boothtown.'

'It sounds bigger than I thought, how many work here?'

'Over three hundred.'

'What does the job pay?'

'We were thinking of £18.'

'With my experience I'd be a fool to myself to work on checking, estimating, production planning, design or jig and tool design for less than £22 basic.'

I spread all the papers across his desk in chronological order. 'That's my last ten years.' He looked at every one thoroughly, skipped the RAF book. 'Higher National and Associate Membership, that's very impressive.' He rang some distant general manager who wouldn't budge beyond £21. I agreed, I'd give a week's notice immediately and start a week Monday. He passed me two Pratt catalogues 'Have a look at these next week, you'll get a good idea of all we make.' We shook hands and passing Eunice I said, 'Got the job, see you a week on Monday.'

'Knew you would, you can eat with me again, Brenda goes home to lunch.' As I passed Brian Laycock, he said, 'Told you you'd get it, have you got your union card?'

'I'm not in it.'

'Will you join?'

Thinking of Lennox and Pratt's skinflint general manager I said, 'Yes, definitely, soon as I start.' He passed me a form. 'Fill it in.'

Arthur Haigh came rushing down the office. 'Nearly forgot, fill this application form in, personnel need your full address and next-of-kin for their records, don't tell anyone what rate you're on!'

'No I won't.'

I found my way out, which was surprising as I have always had a terrible sense of direction, I could get lost in a phone box! Approaching the final passage into the offices I passed a small Genevoise jig borer in its glass cabin, but no air lock at the door. No one was working the machine. On the bus I thought about what I'd seen. Four lads, three draftsmen and two tracers needed a chief draftsman and assistant chief in white coats, three hundred plus employees needed five canteens, with an unused jig borer on the shop floor and a female sales director. Peculiar firm!

It was 12.15 when I got back to the locked office. Strange. I put the catalogues and envelope in my desk and went to the canteen. No sign of Molly, just Olive sitting alone. I asked about Molly. 'She had to go down town.' That's all she said.

Back in the office, George came in. 'Dick rang inviting us to a farewell pie and a pint, his treat. I couldn't find you, where were you?'

'On a vital mission.' He ignored this.

'What are you working on now?'

'Changing the thread miller to take the whirler.'

'Where's that drawing from that Brighouse bloke?'

I pointed, he tore it to shreds and dropped them into my basket.

'I'm not working for that bastard and I don't see why you should either, let him find his own bloody thread whirler!' I took the drawing from the board and tore it up with the scribbled notes giving the vital centre height. All gone. 'What am I supposed to do now then?'

'Read a magazine, but if you find owt interesting don't tell me, I don't want to know. I get my first practice on a bowling green next week!'

It was 2.45 when Molly bounced in, looking immaculate in a striped business suit, white frilly blouse, brooch at her throat and surprisingly, a normal length skirt. Very elegant indeed, and rather elegant legs too.

'You look like a film star, have you been for a screen test?'

With a grin she took a newspaper cutting from her handbag. 'Olive spotted it in Dick's *Yorkshire Post*.' It was a large display advert. A private secretary was urgently required for a director at the Halifax Building Society. The present incumbent was leaving shortly due to approaching motherhood. Mature and discrete applicants were invited to ring extension 4, for an informal discussion. Beneath that was the Halifax head office telephone number (12 lines). Along the lower border ran the legend 'Halifax – The World's Largest Building Society'.

'Did you get the job?'

She laughed. 'Course I did, how could he resist? I get my own office, far bigger than this, two weeks holiday which I can have whenever I want, pension scheme, cheap mortgage if I need one, bank holidays, more pay and a vase of flowers in my office every week. He's the director in charge of all the branches, so there will be some occasional travelling as well. He'll be in his late forties, a photo on his desk showed him and his wife with two teenage daughters. He asked me to copy type a letter and read out another letter to take in shorthand, just said 'Those speeds will be more than adequate.' I told him that I had been private secretary to the chief engineer for eight years since leaving the North of England Secretarial College in Leeds, my boss was retiring tonight and I fancied a change away from all the noise of cranes and big trucks. I told him about my father working at the Halifax years ago and he said he knew the name – it's still printed on the staff internal instruction booklets in their accounts department. He suggested we continue over lunch and I thought we were going into a canteen, instead he took me for a slap up lunch in the White Swan! I had a mad rush this morning, George ran me home to get changed and took me down town. From now on I wear a normal skirt, I've always worn long ones because of that open metal stair-case with men walking about underneath, I'll have to shorten them.'

She went to her desk and typed out her notice.

'Will you do one for me too? I got a new job this morning, as a checker in the drawing office at Pratt Chucks.'

'That was quick, I'm so glad for you. You're very young to be a checker. I'm dying to tell Eric about my job when I get home!'

We took the letters in, George stared at mine 'Bloody hell, you don't hang about, where are you going?' I told him.

'You'll be the youngest checker for miles around and she's got the best woman's job in the town. Anyway, I can't do owt with 'em, you'd best take them to . . . I know, Andrew Hebblethwaite, he'll need to make out your tax certificates. You hand those in to your new employers.'

We both went down to his office. 'By Jove, Molly, you're looking very posh, have you been to a wedding?'

'No, I've been to get another job.' She gave him all the details.

'That sounds like a very good move, there's an old saying that "the nearer you get to the money the more chance of it rubbing off on you", they handle millions of pounds at the Halifax. What are you going to do Donald?' I told him. 'I'm amazed you've both done it so quickly. I'll have your tax certificate made out for next Friday, Molly. I'll have to post yours on to you Donald, and a cheque for your final overtime.' He shook hands with us and wished us a bright future. If we ever needed any help we had just to ring him. A very nice bloke indeed.

George was emptying his desk drawers into the waste bin, he gave me his thick copy of *Machinery Handbook*. 'That'll come in handy the rest of your life, you can tek all those magazines home if you want.'

'I will, many thanks for the "bible"'. This text book was always known as the 'engineer's bible', it was a marvellous gift.

At 5.30 we shook hands, George said 'Any problem any time, ring me at home, I'm in the book.' I went to the outer door with them. Molly just said, 'See you Monday, just think, last Tuesday no one could have guessed all this would happen.'

'Give my regards to Eric.'

I followed down the steps, intent on saying goodbye to Dick and Olive. They were just about to leave. I shook hands with them both, I carried his two bottles of whisky out to the car, telling him about the new job. 'That's excellent news, any problems, ring me.' His wife was sitting in her car, the biggest MG ever built, a long, low slung, four-seater with huge chrome headlamps, long rakish front wings and the hood down. It was finished in deep cream with red leather upholstery.

'Hello, young man, I've heard all the drama, don't know what I'm going to do with him stuck at home all day.' Dick told her about my new job. 'There's a funny woman works there, she's the sales director, so it must be a funny firm.' She started to pull out round the Bentleys. Dick and Olive turned to wave, I waved back. Mrs Asquith, intent on the road, shouted 'Goodbye young man.' She had obviously forgotten my name, not surprising as we had only met at two Christmas functions.

Just then a voice beside me said, 'Must be great to be so well in, do you wash that MG when you've done George's?' It was Selby Rushworth on his way home, he would have seen all the farewell performance as he approached.

'No, and remember I'm not a lying sod, I used to deliver her *Courier* when I was at school. I only see her at Asquith's dinner dance in the White Swan.'

'Is his Bentley broken down, then?'

'No, you don't know the half of it.' Perhaps Selby didn't know that both Bentleys belonged to the firm.

I went back up to the office and leafed through all the huge pile of drawings for the old O.D.1 and Cunliffe radial drilling machines, anything with my red scribble on it I put in a pile to destroy. Tomorrow I would dump them in one of the dustbins outside Goods Inwards and get some cardboard boxes to shift all my stuff home.

At seven I took the screwdriver out of my tool box (I had just one use for that) and took the box home on the bus. On Saturday morning I dumped the roll of old drawings and rooted through the bins for cardboard boxes, filled them with the magazines and the 'bible'. Again I took a box on the bus.

On Monday Molly was back in a long skirt again. We went in and she produced from a carrier bag some hanks in various colours of soft wool. I had to hold my hands out while each was wound into a ball. With pattern and needles she started to create a tiny jacket. 'My cousin in Wibsey is "approaching motherhood" as they say at the Halifax, her first one.'

I rolled up a drawing to add credence to my wanderings. 'I'm going for a walk to see old friends.'

'Come back at half ten for some tea. I'll be on the sewing machine tonight, I've five skirts to shorten and press. I'll be walking home all week.'

'I think the new chief inspector lives in Warley, I'll have a word with him when I'm down there.' I ambled past the dustbins outside Goods Inwards. In this large room the vast variety of small packages of all shapes and sizes were carefully opened, packing notes checked and although by early afternoon it looked chaotic, towards the end of the day a stream of items were being delivered all round the works, offices, foundry and pattern shop. Next was the temperature-controlled gauge room and then the chief inspector's office. I explained Molly's lack of transport. 'Has George's car broken down?'

'No, he retired last Friday and she hasn't passed her test. Just the rest of this week, she's leaving Friday.'

'Tell her I'll pick her up in the morning, I only live round the corner in Warley Lane.'

I ambled over to the REEMA building, found Ronnie, my old racing pal, and told him I was leaving, I'd finished all the new projects. 'You've done well, I thought all t'checkers were old men.' I didn't fully agree with the 'done well'.

'Where's Stanley, in the bog?'

'No, Stanley left a week ago. Some old mate in Akron, Ohio has found a shed with a crane and they're going to start up re-conditioning turret lathes. Reckons America is littered with them, flogged to death during the war and ever since, and they can sell 'em re-built far cheaper than t'new price.'

'Good luck to him, pity I missed him.' I explained that both George and Dick had just retired.

'I wish I could, come up Boothtown Con Club any Saturday night for a pint. I'll sign you in.' We shook hands and I went across to Leslie Buckley, my very first foreman, went through the details, finally shook hands. As I walked away I heard Leslie shout to a crane driver. His gong sounded, then more joined in and hammers were banged, the traditional reactive warning of a top boss entering the building. This time it was my send-off, although few would know why they were banging. You were busy if you sounded busy.

I went back and had some tea with Molly. The tiny yellow coat was so far just a few rows of knitting. 'I'm using yellow because that'll do for a boy or a girl.'

Afterwards, I set off for the diamond grinder shed. I went through the same process with Geoff Toothill. Again the same reaction 'Very young to be a checker.'

'I can do it with one eye shut, they only make lathe chucks.'

I went across to the two engravers, busy as bees, and told them of my imminent exit. Arthur Hill said, 'You and Hoyle did a good job for me. When you can't work you feel like you're on t'scrap heap.' I got out my lighter and on some scrap paper scribbled 'Presented to D. W Ainley

A.M.I Prod.E. by George Hoyle, Chief Engineer, Wm. Asquith Ltd, 1956'. 'You'll have to engrave it longways on three or four lines, very small stencil. I'll fill it with black paint later, can you do that, please?'

'I'll have to split it to get it on, a bit on each side.'

'Right, on one side put 'Presented to D. W Ainley A.M.I Prod.E 1956, the rest in three lines on the other side.'

'Ready late this afternoon, what did he give it you for?'

'Nothing in particular, he just stopped smoking when Robert Asquith died. He used to be a chain smoker before that. I once tried chain smoking but I couldn't get them to light.'

'Eh up, it's Cabaret Time.'

I looked around the room, took in the increased activity I had created. A larger degreasing and a bigger dipping tank had been added, all now worked by two men and a woman. Someone outside banged on the roller shutter, one of the men wound it up to allow the Lister truck to back in with another trailer full of more handwheels to be dipped.

I joined Molly in the canteen. 'How's the knitting?'

'Coming on, I only dropped one stitch all morning, haven't done any for about three years. I knitted a cardigan then for Eric for Christmas. I'm getting faster.'

In the afternoon I ambled round to Bob Sheldrake, told him we would not now be altering the thread miller as there were problems, the 'whirler' was designed to fit on a lathe and we'd likely do that. I deliberately omitted anything else or any mention of dark satanic mills. He just accepted it, and was surprised to learn of Dick and George retiring. I added that I too was leaving to go to Pratts.

'I had a neighbour who cut bevel gears there, but he's dead now.'

'How long have you worked on these?'

'I was apprenticed here long before the war, in those days you had to pay a pound per year to be apprenticed and you didn't get paid 'till the second year. When I'd finished they put me on a capstan lathe, then a Ward 3A turret, when the bloke working these died on holiday they put me on here. I was deferred from call up and during the war all sorts of cripples and unskilled unfit blokes came in, they called 'em 'dilutees'. I've been here ever since. The Acme came here during the war on lease-lend from America, but it was old then.' We both heard this machine change tone, a sure indicator that the four steel bars were near to running out. Time to reload.

'I'll let you get on, Bob, all the best.'

He wiped his hands, we shook and I left as he shouted, 'The same to you.'

I just sat alone, reading engineering magazines, for an hour and a half's overtime. I took home a further box of them. Final one tomorrow and I would take my drawing instruments on Friday night.

Molly was progressing well with the jacket and was now extending the back to form a hood. On the Friday morning I suggested she have a break. 'Carry your scribble pad, I'll have a rolled up drawing so we'll look legit, we'll go say goodbye to John Holmes.'

'Good idea, he's been a pal of George's for years.' We walked up Bob Lane, through the wicket gate beside the roller shutter and down the steps into the quiet tool room. In the glass enclosure I could see the two new jig borers. I was secretly rather proud of those. We went into John's neat glass cabin. 'We're doing a farewell tour, Molly's got a job at the Halifax; I'm going to Pratt Chucks as a checker.'

'Oh, very good, no point staying here.' Typical of John, he made no comment on my age, he'd know full well I could do the job. We sat and chatted about the good old days.

'How's the new borers?'

'Fine, no problems, it's a clever design, who dreamt it up, George or you?'

'Me, all my own work, frightened George to death at first.'

'Ken Kershaw brought some visitors round recently, said they were selling like hot cakes!'

'Yes, Dick said they'd sold eighteen or nineteen in only three months.'

'Ken said Rolls Royce have ordered two, pity you even suggested it, pity you couldn't have patented it and got some other firm to make it for you. Jeff Toothill did that with his tapper.' The tea trolley appeared with the never ending onion pasty squares. 'I'll nip up to the canteen for some cups.' I tore two sheets from Molly's pad, got teas and two pasties. I passed her one 'Watch your clothes, bits of onion drop out.'

'Thanks.'

After careful munching she gave her verdict. 'Super, the pastry is marvellous.' The now-greasy papers went into John's bin, I took the cups back. We had a brief stroll round the tool room, back in John's office we both shook hands with him. 'You ought to give George a ring now and again, he'll want to know how you're going on. Come to t'bowling club some Saturday.'

I would miss this chap and his quiet haven of precise efficiency.

We'd only been back up in the office ten minutes when there was a knock on the door. 'Good morning.' It was the flower delivery woman. Molly said, 'This office is closing down tonight, the chief engineer has retired and we're both leaving Asquiths, so will you cancel the order, please.'

'Shall I take these back then?'

'No, I'll take them home.'

'Right, goodbye then. Good luck in your new jobs.'

We ate in the canteen and back in the office I took pencils from the tray on the drafting machine and put the dust cover over the board. I took the 'Hoffman' calendar from the wall, it could go on our kitchen wall, and started to pack my drawing instruments and some large and small white envelopes.

I unscrewed the name plates from my door and the outer one, dumped them in the bin. I scribbled on the back of an O.D.1 drawing 'CLOSED DOWN DUE TO RETIREMENT' and Molly laughed when I taped it to the outside door. She went on knitting, now working on the tiny one-piece 'overall', which according to the pattern would also have a hood. She had made a red bobble using milk bottle tops and fastened it to the hood on the finished jacket.

To pass the remaining time I went to Cyril Rushworth in the design office, grumpy and suspicious as usual, just the same as his brother, Selby. Their father, Clifford, who worked an orbital grinder, was even more miserable. Cyril growled 'Hullo, what the hell are you changing now?'

'Nothing, I've finished the changes. Just came to say goodbye, I'm finishing tonight. I'll leave you to the tender mercies of your mate Johnson and that clown Lennox.'

'LEAVING?'

No one, but no one, ever left an Asquith drawing board; you retired or died, but you simply didn't leave. (When I was an apprentice one designer, said to be extremely bright, had actually collapsed over his board and died age 28 from a brain haemorrhage. He'd been one of that merry band described by George as 'Johnson's clowns'.)

'Who's that weird bugger in a bow tie?'

'Secretary and chauffeur to Lennox, thought to be a poofter.'

'He must be, wearing a bow tie in an engineering shop. Where are you going?'

'I've got a job as Finance Director of Halifax Building Society.'

'Lying sod. Anyway, tek care.'

I went out, Johnson's glare following my every step, down the stairs, up the other stairs into the jig and tool office. Ignoring the rest, I went into Eric Buckley's office. When I explained my move to him and Glennis, she said, 'My cousin is a typist in their buying office.' I said to Eric, 'Grim about the foundry.'

'Yes, horrible shock, Asquiths have never been known to lay men off. I thought we were going to have some severe union trouble. The two ten ton lines are OK but we can't make heavy borer castings, just the 2 inch machines, but Cunliffe's and Warner Swasey are OK for theirs.' Once again I shook hands and went.

Five thirty came at long last. I looked round the three empty offices, nothing to indicate we'd ever been there except the faint but ever-present smell of Molly's apple blossom perfume in her area. She gave me George's key and her own. 'You'd best leave them with Mr Hebblethwaite.'

'Right'

I locked the door and carried her flowers down as she already had two carrier bags. 'I see you're nicking the vase as well.'

'I'm not! It belonged to George's wife. That's the last time I use those stairs, it's a lift from now on.'

'Me too, there's a lift at Pratts, four floors up to the drawing office on top of an old mill.'

'If you ever ring George, ring at night or weekend, I'll be home and we can have a natter.'

'Right, give my regards to Eric.' The horde began to exit the drawing office so we both quickly signed the timeclock for the last time. I had intended to 'work' Saturday morning but to hell with it.

The low loader was parked right at the far end of the loading bay, engine stopped for once. The chief inspector was approaching from the other end to give Molly a lift home. She put the bags on the floor, hugged me and pecked my cheek to the stares of people coming down the steps. 'Been lovely working with you, take care, 'bye.'

'Likewise, 'bye Molly.' I kissed her cheek.

'Time you got married and settled down.'

'Can't find a rich girl.'

I was just turning to take the keys to Andrew when Cyril Rushworth, queuing at the clock grunted 'Bet you've been having a right old time with her this last week, with George gone.'

'No such luck, she's married.'

'So what, lying sod, they all like some spare.'

'He always was a lying sod.' This from Selby, joining the queue. 'I knew they'd sack you, what are you going to do now?'

'I'm joining Halifax Building Society as Finance Director. One of the secret projects I've been working on at home is a machine for the rapid counting of bank notes, Dick Asquith is backing it, we're going to have them built at Gledhill's Cash Tills. Molly's going with me. I'm going to do what Lennox does, take my secretary with me from job to job.'

'Ha, ha, you lying sod.'

'If you don't believe me, look in the *Courier* next week for a big announcement.' At this they looked at each other, somewhat puzzled. Might as well get the rumour mill into overdrive from Monday, no doubt many eyes would avidly search every page of each evening paper. I was leaving but the 'boy wonder' legend would live on, at least for a week.

I dumped the keys with Andrew, marched boldly out through the main office doors and caught the next bus home, clutching the package of instruments and screwdriver.

Riding home I thought about the wonderful people I'd worked with, and five bastard Londoners. I was so engrossed I passed Newstead and just remembered to get off at Queen's Road. Walking back, past the end of Adelaide and Tierney Streets, the 'Wm. Asquith Ltd.' sign prominent on the end of the machine shop, reminded me of the day I had left school with my first ever certificate. It was just another 'never to happen again' day. Unlike school, where nothing remained to show my presence except a broken desk lid, up the hill and at Tierney Street a great deal remained to show not only had I been present, but I had certainly 'delivered!'

There were drawings recording all the changes, yet my signature on none of these. Robert Asquith had instructed me to keep it secret. Before I reached home I resolved that never again would I go 'above, beyond or even near the call of duty'. Any future employer, certainly one who argued about a pound per week, would have to find their own improvements. I would follow the Yorkshire adage:-

> Hear all, see all and say nowt.
> Eat all, sup all and pay nowt.
> If tha does owt for nowt
> Do it for thiself.

I went home and casually announced, 'I've finished that work at Asquiths; I'm starting just down the road at Pratt Chucks on Monday as a checker in the drawing office. I'll be checking the draftsmen's work to see there are no mistakes, just like a teacher marking books.'

'You've always liked drawing.'

'I like drawing wages too, but I won't get paid as much, it's a far smaller firm.'

I had two days to relax. Contrary to the first day in the office next to Hoyle's, where I didn't know exactly what I was supposed to do, how to do it, what the reaction to it would be or how long the job would last, this time I was totally confident. I was simply to become a checker in a small drawing office in a firm producing much simpler engineering products. I was not to know the pitfalls ahead, nor to imagine that the up–down earnings cycle would continue.

20

'Le Cirque du Galliers-Pratt'

I was five minutes early arriving at Pratts, found the time card and clocked on. From now on I was responsible for the integrity and accuracy of each drawing and had to sign the drawing accordingly. Just that, nothing more. After the boardroom disaster I vowed never again to work flat out at going the extra mile. Why should I, just to benefit distant shareholders?

Pratts' drawing office could best be described as well-worn, particularly the old style extra-wide bare floor boards. Two rows of bare bulbs each with a large once-white round reflector marched down the full length of the ceiling, at one end a dividing glass partition provided two offices, both unoccupied, the two at the opposite end housed Arthur Haigh, chief draftsman, and Lewis Murgatroyd, assistant chief, both for some strange reason wearing long white smocks like hospital doctors. Lewis seemed in awe of Arthur, even subservient, he even called him Mr Haigh to his face. Arthur did the estimating; Lewis, my boss, ran the office.

Old roller drawing boards were spaced the full length of one side of the room, positioned well away from the wall to allow for the deep bench fitted to the wall. More boards ran down the other side, then the double doors, my board and a large flat table, then a few huge steel filing cabinets with shallow drawers to store drawings and blank drawing sheets.

Print room and toilets were on the half floor below in the adjacent mill block. This was to be my working environment, hopefully not for long. Very different from Asquiths, where I had my own office with thick carpet, German drafting machine, fluorescent lights above, filing cabinet, large desk and two first-rate bosses, plus a shared and rather lovely secretary. From fourth floor level you could look out over the rest of Pratts' site and a great deal of Halifax, the distant Beacon Hill forming a backdrop. Beyond that hill my well-loved widowed aunt had for years run a farm, until her three sons were called to the war. After the youngest, Alec, went into the navy she had to give it up. Alec's arm badge proclaimed him to be a stoker in, believe it or not, a submarine!

The drawing office crew comprised Rodney Hemmings, an ex-Asquith estimator who'd moved to continue estimating, working purely for Arthur Haigh. Next along the room were Brenda and Eunice, tracers, and both ex-Asquith. They laboriously copied in black ink on waxed linen from the pencil-on-paper drawings. These copies lasted for years and would stand up to being printed repeatedly. Women were reputed to steal this material to make stiff petticoats, just as after the war women had used surplus parachute material to make various undergarments. Being young, attractive and the only two women in the office, they got away with murder. If one went to the toilet, they both went, no doubt to powder their noses for half an hour. If Lewis sent one on some errand down to the main office block they both had to go. Brenda, who changed into low heels to work, would slip on her high heels and it was easy to imagine the cat-calls and wolf-whistles as they pranced through the shop floors. You didn't see them for an hour. They regularly teased Lewis but he never twigged, nor did he ever query their absence. Perhaps he didn't dare in case they left.

Brenda had been courting a joiner for six years, which sounds a long time but they were intent on building their own house. They had already purchased a plot and he had mates in all the building trades who would help as required. Her mother had stopped working at the Co-op so Brenda went home to lunch. I ate with Eunice as I had done at Asquiths. Eunice was married to a chap who had a market garden at West Vale, between Halifax and Huddersfield, which meant she had to use four buses every day.

Next was Joe Jackson, a quiet, studious but friendly type who made no errors on his drawings. In a few short weeks he left to start a two year BSc course in hydraulics at Manchester University, sponsored by Pratts who would pay him basic draftsman's rate through the course. He had to sign an agreement to work back at Pratts during the long summer holidays and for five years afterwards. I was the last one in this row, with a board and large old table behind me.

On the opposite side, first came Ronnie Baxter, oldest of the squad with prematurely grey hair, who had spent the last year of the war as a bomb-aimer on Liberators, hitting southern Germany and the German army retreating through northern Italy. There was no need by then to aim at the Sweinfurt ball bearing factories as the Americans had finally flattened them, but at enormous cost in aircraft and crews flying the long run from England. After the war he worked at Dargue Bros here in Halifax, the very firm who made the roller drawing board he now worked on every day. He was married with two children and lived on a sprawling new council estate on the edge of town, tacked onto the old village of Mixenden. For some reason he changed into pumps for work. His one hobby was the ATC as an officer of 250 Squadron (Halifax) Air Training Corps. Every Wednesday he came to work in uniform and after over-time went straight to the ATC based with the Territorial Army unit next to the 'Shay' football ground. Because of our common RAF links we became good friends, still are to this day.

Next along the room were four young lads, all ex-Pratt apprentices, prone to making endless errors. Lewis was always nagging them to improve their printing and general neatness. I've only ever remembered the names of three, John and another by the name of Des O'Boyle, and Billy McQueen. Billy walked as though he had large springs fitted in his heels. He lived out at remote Heptonstall, on the edge of Keighley Moor, above Hebden Bridge. To avoid four buses each day he used an old motorbike.

Next came Peter Harrop, ex-Asquith design office but with no knowl-edge of jigs and fixtures but otherwise entirely competent. He left after a while to work at Womersley & Broadbent, a lathe manufacturer in Brighouse. Years later I heard he'd got a teaching diploma and moved to a Scarborough technical college. He'd like the long holidays, much longer than when he had been part of what my recent boss George Hoyle always described as 'Johnson's bloody clowns', Johnson being the chief draftsman at Asquiths.

Pete's immediate colleague was the very quiet Keith Binney, a graduate of the Institute of Mechanical Engineers, hailing from Sheffield. He lived, he said, in a rambling old home near Brighouse. His wife could not have children so they had adopted five, yes five. He was either mad or intent on creating an orphanage. Perhaps not so mad – he didn't pay income tax! Over a period I could never find any errors in his dimensions, but it was quite obvious he had never worked on a shop floor.

I soon began to realise that customer enquiries never gave any indication of the speed at which the chuck would run, the depth or width of cut, rate of feed or even the material being cut. I thought back to what both Lewis and Joe had said during my first week. It was bad practice to run a chuck at high speed with the jaws extended beyond the chuck body, and at speed the centrifugal force created reduced the gripping power of the jaws by up to 60 per cent. I had been amazed it could be so high but knew of no way to dispute the figure. Weeks later when Keith dealt with an enquiry, as usual, I found the figures to be entirely correct but thought I would gently tease him. I took the drawing back to him and quietly pointed out the risk of extended jaws.

'There could be three alternative ways to get round this, simplest is to recommend that the next larger size of chuck be used, or specially-made jaws such that all the jaw teeth are always engaged with the scroll teeth (actually one single endless tooth cleverly cut on the face of a disc to form a scroll) or we could assume say 300 rpm taking a very light finishing cut on 9½ diameter steel and calculate the centrifugal force acting unseen on the gripping step of each jaw. We could work out the shear strength of the step. If the latter was less, we'd have to use either alternative, but the special jaws would cost more and the customer might not want to wait 16 weeks for delivery.' I'd spoken quietly and sensibly, Keith took it all in, thought about it and accepted the challenge.

'I never thought about that, I'll have a go.'

Half an hour later he was back with the drawing and some calculations neatly laid out in best school exercise book style. I checked the figures and agreed the 22 per cent safer than required, so I signed the drawing.

Brian Laycock worked on the next board to Keith. Brian was the union rep. in this office. I had promptly joined on my first day. He made every job last as long as possible simply by putting too much on each drawing. For example, for the simple length of plain steel tube used on their diaphragm chucks (made under licence from the N.A. Woodworth Company in Michigan, USA) he would draw a side view (alone vital), with an end view and section through the tube. He regularly drew totally needless sections but I never commented. It wasn't my job to go the extra mile.

Last in the row was Peter Brooks, known as 'Brooko'. I was to learn over a period that Peter was a law unto himself. He'd disappear for an hour, no-one knew where but by teatime he'd have a stiff brown carrier bag full of wood – bits from used packing cases, damaged wooden patterns, whatever. One day I asked a daft question. 'That's my firewood for tomorrow, I chop it for the wife.' A variation on the old American song 'He was a good, good boy to his momma, he held the lantern while she split the logs!' Late morning he'd leave by the large roller shutter in our building (access to the bar steel storage racks and power saws) to avoid being seen from the main offices. He'd go up Parkinson Lane and along a side street to the shops in Gibbet Street, to return with a sandwich, apple, Mars Bar and small bottle of ginger beer. He didn't use the canteen. When Lewis gave him a job, instead of the abrupt 'Do this one next' which he said to any other draftsman, he'd timorously suggest Peter 'might fit this in when he got time'. It was a curious performance indeed. Next, and finally, was Jack Rostron, about whom at that stage I knew nothing whatsoever.

The remaining member of this happy band was old Harry Howe, who worked the printing machine. At four every day he started to reprint all that day's output, as copies had to be stored at their Bankfield works in case of fire. Even if he had only two to reprint, he still would not continue with normal printing, simply sat on a stool until 5.30. 'Miss Buckley's orders, the insurance company insists, so you can wait 'till morning.' He was a one man union. George Hoyle would have described the place as a 'complete bloody circus'.

First day I started, I was standing staring at a drawing spread out on the old table when Brenda came up behind me. Hidden by drawing boards she wrapped her arms round my stomach and repeatedly rubbed her firm breasts in my back.

'You've never done that before, come round the front and do it!'

'We all live in hope, tea's up at 10.30 do you want sugar and milk and two biscuits or a bun?'

'Both and two biscuits please, you daren't come round.'

'Can't, I'm engaged.' With a 'ha ha ha' she released me.

The first member of the management I saw was a woman of about 50, in a business suit, who came through the double doors with a bunch of yellow forms which she took to Lewis. I got a better view when she returned and felt I had seen her before. It was only when she reappeared on the Friday that I got a longer look and realised she was the Miss Florence Buckley, younger then, who had attended the Methodist church in the village when I was a young lad. She had coached us in rehearsals for the Christmas Nativity play. It was the same woman described by Mrs Asquith as a 'funny woman sales director, must be a funny firm' on the day when Dick Asquith retired. Ronnie Baxter later told me, 'She trained to be a language teacher but the Education Authority could not employ her as she had some medical problem which meant that she could not enter the teacher's pension fund.' I had once overheard her talking down to Lewis as though he was a peasant. I got the impression of an embittered, snobbish sourpuss. Lewis responding in his ever subservient 'yes miss, no Miss Buckley, three bags full Miss Buckley' manner.

The chairman of the company was named Galliers-Pratt. Ronnie told me, 'He rarely appears, lives on a forestry estate at Sutton-on-the-Forrest, near York. Has a saw-mill and joinery firm there, they supply Pratts with the small packing cases. His son Vernon is managing director, he's in most days, used to be a guards officer. That's his Jag parked out front, don't know where he lives but it won't be Mixenden. The technical director is a good bloke, Maurice Ackroyd. Has one draftsman, Derek Greenroyd, working for him in the main office block. The general manager is a miserable old sod, name of Willy Booth. He works the jig borer on the shop floor.' Mrs Asquith was right – it was a weird set-up. 'The buyer, Lister, used to have a milk-round in Mixenden.' Weirder still! 'They have a progress chaser called Joe Concannon, we call him "concussion"! He works for Roy Wood, the planning engineer, with an office by the jig borer. He lives somewhere round Brighouse and uses a motorbike and side-car. He's OK.'

Each of the yellow forms Florence Buckley distributed came to me with each drawing to be checked. It was the sales department's version of the customer's original enquiry and it was Ronnie who returned them, each with a print of the drawing, with the estimate prepared by Arthur or Rodney. That was the system, puzzling to me to use a draftsman in a busy drawing office as an errand boy.

I got home one evening to find a letter with Asquith's postmark – a cheque for my final overtime and tax certificate. Hand written on the 'with compliments' slip was the brief message 'Such a pity, best of luck, Andrew'. It was from Andrew Hebblethwaite, the civilised company secretary.

During my second month at Pratts the dramatic changes started, triggered from London. Our union, then known as the Association of Engineering and Shipbuilding Draftsmen, started pushing to get two weeks annual paid holiday in the north of England drawing offices. They selected Pratts because their subsidiary in Hampshire, Burnerd Chucks, already enjoyed two weeks and Pratts were extremely busy and a strike would hit them hard. Brian passed a letter round the office, from one Ernest Higgins, a full time paid official based in Leeds. He proposed a meeting after overtime in a local pub, to determine if we would actually strike. Eunice gave her very positive reaction: 'I'm all for it, I could do with a break but I've two buses to catch and two meals to cook, so I'm damned if I'm going to any pub.' She signed a form to allow Brian to vote as her proxy.

We met Ernest, had a pint, the vote in favour was unanimous so he said, 'The union HQ will write to give formal notice to the managing director and issue a press release to the national dailies, the *Yorkshire Post,* local papers and Yorkshire Television. The union felt this might boost recruitment if non-members saw the union acting positively against stingy northern employers.'

For some reason Brian said, 'Hear, hear.' I asked Ernest, 'What about any other local firms?'

'We would have liked to attack Asquiths but the union is weak in there, this action might improve that. Union rules call for 75 per cent in favour. We wouldn't get that in Asquiths.' It was only then that I noticed Derek Greenroyd was with us. We drank up and went home. The young lads were thrilled, we older ones more apprehensive, perhaps wondering as to the outcome. Walking home I wondered how the Asquith brothers would have handled this situation.

Brian basked in his new-found glory, he was our link to Ernest, the latter our link to London HQ, who moved very rapidly. Brian showed us a carbon copy of the simple request for two weeks holiday but that was all, no mention of a strike threat. There was also a copy of the reply from Pratts' managing director – an equally simple but very positive 'no'. Such a change would add to costs when they had to stay competitive in export markets, and steel costs were rising, etc. Stalemate. There was a cutting from the *Yorkshire Post*, tucked away at the end of the editorial column the editor thought that such threats were self-defeating, irresponsible and could jeopardise our export trade and lead to a worsening in Britain's already disastrous balance of payments. It read like the world was coming to an end. In contrast, the *Halifax Courier* cutting, which we had already seen, was a big bold spread suggesting that such action would be unique in the proud history of Halifax engineering, occasional shop floor disputes yes, drawing offices never. It went on to outline other glaring differences between north and south. Statistics had even shown that more trains ran late in the north. What the hell this had to do with a possible strike was not at all clear. The reporter must have had a few spare column inches left, so padded it out. Typical press. However there was no mention of the world coming to an end and the paper was sure northern common sense would prevail.

298

There was a scribbled note from Ernest to say that Yorkshire Television had ignored it, there was nothing to film, no dramatic pictures of flat-capped Luddites burning drawing boards.

A week later Brian passed around the ominous warning. The strike would start the following Monday. He took it down to Derek Greenroyd, on return showed it to Arthur Haigh and Lewis. Arthur, looking more serious than ever, bemoaned the fact that things were coming to a pretty pass, whatever that meant. Rodney pointed out to them, 'You'll get two weeks as well and you're not even in the union!'

Lewis just said, 'One week at the wife's mother's place in Bridlington is bad enough!'

The tension mounted. At 2 pm on the Friday Willy Booth, general manager/jig borer, shot through the swing doors. 'Stop working for a minute and pay attention. Mr Pratt senior has agreed to two weeks but cannot get back until Monday morning, he asks that you call off the strike 'till he comes in to explain!'

Brian muttered, 'He might be just stalling, the union will want it in writing, it's a serious matter calling off a strike, after all the organising.'

Brenda surprised us all. 'Ask him to send a telegram, they're written down.'

I said, 'Not just a pretty face, clever with it too. We all get trained to think fast up the hill.'

Both women and Rodney laughed, all the tension swept away. Brenda used her thumb to stick a medal in an interesting position. Booth just looked worried and baffled, no idea what we were laughing at. 'I don't think that's necessary, his son could write a letter straight away.'

The managing director himself brought the letter in double quick time, being an ex-guards officer. 'Who is the union chap?' Brian stepped forward. 'I hope you'll accept this in good faith.'

Brian read it. 'Can I ring the union in Leeds?'

'By all means.' Booth would probably have said 'If you must ring, keep it short as it's long distance.'

Brian rang from Arthur's phone. 'They're quite happy, strike's off.' Pratt Junior shook hands with him and went. Brenda and Eunice joined hands to do a maypole dance in the aisle. Everyone clapped. Lewis, serious as ever, said, 'That's enough you two, I think we should all settle down now and catch up with the work.'

Around 11 am on Monday the double doors opened and in walked Pratt and son. Everyone stopped work and gathered in the aisle. The father did the talking. 'Good morning, I was unable to return on Friday as I was completing an agreement with a French company to manufacture their rotating hydraulic cylinders under licence and also hydraulic tailstocks, plus a range of hydraulic cylinders.' Now I knew why Joe was in Manchester. 'The two weeks paid holiday will commence next summer to bring us in line with Burnerds, we have decided to extend it to all white-collar staff including office girls. We also intend to modernise this office so conditions will improve overall.' Brenda and Eunice started to clap, others joined in and the pair went. Arthur and Lewis went into their respective offices. Brian said, 'All's well that ends well, just shows, it pays to be in the union.'

The episode was headlined in the monthly union newsletter as a triumph and a breakthrough for long overdue reform. The *Halifax Courier* carried a much larger headline 'STRIKE AVERTED', the article below containing dramatic phrases about a 'frantic last minute dash from France', 'saved the day', 'avoided serious consequences' and ended with the much calmer 'Yorkshire common sense had finally prevailed' as they had predicted of course.

Mid-afternoon the doors flew open, and an office girl appeared escorting of all people, Selby Rushworth. He stopped dead, staring at me. The girl muttered, 'I must get back' and promptly went.

'What the hell are you doing here?'

'I'm the checker.'

'It didn't take Halifax Building Society long to rumble you!'

'I soon got fed up of being finance director, too easy, boring in fact.'

'Lying sod, what about that machine you designed for counting banknotes?'

'I sold the patent to IBM, they make it. I'll be getting some good royalties soon, have a Bentley in no time.'

'Lying sod. Where's this Arthur Haigh bloke?'

'That right hand office' (Lewis's of course). He ambled down the room as Brenda shouted, 'Hey Eunice, another refugee.' He knocked on Lewis's door, went in. I saw Lewis rise and point next door. Selby turned, gave me a two finger salute and had a session with Arthur, then stopped by me on his way out. I said, 'I know you'll have got the job, but why did they sack you from Asquiths?'

'Sack my eye, they've stopped the annual bonus and cut the overtime, some blokes get no overtime at all.'

'I never thought you'd lie to me, Selby, I'm deeply shocked. I'll show you a quick way out.' We went down the lift towards the roller shutter. 'You'd better have a sharp pencil when I start checking your drawings. Tell your brother.'

Brooko was loading some sawn-up scaffolding planks into a van. 'I didn't know you had a van.'

'My cousin's, I've borrowed it. I've got a splinter.'

'Brenda will suck it out for you.' He disappeared inside and I directed Selby. 'It's a short cut, left at the end then first left, you can't go wrong. Don't forget, tell your brother I'm the checker.'

'Who's the bloke with the van?'

'One of the draftsmen. Wait 'til you see the jig borer – he's the general manager. It's a circus.'

'Lying sod!' He'd have to walk right down Hopwood Lane, past the Polish White Eagle Club, turn left at the tech, all the way to Lister Lane and up that to get back to Pratts' office block. He could have gone back through the machine shops in a few minutes. I was still laughing as I got out of the lift.

Friday came and Lewis announced 'No overtime in the morning, workmen will be in all weekend.'

Monday morning was amazing. The ceiling and walls were painted white, the cracked window pane had been replaced, frames and all the woodwork painted cream, the whole floor had been laid with grey PVC tiles, the panelled double doors had been covered with hardboard and were also cream, and kicker, hand plates and new chrome handles fitted. The unoccupied drawing boards were left close together at the 'empty' end.

It took some getting used to, so did the reek of paint and whatever they'd used to secure the flooring. During the week an electrician started to progressively fit twin rows of end to end fluorescent lights. Arthur Haigh brought me a big carton. 'You've no window because of the lift shaft, you might need this.' Together we opened the box – an anglepoise lamp.

'Thanks very much, just one problem, there's no socket.'

'When the electrician reaches here he can run a cable down from the lights.'

'Thanks again.'

He took the second carton and put it on the desk in one of the empty offices.

I heard the lift stop and four men came in wearing fawn smocks. They looked all round: one wedged both doors open and they started to drag a new German drafting machine up a steel plate laid over the steps. They then produced a low flat trolley on pneumatic tyres, and loaded it on to trundle it down the room. Two of them went back to the lift to fetch the drawing board, fitted it onto the base, set the rules and finally added the angle lamp. Rodney was the first to receive one, his old roller board and the base drawer cabinet were then taken and left on the lower floor behind the print machine. The trundling continued until every board was replaced, including those unoccupied. The electrician finished the lights and started to fit sockets along the skirting boards.

When Selby arrived the following Monday morning he was amazed at the transformation. He stopped at my desk, staring all round. 'Bloody hell, what happened, did you have a fire?'

'No, I told Arthur Haigh that the place was just as scruffy as Asquith's jig and tool office, so he's had it all done up.'

'It hasn't taken you long to get well in with him then, you lying sod.'

'I had one of these machines up the hill, George bought it for me when I went to work for him, it was the only one in Asquiths.'

'Another bloody lie!'

'If you don't believe me I dare you to unfasten the setting screws to square the rules. See if you can reset it. I can.'

Lewis approached. 'Good morning, we'll get you organised on a board, what was your name?'

302

'The name's Selby.'

'Oh, sorry, what's your first name?'

'Selby, Selby Rushworth.'

'That's an unusual name.'

I just had to say 'He's an unusual fella, too.' I asked Selby, 'What've you got in the case, sandwiches?'

'No, my tackle, and you're not borrowing the big compass!'

I had done so, frequently, when I worked on a board in front of his during the last year of my apprenticeship: on one occasion I had, by mistake, taken it to the tech all day Wednesday, along with my own meagre tackle! The next morning I went in early and slipped it under a drawing on his table. When he started work he said 'Where's my bloody spring-bow, you had it yesterday.'

'How could I? I was at the tech all day.' He found it later. The day I left Asquiths to go into the RAF was when he first christened me 'lying sod'.

Being new to Pratts he couldn't judge whether I was telling the truth, the half truth or nothing like the truth, although he would realise that my term 'circus' was true as with his own eyes he had witnessed Brooko loading wood into a van when he was supposed to be working on a drawing board four storeys above. He certainly didn't believe my horrible sense of direction.

Lewis said the old boards were scrap and would be delivered by Pratts' truck to the nearest kid's bonfire in November. Brooko promptly bagged them but agreed to let me have one board. He borrowed the van again and ran it home for me, the first of his hoard already loaded.

The changes continued, within days three men appeared and the din of hammering, swearing and sawing started as they constructed two cabins on the floor below, opposite the print machine. When glazed and painted the electrician reappeared to fit fluorescents. A labourer brought a huge carton, Lewis directed him to take it into the empty office on our floor. This was a fully upholstered swivel chair which wound into its base to adjust the height. A right luxury job said Lewis, having sat in it and swung right round.

Arthur left the office one morning and returned with a stranger. A tall, erect chap in a neat pin-stripe suit, with crisp, short curled hair and shiny shoes, he reminded me of an actor, Jerry Desmond, who played a department store manager in an old black and white film, a foil for the Marx Brothers. Arthur stopped in the middle of the office. 'Gather round. This is Mr Cope, Harold Cope. From today he is the head of design. I will be chief estimator and Lewis is promoted to chief draftsman.'

Lewis grinned, rare for him as he looked permanently worried. He had once grinned when he saw Brenda trying to remove a splinter from Brooko's finger. The same Brooko now shouted, 'Good old Lewis, I knew you'd make it despite what they say.' This gentle sarcasm went straight past Lewis, who continued to grin, enjoying his moment of glory. 'That's enough, Peter, I'm sure you'll all give him the respect I've enjoyed for so long and work harder still.' He was beginning to sound like an ex-MP at a post-election inquest. Cope grinned. Arthur continued, 'Mr Cope has joined us from down south to strengthen our team. Right, lets get on with it.'

We dispersed and back at our end I said to Selby, 'You're now the head of tool design and I am the chief checker!'

He just looked glum. 'You were right about the "bloody circus", only time you haven't given me a pack of lies.'

Brenda and Eunice set off on another nose powdering trip, as they passed she said, 'We've decided that makes you the chief checker but we aren't going to salute you.' They howled with laughter as they went out and down the steps. I wondered just how much respect Cope would get from these two. What wasn't at all funny were Arthur's words 'from down south!' I had recent experience of a bloke 'from down south', a right bastard who far from strengthening the existing team had done a total demolition job on the whole team. I'd need to be wary of this one.

One day the double doors flew open and an office girl came in with Ronny Hilton, another Asquith jig and tooler. I knew him but had never really talked with him. He would be in his early fifties and worked right at the back of the office on the complex tooling Asquiths fitted to transfer machines for the motor industry. 'Hello, Donald, what are you doing here?' Eunice was just passing and said, 'Hello, Ronnie, he's the chief checker.'

'You're a bit young to be a checker.' The girl took him to Arthur Haigh who promptly sent him to Cope. As he passed I said, 'You'll get the job, for certain.' He spent some time with Cope and on return said 'It'll be the first time in my life I've ever given notice to leave.'

'You'll find the job's a doddle, that bloke Cope is new, don't know what he's like yet.'

Something was going badly wrong up the hill.

The following week I went down to the print room and noticed a woman with black hair in one office, pounding a typewriter and a man in the far office. At lunchtime she met us at the lift. 'Could you direct me to the restaurant, please?' Quiet BBC English, not a trace of cockney. The ever-happy Eunice said, 'That's where we're going, you can sit with us, food's OK.'

In the lift Brian said, 'You're not from Yorkshire' the tone hinting that she was therefore sub-human, even suspect and definitely dodgy.

'No, I've never been in Yorkshire before in my life.' She didn't elaborate on this. During lunch, queuing at the counter, I whispered to Eunice, 'Ask her about her boss, what's his name, what's he supposed to do here?'

'I will'.

We then learned that she was his secretary, he was a specialist in hydraulics, had a degree in this, was French and she had to write his name down on a bit of Brian's scrap paper. 'Jean-Claude Martin de Faulvey BSc'. Brian's reaction: 'That's a mouthful.' She said they both worked for Pratt Precision Hydraulics Ltd. That was an eye-opener. From then on she kept herself to herself although if you met her in the lift there was always a quiet 'Hello, good morning.'

It seemed the two Pratts could really deliver, they perhaps realised that it would be three years before Joe Jackson could be of any real use, and the abrupt arrival of Cope and this French chap showed that they must have planned this some while since. The old man had mentioned the pending French hydraulics units. Here father and son were on a par with the Asquith brothers, carefully strengthening the design team, widening the product range yet still aiming at the same market. The improvements to our lot, prompted we had thought by a threatened strike, were but a small part of a much wider action, despite the twice daily performances by the circus. To me it was reassuring to know that two wise men were in overall charge, Pratt senior quite well off as Ronny Baxter told me he came in a black Rolls Royce on his infrequent visits. I was quite wrong as we knew nothing at the time of the glaring error he had recently made.

Harry Cope started by interviewing each of us separately, probing for strengths and weaknesses, starting with Selby, who returned to his board scowling as usual.

'What's he say? What's he like?'

'Nowt much, seems all right.' That was all I was going to get.

He progressed through everyone, even Lewis and Arthur, although I noticed the door was closed when they attended. He had all four young lads in together, ignored the tracers, I was last.

He opened the personnel file on his desk. 'See you've got Higher National and AMI.Prod.E., I'm in the Mechanicals. You've done well to get Associate Membership.' I briefly explained my last two years' work. 'Just the thing to widen your experience at a young age. When I came out of the army I was seconded by Plessey to work with the control commission in Germany, ferreting out designs and patents Plessey might use. Found very little but the chemical boys had some results with formulae for synthetic rubber and oils. The aircraft companies also got useful stuff about guidance systems for pilotless aircraft from Peenemunde. It could be quite risky rooting about in bombed buildings and prising open buckled filing cabinets. The army got them open for us.'

'Ronnie Baxter was a bomb-aimer during the war.'

'Yes, he told me that. How are you going on with the checking?'

'Fine, no problems, never get errors from Selby or Ronnie Hilton, they're both very experienced tool designers. The four young lads need watching, just to be expected, one or two of the others lack shop floor experience and it shows on their drawings. I only check one in five tracings but they are very experienced, never leave anything off. There's now five of us here, all ex-Asquith.'

'You might like to know that the young lad called Des said you were very strict!'

'You need to be with that bunch, it's the only way they'll learn. I must admit I was just the same at their age, draw first, think later.'

'Right, you're the last, I've done this just to get to know what talent I have available.'

Cope started his daily routine by first getting the pipe alight, then opened his *Telegraph* at the racing page, picked his fancies and then rang his credit bookmaker in Leeds. I was to learn later that he lived in Leeds, his wife was born there and was glad to be back up north again. One day he showed me a letter – stiff crisp cream single page with the heading I knew so well. It was addressed to Lister, Pratts' buyer, short but formal. 'My managing director has instructed me to warn you that we shall procure chucks from other sources should you continue to poach our jig and tool draftsmen.'

'Show it to your Asquith pals.'

Selby said, 'Is that your formal written notice? It hasn't taken him long to rumble you' followed by a cackling laugh.

'They can't sack me, I'm too well in, that woman sales director used to teach me in Sunday School.'

'I suppose you wash her car as well, what else do you do for her?' Another cackle. 'You're a greaser and a lying sod.' I showed the letter to him, he read it and the frown returned.

'Bloody hell.'

'I knew it was only a matter of time, being well in I got wind of it when Eunice and Brenda left. It was only through me you got this job. I had a hell of a problem to get Ronnie in, I got my fellow Masons to help.'

'Bloody lying sod.'

It was my turn to cackle. He now would be stuck wondering if I really was a mason.

'Right, tell me what Lodge you are in.'

'I shouldn't really discuss it with an outsider but it's Blackwall.' (It was very close to where I had first lived in Halifax. It was the only name I knew because I had delivered a glossy magazine there from the paper shop when at school.)

Selby had actually laughed – the two Pratts were changing everything. On Saturday afternoon I was taking a short cut across the car park in town when a face I recognised approached. We met beside a huge, dark blue Austin Westminster, the size the police used on main highways. It was Brian Robinson, he had been two forms above me at the senior school, his elder brother there as well. He had been an apprentice at Asquiths, done national service in the navy, returned to the main design office, then on to estimating. Bored with the life he got a job as a technical representative for the Yorkshire area with the Birmingham firm Tufnel Bearings. They made a resin-based rigid plastic material known for its low co-efficient of friction for bushes needing no lubrication and it had excellent dialectric properties. Asquiths used it as insulation discs protecting the brass distributor ring on radial drills. When machined it came off the tool as swarf with a high dust content, the material was plain chocolate brown yet the swarf was yellow ochre. The women turning it at Asquiths always wore masks over nose and mouth. I knew Brian had married Hilda Hall, the daughter of the electrical superintendent, Arnold Hall. He was now area sales manager for the whole north of England and the big car was his. 'Get a new one every year, the firm leases them. On the road other drivers assume it's an unmarked police car. It can really move. The reps get the Austin Cambridge. You ought to try getting a rep job, see you sometime.' He got in and went. I had a brief glimpse of leather covered seats, big steering wheel and chromed horn ring.

Ambling home I thought about this chance meeting. A rep job with a company car for free might be a way out of Pratts with some benefit to me.

By the time I reached home I was convinced it was worth trying. First I needed a driving licence and telephone. I applied to the GPO who could install one in eight weeks. On Sunday morning I went down town to find the home of a retired bus driver who had a taxi and a little Austin A35 van. He used the latter for teaching driving. He was well known in the town for patiently persevering with would-be drivers who had persistently failed after repeated and costly lessons with the British School of Motoring. I was soon directed to his house, he lived very close to the Warner-Swasey-Asquith works. He was about to depart to give a lesson, but could fit me in Tuesday evening and Thursday. He gave me a

308

Highway Code book. 'Start memorising the road signs and everything in it.' I told him I had learnt first on a Bedford Duple coach, then a Standard Vanguard pickup, all illegal and at night on an RAF airfield, and later driven a huge old American car in Tripoli, with a knob on the steering wheel, an automatic, again quite illegally but the roads were quiet compared with England.

'Have you been with BSM?'

'No'

'Right, must dash, pick you up six on Tuesday.' He jotted down my address. I walked home, stage two now ready to roll. Stage three was to get each Thursday's *Daily Telegraph* and have some CVs typed.

On Monday in the canteen I asked the girls near us, 'Which of you work in the buyer's office?'

'Us three'

'Which of you has a cousin working at Asquiths?'

'I have.'

'I know Glennis, worked in the same office for a year, her boss is a good bloke.'

'Wish ours was, that Lister is a right nagging sod.'

I was right beside her as she went out of the canteen door. 'I need you to do me a favour.'

'Before you start, I'm married.'

'No, it's nothing like that, can you type some CVs for me. I want to get a better job.'

'Bring me a copy tomorrow into the canteen. I did one for Peter Harrop in your place once.'

'Thanks a million, if you ever want a drawing done for a planning application or something else, just ask.'

'Hardly likely, we live with Frank's parents in a council house.'

'I can draw most things but I like drawing wages best. I was thinking of getting you a box of chocolates, milk or plain?'

'Dairy Milk please, that sounds more like it.'

That evening I wrote and re-wrote the CV. Laid out in chronological order it showed careful solid progress. Against each time period I added the resulting certificate, ending with A.M.I.Prod.E., adding some tone to the history by a brief mention of the winter course at Leeds University leading to graduate membership. The RAF activity was just described as 'Senior Aircraftman, loading and balancing transport aircraft' – it gave a better technical impression than 'airborne labourer'. The CV gave no indication of the dramatic and sudden departure from Asquiths. That move could be explained quite logically at an interview by 'the work was completed and the chief engineer and managing director then retired and offered the choice between draftsman and checker the latter was a promotion not available to me at Asquiths.' The ending was just 'Born Altrincham 3.6.31, present age 26. When I passed the test I could add 'clean driving licence'.

I passed my typist friend the copy and by the end of the week she'd typed six. They were immaculate, with ample space for a signature. Underlined below that 'Donald Wm. Ainley A.M.I.Prod.E'. I then concentrated on getting in every spare hour I could in the instructor's little Austin van.

Before the first lesson he stressed, 'During the test the examiner will be constantly watching that you look in the mirror before making any move, and always keep a good look out for any other traffic. The other thing is doing a three-point turn, they're sticklers on it, that's how most people fail. You'll be taking the test in this van so get used to it.' I did, endless 3-point turns in increasingly tight T-junctions, starting on a hill and keeping to 30 mph. Then he started to direct me on a typical test route. He certainly was thorough and patient. The lessons stopped when the snow came, around four inches overnight, it was a week before I could resume.

Christmas came and went. I knew the Highway Code word for word and I booked a test for late January. More snow fell and froze overnight, the main roads were salted but the side streets were interesting to practise skids. This lasted around two weeks and the roads were still slushy. At the driving test centre I found Alf had parked the A35. He said, 'I won't say good luck, luck doesn't come into it. I'm sure you'll pass.' With that he disappeared into the driving centre to keep warm.

The examiner said 'Good morning, are you certain you want to do it in these conditions?'

'Quite sure, I've been driving on this stuff for the last fortnight.'

'Right, lets get started then.'

Very careful about mirrors and hand signal, we started sedately along the broad Huddersfield Road, the 'Shay' football ground on the left, main Ford dealers on the right. 'Take the right fork at the statue.' This life size bronze statue was well known as an oddity. The sculptor had positioned the horse's legs in an unnatural position. Signalling, I moved out to the middle of the wide road, slowing to allow opposing traffic to clear. With no warning, a double-decker bus reversed straight out blocking the road, then pulled back onto the huge tarmac area in front of the bus garage. I stopped and pulled on the handbrake. The examiner said, 'The damned fool, it must be a mechanic, no bus driver would ever do that.' We had both heard the squeal of brakes from a Morris Minor approaching from the opposite direction. The bus was now parking on the garage forecourt, the Minor was at an angle, the driver bawling obscenities across the road. The bus chap alighted and disappeared into the huge garage.

I looked in both mirrors, (bit pointless really but it had become a recent habit) pulled away without skidding and we carried on. We managed to find a dry portion of road across Savile Park and I did an emergency stop, remembering to look in the mirror. Back at the driving centre I read a distant number plate for him. He signed the form, saying, 'I was more than happy when you stopped for that idiot with the bus. Alf is a good teacher, don't know why he doesn't do it full time.'

'I've done quite some hours recently practising in Hebden Bridge in darkness. Alf said it's best to learn the hard way on narrow roads, Savile Park is too easy. Anyway, thanks very much.' Alf ran me back to Pratts and I paid him, with a £10 bonus. 'Thanks for everything.'

I went in very happy with life, clocked in again and went to Lewis. 'I passed it OK. If you fail again try this fellow.' I gave him Alf's card. Lewis intended to book a further course with BSM when the weather eased.

I was checking one of Ronnie's creations when a strange girl came in and asked in a very polite southern accent, 'Excuse me, whom is Mr Cope?'

311

I pointed to the glass cabin, 'The chap with the pipe.'

She went, gave him a file and returned. 'Thank you. I had quite a problem finding this place.' With a 'bye' and a pleasant smile she went. Brian shouted across 'She sounds rich, you want to get after her!'

'Depends how rich, I'm very particular. I rather fancy Miss Buckley, she has a Riley' (a rather up-market car in those days). Minutes later the Frenchman came in, clutching a bundle of drawings: this time a broken accent sought Harry Cope. 'That office there.'

Harry was certainly getting some trade today and I was fast becoming doorman/checker. They both came across to me with the drawings. 'Need to spread these out, can you lower your board, more room than my desk top.' I did, then brought it to the horizontal position. I looked on as they went through all the drawings for the 'Gamet Produits' rotating hydraulic cylinders and rotating oil distributors. The stationary cylinders with a range of end mountings were a very interesting and clean design. I'd seen tipper trucks with welded ends to their hydraulic rams and expected these to be threaded to the tube. Instead they had used a cunning clamp design, which involved a thick wire ring sitting in a half-round groove turned in the tube. On some drawings scribbled translations had been added. No doubt by the Frenchman. The two-way swivel ends were very compact and would call for some crafty machining fixtures. Harry said to me, 'We'll have to get them all re-done in English. Just the job for those four young lads.'

I didn't care for the 'we' – not on my pay level. 'Wouldn't it be a better idea to let Roy Wood have a look at them first, he might want some changes depending on how they'll make them.'

'You might be right, I'll give him a ring.' They left me in peace and Roy Wood was the next to appear.

'Hello, Donald, I hear that French stuff's come, don't know when I'll start on it, I'm swamped out already.'

'It's going to need a hell of a lot of tooling and gauges.' He set off towards Harry's office. 'Oi! The drawings are here on my table.' Doorman, checker, now librarian. If the multi-skilling increased I'd have to be thinking of a pay rise. With no further interruptions I set about checking

Ronnie's latest offering. The yellow flimsy indicated that a Belgian customer wished to purchase a standard 9 inch Pratt scroll chuck with a separate back plate to fit a plain spindle flange with seven bolt holes in it. The chuck to be offset 20 millimetres from the lathe spindle centre line. It looked simple and Ronnie had kept it that way, ignoring the vibration which would certainly be caused by the 20 millimetres off-set. I took it back to him, outlined the problem. 'You'll have to design something to act as a counterweight.'

'How come you know all this and I don't?'

'Five years grafting at the tech.'

'How the hell do I do it?'

I grinned. 'You'll have to ask Lewis, he's your boss, not me.'

'You swine.' I laughed all the way back to my board as he called Lewis to his board and some muttering started. I noticed Lewis glance my way, Ronnie smiling but Lewis just frowning, perhaps even more that usual. Eventually Lewis took the drawing into his office and shut the door. I started to check a grinding mandrel Jack Rostron had designed. I didn't even start to check the dimensions, just did one quick one of my own. 763 lbs. Christ! It was frightening. I just took it back to him. 'You'll have to re-draw all this, Jack, it's totally wrong.'

His reply was very hostile. 'How do you mean, what's so wrong with it?'

'I haven't checked any dimensions, the way it's made is wrong.'

'We were always taught at English Electric that if you can make something out of one piece it's always cheaper than bolting two bits together.'

'Very true Jack, but not in this case!'

'All right then, how would you do it?'

'If I tell you, I'll be checking my own work, how will I know if I'm wrong?'

'Right, we'll see what Lewis says.'

'Don't bother him just yet, he's doing some involved calculations for Ronnie and me.'

'You lot can all bugger off, I'm going to the toilet.' He hid his *Daily Mirror* down his trousers and lurched out.

It was late afternoon when Lewis and Ronnie returned with the now altered drawing and a single piece of paper littered with figures, some crossed out, at the bottom of the sheet two nearly identical figures were deeply underlined. Beneath that the letters 'QED'.

'I didn't know you were well up in Latin, Lewis.'

'What Latin?

'QED: quod erat demonstrandum. Means 'what was to be proven'. Don't you two just wish you were riddled with culture like what I is?'

Selby shouted 'Riddled with guilt more like.' I laughed at this, laughed even more as I studied the drawing. Lewis had decided that one standard jaw would be replaced by a special version, made from an enormous block of 2 inch thick steel. The weight of this would counterbalance the off-set chuck.

'What the hell is so funny?' This from Ronnie, laughing at he knew not what, simply because laughter is so infectious.

Another shout came from Selby. 'Sack him, Lewis, I can't concentrate with all this racket.'

Lewis said, 'All right, seriously, what's wrong with it?'

'Assuming those two weight figures are right then the drawing is right, but you don't know what diameter they will be gripping. If it's a bigger diameter that jaw will be further out and still out of balance.'

Lewis frowned even more, trying to digest this, Ronnie just said, 'He's right, Lewis.'

I said to Lewis, 'Why not see Cope, see what he thinks?'

'I can't ask him, he's the head of design!'

'Well that's what he's there for, he won't bite.'

'Oh, I couldn't, it's not right.'

'Well go and ask Maurice, he's a good bloke.'

'I couldn't do that, Mr Ackroyd is a director!'

'Well it will have to be Harry.' Reluctantly, he went towards Cope's ever-open door, Ronnie, shuffling behind him in his pumps, mouthed the words to me 'You are a swine.'

Selby shouted across, 'Thank God.'

After the three of them had huddled over Harry's desk I caught the words 'Leave it with me, I'll have a go at it.' Lewis came back, looking much relieved. As he passed, Selby said, 'I bet you never had these problems before Donald came here.' I jumped straight in with 'Course he did, he just didn't realise it.'

Jack had returned and he collared Lewis, stuck with his grinding mandrel problem. After some muttering Lewis came to me with the drawing. 'The dimensions seem OK. What's wrong with it?'

'The way it's made, should be a 2 inch bar with a 12 inch flange welded to it, otherwise it'll mean reducing a 12 inch bar weighing nearly 7 hundredweight to 80 per cent swarf.' He went to Jack, told him what to do and Jack just glowered at me.

Some while later Harry banged his window and waved me in. 'Lewis has got this job all wrong, it's the backplate which needs balancing, not the chuck!' He had sketched a considerable extension to the backplate casting with similar weight calculations as Lewis had done. 'That will mean a pattern for a special casting, a neater, cheaper alternative would be to bore a large off-set hole in a standard 15 inch backplate, but it still won't solve the problem!'

'Am I missing something?'

'Yes, we don't know what's going to be held in the chuck, we need Miss Buckley to get some information from the customer'.

I scribbled below his figures:
1. Is it going on a lathe or an internal or cylindrical grinder?
2. Size and weight of the material in the chuck?
3. What is the tolerance on the 20 mm off-set?

'If it's to hold a bar to be turned eccentric the weight of the bar may be far greater than the chuck, and all the bar will run out of balance. There is no way we can counteract this. If it's grinding the spindle speed is so slow, perhaps only 10 rpm so we can ignore balancing and just revert to Ronnie's original drawing, standard chuck on an off-set back-plate.'

'What makes you think it's for grinding?'

'Their drawing of the spindle nose flange. It has the usual sets of three and four holes but also a separate tapped hole for a driving dog.'

'I never noticed that, I'll give it back to her.'

None of the rapid changes which had occurred in Pratts had been my doing, yet I seemed to be leading them all by the hand. My old boss up the hill would have shifted them to labouring on the shop floor, even that might have been risky.

When going to the toilet I'd noticed that the Frenchman was not in his office and later, walking to the canteen, asked his secretary, 'Is your boss away?'

'No, the swine gave false references which this stupid firm only checked after he'd started. Even the BSc was a lie. I'll be leaving at the end of the week, never again will I work in the north of England, and certainly not in engineering. The last job the agency sent me to was an engineering firm in Nottingham. A strike closed that lot down. I'm going to find another agency too!'

The others had drawn well ahead, leaving the two of us to plod through the now quiet machine shop. 'I had to pay three months advance rent on a flat in a pleasant area near the Infirmary, I'll probably lose two months of that, some estate agents with a long winded name.'

'Would it be Crossley, Crosland & Uttley?'

'That's it.'

'We pay our rent to them, my mother paid them for our old house when I was away in the RAF.'

Entering the canteen she put her hand on my arm. 'Please don't tell anyone, I feel such a fool.'

'Certainly not.' We never spoke during lunch, but I kept thinking about the rough deal she'd had at the hands of one crooked Frenchman and two half-French rather stupid Pratts. I knew only too well how rough it could get, up near the top in Halifax engineering.

Later in the afternoon, returning from the toilet, I dodged into her office. She was passing time reading a copy of *Woman's Own*. 'Had an idea. Where's your phone book?' I rang the estate agents, explained who I was and he remembered me, as I was one of very few allowed to pay by cheque. 'If you're wanting a better one, we've got a beautiful semi on Leamington Avenue, Savile Park, the chap's working abroad for a year.' I declined and gave him the whole sob story of the woman I was working with at Pratts.

'By, that's a rough do, no woman should be treated like that. In the circumstances we'll gladly refund the rent when she returns the keys.' 'Many thanks, she'll be very glad.' I gave her the good news.

'I'm grateful, it was very good of you.'

'Not at all, you can do me a favour.' I explained about the CVs I needed to pursue a free company car.

'Glad to, many as you like to pass the time. I'll go back to London to live with my parents, they were a bit worried when I moved up to Nottingham.'

I was tempted to ask her out for a drink but resisted. No much point as she was going back to London. I knew full well how boring it could be to get through a whole week from my own last week at Asquiths, with no boss and nothing to do. At least I had had some very good company to pass the time. It was just one more coincidence in my odd life-style.

Next morning I gave her a CV copy, she read it through and promptly said, 'The phone number should be under your address, I'll get cracking.' At lunch time she whispered 'Done twenty, need any more?' After lunch I collected the clear bold print from a new Remington machine. She put them in a stiff white envelope.

'Have you any envelopes half that size?'

'Stacks, help yourself.'

I took a thick wad, put them in another large one. 'You've done a super job, thanks.'

'When you sorted out the estate agent I was tempted to ask you out for a drink, but I assumed you had a girlfriend.' I just grinned and went. Not versed in the wiles of mature women, I didn't realise she'd given me the open opportunity to ask her the same thing. Perched on the comfy stool, staring at a drawing but seeing nothing, I thought I should have asked her out. I could remember the trim figure I walked behind, up the steps into the canteen, but I could not remember her name! Now, alone with no friends, far from home in a hostile land and in some state of bitter shock from abruptly losing her job through no fault of her own, she would be sorely in need of some deep and sympathetic therapy, the deeper the better. A few drinks in the low-light intimate and lush White

Swan bar could have set the tone, followed by a walk to her flat, which presumably had a bed or at least a sofa-bed. Pitch darkness would have aided the therapy, followed by my lighting two cigarettes in my lips and slipping one between hers, Hollywood style.

The drawing came into focus and I realised all I had left was a file of CVs. I ought to keep one of these as my only memory of what might have been. I started to check a Keith Binney creation. Despite him being a Grad.I.Mech.E. he could not spell 'gauge'. Draughtsmen frequently printed 'guage' instead. That was the only mistake this time. I gave it back to him and started some trig calculations to check a drill jig from Ronnie Hilton.

It was Thursday, the day the *Telegraph* carried all the job adverts. At the end of overtime I stalled, pretending to look for something in each drawer. Everyone moved rapidly to the clock and the lift. I sat, heard the lift grind up and the mesh gates crash closed. It then squeaked downward. In Cope's office I slid the vital sheets from his binned *Telegraph*, folded them to go into one envelope and clocked out, leaving through the side loading bay. I then walked the long way home, clutching the two envelopes, no one at work any the wiser. At home I brewed some tea and began to search through the jobs listed under technical sales. I found four possibles but none involved the sale of machine tools. Three used the vague term 'the north' and the fourth more precisely stated 'Yorks/Lancs/Ches northward incl. Scotland'. One used the term 'field sales', perhaps this was selling to farmers using a Land-Rover and company-issue wellingtons?

I wrote to all four, depleted my mother's stock of stamps, and dropped them into the pillar box next morning. I asked my mother to get two dozen stamps on her next trip to the Queen's Road shops.

Next morning the doors flew open and a bloke in overalls appeared with a small spur gear, some teeth missing, the next tooth badly mauled. 'It's off a turret lathe. Part of the power feed to the turret saddle.'

'Give it that bloke in the white smock in the right hand office.' I saw Lewis listen, peer at the gear and go to Des. The overalls moved to a window to scan the Halifax roof tops. Lewis arrived. 'They've a machine broken down. Will you check the drawing soon as Des has finished it?'

318

'Right, will do.' Des brought it within half an hour but forgot the gear. I took the drawing back to his board, then took the gear to the fitter, still viewing the surrounding roof tops. 'Have you checked the gear meshing with it?'

'Yes, we took it out undamaged.'

'What about the teeth off this?'

'Fished three teeth out of the oil bath.' I took the gear to Brenda.

'Hey Eunice, he's brought me a present, I didn't know he cared.'

'You know I love you, can I borrow your nail file.' I rubbed it firmly across the end of one tooth to reveal shiny steel, then gave it her back. 'I thought you were going to ruin it.'

'I could never ruin anything of yours, I love you too much.' She thumped me right in the ribs.

'Get down the rough end.' She had a vicious right jab, I had first experienced it in Asquith's canteen. I told Des to change the pitch from diametrical to circular and the steel to EN8 instead of the vague term 'mild steel', and change the useless tolerance on the bore to 'to suit shaft'. At least he'd got the width right. Des reacted. 'You don't want much, do you, why circular pitch?'

'Bound to be with only eleven teeth, look at the clearance on the dedendums.'

'I might as well draw it again.'

'Whatever, but fast, that fellow's waiting for it.' I went to this bloke, now staring out of the opposite window with occasional glances at Brenda's legs. 'Won't be long, what's the machine?' He rooted in his overall top pocket for an old cig packet. I took it to Des. 'That's the title, 'Turret Feed Gear for Ward 7A, machine number 37, Bankfield'. Don't forget to give it the next number in the repairs register, which you had forgotten about altogether.'

'We are fussy today.'

'I always am, every day.' I finally signed it, got a print and the man disappeared. In the distance I could hear Lewis berating Des for 'repeated general sloppiness, and you were late this morning.'

At 4 pm the doors flew open again and the Frenchman's ex-secretary came round my board, shook hands and pecked my cheek. 'I'm off now

319

to catch the estate agent and the train. Nice knowing you, pity it was so brief. Thanks for everything, at least I've one good memory of Yorkshire!'

Brian was motionless, his pencil in mid-air, staring amazed. Selby was equally transfixed, leaning on the board, head twisted to catch every word, mouth wide open. A quick squeeze of her hand, 'Must dash, good luck.'

'You too' and she was gone. I've never remembered her name, but she bore a close resemblance to Tessa Peake-Jones, when many years later she played the part of Del Boy's long-suffering live-in girlfriend in the much-loved 'Only Fools and Horses', similar dark hair but cut in a different style.

Brian shouted, 'She might be rich, she comes from London!' Selby's contribution, rubbing his neck, 'It didn't take you long to get greasing round her, have you had her in the lift?'

'Rubbish, you know I'm spoken for, Miss Buckley or no one for me. We go back a long way.'

'Lying sod.' Still rubbing his neck.

I'd noticed Lewis staring down the room. He'd missed the hand-clasp and cheek-peck as her back was to him. He now came purposefully down the room, probably worried as she was secretary to a top boss. Lewis had a very strong sense of 'know thy place' pecking orders. 'What was she nattering about?'

I kept it casual.

'This and that, she eats with us in the canteen.'

Seemingly satisfied he moved away, stopped, and was back. 'I haven't seen her boss for a while.'

'No, he's away on a trip somewhere.' I didn't expand it to 'long gone and far away'.

Even at this late stage, I could have grabbed Harry's phone for a taxi, dashed to the station, bought a platform ticket, found her. Instead I did nothing, couldn't bear to lose the overtime pay. As Harry passed to go home I quietly said, 'I see we've lost our hydraulics wizard.'

'Yes, he was a right bloody fool, so are those two Pratts. Goodnight.'

''Night Harry.'

* * *

320

The following week Miss Buckley brought up the translated answer from Belgium. As usual it was typed on flimsy airmail paper, as was the small print showing a cast-iron sleeve, weight 1.6 kg, outside diameter 180 mm, inside was a smaller partial radius, a solid black triangle pointing to this surface. The phrase beside it Miss Buckley had ringed and translated as 'inside grind?'. There was now a tolerance on the 20 mm of plus or minus 0.1 mm easily jig bored. 'It is internal grinding, I'll give it back to Ronnie to change to his original design. We have no problem left.' Strange how I had had two arguments on the same day, both involving internal grinding.

Harry then introduced his latest idea, again using the ominous 'we'. 'If we vetted every enquiry to see how best to deal with it, only the dimensions would need checking and Lewis could do that. What about tooling?'

'Those two ex-Asquith blokes don't need checking, they've been at it for years.'

'Right then, you stop checking and any really awkward ones, you do 'em, I'll check 'em, there's a weird-looking one here, might be interesting!'

Passing Selby, I stopped. 'Cope's taken me off checking.'

Selby gave a harsh cackle, 'Hey, Brian, Harry's sacked him off checking, I knew it wouldn't be long before he rumbled him.' More cackling.

Brian to me: 'Is that right, are you serious, who's going to do it?'

Me: 'Yes, quite right, Lewis is doing it from now on.'

Brian: 'What are you going to do? If he wants some union trouble he'll get it.'

Me: 'I'm going to do special enquiries.'

Selby: 'Rubbish, he's going to work for his fancy bird, Ma Buckley!' My turn to laugh, we had lots of fun down 'the rough end' as Brenda referred to it. With the boards positioned nearly vertical, we were well hidden from Cope or Lewis and Arthur, well able to chatter away as all three were too far away to hear any of it except Selby's attempt at laughter. Naturally silence reigned whenever the doors flew open.

There were three more drawings on my table to check, I gave them back to each bloke. 'Checking is now stopped, for me anyway, Cope's orders, you'd better see Lewis.' I realised that it was poor Lewis who would be checking the huge total of metric to English size conversions on the mass of French drawings currently being laboriously attempted by the four young lads. Poor Lewis

I looked at the next yellow flimsy translated from the enquiry by Gerhard Telle, Pratt's West German agents. They wanted a three-jaw self-centring chuck with a hole through the middle to clear 300 mm. The three jaws were to be operated by a single hydraulic cylinder. It was to be attached to a self-contained electric welding trolley carrying a diesel-driven generator. A hydraulic pump driven from the diesel would supply power for the cylinder. Operating temperature – 40°C. The trolleys would be used night and day to weld a 2,000 mile natural gas pipeline from Siberia to West Germany. Quote for six units in one delivery.

They didn't want much, to quote Harry 'it might well be interesting'. There was one thing missing, no mention of how they would mount it to the trolley. Miss Buckley would have to swing into action again.

I went to Lewis to get a new blank AO drawing sheet, drew a circle 300 mm in diameter, then just sat staring at it. After a while Selby came across. 'Hey Brian, all he's done in half an hour is draw a bloody circle. Wait while Harry sees it, he'll have him out on his arse.' The raucous cackle started up again.

Me: 'You're rudely interrupting my train of thought. This is a tricky one, it's to operate at minus 40° C.'

Brian: 'I didn't know we had customers in the arctic!'

Me: 'No, the Yanks are taking this one to the moon!'

Selby: 'Rubbish, he's just a non-stop pack of lies.'

Me: 'Shut up, I need to concentrate!'

There are irritating moments when some memory is lurking at the back of your mind and it just won't reveal itself. This was one such occasion. Suddenly it clicked! I closed my eyes to visualise the special fixed steady, built in Asquith's tool room when I worked there on the jig borer. In that case the three self-centring jaws were moved by a lever which could then be locked in position. It was finally fitted on a large cylindrical grinder to grind the radial drill pillars. The hole through that one would have to clear 18 inches. The same design would be a beginning, well worth trying. I laid it out full size until I was stuck – I needed a standard hydraulic cylinder so I retrieved the French drawings of standard cylinders and found the trunion mount version. Pratts could easily make six of these. Eunice cut me a narrow slice of tracing linen and I traced the slot in the moving plate. In each jaw was a hardened pin which was trapped in each of the three angled slots in the swing plate. Moving the swing plate with the hydraulic ram caused the jaws to grip or release the large tube. I traced on the linen and cut out a few views of the slot, playing about swinging them until by trial and error I finalised the slot length required for ½ jaw movement. Selby had been watching this.

'Hey, Brian, fetch Harry to see this, he's cutting out patterns like kids in infants school. Bound to sack him when he sees this!'

Brian said, 'Hey, steady on with that word "sacking", remember we're all in the same union!'

I asked Harry to have a look at my efforts. I'd done a part section view to show the jaw-pin-slot arrangement. He stared intently, sucking the un-lit pipe, then said, 'As I see it, the hydraulic ram moves the plate, the pins in the slots move the jaws in or out.'

'Right, the vital thing we need to know is how they propose to mount it to the welding trolley, and what metric tap size to use for the hose connection to the cylinder. Miss Buckley will have to send it back to the agents.'

'Perhaps you could show on the drawing how it could be mounted and we'll see how they respond. It might be a good idea if you drew the slotted plate as a separate drawing too, makes it clearer for them to see just how it works. Miss Buckley will be coming up tomorrow with another load of stuff to torment us, see if you can finish it for then, we'll go through it with her.'

'Will do – I'll finish it tonight. Might be better to take it down to her in the morning, according to this date stamp we've had it over a week.'

'Good idea, I'll ring her first thing.'

I added a shallow plain recess by increasing the bore to 356 mm × 10 deep with three 16 mm × 1.75 × 80 metric socket screws to mount it to the flange. The bore tolerance I showed as size plus .02 mm, the flange was size minus .02 mm, all this for their benefit. With the plate fully drawn on another sheet I made a list of the vital questions for

Madam to ask of the agents, who in turn would hopefully ferret out some answers from the ultimate customer.

We went down to see her next morning. Spacious neat office, no flowers, large desk, no clutter, two windows and her Riley parked right outside. Harry outlined our problem, she listened politely. I went over the list of questions she needed to translate. 'I don't think there is any point quoting at this stage, until we know more. The fact that there is no mention of any mounting method leads me to think they might intend to weld it to the trolley.'

Harry asked, 'Why that?'

'The enquiry says "steel". Any machine shop could make it but it's bound to be expensive, with every part to machine all over from flame-cut thick boiler plate. Seeing that drawing and eighteen weeks delivery time they might make their own. If they can make the whole welding trolley they can make this.'

'I think a very high price should be quoted, building a huge pipeline they'll be awash with money.'

Miss B said, 'You can be certain of that! We do that occasionally with the Atomic Energy Authority, but they still order.'

I added, 'They are awash with taxpayer's money. By the way, Miss Buckley, if there is no exact German word for "galvanised" use "heavy zinc plated".' I scribbled it in brackets below the title where I had written 'All parts to be . . . except the cylinder bore'.

She asked 'Oh, like dustbins?'

'Yes, only a thicker layer, as used on pylons. Gives long life protection against rust.'

Harry asked, 'Why bother? They can daub it with thick grease.'

'Agreed, but hailstorms or sand blown by hurricane winds will erode it off overnight. It's got to work outdoors in all weathers.'

'Why sand?'

'The Gobi desert is the southern part of Mongolia, and the wind speeds can reach 80 miles an hour. Got all this from an atlas at home last night.' We all laughed. Walking back I said, 'She's quite human after all.'

'I've always found her perfectly OK but she talks to Lewis as though he was a peasant. We'll see what she digs out of the Germans.'

Back in his office I rang Maurice. 'Are the O-rings we fit to air cylinders suitable for use with hydraulic oil?'

'Yes, they are designed for use in hydraulic cylinders.'

The next morning I was woken by a rumble of thunder, the sky very black in the west. I had just boarded the bus when there came the flash of vivid lightning and a much louder growl overhead. By the time the driver was in second gear the rain was pounding the road and bouncing off it. I got off at the boiler works, dashed across to the irate horn blast from a Webster's brewery truck. I'd just started along the side street to Pratts when another horn blasted, right beside me, as a black Riley abruptly halted, the woman driver pointing to me, then the passenger seat. I dashed round and got in.

'What a filthy morning, it was heavy at Caldene Avenue but it had stopped in King Cross.'

'Thank you very much.'

'Not at all, it doesn't do to sit in wet clothes all day.'

I dashed to the loading bay, Selby had turned and was rushing into the machine shop with Eunice and Rodney, beating me to the lift. By the time I got into the office I found Brian and Brooko looking at the latest issue of the union newspaper. Selby was shouting at them. 'It's right I tell you. I saw him with my own eyes getting out of her car just now. She's bringing him to work every day. He's got shacked-up with her.'

'Is that right Donald, Christ, she's old enough to be your mother!'

I just shrugged. 'You were bound to find out sooner or later.'

Brooko said, 'You crafty sod, I've fancied her for years.' Lewis and Arthur walked in so Brooko and Selby retreated to their boards.

Selby carried on in the same vein: 'Hey, I'll tell you summat else. It's only a few weeks back a wench came in, grabbed him and kissed him. God knows what he'd been doing for her. Soon as her boss was sacked he was in her office quick as a flash. I saw him sneak a flat parcel in here covered in a drawing so nobody'd notice. I bet it was a load of rubbers they hadn't had time to use, and I don't mean bloody pencil rubbers either. The day he left Asquiths a very dishy woman hugged him and kissed him. He'd spent the whole week up in her office. God knows what they'd been up to, her boss had retired. Now he's waltzing around in Ma Buck's car; up at Asquiths he greased round the very top bosses. One day I saw Robert Asquith driving his red Bentley, George Hoyle, the chief engineer, sitting in the front with him like a footman. Lord Muck here was lolling in the back seat. Saw it with my own eyes I did. He's allus been a greaser. A greasing, lying womaniser, nowt but. He even used to go to board meetings with 'em, one of t'office girls saw him regular! The office where he worked with Molly had a sign saying 'Keep Out' and it had a lock on it too!'

I couldn't speak, silent laughter was making my eyes water. He 'heard all, saw all but knew nowt'.

It was a week or so later when Miss Buckley came in, straight to me. 'Good morning, Donald, you were right about welding it.' She showed me the translated reply. On the print someone in Germany had crossed out three bolts and the mounting recess. The entry port threads on the cylinder had been marked 20 mm × 1,5 mm.

'Very good, I'll alter the original and get a print for estimating.'

'Yes, please tell Arthur to give it priority, would you give these to Mr Cope. There's a queer looking one from Atomic Energy.' She passed me a sheaf of the yellow flimsies and went.

Selby said, 'Hey Brian, did you hear that?' He tried to imitate in mincing tones 'Good morning Donald, dearest Donald. It's Christian names now, and she normally deals with Harry. Now it's him, dearest Donald. Pretending to us that's the first time she's seen him today. It's nauseating, he's corrupted her already. It's like reading "t'News of the World" only we get it every day in t'week.' He started up the harsh cackling once again.

I took the flimsies to Harry. 'She says there's a dodgy one in that lot, one from Atomic Energy.' I went through the German stuff with him. 'Clever guess about welding, you'd better get straight on with it. It's getting behind.'

'Will do.'

'What's amusing you lot out there?'

'It's Selby, he thinks I'm shacked up with Miss Buckley!'

'My God, he must have a hell of an imagination, you can't be that desperate. The Frenchman's secretary looked quite interesting.'

'She could have been, she was going to ask me out but she assumed I had a girlfriend. I was going to ask her out but I assumed she was sleeping with her boss. We swapped notes just before she left, by then it was too late.'

I altered the drawing, got an airmail print and took it to Arthur. 'This had to go back to Germany for more information. With the delay Miss Buckley said to tell you to give it priority.'

'It's a funny looking chuck.'

'It's just a welding fixture, nothing to it really.'

As I returned past Eunice she said 'What's always so funny down the "rough end", what are you lot always laughing about?'

'No so much of the "rough" my girl, me, Brian and Harry are quite respectable. It's Selby who's rough. He thinks I'm living over the brush with Miss Buckley.'

'I wondered about that. I saw you get out of her car one morning.' Brenda was listening intently. 'She just gave me a lift from the end of the street, it was throwing it down. Anyway there is only one true love in my life.' Both were frowning now with concentration. 'I sometimes cry into the pillow at night, the longing is so intense it's hard to sleep. Sometimes, as I see her walking down the room in high heels and tight skirt the agony of waiting for her to break off that long engagement is so great I feel like jumping off that fire escape to end the anguish forever.'

'I'll give you some agony and anguish.' Brenda's quick fist thumped into my ribs.

'See that, Eunice, they say you always hurt the one you love. Three weeks from now when I look at the bruise I won't mind, I know she cares, just has a vicious way of showing it. At the infirmary when I get the ribs X-rayed I'll tell them it was just a lover's tiff.'

Silence reigned, but not for long as the cackling started up again.

Selby: 'Hey, Brian, can you just imagine 'em at the bottom of the stairs holding hands. "Come, Florence dearest, time for beddy-byes." Florence, what a daft name, sounds like something out of Jane Eyre.'

Brooko: 'Jane Eyre was a prostitute in *A Tale of Two Cities*, you'd know that if you were riddled with culture like me.'

Me: 'I don't call her Florence, I call her Flo, she doesn't like it, neither does her father.'

Brian: 'Christ, does her father live with you?'

Me: 'Course he does, it's his house, next to the last one at the posh end of Caldene Avenue in Mytholmroyd, the one with the double garage, next to the end one with the tennis court.'

Selby: 'Lying sod.'

Brian: 'I know where you mean, I've seen it from the bus. I once bought a wood-turning lathe from a bloke in Hebden Bridge. I know of a big house in Shibden with a tennis court.'

Me: 'I know a house on Savile Park with a tennis court and a private cinema built in the grounds, belongs to Gledhill's Cash Till family.'

Selby: 'I suppose you cut their lawn.'

Me: 'No, I delivered their *Courier*. I used to start at Mackintoshes' big mansion, then Dick Asquiths, Albert Kitchen, Jim Butler and next was Gledhills. I remember Mrs Asquith saying "come in and warm your hands at the fire." She gave me a cup of coffee, a mince pie, a piece of Christmas cake and two quid! It was the best paper round in all Halifax for Xmas tips!'

Selby: 'Dig all those Christian names, started greasing when he was a kid and he's never stopped since!'

Cope banged on his window and waved me to go in.

'That was Willy Booth on the phone. He's on the jig borer, says the drawing is wrong. One of yours, Hilton checked it.'

'A pound says there is nothing wrong with the drawing.'

'Knowing you, ten bob, you're on.'

I went down to the jig borer. Booth sat waiting on an old canteen chair by the machine.

'Hear you've a problem, what's up?'

'When I swing the table 35½ degrees it won't come anywhere near the spindle.' (He meant swing the workpiece). I wasn't surprised, he'd mixed up the setting sequence. The hole was at a compound angle, but off-set on a separate radius at a second angle dimensioned clearly on the drawing from a .500 inch diameter hole marked T.H (a tooling hole used purely for manufacturing the part, as a measuring or setting datum and having no further function once the part was assembled). I wound the machine table back to start from scratch, checked the clamps were secure, re-set and locked both machine and rotary tables. The workpiece was now directly under the spindle.

'Right, you can bore it for the liner bush.'

'I've never seen that done before.'

'They're doing it all day long at Asquiths, got five jig borers up there, I designed two of them.' Knowing he wouldn't believe a word of it, I left him to it.

'Nothing wrong with the drawing at all, the old fool doesn't know how to set up a jig-borer, that's ten bob you owe me! They wouldn't let him use a bench drill in Asquiths.' Cope handed over a ten bob note.

'There can't be many firms this size where the general manager is the jig borer. They'd fall over laughing down south.' I went back to study the weird and wonderful request from the even weirder crew at the Atomic Energy Headquarters.

Meanwhile, at home my pursuit of a company car was getting exactly nowhere. Most firms didn't reply at all, some said they were sorry I hadn't made the short list on this occasion but wished me all success. One kindly opined that I should apply for works manager positions rather than selling. Perhaps they were right?

I was down to the last two CVs and would rapidly need some replacements. My prospects suddenly increased upon receipt of an invitation from some unknown outfit by the name 'J. R. Rose Associates', with a London box number address. Their letter boldly described their function as 'Professional Sales Recruiters to world engineering industries'. The simple reference was HB/01. I knew from *Production Engineer* magazine that there was a southern firm called Hupfield Brothers making plastic injection mouldings machines of up to 1 ounce capacity. The brief *Telegraph* advert stated a new 1¾ ounce machine had been introduced requiring an aggressive salesman to push this in what was described as 'the northern territories'. I also knew from the magazine that another firm called Windsor made a machine which could mould anything up to the size of a dustbin in one squirt, or shot as they put it. The photo had shown a monster 70 ounce machine so large that a man standing on the lower tie bars, with legs outstretched, his fingers could just touch the two upper bars. The hydraulic pump unit beyond the man was enormous. I was invited to 'meet with the undersigned' to discuss this at 7 pm, Room 207, Midland Hotel, Manchester, on Wednesday the following week. It finished with a request that I write to confirm that I could attend (no phone calls please). I rather eagerly did this, dropping it in the post box on the way to the pub.

Wednesday came and forgoing the overtime I shot down to the station, duly arrived at the reception desk at 6.35. 'Could you direct me to room 207, J. R. Rose Associates?'

'Certainly, the lifts are in that corner sir, level two.'

With some time to pass I found the bar and bought a glass of orange juice for three times the cost of a pint of Halifax beer. At five to seven I knocked at room 207, a voice with a slight trace of cockney shouted, 'Enter' and according to the small sign on the desk I was face to face with the Mark Anstruther who had signed the 'invitation to meet'.

'Mr Ainley, do sit down.' We were now facing each other across a typical hotel room writing desk. Behind him huge, fully drawn brown velvet curtains fell right to the carpet. I laid the two references on the desk.

'Your CV was very interesting, good engineering background but no sales experience, any knowledge of plastics?'

'Small plastic mouldings in Christmas crackers, no, however industrial rubbers, yes, but slight.'

'No matter, you'll soon pick it up. Any questions so far?'

'Yes, what's the pay?'

'£800 per annum, but you'll soon top this up to £3000 with excellent commission.'

'What sort of company car?'

'It's a Morris 1100, very versatile motor.'

'What about private use.'

'Well, er . . . within reason, with discretion of course.'

'I was thinking more of holiday use.'

'Oh, yes, just provide your own petrol. These references are very impressive.'

'They should be, they were hard-earned, very hard. Regarding the area, what exactly do you mean by 'northern territories?'

He rooted in a folder and pulled out a map, turning it upright for me. On it a bold line in red crayon went right across the page. This included Lincolnshire, Yorkshire, Lancashire, Cheshire, North Wales, Anglesey, Isle of Man, Northern Ireland and all Scotland. Three other lines chopped up the rest of Britain, indicating presumably four reps for the whole UK.

'Everything north of that line.'

'OK. What about expenses?'

'I'm afraid we do not pay interview expenses.'

'No, I meant working expenses on the job, petrol, hotel bills, customer lunches etc.'

'All paid of course, but naturally don't overdo it. You'll start with a £20 float so you'll be all right for the first month.'

'Right, would I be selling the Hupfield one-ounce machine as well?'

'Yes, and the . . .'

Without warning the curtains parted and a man jumped forward shouting to Anstruther, 'How the hell did he know it was Hupfield Bros?'

Startled, I jumped up from the chair and shouted back, 'Who the hell are you?'

Without even looking at me he snarled, 'I'm the managing director of Hupfields' and repeated 'How the hell did he know?' at Anstruther.

To help the panic-stricken cockney I pointed to the reference. 'HB1 tells me it can only be Hupfields, who else could it be? Do you spend a lot of time hiding behind curtains?'

It was getting worse every minute. I put the vital references back in my envelope. 'I'm wasting my time. A Morris 1100 will be rusted through after one winter on heavily salted northern roads. Next time I go to an interview I'll want all the conditions in writing first and they'll have to be a lot better than this rubbish.' I got up again and simply walked out.

Travelling back in the rattling train I began to wonder if I'd been too hasty. Once I was a rep, getting a better rep job might be easier. Still I

331

wasn't exactly in a frying pan and had no intention of jumping into the fire. Pratts' circus would have to suffice for the moment but I obviously had another learning curve to climb. Picking the brains of an existing technical rep might help.

The first essential was to get some more CVs typed. My friend from London was now back there so I needed to find another typist. I picked the young one who had replaced my first one in the buying office, the one who Brian thought sounded rich and I should 'get after her' as he so diplomatically put it.

I took one of the remaining CVs into work, folded quite small to pass to her secretly, collided with her deliberately when leaving the canteen and promptly apologised, giving me the perfect chance to mention, quite casually of course, that she perhaps could do me a favour. I guided her along the silent machine shop, past the works cat who, vigorously licking itself, completely ignored us, and told her of my quest for a company car. There was no one near us so I could speak quite freely. To my surprise she said her father was a technical rep selling large ovens to bakeries. He had a white Standard Ensign and did an enormous mileage. Overalled characters were starting to arrive at machines. I looked at my watch, 'Better be getting back. Will you come sit at our table tomorrow? I can tell you more about it. If we get through lunch quick enough we'll have more time down here alone.'

'Yes, that would be nice.'

'Thanks a lot.' She waved and hurried away, I hurried too, I could see Arthur approaching from the senior dining room.

In the morning I plodded on with the nuclear wizardry making quick scribbled sketches in an effort to arrive at a workable answer. These efforts led Selby to shout 'He's drawing bloody cartoons now.'

Carole Smith was waiting outside the canteen doors when I got there. Entering the canteen together I grabbed a chair from an empty table and re-arranged ours as the rest of them queued at the counter. The gang reached the table, we joined them and I said, 'We have a guest today, this is Carole Smith.'

The blokes just looked puzzled, Eunice said, 'I'm Eunice Lodge, I work with these layabouts. I worked with Donald at Asquiths, he's got worse since he came here.'

'That's my Eunice, best fan I ever had.'

There were muttered 'Hello, Carole' but they still looked puzzled. Brian continued, 'You get a much better class of diners on this table, Carole.'

I whispered to Carole, 'Skip the sweet, we'll have more time on the shop floor'. We did and left together to puzzled stares. Going down the stairs I passed her the copy. I pointed to the alteration at the bottom. 'I first learned to drive in an RAF bus and Vanguard pick-up on Tripoli airport in the middle of the night in 1954.'

'Where's Tripoli airport?'

'In Libya, North Africa. What it says is exactly true but it reads as though I have had a clean licence since then, whereas I only got it in February this year, passed it first time in the snow.'

'I passed mine first time in Halifax when I was just eighteen.'

'How old are you now?

'Eighteen.'

Twelve minutes left. In that twelve minutes much to my surprise we had arranged that she would come to the top of the lift at ten to six, to allow plenty of time for Harry, Lewis and Arthur to clear the building, I would meet her and she could type the copies on the Remington which the London woman had used. When she was fed up with it, I would clock out, we would go down the lift and out the loading bay. No one in the drawing office would know, and if she would come, we could go to a cinema café for a snack, then into the cinema. 'Yes, what a cunning plan, that would be nice, we must get back.'

'Thanks again.'

Back in the office, Brian now had a field day at my expense, for Selby's benefit.

'You're not going to believe this, but he has now latched on to a young 'un, he doesn't hang about!'

Selby: 'What young 'un?

Brian: 'Her that sounds rich and posh. She once brought some junk up for Harry, but before you came here.'

Selby: 'How young'

Brian: 'Dunno, fifteen, maybe sixteen.'

333

Selby: 'Bloody hell, he should be jailed for baby snatching, not just sacked. Still, that would get rid of him anyway.' He switched on the cackling machine.

Lord, forgive them for they know not. Every time I laughed my bruised ribs hurt.

Our three top men left at half past five, at ten to six I found Carole closing the lift gates. I opened them slightly 'That way no one can come up and find us.' Then I got a shock; Harry Howe was working over to catch up with his copy prints for the Bankfield archives. He asked, 'What is she doing here? Who is it?'

'She's doing some rush typing for Harry Cope, he has no secretary so they sent her up from the office block. I've got to check it as she does each sheet. It's for Miss Buckley, wants it first thing in the morning.' Any mention of Miss Buckley was the rule of law to Harry Howe. Seemingly satisfied he carried on printing. It then dawned on me that if any draftsman used the toilet we would be seen, all my elaborate plan blown. Dick Asquith (ex-Lieut. Col.) would not have been at all happy with my too-hasty planning. Just then I heard foot-steps approaching the double doors. I lit a cigarette, wondering what to do. To my relief it was Rodney, who just stared at the lighted office. 'Who's that? What's she doing?' I gave him the same story Harry Howe had swallowed and he went off to the toilet. I was in the office reading one sheet when he passed back into the drawing office. I breathed again, even if one of my merry gang came down I could get away with it. Even if Selby came down he would not know Carole, and he would get the same story. It was so easy to slip into the 'lying sod' role.

Harry Howe put the lamps out on the printing machine, switched off the cabin lights and shouting 'night' went down in the lift. I heard it halt. Both set of gates opened and closed so I opened the top gates slightly, to disable it once again.

Carole had now done seventeen and agreed to hit twenty, then we'd rush to the cinema. 'It's a beautiful machine, wish I had one downstairs.'

'You've done a lovely job with them.' I stuffed them into the large envelope with the remaining blank sheets as she went to the toilet. The cover back on the typewriter, lights off, door closed and lift gate open for our unseen exit. A real MI6 operator would have wiped every key and the return lever, finally the door handle. Carole reappeared wearing a colourful scarf, make-up repaired and I could smell scent. In the lift she laughed, 'This secret service stuff is good fun, is it always like this with you?'

'Only when necessary, I was nine when I fired my very first bullet. We'll find a phone box, you'd better call your mother, tell her you'll be late.'

'I did before I left the buying office.' Two quick slams of the lift gates and we were off, her arm linked through mine. I had known the best day ever in that circus, now an even better evening beckoned.

It was the first time I had ever walked on a street with a girl on my arm. I kept hearing the high heels clicking faster than my strides, so I slowed a little. We had beans on toast followed by tea and cakes in the cinema café, then went on to find half the short starter film was over. It mattered not as we concentrated on getting to know one another. By the time we kissed goodnight at her bus stop it was agreed that this was to be the first of further such outings. It had been quite an interesting day and progress had been made in a variety of ways.

Next day Harry came up with another idea for change, this change would involve me, and me alone. 'Pratts are to start making three new ranges of products.'

'The French stuff?'

'In addition to that, cone-lok drill jigs under licence from Woodworths in America, and their own permanent magnet chucks, round for lathes, with rectangular ones for surface grinders. Maurice and Derek Greenroyd are designing these at the moment. Roy Wood will be overloaded when planning the French stuff, can you do the production planning for the magnetics?'

'I've no doubt I can do the job, provided I get the same pay as he does!'

'I expected you to say that, I don't blame you but I doubt you'll get it. I'll ask.'

I went back to the radioactive chuck. Despite the in-built problems I had finally solved it. Miss Buckley's 'queer one from the Atomic Energy people' was an understatement, the yellow flimsy read:

A 12 inch diameter 3 jaw power chuck was required with only one set of jaws to grip round, square, triangular, hexagonal and octagonal graphite rods, sizes as sheet 2. Changeover from one shape to another must not involve loose top jaws or loose fasteners, the only operating tool to be a chuck key swivel-mounted on the end of a long spring attached to the lathe headstock. The chuck will operate in a high-level radioactive zone, the chuck key would be handled using remote manipulators by an operator working behind a sealed glass widow set in a thick concrete wall. Spindle nose mounting details and type of lubricant for the chuck to be advised later. Quantity required 1 off only.

They didn't want much.

I started to draw the real thing, commencing with a simple circle, triangle, hexagon, square and octagon superimposed on a common centre. Numbered arrows pointed to the edge of each shape, 0 being the circle, 3 for the triangle, 4 the square and so on. On the face of each revolving top jaw equivalent large engraved numbers indicated the appropriate gripping surface. I drew some open and closed jaws in sectional views and couldn't go any further because I didn't know the promised mounting details. I had nothing as yet to indicate which lathe spindle. I told Harry. 'Ring them up.'

'Don't know who to ask for, I'll ring Miss Buckley first.' I rang her, told her I thought I'd solved the problem, yes it could be made quite easily by jig-milling the top jaws, but it had been a real brain-teaser.

'I expected we'd have to turn it down as impossible.' She gave me the name of D.S. Evans, Buying Department, the number and his extension. Evans got me transferred to one David Hathaway, production engineer in the experimental department. I outlined the problem.

'Oh hell, I'd forgotten! It's to fit on a Dean Smith & Grace centre lathe with an American D6 short taper camlock nose.'

'What about the lubricant for the chuck?'

336

'Forget it, the radioactivity has no effect on the lathe, it's just far too strong for humans to stand.'

'Right, I'll finish the drawing and whip it to the estimators, you'll get a quote in a few days.'

'Sorry to send you a rough one, we're at the mercy of all these scientific boffins in here.'

'It makes life interesting. Cheers.'

I put Harry in the picture and went back to the board.

Selby said, 'We had a squint at that, Harry'll sack you on the spot when he sees a kid's puzzle book. It'll never work, it's pure Walt Disney.'

I replied, 'You're looking at applied science, I'd get a masters degree for that from any decent university.'

'Rubbish, you'll get the sack. Last week it was gas pipes and dodgy Russian bastards, now you're playing about in atomic energy. You'll blow up the bloody world. Brian, you ought to get onto t'union. We ought to get danger money for working near him. Four days he's been messing with that fantasy, and he's corrupting our morals with womanising.'

Brooko said, 'He's started taking that young wench for romantic walks in the machine shop, thinks we don't know.'

'I like to think that Harry and me operate in the real world of international engineering where the going gets tough and we tough ones really deliver,' I said

'Lying sod, it's all Walt Disney make believe. Hey, I've just thought of summat, we ought to write some "anomerous" letters, one to Miss Buckley to tell her about the young wench, one to the young wench to tell her about his Flo, and one to his mother to tell her about both of 'em. We could just put "from a well-wisher"! What did your mother think when you got shacked up with Flo?'

'She doesn't know, thinks I have a flat on Savile Park. The one where that London woman stayed. I thought it was very nice when I stayed overnight sometimes. I only see my mother when I dump my washing on her on Sundays.' Might as well build the legend, fuel their imagination, pile on the Disney make-believe. Jack heard all this repartée but never joined in. I don't think he had ever forgiven me for the grinding arbour episode.

At home there was a letter from a firm called Hellermann Ltd. I dug out their advert, it was very brief: 'The leaders in cable accessories and cathodic protection required a rep for the northern counties. No electrical knowledge required, product training provided. Apply in writing to Theo Smith, Sales Manager.' I was a little worried as I knew the word 'cathode' from cathode ray tubes in TV sets, despite this I had sent off the CV. Theo Smith quickly invited me to an interview in the Queens Hotel, Leeds, and asking that I write back promptly to confirm I could attend at 7.30 on Monday week. I did so, very promptly, posting it on my way to the pub, but this time there was a difference. I asked him the vital conditions and was surprised to receive a very clear reply in the Friday post. The area was precisely Yorks/Lancs/Ches/N.Wales up to the Scottish border. The car a Hillman Minx, renewed on reaching 50,000 miles. Salary £950 paid monthly plus annual profit share, probably not exceeding £50. All expenses paid weekly with a starting £50 float. I could claim for 20 cigarettes a day and seven and six lunch allowance if not entertaining customers. The car was available for 100 personal miles a week which could be accumulated for holidays but not abroad. It was all clear so on Monday I skipped the overtime and went by train to Leeds. Queen's Hotel is built over the main station and towers well above it. I asked at reception and was directed to room 318.

Theo Smith was perhaps 45, neat and compact, pleasant smile and spoke without a trace of cockney. He sat on the bed, allowing me the only chair. He was the sort of bloke who would get on with anyone at any level, totally normal and relaxed. 'Did you get my letter in time?'

'Yes, good of you to send it. Everything seems straightforward. If I'm offered the job I'll certainly accept it.'

'Any questions about what I sent you?'

'No, but I would like to know about cathodic protection.'

'You can forget it, we have two specialist reps who handle just that. It's a form of galvanising for outdoor steelwork, Hellermann took it over from the two men who developed it because they could not afford to sell the system. These two are now the reps. They started up in an old oast-house in Kent.'

'It might interest you to know that one hundred and five people replied to that one advert. Some could barely write English, some wrote an obvious list of lies, one had a clean licence except for once being wrongly convicted for jumping a red light, one wanted to cover Yorkshire only as he couldn't stay away overnight, he had a pub to run in Rotherham! I finally picked three, I saw one earlier who I had to turn down, pleasant chap but finally admitted he was 61 and had given his age as 51. He couldn't get into the firm's pension scheme at 61! I'm getting dry with all the talking, like some coffee?'

'Tea for me please. What happened to the chap who was previously doing this job?'

'His wife had their first child and he wanted to be home every night naturally, so he's taken some design job back with his old firm, English Electric in Bradford. He'd worked for us five or six years.' There was a knock on the door and a waiter brought in tea and coffee with biscuits. 'You're now on a short list of two, I may well give it to this remaining chap as he has been selling to electrical wholesalers for ten years, providing his CV is not a pack of lies.'

I spread the certificates on the bed as he sipped coffee. 'That lot should prove my CV all right.'

Unlike the weird recruiter in Manchester he glanced at every page in the RAF discharge book. 'I well remember that yellow fever jab, knocks you right out for a couple of days. See you were at Idris, it was called Castel Benito when I knew it. Tomorrow morning I'm going to see my sister in Roundhay, her husband and I were in tanks together in the Western Desert. The final chap is due in ten minutes, you've two chances, I'll write – either way, soon as I'm back in Crawley. Goodnight, I'm glad you came.' We shook hands.

'I'm glad I did, thanks for a very pleasant interview.'

His promised letter arrived three days later. He'd felt obliged to give the job to the experienced rep but wished me well. It was disappointing, yet at the same time encouraging to have got so near. I had no inkling that by a strange fluke, within a year I would get to know Theo Smith a lot better.

Back at work Harry passed me one more yellow flimsy. 'One here from your old mob who don't like us poaching their draftsmen.' Warner

Swasey Asquith required two power chucks to fit their D6 short taper American cam-lock spindles, the larger chuck to fit the D8 size, along with the usual air cylinders. A set of three special jaws was required for externally gripping and another set for internally gripping the variety of forged flat discs, two sets per chuck. The Japanese drawings must be returned with the quote *without fail*. In the event of any queries please contact George Barnard. These drawings showed five sizes of discs ranging from 12 inches outside diameter down to 5 inches. On each drawing someone had put a line through some Japanese characters and scribbled the word 'disc', further Japanese lettering was crossed out to show the name 'Datsun'. That's if it was Japanese, might have been Chinese for all I knew.

Harry said, 'I think they are for disc brakes, the coming thing for ve-hicles. They are already used on racing cars.'

'I think we might have a problem fitting this range onto two chucks – 12 inch down to 5, it's a big difference.'

'Have a go then.'

I laid out the barest essentials of 12 and 10 inch chucks, then got some tracing linen and traced each ring and a standard blank jaw per chuck size. Selby came across to have a look and perhaps assess the new risk. 'He's cutting out more fancy patterns, mucking about now with some Japanese stuff, God help us, Brian, ring the union about more danger money!'

'Harry has total confidence in my ability to cope with all these varied challenges, if you'll pardon the pun.' However I juggled the jaw and disc cut outs it would have to be done on 8, 10 and 12 inch chucks, not just two sizes. Standard soft top jaws could be used to have the grip-ping step reduced to three-sixteenths high before hardening. I rang the sales office. 'Yes, that would be no problem. Chucks, cylinders and soft jaws are always in stock.'

The only George Barnard I knew of had been two years above me in the senior school and lived at that time in Norland, a hilltop village across the valley from the school. I rang him and explained that three chucks were required rather than two.

'What's delivery like?'

'Special jaws are sixteen weeks, chucks and cylinders in stock. Will you be making the draw bars?'

'Yes, we normally do, but sixteen weeks is impossible. We were so intent on making the lathes we forgot to order the chucks etc. We need to get the machines on board ship in six weeks for an exhibition in Japan!'

'OK, let me doodle with it, see what I can come up with, I'll ring you later today.'

First I rang Roy Wood and briefly told him the problem. He said, 'No reason why they can't convert soft top jaws themselves, and they've Holt Bros. on the doorstep to do the hardening, but there is just one snag, when we send them into Holt Bros. we instruct them to blank off the serrations with thick clay. This keeps the case-hardening from the serrations, leaving them soft, but the heat still distorts them. When they come back we take a light skim over the serrations to restore them, otherwise they will never mate with base jaw serrations.'

'It's unlikely Warner-Swasey will have a serrated milling cutter, who would they have to ask to borrow one of Pratts'?'

'Willy Booth, leave it to them to organise that, don't you get involved, he's a right cantankerous old sod.'

'OK, many thanks.'

I went through everything with Harry and rang George Barnard, who decided he'd better come straight up to see the drawing. I went to Arthur with the flimsy. 'This one doesn't need any drawing, it can be made from standard stock items with soft top jaws. The customer's due any minute, can you put a price on it but include two off 8 inch chucks for D6 mounting, and one set of inside and outside top jaws for each chuck. He might want to see the prices while he's here.'

'Hang on a minute.' He listed each item with its price in pencil on the flimsy, finally added the total, £1432. Shortly afterwards George arrived, guided as usual by an office girl. We shook hands, vaguely recognising each other from school.

'What did you do when you left school?' I asked.

'I was apprenticed at Stirk Planers, it's now "Cov-Mac".'

'I was at Asquiths.'

I waved to Harry and introduced them. We stood around my board as

I outlined a solution to the problem, showing George just why three chucks would be needed instead of two, did a sketch for him showing the operations required to make the jaws and advised him to arrange to borrow the serration cutter from Willy Booth, the general manager. I showed him the price Arthur had promptly provided.

'Thanks very much, you've got us out of a right mess, I'll get these ordered right away.'

'Don't forget to make the draw bars.'

Off he went, a happier man. Selby said 'He's greasing round outsiders now, sniffing for a job at Warner-Swasey.'

'Rubbish. I went to school with that bloke.'

'Lying sod.'

Two days later Harry banged on his window and waved. 'Shut the door, I've just had Willy Booth on the phone. You may not believe this, but he's suggested I get rid of you as you seem to be doing three people's jobs, therefore you can't be doing your own job properly. Said he'd been pestered by Warner's managing director to lend them a special milling cutter and you'd arranged this.'

'It does take some believing, the stupid old sod. What did you tell him?'

'I told him he'd first have to get me someone just as good and I'd need an order, not just a suggestion, and that would mean Pratts would have to deal with the union!'

'I'll go down and give him a piece of my mind.'

'I wouldn't, you'll just make it worse, but you ought to tell the union so they are in the picture. That bloke will have his knife into you from now on, and you made him look foolish with that thing about the jig borer.'

'There might be a better way, I could appeal to Miss Buckley. She might not know anything about this, she used to teach me in Sunday School but it's years ago.'

'That could be a very crafty ploy, see what her reaction is and only then tell the union. Ring her up.' I did, telling her a problem had developed with the Warner-Swasey enquiry and I'd like her opinion, before going any further with it.

Miss Buckley said. 'They brought an order in yesterday and collected all the equipment. Come on down.'

Harry said, 'That sounds like she knows nothing about it.'

'I'll enlighten her.'

'Be careful, don't start playing hell about Booth, just stick to the facts and nothing else, and don't do any pleading. You might also mention that it puts me in an awkward position with the union. She once told me about you lot threatening to strike for two weeks holiday, she'll not want the union to get involved.'

En route to her office I thought about his words 'have his knife into you'. Exactly echoing Dick Asquith. I could be hanging on the end of a snake again, but this time I had a very strong ladder available – the union.

I explained everything calmly and clearly, told her I was very surprised as I had managed to get Pratts an order for two extra chucks and 18 blank jaws, and ended with Harry's mention of the possible union problem. She listened as ever without interrupting, but she was frowning when she at last replied. 'I am amazed, it sounds so spiteful, so childish. I'm sorry this has happened, I'll go and have a word with Mr Booth right now. Try and forget it. I'll speak to Mr Cope later. You did right to tell me about it.'

'I haven't mentioned it to our union rep as yet. Perhaps the fewer know about it the better.'

'Yes, very wise. I wouldn't wish Mr Pratt to hear of this, he's still smarting over that fiasco with the Frenchman!'

Walking back I realised I had broken my golden rule. I had gone the extra mile for Asquiths. The strong habit developed up the hill was just too strong.

By the time the lift stopped, I had decided exactly what I would do. I went into Harry's office and closed the door.

'Well?'

'She apologised, said she'd have a word with Willy Booth. She thought what he was doing was spiteful and childish. She'll have a word with you later, would like it kept quiet, I haven't told Brian.'

'She is human after all.'

343

'We'll see, she might be just fobbing me off to keep the union out of it.'

'I still think you should get down south, Halifax is too old fashioned. Go make some money while you're young enough.'

I left him and went to Lewis for the next yellow flimsy.

Lewis said, 'This box of bits goes with that enquiry.' I looked into the box to find weird shapes in wood and steel, some looked like misshapen duck eggs, one was flat, each had a short spigot which some idiot in Eire wanted to taper turn and drill. They were heads for a set of golf clubs.

I said, 'We can't machine jaws to hold irregular shapes like that, give it to Arthur, it's impossible.'

I picked the next one and dumped it on my table. Selby muttered, 'Where have you been skiving off to and why are you having closed door sessions with Harry?'

'I popped down to see Flo, she wants to go to the theatre in Manchester tonight, I couldn't very well ring her from his phone.'

'You? Buying theatre tickets, that's a laugh!'

'What makes you think I bought them?' He switched on the cackle, somehow, today it didn't seem at all funny any more. I grabbed some scrap paper and went to Brian. 'Give me the union rag, I've nothing to read in the bog.'

As usual the back four pages of this tabloid were crammed with all manner of engineering jobs. Some quoted £1 per hour, others up to £1.2/6d, with a sprinkling of pension schemes, subsidised travel, luncheon vouchers and other goodies. I copied two, one an American firm in central London, the other a contract tool design firm in Horsham. This one, with a toolroom in Guildford, offered £1 per hour with ample overtime, toolmaking experience preferred. 'There's an interesting story in there about the War Office pleading with Thorneycroft's management to avert a strike as it may delay delivery of tank transporters!'

Brian said, 'Yes, I read it, just shows the strength of our small union.' I knew that strength only too well from experience during the last hour.

I plodded through the work, the next was quite straightforward. DeHavilland Propellers required special top jaws with a larger step cut away to clear the component to be gripped. Once finished, I went over it with Harry and delivered it to Rodney for his estimating process. The next was just as simple, Heald Boring Machines needed special jaws to grip the vee of a vee-pulley whilst finishing the die-cast bore. In this case the chuck was static while the spindle with the boring tool revolved whilst being fed forward.

I left at 5.30 and sped home to get CVs in the post. My stock was down to three, recent ones had produced either rejection or no reply at all. Carole had left Pratts, obtaining a far more pleasant job in the buyer's office at Blakeborough Valve Co in Brighouse, which meant two bus rides a day instead of four, occasionally she even walked to work. Here the chief buyer was Guy Blakeborough, a descendant of the founder. It was unlikely he had ever had a milk-round. They made up to the largest sizes of valve for water and sewage works, power stations, hydro-electric schemes and the nuclear industry. Many were remotely activated and they exported them world-wide.

Carole and I had quickly started going out together at weekends. I had met her parents and two younger brothers, the older, Nigel, attended Bradford Grammar School as a day pupil, and was in the Sea Cadets. The younger brother, Robert, went to the nearby Hipperholme Grammar School. A Bedlington terrier called Lucy was the sixth member of the household. Carole's father had a white Standard Ensign company car, piling up tremendous mileage selling huge conveyor ovens to bakeries. He did this for Spooners, based in Ilkley, who built and installed them for the bulk production of bread, cakes and biscuits. He grew his own tobacco in the back garden, dried the leaves in the cellar and blended it with his normal pipe tobacco. Her mother had a green Morris Minor. They lived in a large semi-detached house, the steep front garden had been dug out for a garage.

Over a period I got to know Carole's large family on her mother's side, around Huddersfield, and occasionally we borrowed her grandmother's old Hillman Minx. Her mother's maiden name was Wimpenny, her great-grandfather founded the family construction firm based in Huddersfield with their own joinery shop, quarry and a variety of tower cranes and heavy building plant, concentrating on large projects, multi-storey car parks, office blocks etc. and were developing a large industrial estate at Normanton, near Wakefield. During the late 1930s they had built a cinema in Huddersfield and after the war sent some dressed stone to London, to repair slight bomb damage on Buckingham Palace.

Carole's father had a twin brother, Francis, who was London Sales Manager for John Summers Steel, a rolling mill at Shotton, near Chester. Summers had an office suite on the top floor of the St Ermins Hotel. Francis and his wife, Betty, had four children. John, the eldest was an apprentice at Jaguar Cars in Coventry, Jennifer was intent on becoming a nurse. Godfrey and Catherine were still at school. They lived in Banstead, Surrey, in the same road where Carole had been born, as did close friends of her mother and father, the Hobills. Bobby Hobill was then manager of the London office of the Ferranti electrical empire.

Carole's mother had a sister, Nancie, whose husband, John, had survived a horrific accident while checking maintenance work atop an electricity pylon. The current should have been switched off, instead 32,000 volts bounced him into the air to land unconscious straddling the lower pylon arm. He sustained a huge area of burnt flesh on his back and suffered recurring bouts of severe depression right through his life. The East Midland Electricity Board were totally liable so he received a huge lump sum and a job for life. With the cash he had a detached house built at Southwell in Nottinghamshire. They had five children, however one died aged three.

Carole and I tried to draw up a family tree of this vast brood, but were defeated by the twin brothers, born in Streatham, south London, marrying two cousins born in Huddersfield, Yorkshire. At the time of writing this, there are still four branches of this family, each with four generations still alive.

Replies to my job applications arrived very promptly. The first was from U.S. Industries (U.K.) Ltd. in offices above Burlington Arcade, inviting me to an interview Monday week. A Richard Girling Snr, design chief, would be available from 8.30 am until 6.30 pm and he asked me to confirm that I could attend. Travelling expenses would be reimbursed. Multi-Development Engineering Co. Ltd. in Horsham also wanted me to attend on exactly the same date. Perfect, I could hopefully fit them both in and craftily claim the rail fares from each firm. One Donald Welton would be there up to 7.30 pm so an exact time was not important. I promptly wrote to both and confirmed the date. I found the London underground map in the back of my mother's diary. Kings Cross to Oxford Circus, change for Bond Street. Bond Street to Green Park, change for Victoria. British Rail Brighton line to Crawley, change for Horsham.

I told Harry I would not be in on Monday. 'Going to interviews, London and Horsham, West Sussex.'

'Best thing you could do.'

Monday I set off early with the little attaché case I had bought in town. In it just pyjamas, shaving-gear, a note of the route, the diary, certificates and both references. I was in Kings Cross by 11 am and went down into the tube, which ran far less frequently during the day. From Bond Street I found the Burlington Arcade and the office entrance between two shops.

Richard Girling Snr was an elderly, wrinkled American. 'I'm glad you have no previous experience of heavy press design, we'll teach you our way.' He unfolded a large print. 'This is a half-scale section across the crankshaft of our largest machine. Will you describe all the parts for me? This is an American drawing but here we use metric dimensions – the machines are built for us in Italy by Innocenti, best known for building English Minis under licence and their own scooters.'

I worked my way across the drawing from the huge four groove vee-belt driving pulley, clutch, double bearing in its housing, double throw crank, a further bearing and massive flywheel. 'These double frames are shown as steel, this long vertical bar presumably works the clutch?'

'You got it. That's fine. Those frames are 1 inch thick welded steel plates. When can you start?'

'I would have to give a week's notice to quit, but there is one other job I want to explore, the chap I need to see is on holiday until next Monday. I'll ring you immediately I've seen him.' Might as well maintain the sobriquet 'lying sod'! 'What's the pay?'

'This office is just temporary, we're relocating into permanent new offices on an estate in Hounslow, near the airport, in six weeks. The pay is £1200 paid monthly plus overtime. This sure is a pricey town. You get luncheon vouchers and travelling expenses of £3 per week. What did today's travelling cost you?'

'Just fourteen pounds for the rail fare.' All he had were five pound notes, so he gave me three and another for 'a meal going back'. I thanked him, signed the expense sheet and promised to ring on Monday week.

I rushed to the tube and finally reached Horsham at 2.30, found a café in the town and had a simple meal, then found the office. It was nice to be in a normal town instead of crowded London. It was a newly-built office block, ground floor occupied by an insurance company, the drawing office on the first floor.

Climbing the stairs I suddenly realised I had never shown the references to the American. No matter. The full office area was littered with drafting machines including three women tracers. In a small glass cabin I found Donald Welton and shook hands. He ran this office, organised the work load and checked the drawings. His partner, Dave Milner, delivered and picked up work for customers, also delivering tools from their Guildford tool room run by the third partner, Eric Mallinson. He was an ex-toolmaker from Hawker Aircraft at Kingston. 'Dave is a cockney who used to sell spare parts for cars.' Donald had also been a toolmaker at Hawkers. They could thus provide a design only, or a design and build service. They were often offered work other than press tools and this is what I would be doing. My predecessor, a Geordie, had returned to Newcastle to work as a checker in Reyrolles electrical firm.

Donald said, 'We pay £1 per hour, £1.2/6d weekday overtime, £1.10/- Saturday and £2 Sundays, paid weekly. We charge the customer £1.2/6 per hour and the same 25 per cent for overtime. I'll give you your travelling costs before you leave, you can live with the widow where the Geordie lodged, it's a bungalow only walking distance from here. The pub next door serve a three course lunch, most of us use it, but not at weekends. How do you feel about it? We are pretty desperate.'

'I'm more than happy, everything you've told me sounds fine. I'll take the job gladly, I'll give a weeks notice tomorrow.'

'I've provisionally booked you a room in the Black Horse hotel, if you can get trains back I'll ring to cancel it. Seeing as you have accepted we'll stand that, just sign their bill in the morning. It's an old coaching inn, we have our office Christmas Dance there, very good food.'

'That's very good of you. I'm a bit puzzled why you trace tool drawings.'

'We don't, those women trace aircraft wiring diagrams for the three V-bombers, we had to buy that steel drawer filing cabinet to keep them overnight, the Air Ministry insist on security and Dave has to deliver them as soon as each is finished. How he got that work I don't know, I think he could sell fridges to Eskimos.'

'Could you do me a sketch map? I'll find the bungalow and have a word with the landlady while I'm here.' He did this, then extended it from the office to the hotel. He scribbled Mrs Williamson, 4 Hengist Close. We shook hands and he unlocked a metal cash box and paid out my rail fares.

'I'll travel down next Sunday and start Monday morning.'

'I'll get you a clock card and you'll have a key to the office.' Once again I had forgotten to show the references.

I found the widow in a small, detached bungalow, one set in a semi-circle of six with a common lawn in front of them. She was perhaps 65, her husband had died shortly after retirement, having worked as the bridge master to Sussex County Council. She wanted £12 per week, didn't provide any meals but I was free to use the kitchen any time. The bungalow was spotless with one spare bedroom, and I could have a spare key.

I found the hotel and booked in, far too early for dinner, so went back to the station to check morning train times. I found the same café and got a cup of tea just before they closed. I ambled round the town centre, most shops were closing and back in the hotel I shaved, had a meal and went into the bar for a couple of pints of some Courage beer which was weird. I had had a hectic day but a very interesting one, and slept like a log.

Riding the nearly empty trains next day I thought about the big changes ahead. I would be out of the circus and even better, I would be working for a toolmaker, and the net pay, even after tax, would be higher than at Asquiths. I'd also made a good profit on the trip. At home, I explained it all to my mother.

Wednesday morning I wrote out the brief notice and gave it to Harry. 'Too late to get a train back, I got both jobs, I'm going to take the Horsham one, a tool design office. The pay is £1 per hour with overtime at the usual rates. They've got a tool room in Guildford, do design and make. Not only that, they paid my hotel bill.'

'Just the job, told you you'd get far more pay. Write that notice out again and change the date to last Saturday, I'll have to hand it to the wages office. I'll get one of their girls to type a very good reference. You'll never regret it.'

'Thanks Harry, I'm very grateful.'

Later, Harry brought me a typed reference. It was excellent – according to him I was versatile, quick and accurate on a drawing board, with a wide knowledge of machining, and would be difficult to replace.

'Very good of you. I'm very grateful.'

When Harry was back in his office Brooko said, 'Harry has just given him his written notice.'

Selby contributed, 'Flo will soon throw him out when he's back working in the scrap yard at Ovenden.' The usual cackling started again.

Mid-morning Harry banged and waved. 'A Richard Asquith for you, want it private?'

'No, it's OK.'

It was an invitation to a pub lunch that very day in the Golden Lion, which I had known so well. George and John Holmes would be with us. Without knowing it, Richard's timing was perfect. I agreed it would be great to see them all again, I'd come up the hill. I cradled the phone.

Harry said, 'Not another job, I thought you'd accepted the Horsham one?'

'No, just a pub lunch for old times sake. Dick and George Hoyle, the chief engineer, both retired the week before I left. It came about at a boardroom row which lasted from 9 am until 3 pm. George and I were told to attend. The other three members of the main board were there too, a stockbroker, an accountant and a solicitor from London. They didn't know a machine tool from a 12 inch rule, but they knew a lot about making money. My work for George was finished and all I could do was to go back into their jig and tool drawing office, so I came to

350

Pratts as a checker on more pay. You'd have fallen over laughing at what went on in that boardroom. Those two and John Holmes, the tool room superintendent, were the best bosses and later the best friends I'll ever have. I could be back a bit late.'

Harry said, 'Who cares, it's your last day, go out the loading bay so no one will know. When you're back I'll sign your clock card for 1.30.'

'Thanks again, I'll have to add you to my list of best friends.'

I slipped out at 12 and the first thing I saw in the pub car park was a black Bentley. Two red Bentleys were across the road. Highroadwell appeared awash with money this Friday. I spotted the low-loader starting to traverse Bob Lane from the far end of the works. Apart from the black Bentley it was as though I had never been away. I saw George's car beyond the Bentley. I found them, shook hands as the landlady started to cut slices of pie.

'I haven't seen you three for ages, your mate just came in,' she said.

'Those two retired, I work at Pratts now.'

She delivered the plates with a cruet to an empty table, then returned with three pints and a double whisky and soda for Dick, who today looked every bit the country squire. Check flat cap and shirt, yellow neckerchief with a paisley pattern, smartly cut hacking jacket, fawn twill slacks and highly polished brown brogues. He was a perfect advert for Sam Stocks Tailors, downtown.

John brought us up to date. Lennox had disappeared about two months after we had left, taking his fancy man with him. The London board members had then recruited two blokes, one from Churchill Machine Tools and the other from Elliot Milling Machines, both mid-forties, very solid clued-up machine tool men. Churchills had soon after ordered one of the Asquith new jig borers. Alf Johnson had retired and the foundry was now limited to producing castings up to ten tons. The main central foundry building had been totally demolished and the pattern shop extended.

I asked Dick what had happened at the AGM of the Asquith Machine Tool Corporation in London.

'No idea, didn't need to attend. The evening I retired I rang George

351

to tell him I was selling all my shares, making a complete break with the company. I put a sizeable chunk into Tube Investments Ltd, and a considerable proportion of my son John's also. The shares have risen nicely and both dividends have been over 10 percent. George did the same, we used a Manchester stockbroker to avoid the Londoners knowing immediately. The Asquith share price had never moved, nor since.'

I said, 'You remember Lennox saying on his first day that we should all set about "kicking Asquiths into shape"? In reality the three of us and Robert, before his tragic death, had already done that, before he arrived.'

Dick said, 'Very true, he was wrong on all counts, and we did a very good job of it too.'

'What about Asquiths Electrics at Colne?'

John said, 'I heard from Arnold Hall that nothing changed, they just carried on as normal. Arnold retired this year.'

'There are now six of us ex-Asquiths at Pratts, but there will be one less from tonight. I'm shifting to work in Horsham, West Sussex, in a jig and tool drawing office, with its own toolroom. With overtime the pay will be higher than I had over the road. Pratts is a strange firm. The buyer used to have a milk round, they have four separate canteens, the general manager is the jig borer, the sales director is a woman who's good at European languages, the managing director is an ex-guards officer! Asquiths sent them a letter threatening to stop buying Pratt chucks if they didn't stop poaching Asquiths jig and tool draftsmen.' The laughter increased the more I told them.

George said, 'I always thought Johnson ran a bunch of clowns but that sounds like a total circus.'

'It gets better, they decided to make hydraulic cylinders, valves etc under licence from a French firm called Gamet Products. They built two glass offices for a French hydraulics wizard and the secretary he brought from a London agency. Well after he started they only then checked his references and found they were all false, even his BSc was faked, so they sacked him. The managing director and his father, the chairman, are called Galliers-Pratt so they must have some French connections.

Pratt senior has a forestry estate near York and sells wood to Pratt Chucks for their packing cases.'

John said, 'I have never heard anything like it. A jig-borer general manager.'

Dick added, 'Perhaps we were all lucky working across the road up to Lennox arriving.' He went to the landlady and paid for everything, including the second drinks we had enjoyed.

With mutual agreement to repeat this happy time and hands firmly shaken we went our ways. Dick dropped me off in Hopwood Lane and I sneaked up the lift, clocked in at 2.20, Harry signed the card and I dumped it back in the rack. Selby shouted across, 'Where the hell have you been?'

'Round and about, just got a lift back in a Bentley, my old mate's got his own black one now.'

'Lying sod!'

I shook hands with Harry for the last time. 'Good luck with the horses, it's been nice knowing you.'

'Get settled down there and you'll never look back.'

I went down the room, asked Brenda, Eunice and Ronnie to come into Lewis's office and to puzzled looks closed the door. I told them the good news and they were somewhat startled.

I said, 'It's been grand working with you all, but I've got to leave you to the fun and games while I get out into the world to make some real money.'

'Come in and see us sometime, where are you going?'

'Horsham, West Sussex, on jig and tool design. Where's Arthur?'

Lewis said, 'He's gone to a funeral this afternoon'.

Four handshakes, four firm pecks on the cheek and I was back at my board loading the valuable *Machinery Handbook* and the instruments into the case. The gang just watched as I emptied rubbish from my drawers.

Selby said, 'He's off, I knew it, Harry's given him the boot at last.' Cackle as usual.

Brian said, 'Hang on, I'll ring the union!'

'It's all right, Brian, I've resigned. Flo's bought me a big hardware shop in Hebden Bridge and her father's going to work for me part-time. Tell Maurice Ackroyd I won't be taking his job when he retires.' For the very first time ever they seemed to believe it, no comments or even a cackle from Selby. I was first at the clock, rode the lift alone and caught the bus into town. I needed to buy a new suitcase, a wallet and an alarm clock. I had known and worked with some very interesting friends, colleagues and bosses in Halifax over the years.

A pleasant surprise occurred one day much later, when briefly back in Halifax, as I parked the company car in a public car park, a woman got out of a green MG sports car beside mine. It was Eunice. She stared and with a cry of delight, hugged me. 'It's Donald, daft time of year to come on holiday.'

Through the biting December air we dashed into Collinsons' Café and over tea and toast she brought me up to date. 'Shortly after you left Pratts I started a night school course and got the ONC in building surveying, I got the idea from Brenda's husband. I now work for the Borough Surveyor, I'm a draughtswoman in the town hall, and the union rep too! You don't get overtime in the town hall, just time off in lieu, that's why I'm off today to do some shopping in Marks.'

'Good for you, I'm glad to hear it. I'm getting married in July, remember Carole who sat with us in the canteen?'

'Course I do, I'll tell Brenda. They finally finished the house and got married, lovely house, he built a fireplace in Lakeland grey slate tapering right up to the ceiling with a copper canopy. We had lots of fun at Pratts, it's all very formal in the town hall.'

I ordered more tea and toast, then explained how I had stayed in the Horsham job less than a year and by an odd fluke now had a job as a sales engineer with a company car. It had come about when I took the week off to return home at Christmas in a hired Ford Consul. Theo Smith, the sales manager at Hellermann Electric Ltd in Crawley had written to my home address offering me a job as northern sales engineer, the job I had just missed after the Leeds hotel interview. The chap who got the job had proved to be an alcoholic and refused to attend a 'dry-out' course so they had told him to resign. My mother had deliberately not forwarded the letter as she knew I was due home within days. I rang Theo who was surprised to learn I was now living only 11 miles from their factory. When I got back I went across to Crawley and got the job!

'Funny how life changes.'

'Yes, but you have to make it change, you did and so have I. The others will be stuck at Pratts for the rest of their lives.'

I paid and we went out into the drab day. Another hug, and as our four hands clasped together she said, 'Thanks, super seeing you, I'll ring Brenda tonight.'

Ronnie Baxter has always kept in touch and only last year rang to tell me the house I'd lived in in Halifax was for sale, for £159,950! During our long chat he told me that Harry Cope died of a heart attack whilst trying to push his car up his sloping and icy driveway in Leeds.

Ronnie had been transferred to Burnerd Chucks in White Waltham, Berks for seven years, then some factory in Scrubbs Lane, London, near Wormwood Scrubbs prison, then Burnerd's Winchester factory and finally back as Pratts' sales engineer for northern England, with of course, a company car.

Brooko and Billy McQueen I saw but once again, when invited to Brooko's retirement lunch in a Halifax pub. He had clocked up 38 years in Pratt's drawing office. I asked him about his constant quest for timber. 'Don't need it now, got gas central heating.' After the lunch we went back to the works where Billy McQueen showed me round the yellow brick extension built on the demolished Hartley & Sugden Boiler Works. Pratts now stretched from the top of Lister Lane right through to Gibbet Street. Bold lettering on the extension announced 'Pratt-Burnerd International'. The whole firm, along with Crawford Collets and Harrison Lathes now part of Geo. Cohen 600 Group, the same Cohens who'd purchased all the scrap in Turners Grease Works. Billy McQueen was now a sales engineer for Pratts, the drawing office and some new Japanese machine tools now computerised.

'What happened to Selby Rushworth?'

'Had a heart attack, recovered and got a part-time job in King's Typewriter shop.'

Back in the office area Billy took me to a door marked 'Dr J F Jackson,

Technical Director'. Inside was the very same Joe Jackson I'd known so briefly when I first started in the circus. After getting his degree in Manchester he'd completed the mandatory five years at Pratts, then moved to the Hydraulic Research Station, somewhere down south. It was he who had authorised Brooko to spend up to £100 on the pub lunch. He was still the same quiet, studious and polite Joe, but now a Doctor of Science. I asked about Willy Booth and Lewis Murgatroyd. 'Pratts did some deal with an Indian firm to make and sell their chucks in Asia. Willy was sent there to set it all up, when he returned he looked ten years older and promptly retired. Lewis has now turned 90 and still writes a weekly article on Labour Party affairs for the *Halifax Courier*.'

During all this visit my wife, Carole, had been sitting and chatting to the receptionist with tea and biscuits. She said that the only three women now working at Pratts were driven into town each evening by one of the staff, as when walking down they had been harassed by Pakistani youths, about which the police had done nothing.

I met Dick Asquith again when I was appointed a magistrate at Halifax Borough Court. By then he had been on the Bench for many years.

Back in 1938 my mother had made a crucial decision not to return to luxury living in Canada, perhaps never realising this would result in poverty and hardship for years ahead. I had made a decision to take a 60 per cent drop in pay to get a company car and be able to live amongst friends back home in Yorkshire. Whether my decision was the right one I still don't know to this day. I had no idea then that for me, it would ultimately be back to the drawing board, working in aircraft design offices in the UK, Israel and finally Paris. Nor was I to know that the only domestic product I ever designed would be accepted by the Design Centre in London, which promptly generated an order for 100 of these from an American department store! I remember looking through the Grattan Mail Order catalogue that winter, and amongst the whole mass of toys it was the only product bearing the distinctive 'Design Centre' label. After producing over 24,000 of these I was sick of the sight of the simple child's blackboard and easel.

Nor was I to know then that even in retirement I was to win £500 and a huge bronze medal in a design competition sponsored by that ancient guild 'The Worshipful Company of Turners' and my old buddies the 'Institute of Production Engineers'! The design was for some attachments for any model engineer to make himself to enhance the versatility of his small lathe.

Today, Keith (ex-Tod) too is retired and plays golf. He is still the same relaxed, fun-loving individual, but now a devoted granddad. Perhaps he was right when he advised 'If you want to do it, do it, if it goes wrong you can allus do summat else.' This was when over a pint with him I was pondering whether to take the Hellermann job.

Why not? You're only on this earth once. I could always go back to the drawing board.